THE ETERNAL QUEST FOR GOD

By the same author
Nell'Universo sulle tracce di Dio
(EDITRICE NÚR, ROME 1988)
Bahíyyih K͟hánum, Ancella di Bahá
(CASA EDITRICE BAHÁ'Í, ROME 1983)

The Eternal Quest for God

An Introduction to the Divine Philosophy of 'Abdu'l-Bahá

Julio Savi

George Ronald · Oxford

George Ronald, Publisher

Copyright © Julio Savi 1989
All Rights Reserved

British Library Cataloguing in Publication Data

Savi, Julio
   The eternal quest for God : an introduction to the divine philosophy of 'Abdu'l-Bahá.
   1. Bahaism. Abd al-Baha ibn Baha All ah, 1844–1921.
   I. Title II. Nell' universo sulle tracce di Dio. English
   297'.8963

ISBN 0–85398–295–3

*To my father
Umberto Savi
with love and gratitude*

*I am especially grateful to Continental Counsellor
Dr. Leo Neiderreiter
without whose loving encouragement
this book would not have been written*

Contents

	page
Introduction	xv

1 THE WAYS OF THE SEARCH: TOWARDS A PHILOSOPHY OF REALITY — 1

The criteria of knowledge	3
Sense perception	3
Intellect	4
Insight	4
The Holy Writings	5
The research method	6
Which truth?	8
Thought and action	10
Natural philosophy and divine philosophy	11
The unity of religion and science	17
Towards a philosophy of reality	19
A conclusion and a preamble	20

2 THE BEGINNING OF ALL THINGS — 22

God is unknowable	22
Differentiation of stages	22
God's all-inclusiveness	23
Human limitations	23
Human incapacity to know the essence of things	23
Limitations of human understanding	23
Rational proofs of Divinity	24
Cosmological proofs	24
On the grounds of movement and the principle of efficient cause	24
On the grounds of the different degrees of perfection	25
Teleological proofs	25
The perception of the indwelling Spirit	27

3	**THROUGHOUT THE UNIVERSE IN SEARCH OF GOD**	29
	Creation	31
	The world of God	32
	The world of the kingdom	34
	God's transcendence and pre-existence	34
	God and His creatures	34
	Different degrees in the world of existence	35
	The world of the Kingdom	36
	Pre-existence of the world of the Kingdom	37
	The world of the Kingdom and spirit	38
	Degrees of the spirit	40
	The world of creation	41
	Relation between the world of the Kingdom and the world of creation	42
	Nature and the Will of God	44
	Distinctive features of the world of creation	44
	The atom	51
	Evolution	56
	The creative plan of God	56
	General features of the creative plan of God	57
	Evolution in the world of creation	58
	Evolution in the four kingdoms of the world of creation	62
	Evolution according to Plotinus, in the Bahá'í texts	64
	Evolution as an educative process	65
	Evolution in the different planes of the world of existence	66
	Limitations of some modern concepts of evolution	67
4	**THE WONDERS OF EVOLUTION**	71
	The origin of the universe	71
	Evolution in the mineral kingdom	73
	Living systems	75
	Animals	78
	Qualities of the animals	79
	Sense perception	79
	Memory	79
	Learning	80
	Voluntary movements	81
	Natural emotions	81
	Animal limitations	81

Contents

5 MAN: THE FRUIT OF PHYSICAL EVOLUTION   84
   His animal nature   87
   His human nature   89
   His divine nature   91
   Human greatness and limitations   93
   His evolution and his divine nature   96

6 THE PERFECT MAN: THE MANIFESTATION OF GOD   100
   The Manifestations of God in the history of mankind   100
   Their threefold reality   102
     Material   102
     Human   102
     Divine   103
   The Essence of God and the Manifestations of God   104
   Their names   106
   Relations between the Manifestations of God   107
     The station of unity   107
     The station of distinction   108
   Their purpose   111
   Their proofs   112
   Denial   114

7 STRIVING TOWARDS PERFECTION: DYNAMICS OF HUMAN TRANSFORMATION   115
   The method   115
   Prerequisites of human transformation   118
     Voluntary submission to the will of God   118
     Purity   118
     Endeavour   119
     Directions of human endeavour   119
     The special meaning of the Revealed Word   120
     Serving mankind   121
     Means of entrance into the Kingdom   125
     Qualifications of the enlightened souls   125
   Obstacles to human transformation   126
     Self or self-centredness   126
     Estrangement   128
     Malice   128
     Envy   129
     Backbiting   129
     Exceeding in words   129
   Meanings of sorrow and sacrifice   130

	Meanings of sorrow	130
	An instrument of human perfection	131
	An instrument of self-knowledge	131
	An instrument of detachment from the world of creation	131
	Meanings of sacrifice	132
	Conquering the natal self	132
	Self-sacrificing for a universal cause	132
	Attaining the qualities of the world of the Kingdom	133
	Human transformation as spiritual progress	133
	Spirituality as love in action	134
	The second birth	135
8	**THE SOUL: THE REALITY OF MAN**	138
	Rational proofs of its existence and immortality	138
	Proofs of its existence	139
	Human rational faculty	139
	Inner perception	139
	Human inner reality	139
	Metaphysical proofs of its immortality	140
	On the grounds of movement	140
	On the grounds of the soul defined as substance	141
	On the grounds of the soul being simple as substance	142
	On the grounds of the presence of truth within the soul	143
	On the grounds of its natural aspiration for immortality	143
	On the grounds of the idea of mortality	143
	Moral proofs of its immortality	143
	As a requirement of human moral life	143
	On the grounds of consensus gentium	144
	What is the soul?	145
	Its individuality	148
	Its dual nature	150
	The oneness of the spirit	152
	Soul and body	153
	Its bounties or powers	154
	The soul as coordinator and motor of the body	154
	Knowledge	155
	Sense perception	156
	'Reasonable perception' or 'intellection'	156

Contents

'Inner perception or insight' or 'intuitive knowledge'	157
Self-consciousness	159
Love	160
The capacity of feeling joy and pain	161
The power of love	163
Love and knowledge	164
Love and courage	164
The growth of love	164
Will	165
Action	167
The dynamics of the choice	169
The soul as the mirror of human choice	171
Spiritual knowledge	172
Spiritual feelings	172
Spiritual deeds	174
Spiritual words	174
The journey of the soul	176

9 HUMAN EVOLUTION — 179

Individual evolution	179
Material evolution	179
Intellectual evolution	180
Spiritual evolution	181
Human education	182
Material education	184
Intellectual education	187
Spiritual education	188
Evolution of mankind	189
Material evolution	190
Intellectual evolution	193
Spiritual evolution	196
Contemporaneousness of material, intellectual and spiritual evolutionary processes	199
Discontinuity of evolutionary processes	199
Social evolution	200

10 THE WORLD OF THE KINGDOM — 205

The world of the Kingdom within the creatures	205
The world of the Kingdom within man	209
The world of the Kingdom within society	213
The world of the Kingdom as the world beyond	215
It transcends time and space	215

	Metaphors of the world of the Kingdom in the Bahá'í texts	216
	Qualities of the world of the Kingdom	217
	Human souls in the world of the Kingdom	218
	Relations between this world and the other	220
	Relations between human souls in the world of the Kingdom	222
	Relationship between human souls in this world and in the other	223
11	GOD: THE BEGINNING AND THE END OF ALL THINGS	224
	The knowledge of God	224
	God within human hearts	225
	God within the universe	228
	God in His Manifestations	230

A CONCLUSION — 236

BIBLIOGRAPHY — 238

INDEX — 245

Notes and Acknowledgements

Italics are used for all quotations from the Bahá'í Sacred Scriptures, namely, 'any part of the writings of the Báb, Bahá'u'lláh and the Master'. (Letter on behalf of Shoghi Effendi, in *Seeking the Light of the Kingdom* (comp.), p. 17.) Italics are not used for recorded utterances by 'Abdu'l-Bahá. Although very important for the concepts and the explanations they convey, when they have 'in one form or the other obtained His sanction' (Shoghi Effendi, quoted in *Principles of Bahá'í Administration*, p. 34) – as is the case, for example, with *Some Answered Questions* or *The Promulgation of Universal Peace* – they cannot 'be considered Scripture'. (Shoghi Effendi, *Unfolding Destiny*, p. 208.)

Quotations from Italian publications are translated by the author, unless otherwise indicated.

This book was, in a way, written twice: first in Italian, and then again in English. For the English version I am particularly grateful to Guitty Payman Galeotti, who encouraged me to accomplish this task, which I thought to be out of my reach. I wish to express my gratitude also to May Hofman Ballerio for her precious help in revising and editing the manuscript. Last but not least, I gratefully remember the patience of my wife Paola, who accepted my absence during the long hours I dedicated to this work.

Introduction

The Bahá'í Faith presents itself to modern man as a solution to the manifold problems which afflict him on the social and individual level. It does not claim to be a sort of magic wand, which could suddenly transform our imperfect world into an improbable utopia, but it presents itself as a cause entitled to indicate goals and methods and to furnish ideas and energies necessary for a transformation to take place. This transformation will certainly be difficult and slow and will proceed according to the unchangeable laws of social development, until it brings man to a higher stage of civilization.[1]

The Bahá'í Faith offers a particular vision of man and the universe; on the one hand, it suggests a specific code of ethics whose application raises man to a higher level of maturity than hitherto; on the other, it suggests principles, structures, and methods in the social and political sphere which would enable man — as, by increasingly applying this ethic, he grows in his feelings and behaviours — to build a world of peace and cooperation between the peoples of the earth. This kind of world is the only cradle in which

---

1. 'Abdu'l-Bahá writes: '. . . *the cause of Bahá'u'lláh is inclusive of all perfections and supplies all the needs of the world of humanity. But this cannot be accomplished in a short time. Time is needed. This will gradually be realized.*

   '*When a divine farmer sows the seed, the crops cannot be immediately gathered in, but it is certain that the seed will develop into a harvest. The seed which His Holiness Christ — may my soul be sacrificed for Him! - sowed, grew into a harvest within three hundred years.*

   '*We are now at the commencement of the shining forth of the Sun of Reality. It is the time which His Holiness Christ calls the "days of marriage". No doubt the house is not in order, but the time will come when it will come under order.*' ('It is the time which His Holiness Christ calls the "Days of Marriage" ', in *Star of the West*, XII, p.194.)

   The parable of the wedding feast 'Abdu'l-Bahá refers to is in *Matt.* 22:1—14.

an infant human intellect (infant in relation to the millions of years of man's existence on the planet) can develop and prosper, and gradually manifest the infinite potentialities with which man has been endowed.

Modern readers have been undoubtedly disappointed and wearied by the different ideas for the improvement of man and society, expounded down the centuries by philosophers, politicians, sociologists, and others. Their trust in religion has been seriously shaken by many unfortunate events. It is hoped, however, that despite these obstacles they may be induced to a preliminary investigation of the Bahá'í teachings and their proposed reforms.

To appreciate, let alone accept, an idea at its inception, is undoubtedly more difficult than appreciating an idea that is already producing concrete and visible results.[2] It could be, in fact, considered the undertaking of a pioneer. But it is the pioneers who move the world and mark the paths of history: Columbus with his trust in the world being round; Galileo with his determination to follow the as yet unexplored paths of the scientific method in the study of nature and its phenomena; Pasteur and Koch with their diligent studies of the world of microorganisms, then unknown and almost inaccessible; the Bahá'ís of today, with their faith in a human nature moving towards perfection, in the attainability of peace and justice – not utopia, but concrete goals to live and struggle for.

* * *

In 1912 during His historic travels in North America, 'Abdu'l-Bahá said: 'We must also render service to the world of intellectuality in order that the minds of men may increase in power and become keener in perception, assisting the intellect of man to attain its supremacy so that the ideal virtues may appear. Before a step is taken in this direction [1] we must be able to prove Divinity from the standpoint of reason so that no doubt or objection may remain for the rationalist. Afterward, [2] we must be able to prove the existence of the bounty of God – that the divine bounty encompasses humanity and that it is transcendental. Furthermore, [3] we must demonstrate that the spirit of man is immortal, that it is not subject to disintegration and that it comprises the virtues of humanity.'[3]

2. Bahá'u'lláh writes: *'When the victory arriveth, every man shall profess himself a believer and shall hasten to the shelter of God's Faith. Happy are they who in the days of world-encompassing trials have stood fast in the Cause and refused to swerve from its truth.'* (*Gleanings*, p.319.)

3. *Promulgation*, pp.325–6. He says in the same passage: 'This is, in reality, the science of Divinity.' (ibid. p.326.) Numbers in brackets are added by the author.

Introduction   xvii

This book is an attempt to respond to 'Abdu'l-Bahá's exhortations. To this end, Bahá'í texts available in English have been perused in order to find passages which provide:
1. rational proofs of the existence of God;
2. explanations of the concept of 'the bounty of God';
3. guidance for tracing the spirit in the phenomenal world;
4. rational proofs of the existence and immortality of human soul;
5. explanations of the nature of man and the meaning of his individual and collective existence.

In collecting these passages it became evident that the Bahá'í texts describe criteria and methods we should conform to, if we want to obtain useful results in our intellectual endeavours. An introductory chapter was therefore written, dealing with research criteria and methods.

Though the concepts presented in these introductory pages may seem abstract and even difficult to understand, it is hoped that they will be useful for a fuller comprehension of subjects which are dealt with further on, subjects which — since they concern man, his nature, his soul and his faculties — are, perhaps, not only easier to understand but also of more immediate interest to the reader. Through the entire research and writing runs a common thread — the consciousness that, in the words of the Universal House of Justice, 'no Bahá'í at this early stage in Bahá'í history can rightly claim to have more than a partial and imperfect understanding', of 'a Revelation of such staggering magnitude'.[4]

It is hoped that these concepts, which have been expounded by 'Abdu'l-Bahá, will assist the reader to understand, appreciate, and put into practice the practical and concrete suggestions which the Bahá'í Faith offers to individuals and societies for achieving a world of justice and peace.

JULIO SAVI
Bologna, 23 May 1987
to 12 August 1988

---

4. 'The Challenge and Promise of Bahá'í Scholarship', *Bahá'í World*, XVII, pp. 195–6.

A Bahá'í scholar . . . will not make the mistake of regarding the sayings and beliefs of certain Bahá'ís at any one time as being the Bahá'í Faith. The Bahá'í Faith is the Revelation of Bahá'u'lláh: His Own Words as interpreted by 'Abdu'l-Bahá and the Guardian. It is a Revelation of such staggering magnitude that no Bahá'í at this early stage in Bahá'í history can rightly claim to have more than a partial and imperfect understanding of it.

The Universal House of Justice[4]

1 The Ways of the Search: Towards a Philosophy of Reality

Whenever 'Abdu'l-Bahá[1] set forth, whether in His Writings or in His talks, a concise exposition of the principles taught by Bahá'u'lláh,[2] consistently among the first to be mentioned was the exhortation to free and independent search after truth.[3] This search, according to the Bahá'í teachings, is the beginning of man's true life and the key to all his attainments. Bahá'u'lláh exhorts man to make an independent search after truth, so that he may fulfil his purpose of knowing truth, and He informs him of the criteria and methods he should follow in order that the results of his search may be reliable.

The criteria and methods recommended for the investigation of physical (or material) and metaphysical (or spiritual) reality are the same, for, as 'Abdu'l-Bahá writes: *'reality is one and cannot admit of multiplicity'*.[4] The process of investigation is knowledge; its fruit is

---

1. 'Abbás Effendi, known as 'Abdu'l-Bahá (1844–1921); son of Bahá'u'lláh (*see* below p.1, no.2) Who appointed Him Centre of His Covenant and authorized Interpreter of His Words; after Bahá'u'lláh's passing He was the Head of the Bahá'í Community. For a study of His life, mission and writings *see* Shoghi Effendi, *God Passes By*, chapters XIV–XXI; H. M. Balyuzi, *'Abdu'l-Bahá*.

2. Mírzá Ḥusayn-'Alí, known as Bahá'u'lláh (1817–1892), Founder of the Bahá'í Faith. For His life, mission and writings, *see* Shoghi Effendi, *God Passes By*, chapters V–VIII; H. M. Balyuzi, *Bahá'u'lláh, the King of Glory*; A. Taherzadeh, *The Revelation of Bahá'u'lláh*, Vols. I–IV.

3. *See* 'Abdu'l-Bahá, *Selections*, pp.107, 248, 298; *Promulgation*, pp.62, 105, 127, 169, 180, 314, 372, 433, 440, 454; *Paris Talks*, pp.129, 135; *Divine Philosophy*, p.77; *'Abdu'l-Bahá in London*, p.27.

4. *Selections*, p.298. *See* also *Promulgation*, pp.63, 126, 287, 297, 313, 344, 364, 373; 'Talks by 'Abdu'l-Bahá in the Holy Land', in *Star of the West*, IX, p.135.

science, which is defined by 'Abdu'l-Bahá, in this context, as 'the outcome of this intellectual endowment';[5] the process of investigation and its fruits can be together defined as philosophy, according to the following definition given by 'Abdu'l-Bahá: 'Philosophy consists in comprehending the reality of things as they exist, according to the capacity and power of man.'[6]

From this concise definition we can infer four fundamental elements:
(i) the purpose of philosophy: to understand reality;
(ii) its subject: the reality of things;
(iii) its risks: things as they exist, and not (it seems implicit) as they appear or are supposed to be;
(iv) its limits: according to the capacity and power of man.

Nevertheless, this definition of philosophy could be misleading in the context of modern Western civilization; we could be brought to believe that a philosophy (and with it the search for truth), whose aim is 'comprehending the reality of things', is, and should be, a merely theoretical activity; that as such it serves its own purposes and is therefore doomed to remain in the sphere of thoughts and words. Bahá'ís, therefore, who strive to achieve 'all the perfections of man in activity'[7] and to emulate 'Abdu'l-Bahá in treading 'the mystical way with practical feet',[8] could be easily tempted to relegate philosophy to those useless sciences which, beginning and ending in words, have been peremptorily banished by Bahá'u'lláh.[9]

Bahá'u'lláh, on the contrary, praised great philosophers, stating that they *'stand out as leaders of the people and are prominent among them'*;[10] whereas 'Abdu'l-Bahá, referring to Bahá'u'lláh, writes: *'In His Tablets He has encouraged and rather urged [people] to study philosophy. Therefore, in the religion of Bahá'u'lláh philosophy is highly esteemed'*;[11] moreover, He says that 'the philosophers have founded

---

5. *Promulgation*, p.29.
6. *Some Answered Questions*, p.221.
7. Quoted in Esslemont, *New Era*, p.71.
8. This statement on 'Abdu'l-Bahá was uttered by Dr. David Starr Jordan, President of the Leland Stanford Junior University of Palo Alto, California, while he was commenting upon a talk delivered by 'Abdu'l-Bahá in that University during His visit of 18 October 1912. Quoted in *Bahá'í World*, VI, p.480.
9. Bahá'u'lláh writes: *'The knowledge of such sciences . . . should be acquired as can profit the peoples of the earth, and not those which begin with words and end with words.'* (*Tablets*, p.169.) And moreover: *'The learned of the day must direct the people to acquire those branches of knowledge which are of use, that both the learned themselves and the generality of mankind may derive benefits therefrom. Such academic pursuits as begin and end in words alone have never been and will never be of any worth.'* (ibid. p.169.)
10. *Tablets*, p.147.
11. 'It is the time His Holiness Christ calls the "Days of Marriage" ', in *Star of the West*, XIII, p.194.

material civilization';[12] whereas Shoghi Effendi[13] wrote through his secretary: 'Philosophy . . . is certainly not one of the sciences that begins and ends in words. Fruitless excursions into metaphysical hair-splitting is meant, not a sound branch of learning like philosophy . . . he would advise you not to devote too much of your time to the abstract side of philosophy, but rather to approach it from a more historical angle.'[14] All these statements encourage us, therefore, to search the Bahá'í texts for references to philosophy which will give us a clearer understanding of the reasons why it is so highly regarded, so that we may be guided along its path, strictly adhering to the advice with which the Bahá'í texts will certainly equip us.

The criteria of knowledge

When the aim of philosophy is understood as 'comprehending the reality of things', it is of paramount importance to know which criteria of knowledge man has been endowed with.

'Abdu'l-Bahá specifies four criteria of human knowledge: sense perception, intellect, insight or inspiration and Holy Writings or tradition.[15] Examining these four criteria, He concludes that — each one of them being limited — any single one can lead to fallacious results. Thus any object of human investigation should be studied in the light of all these four criteria: only after such a thorough process can one be assured that reliable knowledge is gained. The effort exerted in this process is man's task; the results depend on the way this effort is exerted, on the ardour with which it is made, and on the divine gift of knowledge.

Sense perception. The senses are the most immediate instrument through which man keeps in touch with physical reality. Shared by men and animals — which in this respect are often more generously endowed than men — the senses are the instruments of sense perception, which, in the words of 'Abdu'l-Bahá, is 'the lowest degree of perception'.[16] That senses can be deceived, producing a distorted perception of reality, is a well-known fact.

---

12. *Promulgation*, p.375.
13. Shoghi Rabbani, known as Shoghi Effendi (1898–1957), grand-grandson of Bahá'u'lláh, appointed by 'Abdu'l-Bahá Guardian of the Cause of God and His successor, led the Bahá'í community from 1921 to 1957. For his life, mission and writings *see* R. Rabbani, *The Priceless Pearl*; and U. Giachery, *Shoghi Effendi: Recollections*.
14. *Unfolding Destiny*, p.445.
15. See *Some Answered Questions*, pp.297–9; *Promulgation*, pp.20–2, 253–5; *Divine Philosophy*, pp.88–90.
16. *Some Answered Questions*, pp.217.

(Think, for instance, of the phenomena of optical illusions). Sense perception alone is not, therefore, totally reliable.[17]

Intellect. Intellect is the instrument through which man can know abstract reality. This distinctive human faculty differentiates men from animals. 'Abdu'l-Bahá asserts that intellect is assumed by Eastern philosophy[18] as the only criterion for truth. It is an important agent of knowledge, because it allows man to transcend some of the limitations of sense perception which can, as we have seen, involve a fallacious perception of reality. Nevertheless, intellect has its own limits and can likewise be misleading. If this were not the case, why have so many hypotheses supported by eminent scientists been proven false by subsequent studies? Why is it that not even the greatest scholars agree among themselves on many of the most important issues?

Intellect is particularly limited when spiritual reality is ignored i.e. when intellect is confined to a mere analysis of those cognitive data which are produced through sense perception, however vital these may be. Intellect should, on the contrary, be used to analyze spiritual reality[19] also, which it can know through the guidance provided by the Holy Writings.

This is one of the most important limitations of the modern Western world: it does not avail itself of a methodical use of insight; it overlooks the data provided by the Holy Writings; it disregards transcendency; it claims that an unbridgeable gap exists between 'natural science and the reflections of man on the meaning of life';[20] it suggests that within creation there are two spheres – seen as opposed to each other – requiring different means and methods for their analysis. What a cleft in human life and society! What dire consequences in human history!

Insight.[21] There is in man a power which directly 'discerns the

---

17. At the time of 'Abdu'l-Bahá materialistic trends of opinion (for example positivism) were in great favour; they maintained sense perception as their main criterion of knowledge. 'The basis of all their conclusions' – says 'Abdu'l-Bahá – 'is that the acquisition of knowledge of phenomena is according to a fixed, invariable law – a law mathematically exact in its operation through the senses.' (*Promulgation*, p.20.) He criticizes this kind of philosophy (*see* below pp.15–16) whose narrowness is today mostly recognized not only from a theoretical standpoint, but also for its nefarious consequences on human life.

18. He includes among Eastern philosophers also the philosophers of Ancient Greece. See *Promulgation*, pp.356–7, and below p.16, n.80.

19. For the concept of spiritual reality *see* below pp.41–2.

20. I. Prigogine and A. Danzin, 'Quale scienza per domani?' (Which science for tomorrow?) in *Corriere Unesco*, no.2, 1982. Ilya Prigogine writes, 'Nothing must be left out of account, if we are to be successful in reconciling the natural sciences with man's reflections about why he is alive.'

21. For the concept of insight, *see* 'Abdu'l-Bahá, *Selections*, p.44; *Some Answered*

The Ways of the Search

reality of things', independent of deductive or inductive mental processes: this is insight or, as 'Abdu'l-Bahá sometimes calls it, inspiration or the 'meditative faculty'. In explaining the nature of insight, 'Abdu'l-Bahá mentions the school of 'the Illuminati or followers of the inner light . . . Meditating and turning their faces to the Source of Light, from that central Light the mysteries of the Kingdom were reflected in the hearts of those people'.[22] Most people think that such a power can only be used in the mystic field; yet it is well known that several great scientists have discovered physical laws through intuition rather than reasoning and deduction: Newton, with his famous apple; Galileo, with the well-known episode of the swinging chandelier in the Cathedral of Pisa; and more recently Einstein, with his dream in which he conceived the theory of relativity. The Bahá'í writings urge us to train ourselves in the intuitive process by daily practice of meditation and to use this faculty in our endeavours to understand both physical and spiritual reality, for insight – like a mirror – faithfully reflects whatever is placed in front of it.[23]

However, insight can be misleading too: how can we distinguish between idle fantasies or fanciful dreams, and reality? Certainly, testing intuitive data through the senses and the intellect and checking them against facts will help us to distinguish tinsel from gold.[24]

The Holy Writings. Even though the Holy Scriptures are infallible, it is sometimes difficult to understand their meaning, since they are often written in metaphorical language: the limits of this criterion are therefore the limits of human intellect. Mistakes in the interpretation of the Holy Writings have been the cause of endless wars and conflicts. One finds even today, in certain circles, a desire to have the Holy Scriptures literally read, even against

---

Questions, p.157; *Paris Talks*, pp.86–7; 173–6; *Divine Philosophy*, p.122 and below pp.135–6, 139–40, 157–8, 172.
22. *Paris Talks*, pp.175, 176, 173.
23. Regarding the concept of meditation, see below pp.120, 158. 'Abdu'l-Bahá says: 'The meditative faculty is akin to the mirror: if you put it before earthly objects it will reflect them. Therefore if the spirit of man is contemplating earthly subjects he will be informed of these.

'But if you turn the mirror of your spirits heavenwards, the heavenly constellations and the rays of the Sun of Reality will be reflected in your hearts, and the virtues of the Kingdom will be obtained.' (*Paris Talks*, p.176.)

24. Regarding this issue, Shoghi Effendi's secretary wrote on his behalf: 'The inspiration received through meditation is of a nature that one cannot measure or determine . . . We cannot clearly distinguish between personal desire and guidance, but if the way opens, when we have sought guidance, then we may presume God is helping us.' (quoted in *Bahá'í Institutions* (comp.), p.111.) *See* also ibid. pp.109, 111–12.

reason itself — almost as if the measure of one's faith were the capacity to believe in the unbelievable. Tertullian's *credo quia absurdum*[25] is still a source of perplexity and grief. Some creationists for example will have us believe that God has purposely placed fossils in the bowels of the earth to test man's faith in the literal interpretation of the first book of *Genesis*. We could consider this attitude simply ridiculous, were it not for the personal and social tragedies which this mentality has caused and continues to cause in the world today.[26]

Bahá'í texts explain that the Holy Scriptures should not, generally speaking, be taken literally,[27] and that these literal interpretations have been the primary cause of conflicts and divisions in past centuries; even today, followers of the major revealed religions engage in strife despite the fact that their religions are all revelations from the same God. The Bahá'í Faith invites man to read the Holy Scriptures through his senses, intellect and insight, and especially to put them into practice: only then will the purity and ardour of the intellectual and practical efforts be rewarded by an ever deeper understanding of the truths the Scriptures offer.

The research method

Knowledge is a process which requires endeavour, at times a long and laborious endeavour. The reason why man is ready to make this effort is that God has endowed him with a 'love of reality'[28] which urges him on in his research; the greater the effort, the better the results. However, the intensity and ardour of the effort are not enough to ensure the results, if the effort is expended in the wrong way. The Bahá'í texts are rich in counsels for anyone who wants to follow the path of search, counsels which are valuable no matter what the object of research may be. For evidently — as has been already said — it is always reality that man is investigating, whether

25. Tertullian, *De Carne Christi*, v.
26. Regarding this concept F. Facchini writes: 'Advocates of scientific creationism, keeping to literal interpretations of the first chapters of Genesis, claim the scientific nature of its account of creation . . . Though the scientific nature of the 'creationistic theory' is upheld by its advocates, nevertheless they adopt an unscientific approach, in the strict meaning of the word, and in their eagerness to give at least a scientific semblance to their claims, they advance opinions on the theory of evolution, denouncing paleontological gaps and not yet explained issues of biological theory. Their statements are amazing, even ridiculous: for instance they maintain that fossils were created by God in order to test believers' faith.' (*Il Cammino dell'Evoluzione Umana*, p.224.)
27. *See* Bahá'u'lláh, *Kitáb-i-Íqán*, pp.53–69; 'Abdu'l-Bahá, *Some Answered Questions*, pp.83–6. Moreover Saint Paul says: 'The letter killeth, but the spirit giveth life.' (II *Corinthians* 3:6.)
28. *Promulgation*, p.49.

The Ways of the Search

his researches are carried out on the physical or on the spiritual level.

A long passage in the *Kitáb-i-Íqán*, the *Book of Certitude*, one of the most important of Bahá'u'lláh's Writings, is dedicated to the conduct which the *'true seeker'* must maintain if he wants to reap the longed-for harvest of knowledge.[29]

Above all, the greatest obstacle to overcome in the search for truth is prejudice; Bahá'u'lláh calls prejudice *'the obscuring dust of all acquired knowledge'*.[29] He defines it as *'imitation, which is following the traces of . . . forefathers and sires'*.[30] 'Abdu'l-Bahá affirms that prejudice's *'rootcause . . . is blind imitation of the past'*, and that it springs from *'selfish motives'*;[31] in Bahá'u'lláh's words, from *'shadowy and ephemeral attachments'* or from attachment to people[32] and, more often, ideas – a *'remnant of either love or hate'*.[33] 'Abdu'l-Bahá writes moreover that *'the imitator saith that such a man hath seen, such a man hath heard and such a conscience hath discovered: in other words he dependeth upon the sight, the hearing and the conscience of others and has no will of his own'*.[34] And Bahá'u'lláh warns us in His *Hidden Words*: *'The best beloved of all things in My sight is Justice: turn not away therefrom if thou desirest Me, and neglect it not that I may confide in thee. By its aid thou shalt see with thine own eyes and not through the eyes of others, and shalt know of thine own knowledge and not through the knowledge of thy neighbour.'*[35]

Other powerful obstacles in the path of search are, on the one hand, the desire for human approval and, on the other, pride and vainglory; a true man of science does not descend to compromise, but acts in full freedom from inner and outer pressures; however, he should not imagine himself better than others, for, as 'Abdu'l-Bahá says: 'As soon as one feels a little better than, a little superior to, the rest, he is in a dangerous position.'[36]

---

29. The interested reader would do well to read this passage for himself. (*Kitáb-i-Íqán*, pp. 192–8.) *See* ibid. pp. 192. Another important quotation on this subject can be found in Bahá'u'lláh's *Seven Valleys*, the Valley of Search (*Seven Valleys*, pp. 5–8.)
30. *Seven Valleys*, p. 5.
31. *Selections*, pp. 234, 300.
32. Regarding this issue, Shoghi Effendi's secretary wrote on his behalf: '. . . we must reach a spiritual plane where God comes first and great human passions are unable to turn us away from him. All the time we see people who either through the force of hate or the passionate attachment they have to another person, sacrifice principle and bar themselves from the Path of God . . .' (quoted in *Living the Life* (comp.), p. 10.) This idea of detachment, though it is here intended in the way of living, nevertheless can be referred also to the path of search, where Truth or Reality must come before any other thing.
33. *Kitáb-i-Íqán*, p. 192.
34. *Selections*, p. 29.
35. *Hidden Words*, Arabic, no. 2.
36. quoted in Esslemont, *New Era*, p. 84. *See* below pp. 126–7.

Of great assistance to the searcher are, moreover, the following spiritual qualities: patience, eagerness, detachment, resignation, moderation, compassion towards man and animals, honesty and trustworthiness, the capacity to forgive, to avoid empty discourse and finally to choose good company.[37]

A more detailed analysis of this important theme is beyond the scope of this book. However, it seems that these texts – written as they are in the metaphorical language of Revelation – suggest a scientific research method: there is a deliberate, conscious, repeated, organized and systematic use of the cognitive powers; certain standards of inner integrity of thought and behaviour are observed. It is in this perceptive that Shoghi Effendi describes the Bahá'í Faith as 'scientific in its method'.[38]

When this method is followed and these standards are observed, then, 'Abdu'l-Bahá says, 'By the breaths and promptings of the Holy Spirit, which is light and knowledge itself . . . the human mind is quickened and fortified into true conclusions and perfect knowledge':[39] in fact, man's cognitive powers are like eyes and the Holy Spirit like light, in whose absence eyes cannot see.[40]

This Bahá'í concept of 'knowledge as enlightenment' will be further clarified in the light of the concepts of creation, spirit, evolution and human development enshrined in the Bahá'í texts, which we have attempted to study, recording in the following pages our preliminary, incomplete results.

Which truth?

Even if this method is followed and these standards are observed, will man's claim to know truth be justified? 'Abdu'l-Bahá explains that 'our knowledge of things . . . is knowledge of their qualities and not of their essence' and He adds that 'the essential reality underlying any given phenomenon is unknown'. In fact, 'the realities of material phenomena are impenetrable and unknowable and are only apprehended through their properties and qualities'. Knowledge, He explains, whether an outcome 'gained by reflection

---

37. How will these qualities assist a man in his search? The concept will be more fully examined further on. It is here enough to say that these qualities are an outcome of spiritual progress and that this spiritual progress quickens intuitive faculties which are a powerful means and criterion of knowledge. *See* below pp. 172–3.

38. *World Order of Bahá'u'lláh*, p. ix. W. S. Hatcher writes: '. . . scientific method is the systematic, organized, directed and conscious use of our various mental faculties in an effort to arrive at a coherent model of whatever phenomenon is being investigated.' (W. S. Hatcher, 'Science and the Bahá'í Faith', in *Bahá'í Studies* II, 32.)

39. *Promulgation*, p. 22.

40. In the 4th century AD St Augustine set forth a very similar concept in his well-known doctrine of enlightenment: God is Light that enables man to know.

or by evidence',[41] or a fruit of insight gained through meditation and spiritual growth, depends mostly on our efforts. Therefore it is achieved by degrees, as the efforts proceed and bring results, and as experience — by similarity or by contrast[42] (*'the limited is known through the unlimited'*[43]) — enables us to bring it to the stage of judgement. Truth, therefore is a goal toward which we strive: moreover it is only one, because, as 'Abdu'l-Bahá writes, *'reality is one and does not admit of multiplicity'*.[44]

Man is guided, individually and collectively, however, in his efforts toward truth, by Revelation. In the various stages of his individual and collective growth he is thus directly or indirectly guided to an ever wider and deeper understanding of reality, and enabled to correct previous positions and adjust old and partial understandings. Though his yearning for truth spurs him on in his efforts towards this ultimate goal, his finite nature prevents him from ever grasping it in its essence or entirety. His truth is always relative and his science only 'a mirror wherein the images of the mysteries of outer phenomena are reflected',[45] and not Reality or Truth itself.

It seems after all that knowledge is a kind of faith: what man knows is what he has understood through the instrumentality of his cognitive powers and criteria. The certitude of his knowledge is dependent on the harmonization of his newly acquired information with his previously acquired data, in which context new information acquires meaning and value. In this perspective it is not difficult to understand how faith is described in a Bahá'í text as *'conscious knowledge'*. Having faith in something means accepting it as truth in the light of a series of considerations of which we are certain.[46]

---

41. *Some Answered Questions*, pp.220, 157.
42. See *Promulgation*, pp.295, 82–3.
43. 'Abdu'l-Bahá, 'Tablet to Dr. A. Forel', in *Bahá'í World*, XV, p.37.
44. *Selections*, p.298.
45. *Promulgation*, p.29.
46. W. S. Hatcher writes: 'We can define an individual's faith to be his total emotional and psychological orientation resulting from the body of assumptions about reality which he has made (consciously or unconsciously) . . . However, the quality of men's faiths differs considerably depending on the degree to which the basic assumptions on which a given faith is based are justified.' (W. S. Hatcher, 'Science and Religion', in *World Order*, III, pp.3, 14.)

Regarding the definitions of faith recorded in the Bahá'í texts three aspects are considered: knowledge, love and will or action. 'Abdu'l-Bahá writes: '*By faith is meant, first, conscious knowledge, and, second, the practice of good deeds.*' (*Tablets*, p.549.) Elsewhere He writes: '*Know that faith is of two kinds. The first is objective faith that is expressed by the outer man, obedience of the limbs and senses. The other faith is subjective, and unconscious obedience to the will of God. . . This condition of unconscious obedience constitutes subjective faith. But the discerning faith . . . consists of true knowledge of God and the comprehension of divine words*

However, the world of creation, being a dynamic reality, presents us with innumerable facets which defy man's often too strict schemes and definitions.[47] It is precisely because of the manifold facets and the changeability of reality that a confrontation of understanding is useful. Different intellects identify different facets of the same reality, and thus, in the exchange of ideas which Bahá'í often call consultation, they can help each other in a joint intellectual effort. In fact, the manifold facets of reality require us to be tolerant (i.e. to understand others' points of view) and to shun fanaticism, that stubborn assertion of personal truth as though it were absolute – whereas, in fact, every human truth is always partial.

Thought and action

In the Bahá'í texts *truth* is *reality*; thus the coincidence between what is (reality) and what man understands (knowledge) is the guarantee of every human truth. Such coincidence becomes evident when knowledge is put on trial in daily living. 'Abdu'l-Bahá writes: *'Many ideas spring out from the mind of man: some concern the truth and some falsehood. Of these ideas those which owe their origin to the Light of Truth are realized in the external world, while the others from different origins vanish, they come and they go like the waves of the sea of fantasy and do not find fulfillment in the world of existence.'*[48] This concept reminds us of Karl Popper's principle of refutability or the method of falsification, proposing that only what can be refuted through experience is scientific.[49] In the Bahá'í view, for an idea to be accepted as true, it must produce results of unity and peace before the tribunal of life and history, whereas prejudices – erroneous interpretations of reality[50] – have always been 'the foundation of dissension, the cause of obstinacy, the means of war and struggle'.[51]

. . .' (quoted in *Bahá'í World Faith*, p.364.) Moreover, 'Abdu'l-Bahá says: '. . . the love that flows from man to God . . . is faith, attraction to the Divine, enkindlement, progress, entrance into the Kingdom of God, receiving the Bounties of God, illumination with the lights of the Kingdom. This love is the origin of all philanthropy; this love causes the hearts of men to reflect the rays of the Sun of Reality.' (*Paris Talks*, p.180.)
47. Regarding the concept of dynamism of the world of existence *see* below, p.59.
48. *Tablets*, p.301.
49. *See* Karl Popper, *The Logic of Scientific Discovery*.
50. In one of His writings, 'Abdu'l-Bahá mentions five main types of prejudice: '*religious, racial, political, economic and patriotic*'. (*Selections*, p.299.) In the same passage He writes that these prejudices '*result from human ignorance and selfish motives*'. (ibid. p.300.)
51. 'Abdu'l-Bahá, 'Talks by Abdul-Baha in the Holy Land', in *Star of the West* IX, p.135. 'Abdu'l-Bahá says: 'Wars – religious, racial or political – have arisen from human ignorance, misunderstanding and lack of education.' (*Promulgation*, p.116.)

In the Bahá'í texts 'the thought which belongs only to the world of thought' is disapproved, because, as 'Abdu'l-Bahá states, 'if these thoughts never reach the plane of action they remain useless'.[52] Even more severely admonished is he who does not live up to his own words. Bahá'u'lláh sternly warns: '*he whose words exceed his deeds, know verily his death is better than his life*'.[53] And 'Abdu'l-Bahá has little esteem for those philosophers who 'are unable or unwilling to show forth their grand ideas in their own lives'.[54]

Philosophy, therefore, is only meaningful if, having brought man to an understanding of 'the reality of things as they exist, according to the capacity and power of man',[55] it can be translated into beneficial actions in the world of existence. This translation into action is both the necessary prerequisite of every philosophy which is more than mere talk, and the proof and demonstration of its validity: 'Whatever is conducive to the unity of the world of mankind is acceptable and praiseworthy; whatever is the cause of discord and disunion is saddening and deplorable.'[56] The tribunal of life and history is undoubtedly most just and implacable. Knowledge of reality, its practical application, and its consequences of co-operation and unity among men: these are the fundamental prerequisites of a philosophy worthy of man.

Natural philosophy and divine philosophy

Philosophy, aiming at 'comprehending the reality of things', should not limit the sphere of its investigation. It is clear that it cannot and should not exclude the investigation of physical reality, which is also called material, objective, contingent, outer, visible, earthly, sensible, or phenomenal. The branch of philosophy that concerns itself with physical reality, 'Abdu'l-Bahá calls 'natural philosophy': this is 'the investigation of natural phenomena' and 'the discovery of the realities of things'; it 'seeks knowledge of physical verities and explains material phenomena'; it examines and understands created objects and their laws; 'it discovers the occult and mysterious secrets of the material universe':[57] this is what is today called science. 'Abdu'l-Bahá says that science, being 'the outcome of this intellectual endowment' which is characteristic of man, is his 'most noble virtue' and 'highest attainment' and is what

---

52. *Paris Talks*, p. 18.
53. *Tablets*, p. 156. See below, pp. 126–30.
54. *Paris Talks*, p. 18. 'Abdu'l-Bahá however says also that 'A philosopher's thought may . . . in the world of progress and evolution, translate itself into the actions of other people . . .' (ibid. p. 18.)
55. *Some Answered Questions*, p. 221.
56. *Promulgation*, p. 56.
57. *Promulgation*, pp. 326, 138, 348, 326, 29.

distinguishes him from animals; He describes it as 'a mirror wherein the images of the mysteries of outer phenomena are reflected' and 'the one agency by which man explores the institutions of material creation'. Science is, at the same time, a gift from God – in 'Abdu'l-Bahá's words, 'an effulgence of the Sun of reality' – and 'the most noble and praiseworthy accomplishment of man'.[58] It is a gift because all knowledge is a gift from God, and it is an accomplishment because only through his own efforts is man accorded this divine gift.

The power which man acquires through natural philosophy or science is great: 'science is the discoverer of the past' and 'from its premises of the past and present' man can 'deduce conclusions as to the future'.[59] In fact, says 'Abdu'l-Bahá, 'he can frequently, through his scientific knowledge, reach out with prophetic vision'.[60] Science permits man to 'penetrate the mysteries of the future and anticipate its happenings' and to 'modify, change and control nature according to his own wishes and uses'. Through science, man 'is informed of all that appertains to humanity, its status, conditions and happenings'. It is because of science that man is 'the most noble product of creation, the governor of nature'.[61]

The fruit of progress in the sphere of natural science is a civilization which 'Abdu'l-Bahá calls *'material'*,[62] a civilization which is typical of the modern age. The Bahá'í teachings appreciate this material progress, which in its best aspects results in control over the environment and the production of things which are useful, often enhancing the quality of human life. 'Abdu'l-Bahá therefore praises the scientist in these terms: 'The man of science is perceiving and endowed with vision . . . attentive, alive . . . a true index and representative of humanity'. He considers science 'the very foundation of all individual and national development', 'the means by which man finds a pathway to God', an instrument in whose absence 'development is impossible'.[63]

The Bahá'í teachings condemn, however, the abuse of this progress in the production of things which do not benefit humanity but on the contrary destroy it: directly, as in the case of armaments, or indirectly, as in the case of waste of the earth's resources and the devastation and pollution of the environment; or in its more subtle,

---

58. *Promulgation*, pp.29, 49, 138, 49, 29, 49, 29.
59. ibid. p.29.
60. *Paris Talks*, p.41.
61. *Promulgation*, pp.49, 30, 50, 30.
62. *Selections*, p.132. See ibid. pp.132–3, 303–4; *Promulgation*, pp.2, 101, 130, 375; *Paris Talks*, pp.72–3.
63. *Promulgation*, pp.50, 49, 50.

though not less dangerous, perversion of pride and prejudice: pride in that tiny bit of knowledge man may have acquired, prejudice, in his pretension of being immune from mistakes.[64]

'Divine philosophy', also called 'divine science' or 'spiritual science',[65] is concerned with spiritual reality, which can also be called metaphysical, subjective, transcendent, inner, invisible, celestial or ideal. This is the study of what 'Abdu'l-Bahá calls 'ideal verities and phenomena of the spirit'. Its aims are: 'the discovery and realization of spiritual verities', 'the discoveries of the mysteries of God, the comprehension of spiritual realities, the wisdom of God, inner significances of the heavenly religion and foundation of law'. 'Abdu'l-Bahá states that since the teachings of all revealed religions 'constitute the science of reality',[66] divine philosophy cannot ignore revealed religion, which — in His words — is 'the truest philosophy'.[67]

However, 'the philosophers . . . are educators along the lines of intellectual training' and according to 'Abdu'l-Bahá, 'they have been incapable of universal education', because philosophy, as such, is limited to the development of the mind,[68] and has no effect on

---

64. Bahá'u'lláh writes: *'Know verily that knowledge is of two kinds: Divine and Satanic. The one welleth out from the fountain of divine inspiration; the other is but a reflection of vain and obscure thoughts. The source of the former is God Himself; the motive-force of the latter the whisperings of selfish desire . . . The former bringeth forth the fruits of patience, of longing desire, of true understanding, and love; whilst the latter can yield naught but arrogance, vainglory and conceit . . .' (Kitáb-i-Íqán, p.87.)*

'Abdu'l-Bahá writes: *'If a person be unlettered, and yet clothed with Divine excellence, and alive in the breaths of the Spirit, that individual will contribute to the welfare of society, and his inability to read and write will do him no harm. And if a person be versed in the arts and every branch of knowledge, and not live a religious life, and not take on the characteristics of God, and not be directed by a pure intent, and be engrossed in the life of the flesh — then he is harm personified, and nothing will come of all his learning and intellectual accomplishments but scandal and torment.'* Quoted in *Bahá'í Education* (comp.), p.42.

These concepts are commented upon by J. McLean in 'The Knowledge of God: An Essay on Bahá'í Epistemology' (in *World Order*, XII, pp.3, 38.) He writes: 'Bahá'u'lláh, however, is not suggesting that one stop learning, reading, or working because it involves being caught up in acquired knowledge. Such antiworldliness would constitute obvious contradictions to other explicit teachings of Bahá'u'lláh. [Universal compulsory education, higher learning, and the sacred character of work are all to be found in Bahá'u'lláh's Teachings.] It simply means that one does not apply these forms of knowledge in the search after the knowledge of the Manifestation.' (J. McLean, ibid. p.49.)

In the writer's opinion, this means also recognizing the paramount importance of deeds productive of peace, unity and co-operation among men and the importance of making any human activity, even knowledge, conditional upon this fundamental practical outcome.

65. *Promulgation*, pp.326, 138. See also *Promulgation*, pp.31, 87, 253, 284, 329, 349.
66. *Promulgation*, pp.326, 138, 297. See also below, p.104.
67. *Paris Talks*, p.31.
68. *Promulgation*, pp.85, 213.

spiritual development. It is not, therefore, capable of exerting an influence equal to that of divine teachings. 'What philosophy has ever elevated a whole nation and influenced humanity? Philosophy of necessity is restricted to a small school and cannot have an essentially moral influence.'[69] Moreover, whereas intellectual knowledge, becoming sometimes a cause of pride and prejudice, may, like a veil, shut men out from God, religion assists them in approaching *'the highest and last end of all learning'*, that is *'the recognition of Him Who is the Object of all knowledge'*.[70]

'Abdu'l-Bahá enumerates some fundamental themes and principles of divine philosophy: 'the unity of mankind . . . the tie of love which blends human hearts' which He defines as 'the most important principle of divine philosophy'; the concept of existence being 'composition' and non-existence 'decomposition'; 'the intrinsic oneness of all phenomena', which is explained by the atomic concept of the universe; the assertion that 'the world of nature is incomplete . . . nature seems complete, it is, nevertheless, imperfect because it has need of intelligence and education'.[71] Other themes of divine philosophy which He cites are: 'the problem of the reality of the spirit of man; of the birth of the spirit; of its birth from this world into the world of God; the question of the inner life of the spirit and of its fate after its ascension from the body . . . the essential nature of Divinity, of the Divine revelation, of the manifestation of Deity in this world'.[72]

Divine philosophy sets high moral goals which 'Abdu'l-Bahá thus enumerates: 'the training of human realities so that they may become clear and pure as mirrors and reflect the light and love of the Sun of Reality . . . the true evolution and progress of humanity'; and furthermore, 'the sublimation of human nature, spiritual advancement, heavenly guidance for the development of the human race, attainment to the breaths of the Holy Spirit and knowledge of the verities of God'.[73]

Mankind's progress in this field leads to the flourishing – thanks to the impulse of Revelation – of a spiritual *'divine civilization'*.[74] This is the highest aim of the world order proclaimed by the Bahá'í Faith, and in general of all revealed religions.[75]

69. *Divine Philosophy*, pp.84–5.
70. Bahá'u'lláh, in *Synopsis*, p.23.
71. *Promulgation*, pp.31, 87, 329.
72. *Paris Talks*, p.174.
73. *Promulgation*, pp.59, 326–7.
74. 'Abdu'l-Bahá, *Selections*, p.132.
75. Shoghi Effendi's secretary wrote on his behalf: 'In the *Bayán*, the Báb says that every religion of the past was fit to become universal. The only reason why they failed to attain that mark was the incompetence of their followers.' (quoted in *Living the Life* (comp.), p.4.)

We should therefore not be surprised to find that in the Bahá'í texts the philosophers of ancient Greece are praised. Commenting on His *'contemporary men of learning'* Bahá'u'lláh wrote that *"most of [their] learning hath been acquired from the sages of the past, for it is they who have laid the foundation of philosophy, reared its structure and reinforced its pillars'*. He writes moreover that *'the sages aforetime acquired their knowledge from the Prophets . . . The essence and the fundamentals of philosophy have emanated from the Prophets'*.[76] These are affirmations, accepted by Islamic culture, which can and should be verified through an attentive study of history and of the history of philosophy.[77] The philosophers of Greece, 'Abdu'l-Bahá said, 'were devoted to the investigation of both natural and spiritual phenomena. In their schools of teaching they discoursed upon the natural as well as the supernatural world. Today the philosophy and logic of Aristotle are known throughout the world. Because they were interested in both natural and divine philosophy, furthering the development of the physical world of mankind as well as the intellectual, they rendered praiseworthy service to humanity . . . Man should continue both these lines of research and investigation so that all human virtues, outer and inner, may become possible.'[78] This is an exhortation which presents every would-be Bahá'í philosopher with clear and specific indications for the goals of his or her study.

On the other hand, 'Abdu'l-Bahá disapproves of *'that group of materialists of narrow vision who worship that which is sensed, who depend upon the five senses only, and whose criterion of knowledge is limited to that which can be perceived by sense'*, for whom *'all that can be sensed is real, whilst whatever falleth not under the power of the sense is either unreal or doubtful. The existence of the Deity they regard as wholly doubtful'*.[79] In speaking of these philosophers, 'Abdu'l-Bahá, known for His charitable indulgence, His deep love for every human being, and His great tolerance of others' ideas, expresses Himself with a subtle irony, witty and pungent, but at the same time also loving and good-natured: 'Strange indeed that after twenty years

---

76. *Tablets*, p.144.
77. Shoghi Effendi's secretary wrote on his behalf: 'We have no historical proof of the truth of the Master's statement regarding the Greek philosophers visiting the Holy Land, etc. but such proof may come to light through research in the future.' (*Unfolding Destiny*, p.445.) And elsewhere: 'Historians cannot be sure Socrates did not visit the Holy Land. But believing as we do that 'Abdu'l-Bahá had an intuitive knowledge quite different from our own, we accept His authority on this matter . . .' (on behalf of Shoghi Effendi, in *Arohanui*, p.88.)

For a comment on relations between Israel and Greece in ancient times *see* J. R. Cole, 'Problems of Chronology in Bahá'u'lláh's Tablet of Wisdom', in *World Order*, XIII, pp.3, 14.

78. *Promulgation*, p.327.
79. 'Tablet to Dr. A. Forel', in *Bahá'í World*, XV, p.37.

training in colleges and universities man should reach such a station wherein he will deny the existence of the ideal or that which is not perceptible to the senses. Have you ever stopped to think that the animal has graduated from such a university? Have you ever realized that the cow is already a professor emeritus of that university? For the cow without hard labour and study is already a philosopher of the superlative degree in the school of nature. The cow denies everything that is not tangible, saying, "I can see! I can eat! Therefore I believe only in that which is tangible!" Then why should we go to the colleges? Let us go to the cow.'[80]

Naturally this praise of divine philosophy and ironic view of materialistic philosophy should be seen in the context of the Bahá'í Revelation, in which ancient concepts have been overturned and words have often assumed new meanings. Regarding this point, it is important to remember a corollary of the principle of the independent search after truth, i.e. the abandonment of all prejudices. This principle — apparently obvious to the point of banality — put into action with determination, will result in enormously important consequences. Above all, it requires that any would-be philosopher make an unbiased examination of reality, an examination which holds high neither the standards of current thought nor those of ancient traditions. Everything must thus be analyzed through a rigorous cognitive inquiry, retaining only what can hold up under this close examination and yield fruits of unity and progress. How many of the concepts modern philosophers and scientists condemn in those self-styled divine or religious philosophies would remain after such an upsetting revision?

---

80. *Promulgation*, p.361. *See* also ibid. pp.263, 311–12. The words with which He describes in another of His recorded talks the materialistic philosophers, defining them as 'bats' (*Promulgation*, p.179), should be viewed in the same perspective. *See* below, pp.110.

As to the idea advanced by some Westerners that all Western philosophers are considered materialistic by 'Abdu'l-Bahá, He Himself wrote the following words to Dr. Auguste Forel: '*It is as thou hast written, not philosophers in general but narrow-minded materialists that are meant. As to deistic philosophers, such as Socrates, Plato and Aristotle, they are indeed worthy of esteem and of the highest praise, for they have rendered distinguished service to mankind. In like manner we regard the materialistic, accomplished, moderate philosophers, who have been of service (to mankind).*' (in *Bahá'í World*, XV, p.37.)

Shoghi Effendi's secretary wrote the following words on his behalf, on the same topic: 'We must not take many of 'Abdu'l-Bahá's statements as dogmatic finalities, for there are other points which when added to them round out the picture. For instance, when He calls Aristotle and Plato philosophers of the East, He is obviously placing them in that category because He believes they belong more correctly to Eastern culture than to Central European and the New World cultures of the West. When He calls the philosophers of the West materialistic [*See Promulgation*, pp.355–6] this does not for a moment mean He includes all Western philosophers for, as you truly point out, many of them have been very spiritual in their concepts . . .' (quoted in *Arohanui*, p.88.)

Next, the researcher must disregard even his own self, so that he may be as objective as possible: what counts is reality and the knowledge of that reality; in its light every particularity or selfishness must melt like snow under the sun.[81] The Bahá'í principle of balance between science and religion and all statements similar to that of 'Abdu'l-Bahá on materialistic philosophers should be read in such a context.

Ultimately, the Bahá'í philosopher resembles the ancient sage or man of learning, rather than any modern philosopher who is more interested in intellectual games than in the results of his research. 'Abdu'l-Bahá has thus described the Bahá'í philosopher, in His political treatise, *The Secret of Divine Civilization*: '*Again, there are those famed and accomplished men of learning, possessed of praiseworthy qualities and vast erudition, who lay hold on the strong handle of the fear of God and keep to the ways of salvation. In the mirror of their minds, the forms of transcendent realities are reflected, and the lamp of their inner vision derives its light from the sun of universal knowledge. They are busy by night and by day with meticulous research into such sciences as are profitable to mankind, and they devote themselves to the training of students of capacity. It is certain that to their discerning taste, the proffered treasures of kings would not compare with a single drop of the waters of knowledge, and mountains of gold and silver could not outweigh the successful solution of a difficult problem. To them, the delights that lie outside their work are only toys for children, and the cumbersome load of unnecessary possessions is only good for the ignorant and the base. Content, like birds, they give thanks for a handful of seeds, and the song of their wisdom dazzles the minds of the world's most wise.*'[82]

The unity of religion and science

Science being, in the Bahá'í view, 'the discovery of the reality of things', philosophy is science. Science and philosophy cannot ignore the teachings of religion, for — as 'Abdu'l-Bahá says — science and reason are realities, and religion itself is the Divine Reality unto which true science and reason must conform'. Furthermore, He says: 'true science is reason and reality, and religion is essentially reality and pure reason; therefore the two must correspond. Religious teaching which is at variance with science and reason is human invention and imagination unworthy of acceptance, for the antithesis and opposite of knowledge is superstition born of the ignorance of man. If we say that religion is opposed to

---

81. 'Abdu'l-Bahá writes: '. . . universality is of God and all limitations earthly.' (*Will and Testament*, p.13.)
82. *Secret of Divine Civilization*, pp.21–2.

science, we lack knowledge of either true science or true religion, for both are founded on the premises and conclusions of reason, and both must bear its test.'[83]

It is here that we have the reconciliation of a painful division which has afflicted our society for centuries: spirit–matter, religion–science, faith–reason. In fact, *'reality is one and cannot admit of multiplicity'*:[84] man is one, even though the instruments and criteria he uses for obtaining knowledge are many; the method for investigating that single reality is one, the scientific method; the result of his intellectual effort is one, science; the test of the validity of science is one, its outcome of unity and peace in human life.

This single *'reality'* which is the object of science, philosophy and religion, is also described by 'Abdu'l-Bahá as 'the love of God . . . the knowledge of God . . . justice . . . the oneness or solidarity of mankind . . . international peace . . . the knowledge of verities. Reality unifies mankind.'[85] In another passage we find: 'reality is the divine standard and the bestowal of God. Reality is reasonableness, and reasonableness is ever conducive to the honourable station of man. Reality is the guidance of God. Reality is the cause of illumination of mankind. Reality is love, ever working for the welfare of humanity. Reality is the bond which conjoins hearts. This ever uplifts man towards higher stages of progress and attainment. Reality is the unity of mankind, conferring everlasting life. Reality is perfect equality, the foundation of agreement between the nations, the first step towards international peace.'[86]

---

83. *Promulgation*, pp.348, 373–4, 107. It could be interesting to examine some of the definitions of religion given by 'Abdu'l-Bahá. 'By the word religion I do not mean the present dogmatic and theological superstitions which are in the hands of people. By religion I mean the world of celestial attributes.' *(Divine Philosophy*, p.171.) 'Religion is the outer expression of divine reality.' (*Promulgation*, p.140.) 'Religion is the essential connection which proceeds from the realities of things.' (*Some Answered Questions*, p.158.) '. . . by religion is meant that which is ascertained by investigation and not that which is based on mere imitation, the foundations of Divine Religions and not human imitations.' (*Selections*, p.303.) 'Religion . . . is not a series of beliefs, a set of customs; religion is the teachings of the Lord God, teachings which constitute the very life of human kind which urge high thoughts upon the mind, refine the character, and lay the groundwork for man's everlasting honour.' (ibid. pp.52–3.) 'By religion is meant those necessary connections which unite the world of mankind. This has always been the essence of the Divine Religions. This is the object of the Divine laws and doctrines. This is the light of Eternal Life.' (quoted in A. Bausani, *'Unità delle Religione'*..)

Harmony between science and religion is one of the principles brought by Bahá'u'lláh. See *Selections*, pp.107, 280; *Promulgation*, pp.62, 105, 127, 169, 180, 314, 372, 433, 440, 454; *Paris Talks*, pp.130–31, 141; *Divine Philosophy*, p.77; *'Abdu'l-Bahá in London*, p.27.

84. 'Abdu'l-Bahá, *Selections*, p.298.
85. *Promulgation*, p.372.
86. *Promulgation*, p.376.

Such is the reality[87] which man is invited to investigate and such are the fruits of his investigation.

Towards a philosophy of reality

In philosophy, so it appears from this initial study of some Bahá'í texts, three fundamental aspects can be discerned:
(i) man's efforts, which consist in the use of cognitive criteria following a set of norms and a method that is, after all, scientific;
(ii) the divine gift of enlightenment/knowledge which God confers on those who exert the effort required and behave in the proper way;
(iii) the results of human effort, not only in terms of theoretical knowledge, but also in terms of the material and spiritual progress of individuals and society — in other words, civilization. Such civilization will be balanced whenever man equally investigates physical reality, producing material philosophy or science, as we call it today, and spiritual reality, producing divine philosophy.

In all this effort, man should apply the data provided by Revelation, that God-given guidance enabling him to accomplish his difficult but fascinating allotted task — a task which is both ethical and theoretical, practical and cognitive.

This global knowledge is indispensable for the creation of a true civilization worthy of man. For 'the attainment of any object is conditioned upon knowledge, volition and action. Unless these three conditions are forthcoming, there is no execution or accomplishment.'[88] We could compare the search for material and spiritual knowledge to the process of assimilation through which an embryo in the womb acquires the substances necessary for its development. If that poor embryo did not take the necessary atoms and molecules from its mother's blood, it would never become a foetus, let alone an infant and much less an adult. What will happen, then, to that man who cannot or will not use his cognitive instruments and criteria to draw from daily living those ideas he needs in order to be able to understand the reality by which he is surrounded? or to him who assimilates them in an incomplete or distorted way?

This search is indispensable, for — like the mythical Ulysses — man can find no peace in his unending search for distant goals; his

---

87. 'Abdu'l-Bahá says: 'truth or reality'. (*Promulgation*, p.62). In the Bahá'í texts the word 'reality' is used also in the meaning of substance, called also essence or identity.
N. Abbagnano gives the following definitions of the word 'reality':
'1. The way of being of things, as they exist outside of, and independently from, human kind. 2. Being, in anyone of its existential meanings. 3. That which . . . is *de facto* in existence.' (*Dizionario di Filosofia*, pp.733–5.)
88. *Promulgation*, p.157.

life is naught but a journey, a quest for the far-away Pillars of Hercules, the seemingly ever more distant and mysterious frontier of his possibilities of experience and knowledge.[89]

A conclusion and a preamble

The task of would-be Bahá'í philosophers today is thus an important one:

(i) first of all, to undertake the formidable task of studying and learning the Bahá'í texts. Bahá'u'lláh revealed texts that fill over a hundred volumes; there are innumerable Writings of His Herald and Forerunner, the Báb;[90] His authoritative Interpreter, 'Abdu'l-Bahá, wrote copiously and many of His talks are recorded; there is moreover an abundance of comments and explanations given by the Guardian of the Cause, Shoghi Effendi. All of these texts must be examined and studied in depth;

(ii) secondly, philosophical and religious traditions ought to be given proper appreciation,[91] and modern scientific discoveries ought to be evaluated in the light of the Bahá'í texts;

(iii) last, but not least, it is necessary to compile and present those texts which are relevant to the most urgent problems of modern man, in such a way that they can be understood and gradually put into practice throughout the world for the wellbeing of mankind.

These tasks seem quite similar to those which the Universal

---

89. We are reminded of Ulysses' words as imagined in Dante's *Commedia*: 'for brutish ignorance your mettle was not made; you were made men, to follow after knowledge and excellence.' (*Hell*, XXVI, 119–120. Translated by Dorothy L. Sayers.)

90. Siyyid 'Alí-Muḥammad, known as the Báb (1819–1851), founder of the Bábí Faith and Forerunner of Bahá'u'lláh. For a study of His life, mission and writings, see 'Abdu'l-Bahá, *A Traveller's Narrative*, Shoghi Effendi, *God Passes By*, chapters I–V, Nabíl-i-A'zam, *The Dawn-Breakers*; H. M. Balyuzi, *The Báb*.

91. Shoghi Effendi's secretary wrote on his behalf: 'As to correlating philosophy with the Bahá'í teachings; this is a tremendous work which scholars in the future can undertake. We must remember that not only are all the teachings not yet translated into English, but they are not even all collected yet. Many important Tablets may still come to light which are at present owned privately.' (quoted in *Unfolding Destiny*, p.455.)

The Universal House of Justice (see below, n.92) has since 1964 encouraged the collection and collation of all the Writings of the Central Figures of the Faith: The Báb, Bahá'u'lláh, 'Abdu'l-Bahá and Shoghi Effendi. By 1983, 60,000 documents had already been collated. At the same time the supreme Bahá'í body guides and encourages the Bahá'í world community in its studies of these vital documents.

92. 'The Universal House of Justice, the supreme governing body of the Bahá'í Faith, was created by Bahá'u'lláh, the Founder of that Faith in his written text.

'There are no clergy in the Bahá'í Faith. The Community is administered by institutions which function at local, national and international levels. These councils have each nine members elected by the free choice of the voters . . .

'The chief duty of the Universal House of Justice is to promote the transformation of human society from its present chaos and conflict into a world order of peace and justice . . .' (from a statement issued by the Universal House of Justice, 9 October 1985.)

The Ways of the Search

House of Justice[92] has indicated for the 'Bahá'í scholar'.[93] Should we, in fact, prefer the word scholar to philosopher? — philosophy today being considered a science of words and not of actions, what A. J. Ayer calls 'talk about talk'.[94] However, when we choose to use the word philosophy in this book, we do it from the Bahá'í standpoint, where philosophy belongs not only to the realm of thought but also to the realm of action.

In the following pages a presentation will be made of quotations from Bahá'í texts found on the themes which are fundamental to the understanding of 'the reality of things as they exist'.[95] It is offered with an awareness of its limitations, especially in this early stage of the development of the Bahá'í Faith, in the hope of not disturbing any heart and the desire to awaken in the reader's heart — as others did in ours — the urge of 'this love of reality'[96] with which God has endowed every man.

---

93. 'The Challenge and Promise of Bahá'í Scholarship', *Bahá'í World*, XVII, pp. 195–6.
94. *The Concept of a Person and Other Essays*, p. 3.
95. *Some Answered Questions*, p. 221.
96. *Promulgation*, p. 49.

2 The Beginning of All Things

'*The beginning of all things is the knowledge of God . . .*':[1] with this epigrammatic statement Bahá'u'lláh indicates in God the centre of human life. In '*the knowledge of God*' is '*the beginning of all things*' such as knowing, being aware, acting, working, educating, governing, making art. Therefore Bahá'í scholars or would-be philosophers must necessarily move from this '*beginning*' in their efforts to relate the pregnant concepts of 'divine philosophy' enshrined in the Bahá'í texts with the great discoveries made by human intellect during this century described by 'Abdu'l-Bahá as 'a century of the revelation of reality', 'the century of science, inventions, discoveries and universal laws'.[2]

God is unknowable

'. . . *man cannot grasp the Essence of Divinity* . . .': this is the first statement Bahá'í scholars or would-be philosophers are bound to utter. Similar statements are numerous in the Bahá'í texts. Here follow some of the explanations set forth in the Bahá'í texts to justify such human incapacity:

Differentiation of stages. Bahá'u'lláh writes: '*Whatsoever in the contingent world can either be expressed or apprehended can never transgress the limits which, by its inherent nature, have been imposed upon it*';[3] and moreover: '*Every attempt which, from the beginning that has no beginning, hath been made to visualize and know God is limited by the*

---

1. *Gleanings*, p.5.
2. *Promulgation*, pp.326, 29, 188.
3. *Gleanings*, p.151.

exigencies of His own creation . . .'[4] And 'Abdu'l-Bahá explains that '*. . . differentiation of stages in the contingent world is an obstacle to understanding. Every superior stage comprehendeth that which is inferior and discovereth the reality thereof, but the inferior one is unaware of that which is superior and cannot comprehend it. Thus man cannot grasp the Essence of Divinity . . .*'[5]

God's all-inclusiveness. '. . . the Divine Essence surrounds all things. Verily, that which surrounds is greater than the surrounded, and the surrounded cannot contain that by which it is surrounded, nor comprehend its reality'.[6]

Human limitations. '. . . whatsoever can be conceived by man is a reality that hath limitations and is not unlimited; it is circumscribed, not all-embracing, It can be comprehended by man, and is controlled by him.'[7]

Human incapacity to know the essence of things. 'As our knowledge of things, even of created and limited things, is knowledge of their qualities and not of their essence, how is it possible to comprehend in its essence the Divine Reality, which is unlimited?'[8]

Limitations of human understanding. 'It is evident that the human understanding is a quality of the existence of man, and that man is a sign of God: how can the quality of the sign surround the creator of the sign? that is to say, how can the understanding, which is a quality of the existence of man, comprehend God?'[9]

The same idea is set forth also in other words: '*These people, all of them, have pictured a God in the realm of the mind, and worship that image which they have made for themselves. And yet the image is comprehended, the human mind being the comprehender thereof, and certainly the comprehender is greater than that which lieth within its grasp; for imagination is but the branch, while mind is the root; and certainly the root is greater than the branch.*'[10]

* * *

To the question 'How shall we know God?', 'Abdu'l-Bahá answers: 'We know Him by His attributes. We know Him by His signs. We know Him by His names.'[11] Man can know God '*. . . by his reasoning power, by observation, by his intuitive faculties and the revealing*

---

4. ibid. p.318.
5. 'Tablet to Dr. A. Forel' in *Bahá'í World*, XV, p.37.
6. *Some Answered Questions*, p.146.
7. 'Tablet to Dr. A. Forel' in *Bahá'í World*, XV, p.37.
8. *Some Answered Questions*, p.220.
9. ibid. pp.146–7.
10. *Selections*, p.53.

power of his faith': he will be thus enabled to '*believe in God, discover the bounty of His Grace . . . become[th] certain that . . . conclusive spiritual proofs assert the existence of that unseen reality*'.[12] This is the true 'science of Divinity', a set of 'intellectual proofs . . . based upon observation and evidence', 'logically proving the reality of Divinity, the effulgence of mercy, the certainty of inspiration and immortality of the spirit'.[13]

Therefore, though God is inaccessible in His Essence, man is able nevertheless to understand that He exists. He can achieve this understanding by treading a threefold path:
(i) the path of his reasoning power, through which he can formulate theoretical, rational proofs of His existence;
(ii) the path of observation, through which he can discover His traces throughout the universe and in human history;
(iii) the path of his insight and faith, through which he can obtain a spiritual perception of His existence and confirm the results achieved through reason and observation.

Rational proofs of Divinity

Rational or 'intellectual proofs of Divinity'[14] abundantly set forth in 'Abdu'l-Bahá's Writings and recorded talks[15] can be divided into two groups: cosmological and teleological.

Cosmological proofs[16]

On the grounds of movement and the principle of efficient cause. Bahá'u'lláh writes: '*All that is created, however, is preceded by a cause. This fact, in itself, establisheth, beyond the shadow of a doubt the unity of the Creator*';[17] and 'Abdu'l-Bahá explains: '*. . . we observe that motion without a motive force, and an effect without a cause are both impossible: that every being hath come to exist under numerous influences and*

---

11. *Promulgation*, p.422.
12. 'Tablet to Dr. A. Forel' in *Bahá'í World*, xv, p.40.
13. *Promulgation*, p.326. The 'Science of Divinity' is usually called theology. See above, p.XVI and no. 3.
14. *Promulgation*, p.326.
15. *See Selections*, pp.48–9; 'Tablet to Dr. A. Forel' in *Bahá'í World*, xv, pp.40–42; *Some Answered Questions*, p.5; *Promulgation*, pp.17–18, 79–83, 423–5; *Divine Philosophy*, pp.98–103.
16. By cosmology philosophers mean an investigation 'of the origin, the formation, the order and the aims of the cosmic world'. (S. Battaglia, *Grande Dizionario*, III, p.888.) The proofs we have mentioned here are called cosmological because they demonstrate God's existence on the grounds of the observation of the cosmos: movement, the principle of efficient cause, the different degrees of perfection. These proofs were set forth by Aristotle in his *Physics* and *Metaphysics* and revised by St Thomas Aquinas and Avicenna in their writings.
17. *Gleanings*, p.162.

The Beginning of All Things

continually undergoeth reaction. These influences, too, are formed under the action of still other influences . . . Such process of causation goes on, and to maintain that this process goes on indefinitely is manifestly absurd. Thus such a chain of causation must of necessity lead eventually to Him Who is the Ever-Living, the All-Powerful, Who is Self-Dependent and the Ultimate Cause.'[18]

On the grounds of the different degrees of perfection.'*. . . limitation itself proves the existence of the unlimited, for the unlimited is known through the limited, just as weakness itself proveth the existence of power, ignorance the existence of knowledge, poverty the existence of wealth*';[19] '*. . . our need is an indication of supply and wealth. Were it not for wealth, this need would not exist . . . In other words, demand and supply is the law and undoubtedly all virtues have a centre and a source. That source is God, from Whom all these bounties emanate.*'[20]

Teleological proofs[21]

(i) '*. . . every arrangement and formation that is not perfect in its order we designate as accidental, and that which is orderly, regular, perfect in its relations and every part of which is in its proper place and is an essential requisite of the other constituent parts, this we call a composition formed through will and knowledge . . .*'[22]

(ii) The universe is a '*Great Workshop*'; '*though (its) infinite realities are diverse in their character, yet they are in the utmost harmony and closely connected together.*' '*Thus to connect and harmonize these diverse and infinite realities an all-unifying Power is necessary . . .*' In other words, '*. . . interaction, co-operation and interrelation amongst beings are under the direction and will of a motive Power which is the origin, the motive force and the pivot of all interactions in the universe*'.[23]

(iii) '*. . when you look at nature itself, you see that it has no intelligence, no will . . .*';[24] 'Inasmuch as we find all phenomena subject to an exact order and under control of universal law, the question is whether this is due to nature or to divine and omnipotent rule.'[25]

---

18. 'Tablet to Dr. A. Forel' in *Bahá'í World*, XV, p.41.
19. ibid.
20. *Promulgation*, p.83.
21. Teleology is that part of natural philosophy which aims at explaining the object of things; teleological proofs, called also physical-teleological, study the universe, discover its order and design and from this order infer an Intelligent Being which is its Ordainer.
22. 'Tablet to Dr. A. Forel' in *Bahá'í World*, XV, p.42.
23. ibid. pp.40, 42.
24. *Some Answered Questions*, p.3.
25. *Promulgation*, pp.80, 82.

'. . . from the premises advanced by naturalists,[26] the conclusions are drawn that nature is the ruler and governor of existence and that all virtues and perfections are natural exigencies and outcome'.

'. . . man is but a part or member of that whereof nature is the whole'.

'Man possesses certain virtues of which nature is deprived.'

'Man, the creature, has volition and certain virtues. Is it possible that his Creator is deprived of these?'

'. . . the Creator of man must be endowed with superlative intelligence and power in all points that creation involves and implies'.[25]

(iv) '. . . *formation is of three kinds and of three kinds only: accidental, necessary and voluntary. The coming together of the various constituent elements of being cannot be compulsory, for then the formation must be an inherent property of the constituent parts and the inherent property of a thing can in no wise be dissociated from it, such as light that is the revealer of things, heat that causes the expansion of elements, and the solar rays which are the essential property of the sun. Thus under such circumstances the decomposition of any formation is impossible, for the inherent properties of a thing cannot be separated from it. The third formation remaineth and that is the voluntary one, that is, an unseen force described as the Ancient Power, causeth these elements to come together, every formation giving rise to a distinct being.*'[27]

The rational proofs of God's existence set forth by 'Abdu'l-Bahá are not, evidently, new in the context of Western and Islamic philosophy. In this respect, it should be noted that 'Abdu'l-Bahá's authoritative exposition of the Bahá'í teachings – set forth in His Writings and recorded talks – is often worded in a Western, mostly Aristotelian and Plotinian, philosophical language. He uses this language – as Bahá'u'lláh said addressing a Sufi audience in a Sufi philosophical language – '*out of deference to the wont of men and after the manners of the friends*':[28] in other words He is willing to adapt His language to the understanding and culture of the audience He is addressing.[29]

---

26. By naturalists, materialistic philosophers are meant.
27. 'Tablet to Dr. A. Forel' in *Bahá'í World*, XV, p.40–41.
28. *Seven Valleys*, p.26.
29. Thus J. R. Cole explains the reasons why a certain philosophical language is sometimes used in the Bahá'í texts: 'The Bahá'í Manifestation of God, Bahá'u'lláh, wrote in Arabic and Persian, and his immediate audience consisted for the most part of nineteenth-century Middle Eastern Muslims. The theological and philosophical ideas familiar to His audience owed a great deal, not only to the Judeo-Christian and Islamic religious traditions, but also to the Greek and Hellenistic philosophical heritage. For this reason, much of the psychology and the cosmogony of the Bahá'í writings is framed in broadly Aristotelian terms. Their image of the prophet bear likeness in certain respects

The perception of the indwelling Spirit

Though 'Abdu'l-Bahá says that these rational proofs are 'a decisive argument',[30] nevertheless He does not present them as an irreplaceable demonstration of God's existence, nor does he say that they may alone inspire an atheist with faith in God. 'These obvious arguments', He states, 'are adduced for the weak souls; but if the inner perception is open, a hundred thousand clear proofs become visible. Thus, when man feels the indwelling spirit, he is in no need of arguments for its existence; but for those who are deprived of the bounty of the spirit, it is necessary to establish external arguments.'[31] He wrote, however: '. . . *apply thyself to rational and authoritative arguments. For arguments are a guide to the path and by this the heart is turned unto the Sun of Truth. And when the heart is turned unto the Sun, then the eye will be opened and will recognize the Sun through the Sun itself. Then (man) will be in no need of arguments (or proofs) for the Sun is altogether independent . . .*'[32]

In other words, these rational proofs, as promoters of faith in God, are only relatively effective. Inasmuch as '. . . the reality of Divinity is evidenced by virtue of its outpourings and bestowals',[33] rational proofs should be confirmed through the other two above-mentioned paths (i.e. observation, and insight and faith) which — because they can lead to the recognition of God's traces throughout the universe — open 'the inner perception'[34] to His existence and are therefore a more effective path towards a strong faith in Him.

Bahá'u'lláh writes: '*Every created thing in the whole universe is but a door leading unto His knowledge, a sign of His sovereignty, a revelation of His names, a symbol of His majesty, a token of His power, a means of admittance into His straight path . . .*'[35] And 'Abdu'l-Bahá says: 'If we wish to come in touch with the reality of Divinity, we do so by recognizing its phenomena, its attributes and traces, which are widespread in the universe. All things in the world of phenomena

---

to the philosopher-king of Plato and al-Farabi. The mystical theology of Plotinus (203–269/70 A.D.), the founder of Neoplatonism, particularly influenced the cultural context of the Bahá'í writings. Plotinus taught God's unknowability, the emanation doctrine of creation, and the coeternity of the universe with God. He also asserted the existence of a Universal Intellect as a metaphysical principle between God and the physical universe. In their own particular manner, the Bahá'í writings affirm many of these ideas, as well.' ('The Concept of the Manifestation in the Bahá'í Writings' in *Bahá'í Studies*, IX, pp.2–3.) The same concept can be applied also to the Writings and the recorded talks of 'Abdu'l-Bahá, which were addressed not only to Eastern, but also to Western audiences.

30. *Promulgation*, p.326.
31. *Some Answered Questions*, p.6.
32. *Tablets*, p.168.
33. *Promulgation*, p.313.
34. *Some Answered Questions*, p.6.
35. *Gleanings*, p.160.

are expressive of that one reality'; because God '. . . has bestowed (His) bounties upon all kingdoms of the phenomenal world, and evidences of spiritual manifestation are witnessed throughout the realms of contingent existence . . .'[36] '*And whensoever*', He writes moreover, '*thou dost gaze upon creation all entire, and dost observe the very atoms thereof, thou wilt note that the rays of the Sun of Truth are shed upon all things and shining within them, and telling of that Day Star's splendours, Its mysteries and the spreading of Its light.*'[37]

The perception of the 'indwelling spirit'[38] bestowing the inner assurance of God's existence is mostly unknown to modern man, who very often treads the materialistic path, assuming sense perception to be the measure of all things and denying anything sense perception cannot grasp: 'We are not captive of superstitions', are the words 'Abdu'l-Bahá properly ascribes to His contemporary materialistic philosophers, 'we have implicit faith in the impressions of senses and know nothing beyond the realm of nature, which contains and covers everything.'[39]

But, 'Abdu'l-Bahá declares, 'The bestowals of God which are manifest in all phenomenal life are sometimes hidden by intervening veils of mental and mortal vision which render man spiritually blind and incapable; but when those scales are removed and the veils are rent asunder, then the great signs of God will become visible, and he will witness the eternal light filling the world. The bestowals of God are all and always manifest.'[40]

This is a clear invitation to seek throughout the universe God's traces, adopting the criteria of a free and independent search after truth; as man discovers those traces, '. . . *he will find himself endowed with a new eye, a new ear, a new heart and a new mind. He will contemplate the manifest signs of the universe, and will penetrate the hidden mysteries of the soul . . . he will perceive within every atom a door that leadeth him to the station of absolute certitude. He will discover in all things the mysteries of Divine Revelation and the evidence of an everlasting manifestation*':[41] he will be thus enabled to acquire that '*knowledge of God*' in which Bahá'u'lláh indicates '*the beginning of all things*'.[42] This might well be the second stage on the path trodden by Bahá'í scholars or would-be philosophers: pursuing God's traces throughout the Universe or, in other words, searching out 'the indwelling spirit'.[43]

36. *Promulgation*, p.422, 173.
37. *Selections*, p.41.
38. *Some Answered Questions*, p.6.
39. *Promulgation*, p.312.
40. ibid. p.90.
41. Bahá'u'lláh, *Kitáb-i-Íqán*, p.196.
42. *Gleanings*, p.5.
43. *Some Answered Questions*, p.6.

3 Throughout the Universe in Search of God

It was Galileo Galilei (1564–1643) – the founder of the modern scientific method – who said that, since both nature and the Holy Writings arise from the same divine truth and reason, no conflict can exist between what the former shows and the latter states. Nevertheless, in Galileo's opinion, students of nature and of the Holy Writings aim at two quite different goals: the former investigate natural reality, the latter the purposes of men. Therefore he advocated a complete mutual autonomy between scientific and religious truth, and at the same time he maintained that though science and religion pursue two different goals, it is possible for their results not to disagree.

Galileo lived in times when religious dogmatism was grievously interfering with the progress of science. The vicissitudes of his life and the humiliation he was exposed to when he was forced by the religious authorities to recant his theories on 'the two greatest world systems'[1] in the name of dogmatic truth, are well known. Therefore his assertion is amply justified by the conditions prevailing in his time.

During the last three centuries, science has become emancipated from the fetters of a primitive knowledge founded on theological and philosophical assumptions set forth by human minds, minds which were often very acute but – being human – were also limited

---

1. After Galileo published his *Dialogues about the Two Greatest Systems in the World* (1632), in defence of the Copernican system against the Ptolemaic system, he was put on trial for heresy. The trial went on till 22 June 1633, when it ended in Galileo's forced abjuration of his theories.

and therefore liable to error. And yet it cannot be said that such separation between religion and scientific truth has produced good results only, for the cause of the peace and unity of mankind. Even science has made mistakes: many of its theories, though elaborated through the scientific method, were proved later to be false in the light of subsequent discoveries and more accurate observations. And grievous consequences have come from an implicit faith in science which, on the one hand, has resulted in a prevailing and deprecated crisis of spiritual values and, on the other, created a technology, bearer of abundant gifts, but also of such destruction, death and injustice as have brought mankind to the verge of the apocalypse. Obviously it is unfair to criticize the fundamentals of modern science on these grounds; but the urgency is felt to reconcile that ancient separation, so that modern culture may deepen its roots in a knowledge capable both of describing nature and of comprehending spiritual values.

It is in this perspective that the Bahá'í teachings urge Bahá'í scholars to give due consideration, while they pursue their studies, to Revelation.[2] In conformity with the Bahá'í principle of harmony between science and religion, scholars are invited to stay away from the two extremes: the one of creating man-made dogmas about the Words of the Revelation while ignoring the results of science (superstition), and the other of working out self-styled scientific theories on the basis of intellectual and empirical observations while ignoring the Revealed Truth (materialism).[3] Therefore, if a conflict is found in the results of any scientific research it might be useful not only to try to understand better the revealed Words, but also to make a deeper analysis of the results of that empirical and intellectual research.

In the Bahá'í view, whoever thinks he should investigate reality from the standpoint only of the natural sciences, which rationally examine physical reality and all its measurable phenomena, is

---

2. On 15 May 1979 the Universal House of Justice issued a message to the Bahá'ís of the world, establishing some fundamental principles for Bahá'í scholars: 'the principle of harmony of science and religion means not only that religious teachings should be studied in the light of reason and evidence as well as of faith and inspiration, but also that everything in creation, all aspects of human life and knowledge, should be studied in the light of revelation as well as in that of purely rational investigation. In other words, a Bahá'í scholar, when studying a subject, should not lock out of his mind any aspect of truth that is known to him.' (The Universal House of Justice, 'The Challenge and Promise of Bahá'í Scholarship', in *Bahá'í World*, XVII, pp. 195–6.)

3. 'Abdu'l-Bahá says: 'Religion and science are the two wings upon which man's intelligence can soar into the heights, with which the human soul can progress. It is not possible to fly with one wing alone! Should a man try to fly with the wing of religion alone he would quickly fall into the quagmire of superstition, while on the other hand, with the wing of science alone he would also make no progress, but fall into the despairing slough of materialism.' *(Paris Talks*, p. 143.)

behaving like those blind men who in the famous apologue[4] meet an elephant and have the nerve to believe they can describe it without seeing it. Studying the Holy Scriptures, which explain the origin and the purpose of reality, can be viewed as a healing balm having the power of curing blindness; in fact in the Holy Scriptures can be traced an organic vision of created things, in whose context any scientific discovery achieved through experimental means is not denied, but integrated. Another example may be suggested to describe that modern scholar or scientist who follows the path of intellectual search, and rejects the guidance of Revelation: a man persuaded that he can examine the contents of a completely dark room (reality) by means of a single ray of light. Such a man will be able to see in that room only single details, and can therefore hardly have an organic vision of that room or an understanding of the meaning of each detail, though he may have carefully studied them one by one. But if he illuminates the room by means of a lamp – and this is the purpose of Revealed Truth – he will undoubtedly be more successful in availing himself of his cognitive instruments and will more easily understand the meaning of those details. Finally, paraphrasing the famous myth of the cave proposed by '*the divine Plato*',[5] Revelation bestows upon man such knowledge as enables him to come out of the cave where he was confined, and to behold reality itself, not its shadow.

This is a very good starting point for Bahá'í scholars or would-be philosophers: on the one hand, they observe nature through modern and reliable scientific writings (in fact, in 'Abdu'l-Bahá's words, science is both '. . . the one agency by which man explores the institutions of material creation' and '. . . the means by which man finds a pathway to God'); on the other, they peruse the Holy Writings (where 'the science of reality' is enshrined);[6] on the one hand, they analyze the details of physical reality, on the other, they look into the Writings for an Ariadne's thread which might enable them to escape from the labyrinth of detail; on the one hand they carefully study each detail of reality, on the other, they try to make a philosophical synthesis, so that they may not lose sight of the forest while struggling to study a single tree.

Creation

God is the Creator: if we want to find His traces in the universe

---

4. See Hakim Sana'i, 'Apologo dell'Elefante e dei Ciechi' in M. M. Moreno, *Antologia della Mistica Arabo-Persiana*, p.29.
5. Bahá'u'lláh, *Tablets*, p.147. See Plato, *Republic*, Book VII.
6. *Promulgation*, pp.29, 49, 297.
7. ibid. p.272.

the first issue we should try to clarify is the creational relation between Him and the universe.

A full understanding of the great mystery of creation is undoubtedly beyond the reach of any creature: it is a question which will for ever disappoint all human effort. And yet the Bahá'í texts set forth many explanations on this issue: we will try to summarize some of them. Undoubtedly others will peruse these texts with greater skill, the more so in the future when those numerous texts will become available which cannot be studied today by most Western readers because they are as yet unpublished in Western languages or even in the original text.

The world of God

God in His Essence is unknowable, inaccessible to man: we can only say that He exists, but we cannot know anything else about Him, not even what 'to exist' means for Him.

And yet, we are used to ascribe to Him names and attributes: Creator, All-Knowing, Provider, or Word, Will, Love, and so on. The meaning of this ascription of names and attributes is explained in the Bahá'í texts in two ways:

(i) The names and attributes we ascribe to God refer to what we understand of them in the world of creation. 'Abdu'l-Bahá says: 'Their [the attribute's] existence is proved and necessitated by the appearance of phenomena':[7] we see that the universe follows a harmonious and ordered way, and we say that God is its Ordainer; we see creatures, and we say that God is their Creator. But our understanding of these attributes is only what *we* have understood, in the plane of the world of creation, of these spiritual truths which are far beyond our minds. This is what Western philosophers call *via eminentiae*.

(ii) The names and attributes we ascribe to God '*are only in order to deny imperfections, rather than to assert the perfections that the human mind can conceive*'.[8] For example, we say that He is the Almighty, meaning that He is not powerless, as His creatures are. This is what Western philosophy calls *via negationis* or *remotionis*.

From both these explanations, we understand that man comprehends the attributes of God in his own degree of existence – the world of creation – and not in God's degree of existence – the world of God. Bahá'u'lláh writes: '. . .*the highest praise which human tongue or pen can render are all the product of man's finite mind and are conditioned by its limitations*'[9] and 'Abdu'l-Bahá declares: 'However

---

8. 'Tablet to Dr. A. Forel' in *Bahá'í World*, XV, p.41.
9. *Gleanings*, p.62.

far mind may progress, though it may reach to the final degree of comprehension, the limit of understanding, it beholds the divine signs and attributes in the world of creation and not in the world of God.'[10]

The attributes we ascribe to God fall in the Bahá'í texts (as well as in the Islamic tradition) into two categories: essential and active attributes.[11] But, whereas in the Islamic tradition the two categories of attributes are clearly distinguished from each other, i.e. a Divine attribute is either essential or active, in the Bahá'í texts the same attribute can be viewed as essential (i.e. in its own reality) or as active (i.e. as expressed in action), depending on the plane in which it is seen.[12]

The Bahá'í texts state moreover that we understand but a faint reflection of God's active attributes in the world, and that we cannot understand anything at all of His essential attributes. In fact, 'Abdu'l-Bahá says that 'the essential names and attributes of God are identical with His Essence . . .' and sets forth a concise, rational explanation of His statement:

(i) God is absolutely preexistent. i.e. He 'is not preceded by a Cause', and therefore His is 'essential pre-existence'; moreover He 'is without beginning', and therefore He has also 'preexistence of time'.[13]

(ii) 'If the attributes are not identical with the Essence, there must also be a multiplicity of preexistences';[13]

(iii) '. . . as Preexistence is necessary (essential), therefore the sequence of preexistence would become infinite. This is an evident error.'

Inasmuch as Divine Essence and divine essential names and attributes are one and the same thing, it follows that:

(i) God's essential names and attributes are incomprehensible as well as His Essence.[14]

(ii) 'As the divine entity is eternal, the divine attributes are coexistent, coeternal'[15] and 'co-equal'[16] with and to Him.

(iii)'. . . His attributes are infinite.'

---

10. *Some Answered Questions*, p.146.
11. In Islamic tradition the essential attributes are might, science, life, will, hearing, sight and word; the active attributes are love, command, perception, and – according to some scholars – will and word.
12. For a preliminary study of divine attributes as presented in Islamic tradition and in the Bahá'í Faith, *see* J. R. Cole, 'The Concept of Manifestation in the Bahá'í Writings', in *Bahá'í Studies*, IX, pp.3–5, 25–9.
13. *Some Answered Questions*, pp.148, 280, 148–9.
14. See *Some Answered Questions*, pp.148–9.
15. *Promulgation*, p.159.
16. *Divine Philosophy*, p.145.

(iv)'. . . . the names of God are actually and forever existent and not potential',[17] otherwise God would be imperfect.

It is therefore possible to conceive a station where only God, Who is essentially preexistent and preexistent of time, exists, with His incomprehensible, 'coexistent, coeternal', 'co-equal', 'infinite', 'actually . . . existing' essential Names and Attributes.

Bahá'u'lláh alludes thus to such station: *'He was a hidden treasure . . . This is a station that can never be described, not even alluded to'*.[18]

The world of the Kingdom

If God is inaccessible in His Essence, if He transcends His creatures and is sanctified from any other reality, what is the relation binding His creatures to Him?

'Abdu'l-Bahá says: 'The dependence of the creatures upon God is a dependance of emanation – that is to say, creatures emanate from God; they do not manifest Him'.[19]

Creation as emanation – as the Bahá'í texts explain it – implies the following fundamental points:
(i) God is absolutely transcendental and preexistent;
(ii) creatures do not manifest God's Essence, from which they emanate; but they mirror forth its active attributes;
(iii) creatures have their existence in different degrees.

God's transcendence and pre-existence. This concept was previously discussed:
(i) God is unknowable in His Essence and in His essential attributes;
(ii) God has absolute preexistence:
– He is not preceded by a cause (essential preexistence)
– He is not preceded in time by other realities (preexistence of time).
(iii) the attributes we ascribe to Him are intended to deny His imperfection (*via negationis* or *remotionis*).

God and His creatures. 'Abdu'l-Bahá explains: '. . . creatures emanate from God; they do not manifest Him.' He says moreover that if creatures would appear 'through manifestation',[19] then it would follow that the Essence of Divinity had descended in them, transforming Itself into them; but this is impossible, otherwise God – taking on phenomenal attributes – would reduce Himself to imperfection. 'Abdu'l-Bahá explains the meaning of such a concept of manifestation, through the metaphor of a seed and a

17. *Promulgation*, pp.274, 219.
18. *Tablets*, p.140.
19. *Some Answered Questions*, p.202.

tree.²⁰ The tree manifests the seed because the essence of the seed has gone into branches, leaves, roots and flowers forming the tree. This concept cannot apply to creation. He explains the meaning of the concept of emanation through other metaphors: the sun and its rays, an actor and his action, a writer and his writings, a speaker and his speech. Under those circumstances, the essence of the creator does not go into the created objects, but his active attributes appear in them. The relation between God and His creatures is similar: this relation is not through the Essence of the Creator, nor through His essential attributes, but through His active attributes. These active attributes, while expressing themselves, emanate or radiate from the Creator and appear in His creatures as symbols of His perfections. The whole creation can be therefore viewed as *'evidences that proclaim the excellence and perfection of their author'*.²¹

Different degrees in the world of existence. The process of creation as emanation implies the existence of many different realities which, though all emanating from God – 'Supreme Centre'²² – differ from each other because of their different degrees. Bahá'u'lláh writes: *'Furthermore, consider the signs of the revelation of God in their relation to one another. Can the sun, which is but one of these signs, be regarded as equal in rank to darkness . . . Consider your own selves. Your nails and eyes are both parts of your bodies. Do ye regard them of equal rank and value? . . . every created thing should be viewed in the light of the station it hath been ordained to occupy.'* He writes moreover that God *'. . . hath entrusted every created thing with a sign of His knowledge, so that none of His creatures may be deprived of its share in expressing, each according its capacity and rank, this knowledge. This sign is a mirror of His beauty in the world of creation.'*²³

There are still long studies to be done in order to better understand this concept, the more so as many Bahá'í texts – as has already been mentioned – are as yet unpublished, both in translation into Western languages and in their original version. Nevertheless, a concept appears even now very clear: three fundamental levels may be perceived in the world of being: (1) the world of creation; (2) an intermediary world which has been called the world of the Kingdom (or First Mind, First Will or Primal Will, Word of God, Logos, Identity or Self or Soul of God);²⁴ (3) the world

---

20. See *Some Answered Questions*, pp. 202–4.
21. *Gleanings*, p. 337. From this point of view, the physical world might be seen – according to J. S. Hatcher – as a metaphor of the spiritual world. *See below*, pp. 206–9.
22. *Promulgation*, p. 15.
23. *Gleanings*, pp. 188, 262.
24. The Persian word *nafs* is translated into English in the Bahá'í literature sometimes as 'self', sometimes as 'soul'. The term *Soul of God* translates the Persian *nafs-i-raḥmaníyyih*, i.e. literally, 'the Soul of the Merciful.'

of God. These three levels seem to be the same as the three conditions of existence mentioned by 'Abdu'l-Bahá:'. . . servitude . . . prophethood . . . and . . . Deity'.[25] While the world of God is a world of Absolute Unity, wholly unknowable for man, many degrees of reality can be discerned, both in the world of the Kingdom and in the world of creation.

The world of the Kingdom. 'The first emanation from God is the bounty of the Kingdom', says 'Abdu'l-Bahá; and elsewhere He explains in Plotinian terms:[26] 'The first thing which emanated from God is that universal reality, which the ancient philosophers termed the "First Mind", and which the people of Bahá call the "First Will". . .'.[27] The station of this first emanation, where the whole process of existence has its beginning, is alluded to by Bahá'u'lláh in one of His famous aphorisms: *'Veiled in My immemorial being and in the ancient eternity of My essence I knew My love for thee; therefore I created thee . . .':*[28] God, unattainable in His unfathomable Essence, is conscious (He is, indeed, the All-Knowing) of Himself and of His own essential names and attributes, one of which is Love. This Love, on the one hand, implies — just as any other of God's attributes and names which are 'actually . . . existing and not potential'[29] — the existence of a recipient upon which it may be bestowed; on the other — being perfect — it implies also that God is willing to bestow it. Bahá'u'lláh alludes to such spiritual reality with His words ' *"I did wish to make Myself known"* '.[30]

In these words Bahá'u'lláh is, apparently, alluding to a station of existence, more than describing a reality in time and space. Next to the station of Absolute Divine Unity, a station is described in

---

25. *Some Answered Questions*, p.230. This tripartition of being is a pattern which can be perceived in many aspects of reality. While explaining the Christian concept of Trinity, 'Abdu'l-Bahá writes in one of His Tablets: '. . . *there are necessarily three things: the Giver of the Grace, and the Grace, and the Recipient of the Grace; the Source of the Effulgence, the Effulgence, and the Recipient of the Effulgence; the Illuminator, and the Illumination, and the Illuminated.*' (*Tablets*, p.117.) Further, He likens these three '*things*' to the sun, its rays and the objects on which these rays fall. The same pattern and the same explanation apply also in other circumstances: God, the world of the Kingdom, the world of creation; God, the outpouring of His active attributes, the world of the Kingdom; the world of the Kingdom, spirit, the world of creation; God, the Most Great Spirit, the Manifestation of God; the Manifestation of God, the spirit of faith, man; spirit, human soul, human body; soul, its mental faculties, human body. These concepts will be explained further on.
26. As for the philosophical language used in the Bahá'í texts, *see* above, p.26 and n.29.
27. *Some Answered Questions*, pp.294, 203.
28. *Hidden Words*, Arabic no. 3.
29. *Promulgation*, p.219.
30. *Tablets*, p.140.

which the essential attributes of God express themselves as active attributes: Love, as the act of loving; Knowledge, as the act of knowing; Will, as the act of willing. In this station the primal unity splits into a couple, a subject and an object, which in reality are identical: it is God Who knows and loves Himself. In fact, His essential attributes are identical with His Essence and His active attributes are but His essential attributes in their active expression.

Whereas the ancient philosophers called this station 'First Mind', thus emphasizing the attribute of Knowledge, the Bahá'í texts prefer the term 'Primal Will or First Will':[31] God is Love (essential attribute), He loves Himself (active attribute), therefore He wants to bestow His Love (First Will). In this regard, Bahá'u'lláh writes: *'The Cause of creation of all contingent beings has been love, as it is mentioned in the famous tradition: "I was a hidden treasure, and I loved to be known. Therefore I created the creation in order to be known"* ';[32] and 'Abdu'l-Bahá says that every love existing in the whole universe comes from 'the love of God towards the Self or Identity of God', a love He describes as 'the reality of Love, the Ancient Love, the Eternal Love'.[33] Elsewhere He says that love is 'the source of all the bestowals of God', the cause of the creation of the phenomenal world', and 'the axis round which life revolves', 'the eternal sovereignty . . . the divine power', 'the first effulgence of divinity and the greatest splendour of God', 'the greatest bestowal of God' and 'the conscious bestowal of God',[34] '. . . the transfiguration of His beauty, the reflection of Himself in the mirror of His creation'.[35]

Pre-existence of the world of the Kingdom. Explaining the station of the

---

31. *Some Answered Questions*, p.203.. Bahá'u'lláh writes: *'All that is in heaven and all that is in the earth have come to exist at His bidding, and by His Will all have stepped out of utter nothingness into the realm of being.'* (*Gleanings*, p.318.)

32. Quoted in *Star of the West*, VII, p. 100. When 'Abdu'l-Bahá was still a youth He wrote a famous commentary on this well-known tradition ascribed to the Prophet Muḥammad Himself. This commentary, entitled *Tafsír-i-Kuntu Kanzan Makhfiyyan*, has not yet been translated into Western languages. J. R. Cole gives a short summary of its contents in his 'The Concept of Manifestation in the Bahá'í Writings', in *Bahá'í Studies*, IX, pp.25–9.

33. *Paris Talks*, p.180.

34. *Promulgation*, pp.15, 297, 268, 211, 397, 15, 255. In another passage, 'Abdu'l-Bahá says: 'God is love and all phenomena find source and emanation in that divine current of creation. The love of God haloes all created things. Were it not for the love of God, no animate being would exist.' (ibid. p.315.)

He writes, moreover, that true joy is *'spiritual happiness'* and that this happiness is *'the love of God'. This happiness is but the eternal might, the brilliant traces of which are shining forth unto the temples of unity. Were it not for this happiness the world of existence would have not been created.'* (quoted in M. M. Rabb, 'The Divine Art of Living', in *Star of the West*, VII, p.163.)

35. *Paris Talks*, p.180.

world of the Kingdom, 'Abdu'l-Bahá says: 'This emanation, in that which concerns its action in the world of God, is not limited by time or place; it is without beginning or end — beginning and end in relation to God are one.' Then He adds: 'Though the "First Mind" is without beginning, it does not become a sharer in the preexistence of God, for the preexistence of the universal reality in relation to the existence of God is nothingness, and it has not the power to become an associate of God and like unto Him in preexistence . . . .'.[36]

He describes the world of the Kingdom as an intermediate spiritual reality, which, on the one hand, cannot be identified with God, Who is unfathomable in His Essence; and, on the other, is eternal and infinite, because it emanates directly from Him. This reality is not essential preexistence, because it is preceded by a Cause that is God Himself; but it is temporal preexistence, because it has no beginning. For even as the essential attributes of God are 'coexistent, coeternal' with God, so also the world of the Kingdom — which is the expression of these essential attributes as active attributes — is coeternal with God. In fact the divine attributes are 'actually and forever existent and not potential',[37] or else God would be imperfect. Bahá'u'lláh writes: *'His name, the Creator, presupposes a creation'*; and moreover: *'The one true God hath everlastingly existed, and will everlastingly continue to exist. His creation, likewise, has no beginning, and will have no end.'*[38] And 'Abdu'l-Bahá explains: '. . . just as the reality of Divinity never had a beginning — that is, God hath ever been a Creator . . . — so there hath never been a time when the attributes of God have not had an expression.'[39] Therefore God is both preexistent and uncreated, whereas the world of the Kingdom is preexistent, but created.

The world of the Kingdom and spirit. The world of the Kingdom is often likened by 'Abdu'l-Bahá to the sun:[40] 'The outer sun is a sign

---

36. *Some Answered Questions*, p.203.
37. *Promulgation*, pp.159, 219.
38. *Gleanings*, pp.150, 162.
39. *Promulgation*, p.462.
40. That the world of the Kingdom is also referred to as Sun of Truth or Sun of Reality may well astonish or perplex Western readers, accustomed as they are to a univocal and schematical language. But in the Bahá'í texts metaphors are not used as though they were rigid symbols. The same metaphor is suggested, in different contexts, to convey different spiritual concepts. Such a flexible use of metaphors is typical of Islamic literary style both in Arabic and Persian. (For the Islamic and Persian literary styles *see* A. Bausani, *Persia Religiosa*, pp.347–50, and J. S. Hatcher, 'The Metaphorical Nature of Material Reality', in *Bahá'í Studies*, III.)

In this context, therefore, the sun — which is often presented as a metaphor for the Essence of God — indicates His First Emanation, the world of the Kingdom. Therefore, in this context, the essence of the sun seems a metaphor for the Essence of God; the or symbol of the inner and ideal Sun of Truth, the Word of God'; and moreover: 'In our solar system the centre of illumination is the sun itself. Through the Will of God, this central luminary is the one source of the existence and development of all phenomenal things . . . But if we reflect deeply, we will perceive that the great bestower and giver of life is God; the sun is the intermediary of His will and plan . . . Likewise, in the spiritual realm of intelligence and idealism there must be a center of illumination, and that center is the ever-lasting, ever-shining Sun, the Word of God.'[41] As the sun radiates light and heat bestowing life upon the phenomenal world, so spiritual reality pours out its divine bounties (spirit), bringing into existence all created things.

This metaphor, frequently used in the Bahá'í texts, enables us to understand other concepts about the world of the Kingdom: the process of creation as emanation is a continuous, gradual and descending process. From the 'Supreme Centre',[42] — the Essence of Divinity, Absolute Preexistence, uncreated, unattainable in its essential attributes (and this is not — it should be noted once again — a place or a time, but a station), emanates the world of the Kingdom, preexistent in time but created, which is the manifestation as emanation of God's active qualities and attributes. The world of the Kingdom has, likewise, its essential attributes, which are beyond human reach. They are emanations of God's active attributes and in the Bahá'í texts they are sometimes termed, as a whole, Soul, or Self, or Identity of God.[43] These essential attributes of the world of the Kingdom express themselves, in their turn, as active attributes. Bahá'u'lláh seems to refer to this emanation of attributes from God to the world of the Kingdom, and from the world of the Kingdom to the world of creation, in the following passage: '*A drop of the billowing ocean of His endless mercy hath adorned all creation with the ornament of existence* . . .'[44] 'Abdu'l-Bahá describes it with such locutions as 'the bestowals of God', 'the bounty of God', 'the divine bounties of the Sun of Realities', 'the bestowal and grace of God',[45] 'Divine Mercy'.[46] He says moreover: 'The world of existence is an emanation of the merciful attribute of God'

---

image of the sun which our eyes perceive in the sky seems to refer to the world of the Kingdom; the rays of the sun are the bounties emanating from the world of the Kingdom, bounties that in the Bahá'í texts are often termed spirit.

41. *Promulgation*, pp.74, 93–4.
42. ibid. p.15.
43. In Persian *nafs-i-rahmaníyyih*. See above, p.35, n. 24.
44. *Gleanings*, p.61.
45. *Promulgation*, pp.313, 286, 273, 88.
46. *Paris Talks*, p.25.

and 'the bestowal and grace of God have quickened the realm of existence with life and being.'[47]

This metaphysical reality emanating from the world of the Kingdom and enlightening the inferior degrees of existence is often termed, in the Bahá'í texts, spirit: a power conveying the divine gifts to the world of creation. 'Abdu'l-Bahá says that the bestowal of God, or spirit, is a 'divine breath which animates and pervades all things', 'one power animating and dominating all things, and all things are but manifestations of its energy and bounty. The virtue of being and existence is through no other agency.'[48] He writes moreover that spirit is *the power of life*,[49] the eternal 'radiation of the light and heat of the Sun of Reality'.[50]

Degrees of the spirit. Spirit is one, if it is viewed in the station of the world of the Kingdom; but it specializes itself in different degrees in the inferior planes of existence, assuming different features, just as the light of the sun shines in different ways depending on the object by which it is mirrored; or as electric power appears in different ways depending on the different instruments it works. In the mineral kingdom, spirit appears as 'power of attraction';[51] in the vegetable kingdom it appears as 'power of growth';[52] in the animal kingdom it appears as 'power of sense perception'.[53] In the human kingdom, says 'Abdu'l-Bahá, it 'is given different names, according to the different conditions wherein it is manifested. Because of its relation to matter and the phenomenal world, when it governs the physical functions of the body it is called the human soul; when it manifests itself as the thinker, the comprehender, it is called the mind. And when it soars into the atmosphere of God and travels in the spiritual world, it becomes designated as spirit.'[54]

---

47. *Promulgation*, pp.390, 88.
48. ibid. pp.58, 286.
49. *Tablets*, p.611.
50. *Promulgation*, p.271.
51. ibid. p.268.
52. *Some Answered Questions*, p.143.
53. *Promulgation*, p.29.
54. 'Survival and Salvation', in *Star of the West*, VII, p.190. Any student of the Bahá'í teachings on spirit, soul, mind, etc. is faced by a certain difficulty of language, which Shoghi Effendi himself pointed out, writing through his secretary: 'When studying at present, in English, the available Bahá'í writings on the subject of body, soul and spirit, one is handicapped by a certain lack of clarity, because not all were translated by the same person, and also there are, as you know, still many Bahá'í writings untranslated. But there is no doubt that spirit and soul seem to have been interchanged in meaning sometimes; soul and mind have, likewise, been interchanged in meaning, no doubt due to difficulties arising from different translations. What the Bahá'ís do believe though, is that we have three aspects of our humanness, so to speak, a body, a mind and an immortal identity — soul or spirit. We believe the mind forms a link

In the world of the Kingdom it appears as the *Most Great Spirit*,[55] the creative agency of the universe, which manifests itself in such universal Manifestations of God[56] as Bahá'u'lláh; as the Holy Spirit, which manifests itself in such great Manifestations of God as Moses, Christ, or Muhammad; as the spirit of faith, which manifests itself in such extraordinary men as Elijah or John the Baptist.[57]

The world of creation

The world of the Kingdom is that station where all the essential names and attributes of Divinity appear as active attributes. Since they are active attributes, they imply the existence of objects upon which they are bestowed. 'Abdu'l-Bahá says: 'all the names and attributes of God require the existence of objects or creatures upon which they have been bestowed and in which they have become manifest'; 'otherwise, they would be empty and impossible names':[58] this object-receptacle of the bestowals of the world of the Kingdom is the world of creation.

The world of the Kingdom involves, therefore, the specification of two planes of reality: on the one hand, a sensible reality, i.e. matter; on the other hand, a metaphysical reality, i.e. spirit, which moves and directs that sensible reality. The former is a passive

---

between the soul and the body, and the two interact on each other.' (quoted in *Arohanui*, p.89.)

Moreover, these difficulties increase because of certain differences between Western and Islamic terminology and of the different meanings ascribed within these two cultures to such words as spirit, soul and mind. An explanation of the meanings of the words spirit, soul and mind as they are used in this book may be found at pp.40, 145, 156 respectively.

Such difficulty of language obliges any scholar who intends to achieve a deeper comprehension of these concepts to be always mentally alert, in his efforts to understand the real meaning of any statement beyond any precise and rigid definition of such terms as spirit, soul, mind. These mental exertions, somehow, train them in avoiding any rigidity and schematism, which is always detrimental whenever such subtle spiritual themes are studied. In fact spirit, as a living reality, is ever-changing in its manifestations; therefore – within its scope – any definition, which is perforce rigid, is inadequate. It follows that whenever such words as spirit, soul, mind are mentioned, it should be kept in mind that they indicate different aspects of a single reality in its different functions. For example in quotation no.54, p.40, the word spirit seems to indicate the soul of man when the divine reality has appeared in it; whereas the word soul seem to indicate the soul in its relationship with the body. In other texts (*see Some Answered Questions*, p.264) the terms rational soul and human spirit seem to indicate the soul of man in its usually accepted meaning.

55. *See* Shoghi Effendi, *World Order of Bahá'u'lláh*, p.109.
56. Regarding the concept of the Manifestation of God, *see* below, pp.100–114.
57. *See* 'Abdu'l-Bahá, *Tablets*, p.117. The Bahá'í Faith vigorously upholds the concept of the oneness of the Manifestations of God. *See* below, pp.107–10.
58. *Promulgation*, pp.219, 272.

reality, a receptive pole; the latter is an active reality, an active pole. Therefore the world of the Kingdom is also the station where God is the creator both of the visible material world and of the invisible, metaphysical world, i.e. of spirit and matter, which in this station find their unity.

Relation between the world of the Kingdom and the world of creation. 'Abdu'l-Bahá explains the relation between the world of the Kingdom and the world of creation through the metaphor of the sun and the earth. He writes: '*The Lord of the Kingdom and the Sun of Truth hath set forth a splendour and effulgence upon the world and the universe. All the contingent things found life and existence from the rays of that effulgence, entered and became manifest in the arena of being. Therefore all the objective phenomena are as surfaces of mirrors upon which the Sun of Truth hath cast the rays of the outpouring of bounty. All these surfaces (different stages of life) are mirrors reflecting the rays of the Sun of Truth. The outpouring and diversified mirrors are different from one another. Some of them are in a state of the utmost purity and clearness, reflecting the rays of the Sun of Truth, and the effulgence of the Luminary is manifested and visible in them. On the other hand, there are mirrors full of dust and therefore dark: consequently, they are deprived and bereft of any radiation.*'[59] In one of His talks, He said moreover: '. . . the bounty of the Kingdom . . . is reflected in the reality of the creatures, like the light which emanates from the sun and is resplendent in creatures; and this bounty, which is the light, is reflected in infinite forms in the reality of all things, and specifies and individualizes itself according to the capacity, the worthiness and the intrinsic values of things.'[60] In one of His writings, He explains this concept through the metaphor of rain: '*Although the reality of Divinity is sanctified and boundless, the aims and needs of the creatures are restricted. God's grace is like the rain that cometh down from heaven: the water is not bounded by the limitations of form, yet on whatever place it poureth down, it taketh on limitations – dimensions, appearance, shape – according to the characteristics of that place . . . .*'[61] '. . . [T]he bestowals of God', He says elsewhere, 'are moving and circulating throughout all created things. This illimitable divine bounty has no beginning and will have no ending. It is moving, circulating and becomes effective wherever capacity is developed to receive it.'[62] And He says also: '. . . all creatures are favoured by the

---

59. Quoted in M. M. Rabb, 'The Divine Art of Living' in *Star of the West*, VIII, p.123.
60. *Some Answered Questions*, p.295.
61. *Selections*, p.161.
62. *Promulgation*, p.160.

bounty of resplendency through emanation, and receive the lights, the perfection and the beauty of Its Kingdom, in the same way as all earthly creatures obtain the bounty of light of the rays of the sun, but the sun does not descend and does not base itself to the favoured realities of earthly beings.'[63]

From these words we understand that from the world of the Kingdom two realities emanate: on the one hand, His bestowals, i.e. spirit, and on the other, the recipients of these bestowals, i.e. material or sensible reality. Spirit emanating from the world of the Kingdom has neither beginning nor end, because it belongs to that world. It pervades all sensible reality, but is distinct from it, even as the sun which enlightens the world by its rays, but does not descend into the world in its essence.

'Abdu'l-Bahá says that 'spirit in itself is progressive',[64] a characteristic which is mirrored forth in the sensible world. In fact, spirit moves and guides sensible reality, which — in its moving according to the guidance of the spirit — grows in its capacity to receive the gifts of that same spirit. Thus, sensible reality manifests in different degrees on its own sensible level the attributes of spirit, i.e. of the world of the Kingdom. Such a manifestation becomes more and more refined and perfect as the creatures of the sensible world grow, by virtue of their transformation, in their capacity to receive those same gifts. Here we find *in nuce* the meaning and the direction of evolution.

The world of the Kingdom and the world of creation are, therefore, strictly interrelated. They belong to the same creation, inasmuch as their origin is one and the same. Nevertheless, the world of the Kingdom — which is the cause of the existence of the world of creation — is totally different from that world: a world of unity, the former; a world of multiplicity, the latter. Both the world of the Kingdom and the world of creation do exist; nevertheless, they differ from each other in degree, whereas there is no dualistic opposition between spirit and matter.

Since the spiritual world belongs to a superior level, it is higher in degree than the physical world; the physical world does really exist, though on an inferior level to the spiritual world. In this sense Bahá'u'lláh writes: *'The world is but a show, vain and empty, a mere nothing, bearing the semblance of reality . . .';*[65] and 'Abdu'l-Bahá

---

63. *Some Answered Questions*, p.296. This divine presence throughout creation is called by Bahá'u'lláh *'Universal Revelation'*. (*Kitáb-i-Íqán*, p.139.) A short explanation of this concept is given by J. R. Cole in 'The Concept of Manifestation in the Bahá'í Writings', in *Bahá'í Studies*, IX, pp.18–20.
64. *Promulgation*, p.101.
65. *Gleanings*, p.328.

writes: '*Reality is pure spirit, it is not physical*',[66] and He says moreover: 'Only the spirit is real; everything else is as shadow.'[67]

Nature and the Will of God. The relation between the world of the Kingdom and the world of creation is still more precisely explained in the Bahá'í texts. Alluding to the Word of God — which, as has already been mentioned, is the same as the world of the Kingdom — Bahá'u'lláh writes: '. . . [it] *is none but the Command of God which pervadeth all created things*', and further on He states that it is not only '*the Cause which hath preceded the contingent world*', i.e. the creative impulse which brings into existence physical reality, but also the universal law pervading the entire creation. Therefore the Word of God is termed '*Nature*', meaning '*God's Will and its expression in and through the contingent world . . . a dispensation of providence ordained by the Ordainer, the All-Wise*'[68] or else — in 'Abdu'l-Bahá's words — '*. . . those inherent properties and necessary relations derived from the realities of things*',[69] and at last '*the manifestation of the divine laws and disciplines which are essential to the realities of beings . . . .*'[70]

In other words, the world of the Kingdom creates, moves and guides the world of creation: it brings it into existence; it imparts to it the necessary impulse, so that it may move and proceed in its motion and transformations, it gives a meaning to any existing thing; it provides that logic of motion we can trace in natural laws, which are those same '*necessary relations derived from the realities of things*' which science calls natural laws and 'Abdu'l-Bahá terms nature, as the will of God.

Distinctive features of the world of creation. From these premises some general distinctive features of the world of creation may be inferred: (i) creation '*is infinite in its range and deathless in its duration . . . The process of His creation hath had no beginning and can have no end*',[71] writes Bahá'u'lláh. Creation is out of time and continuous: otherwise, the attribute Creator would be an empty name and God would be imperfect. 'Abdu'l-Bahá writes in this regard: '*As to life*

---

66. 'How is it possible to imagine life after death?' in *Star of the West*, XI, p.316.

67. *Divine Philosophy*, p.133. In the Bahá'í view the material world, when compared to the spiritual world, is but a shadow; but it has its own existence. *See* below, pp.49, 60, 216.

68. *Tablets*, p.142.

69. 'Tablet to Dr. A. Forel' in *Bahá'í World*, XV, p.39.

70. 'It is the time which His Holiness Christ calls the "Days of Marriage"', in *Star of the West*, XII, p.194. 'Abdu'l-Bahá also gives another meaning to the word 'nature', i.e. the animal kingdom or 'world of nature', as different from, and inferior to, the 'human kingdom or world of reason'. (*Promulgation*, pp.309, 312, 356–7.)

71. *Gleanings*, p.61.

... it has had no beginning nor will it have end. *The eternal grace of God has always been the cause of life. It has had no starting and it will not approach any end.*'[72]

(ii) '... *the worlds of God are countless in their number, and infinite in their range. None can reckon or comprehend them, except God, the All-Knowing, the All-Wise*'; '... *the creation of God embraceth worlds beside this world; and creatures apart from these creatures*',[73] writes Bahá'u'lláh. And 'Abdu'l-Bahá says: 'The universe hath neither beginning nor ending'; 'Consider the endless phenomena of His creation. They are infinite; the universe is infinite';[74] 'this universe contains many worlds of which we know nothing', and moreover: '... how is it possible to conceive that these stupendous stellar bodies are not inhabited? Verily, they are peopled, but let it be known that the dwellers accord with the elements of their respective spheres', and also: 'The forms of life are infinite.'[75] And finally, He writes: '*Know then that the Lord God possesseth invisible realms which the human intellect can never hope to fathom nor the mind of man conceive.*'[76]

That the universe is infinite in time, in space and in the variety of its phenomena, is a corollary of its Creator's perfection. It is impossible to conceive a time when creation was not existing as a whole: it would be tantamount to say that God is not Creator. It is also impossible to maintain that the universe is limited: if such was the case, what does exist beyond its borders? Finally, this universe cannot but contain an infinite number of phenomena, otherwise it would be finite. Therefore, the 'original matter' is eternal and infinite; nevertheless, it is subordinated to God Who is its Creator and to the world of the Kingdom which moves and guides it.

'Abdu'l-Bahá expounds these same concepts through a different logical argument: 'absolute nonexistence cannot become existence' or else 'absolute nothingness cannot find existence, as it has not the capacity of existence'.[77] Therefore that which exists has always been in existence, though in a different shape.[78] In other words we could say: 'nothing is created, nothing is destroyed, everything changes', which is a well-known scientific principle.[79]

(iii) Bahá'u'lláh writes: '... *each and every created thing hath,*

---

72. 'It is the time which His Holiness Christ calls the "Days of Marriage" in *Star of the West*, XII, p.194.
73. *Gleanings*, pp.151–2, 152.
74. *Promulgation*, pp.220, 274.
75. *Divine Philosophy*, pp.136, 110, 162.
76. *Selections*, p.185.
77. *Some Answered Questions*, pp.183, 180, 281.
79. See *Some Answered Questions*, pp.180, 204, 281; *Promulgation*, pp.87–9.

according to a fixed degree, been endowed with the capacity to exercise a particular influence, and been made to possess a distinct virtue.'[80] Thence, 'Abdu'l-Bahá explains that the universe is a world of 'absolute order and perfection';[81] 'in the possible world there is nothing more wonderful than that which already exists . . . the universe has no imperfection.'[82]

The perfection of the Creator is reflected in the perfection of the universe: in Bahá'u'lláh's words, His *'image is reflected in the mirror of the entire creation'*. In its own degree and as a whole, the universe is perfect, and perfect is also each created thing, as long as it is *'viewed in the light of the station it has been ordained to occupy'*.[83] Therefore, nothing whatsoever in existence is evil,[84] since every created thing has its own place and meaning in the 'creative plan of God'.[85] Nevertheless, 'Abdu'l-Bahá explains, 'this material world of ours is a world of contrast . . . It is all the time changing . . .',[86] therefore the universe is also a realm of imperfection, an imperfection which becomes manifest when the various degrees of existence are compared with one another: this is the reason why we find throughout the universe '. . . contradictions . . . opposites'.[87] Though its qualities are good and perfect in themselves and in view of their intended purpose, nevertheless they are not perfect, when they are compared to other qualities. *'Consider the effect of poison,'* writes Bahá'u'lláh. *'Deadly though it is, it possesseth the power of exerting, under certain conditions, a beneficial influence.'*[88] A further

---

79. This is one of those principles or theorems of conservation, stating the constancy in time of such physical dimensions as mass, energy, quantity of movement, momentum. These theorems, originally enunciated as philosophical statements, were afterwards expressed in scientific terms, thanks to the discoveries made by Lavoisier (1743–1794).
80. *Gleanings*, p.189.
81. *Promulgation*, p.79.
82. *Some Answered Questions*, p.177.
83. *Gleanings*, pp.166, 188.
84. The Bahá'í concept of good and evil is that '. . . there is no evil in existence; all that God created He created good. This evil is nothingness; so death is absence of life . . . darkness is the absence of light.' (*Some Answered Questions*, p.264.) See also *Some Answered Questions*, pp.215, 263–4; *Promulgation*, p.259; and W. S. Hatcher, 'A Logical Solution to the Problem of Evil', in *Zygon*, IX, p.3.

Regarding the concept of the non-existence of evil explained by 'Abdu'l-Bahá, Shoghi Effendi wrote through his secretary: 'We must never take one sentence in the Teachings and isolate it from the rest . . . We know the absence of light is darkness, but no one would assert darkness was not a fact. It exists even though it is only the absence of something else. So evil exists too, and we cannot close our eyes to it, even though it is a negative existence. We must seek to supplant it by good.' (*Unfolding Destiny*, pp.457–8.) See also below, p.89.
85. *Promulgation*, p.293.
86. 'Divine Contentment' in *Star of the West*, XIV, p.168.
87. *Paris Talks*, p.90.
88. *Gleanings*, p.189.

example: the law of the struggle for existence is good in the world of nature, but it is blameworthy in human society. Therefore 'Abdu'l-Bahá pronounces an apparently contradictory statement: 'nature seems perfect, it is nevertheless imperfect, because it has need of intelligence and education.'[89] This imperfection of nature is in comparison to a relatively greater perfection of human beings.

(iv) '. . . the divine and the contingent perfections are unlimited', says 'Abdu'l-Bahá; 'therefore you cannot find a being so perfect that you cannot imagine a superior one.' In fact, 'if it were possible to reach a limit of perfection, then one of the realities of the beings might reach the condition of being independent from God, and the contingent might attain to the condition of the absolute. But for every being there is a point which it cannot overpass . . .'[90]

(v) '*All parts of the creational world are part of one whole*',[91] a 'vast machinery of omnipresent power',[92] 'one laboratory of might'; 'The organization of God is one; the evolution of existence is one; the divine system is one.'[93]

The Creator is the Unifier of the infinite universe He Himself has created. He established in His universe one Law – His Command acting through the agency of the spirit – therefore the universe can be viewed as a great laboratory, whose working criteria are everywhere the same.

The concept of the unity of the laws of the universe is upheld also by many modern scientists and has found a scientific formulation in the cosmological principle, which says: There is in nature a fundamental unity or uniformity, wherefore (with the exception of certain peculiar situations which are limited in time and space) the universe is everywhere the same; indeed the natural laws governing the fundamental phenomena appearing throughout the universe, as well as the atomic and sub-atomic structure of matter, are uniform.[94]

(vi) 'all things are involved in all things',[95] says 'Abdu'l-Bahá. This concept will be better understood in the light of the atomic conception expounded by 'Abdu'l-Bahá, which will be described in the

---

89. *Promulgation*, p.329.
90. *Some Answered Questions*, p.230.
91. 'Abdu'l-Bahá in *Bahá'í World Faith*, p.364.
92. *Promulgation*, p.463.
93. *Some Answered Questions*, pp.182, 199.
94. It is on the grounds of this cosmological principle that many scientists are today trying to explain the oneness of the four fundamental forces in the universe: gravity, the electro-magnetic fields, the weak interactions of Fermi and strong interactions (or nuclear forces). For the time being this oneness is far from having been proved. But the fact itself that physicists are making efforts in this direction demonstrates their trust in the cosmological principle.
95. *Promulgation*, p.349.

following pages. Suffice to say here that, in 'Abdu'l-Bahá's words, 'Fundamentally all existing things pass through the same degrees and phases of development, and any given phenomenon embodies all others.'[95] He says that the world of creation is a uniform and organic reality – *'reality is one and cannot admit of multiplicity'*,[96] He writes – whose components, parts of the same organism, obey the same laws and are strictly interrelated, so that any change in any of their parts influences the whole and viceversa. In other words, 'All the visible material events are inter-related with invisible spiritual forces. The infinite phenomena of creation are as interdependent as the links of a chain.'[97] He writes moreover: '. . . *every part of the universe is connected with every other part by ties that are very powerful and admit of no imbalance, no slackening whatever.*'[98]

This interdependence of phenomena appears with strong evidence in the ecological equilibrium prevailing on the earth, to which 'Abdu'l-Bahá refers in the following words: '. . .*all created things are closely related together and each is influenced by the other or deriveth benefit therefrom, either directly or indirectly.*

'*Consider for instance how one group of created things constituteth the vegetable kingdom, and another the animal kingdom. Each of these two maketh use of certain elements in the air on which its own life dependeth, while each increaseth the quantity of such elements as are essential for the life of the other. In other words, the growth development of the vegetable world is impossible without the existence of the animal kingdom, and the maintenance of animal life is inconceivable without the co-operation of the vegetable kingdom. Of like kind are the relationships that exist among all created things. Hence it was stated that co-operation and reciprocity are essential properties which are inherent in the unified system of the world of existence, and without which the entire creation would be reduced to nothingness.*'[99]

And elsewhere He writes on the same theme: '*In the physical realm of creation, all things are eaters and eaten: the plant drinketh in the mineral, the animal doth crop and swallow down the plant, man doth feed upon the animal, and the mineral devoureth the body of man. Physical bodies are transferred past one barrier after another, from one life to another, and all things are subject to transformation and change . . .*

'*Whensoever thou dost examine, through a microscope, the water man drinketh, the air he doth breathe, thou wilt see that with every breath of air, man taketh in an abundance of animal life, and with every draught*

---

96. *Selections*, p.298.
97. *Divine Philosophy*, p.111.
98. *Selections*, p.157.
99. Quoted in *Ḥuqúqu'lláh* (comp.), no. 61.

of water, he also swalloweth down a great variety of animals. How could it ever be possible to put a stop to this process? For all creatures are eaters and eaten, and the very fabric of life is reared upon this fact. Were it not so, the ties that interlace all created things within the universe would be unravelled.'[100] And elsewhere He says on the same subject: 'If it were not so, in the universal system and the general arrangement of existence, there would be disorder and imperfection.'[101]

(vii) 'The worlds of God are in perfect harmony and correspondence one with another. Each world in this limitless universe is, as it were, a mirror reflecting the history and nature of all the rest. The physical universe is, likewise, in perfect correspondence with the spiritual or divine realm. The world of matter is an outer expression or facsimile of the inner kingdom of the spirit,'[102] says 'Abdu'l-Bahá. Matter takes on manifold shapes, guided in its transformation by the Command of God which is present in it: therefore, it cannot but mirror forth its qualities, though on a different level.[103] We could wrongly see in these concepts a new formulation of the Platonic concept of the world of Ideas and of the material world. But whereas Plato's conception may suggest a dualism between spirit and matter, there is no dualism in the Bahá'í texts. The physical world (the world of creation) reflects the metaphysical world (the world of the Kingdom) in different degrees, according to the capacities matter has acquired in its continuous transformations, induced and guided by spirit emanating from the world of the Kingdom. The world of the Kingdom and the world of creation have their existence on different levels, but both of them are real. The world of creation reflects on its own plane the qualities of the world of the spirit, expressing them, according to its capacities. Therefore, as Bahá'u'lláh writes, *'Every created thing in the whole universe is but a door leading into His knowledge, a sign of His sovereignty, a revelation of His names . . .';*[104] and 'Abdu'l-Bahá urges us to search out, throughout the sensible universe, the traces of the 'indwelling spirit'.[105] Nevertheless, when it is compared to the world of the Kingdom, *'the world is but a show, vain and empty'*.[106]

(viii) '. . . *the whole attracteth the part, and in the circle, the centre is the pivot of the compasses,'* writes 'Abdu'l-Bahá. This is the expression in the world of creation of another universal law, i.e. one of the

---

100. *Selections*, p.157.
101. *Some Answered Questions*, p.247.
102. *Promulgation*, p.270.
103. '. . . within it lieth the true explanation of pantheism', says 'Abdu'l-Bahá. (*Promulgation*, p.286.) See *Some Answered Questions*, pp.290–96; *Promulgation*, pp.284–9.
104. *Gleanings*, p.160.
105. *Some Answered Questions*, p.6.

laws of love: '... *any movement animated by love moveth from the periphery to the centre, from space to the Day-Star of the universe.*'[107]

(ix) 'The sign of singleness is visible and apparent in all things,' says 'Abdu'l-Bahá; and moreover: 'As the proof of uniqueness exists in all things, and the Oneness and Unity of God is apparent in the reality of all things, the repetition of the same appearance is absolutely impossible.'[108]

In this infinite universe, whose phenomena are infinite, the variety of beings is also infinite; therefore, as an earthly sign of the Divine Oneness and Unity manifest in all things, 'there are no repetitions in nature': every individual is itself and, as such, unique.[109]

(x) 'The world of existence is progressive,' says 'Abdu'l-Bahá, and 'is dependent for its progress on reformation', a reformation that, 'Abdu'l-Bahá says, is an educational process: 'the world of nature is incomplete and imperfect until awakened and illumined by the light and stimulus of education,' and moreover: 'the world of nature is inherently defective in cause and outcome ... the defects therein must be removed by education.'[110]

(xi) '... *change is a necessary quality and an essential attribute of this world, of time and place.*'[111]

From the Bahá'í texts the world of creation appears as a reality which — eternal, infinite and perfect as a whole, and in its individual components, provided they are viewed in their own degree — is subject to one unifying law, according to which all realities are strictly interrelated, so that a marvellous harmony and correspondence exist among them. This law is the law of evolution: the change brought into the world of creation by the power of spirit, which transforms creatures bringing them to even higher levels of perfection, and which is in that respect an educational process.

The spirit is the true reality of the world of creation: what we see and understand of this world is but '*images reflected in water*'[112] of the superior reality of the world of the Kingdom. Such is the reality through which we shall be satisfied: those same traces of God in the universe which Bahá'í scholars or would-be philosophers should search and may discover.

106. *Gleanings*, p.328.
107. *Selections*, pp.63, 197–8.
108. *Some Answered Questions*, p.283.
109. This concept is the foundation of the arguments advanced by 'Abdu'l-Bahá against the concept of reincarnation. See *Some Answered Questions*, pp.283–4.
110. *Promulgation*, pp.285, 378, 279, 309, 400.
111. Quoted in *The Establishment of the Universal House of Justice* (comp.), p.47.
112. *Selections*, p.178.

The atom

Since the time of Democritus of Abdera (5th to 4th century BC) philosophy has hypothesized that the sensible universe may be formed by indivisible, eternal units which cannot be directly perceived through the senses, but which are within the reach of human reason, units that have been called atoms, i.e. 'that cannot be divided or split'. Throughout the centuries this hypothesis has been specified, until it was given scientific formulation in the modern conception of the structure of matter.

'Abdu'l-Bahá says that the sensible universe is formed by 'elemental atoms', and expounds an atomic conception whose broad lines can be found in the following quotations from His Tablets and recorded talks:[113]

(i) 'It is evident that each material organism is an aggregate expression of single and simple elements', which He terms 'elemental atoms' or 'individual atoms';[114]

(ii) '. . . it is a philosophical axiom that the individual or indivisible atom is indestructible'; 'it retains its atomical existence and is never annihilated nor relegated to nonexistence'; '. . . atoms . . . continue to exist because they are single, individual and not composed. Therefore it may be said that these individual atoms are eternal.' In fact, 'existence implies the grouping of material elements in a form or body, and nonexistence is simply the decomposing of these groupings',[115] therefore that which is not composed cannot be decomposed, that is, it does not perish.

(iii) 'The elemental atoms which constitute all phenomenal existence and being in this illimitable universe are in perpetual motion, undergoing continuous degrees of progression', they 'are transferable from one form of existence to another, from one degree and kingdom to another, lower or higher'.[116]

(iv) 'Because they have affinity for each other, the power of life is able to manifest itself, and the organisms and phenomenal world become possible. When this attraction or atomic affinity is destroyed, the power of life ceases to manifest; death and nonexistence result.'

The nature of such an affinity is thus explained by 'Abdu'l-Bahá:
—— 'By a divine power of creation the elements assemble together in affinity, and the result is a composite being . . . this affinity of the inanimate elements is the cause of life and being.'

113. See *Selections*, pp.289–90; *Promulgation*, pp.160, 284–6, 306, 350; *Paris Talks*, pp.90–91.
114. *Promulgation*, pp.349, 306.
115. ibid. pp.306, 88, 306, 87.
116. ibid. pp.284, 87.

―― '. . . the phenomena of the universe find realization through the one power animating and dominating all things, and all things are but manifestations of its energy and bounty.'

―― 'We declare that love is the cause of the existence of all phenomena and that the absence of love is the cause of disintegration and nonexistence. Love is the conscious bestowal of God, the bond of affiliation in all phenomena.'

―― 'This quickening spirit emanates spontaneously from the Sun of Truth, from the reality of Divinity, and is not a revelation or manifestation. It is like the rays of the sun . . .'

―― '. . . the greater power in the realm and range of human existence is spirit — the divine breath which animates and pervades all things.'[117]

(v) 'each elemental atom in the universe is possessed of a capacity to express all the virtues of the universe . . . every atom in the universe possesses or reflects all the virtues of life . . .'[118]

(vi) '. . . the constituent elemental atoms of phenomena undergo progressive transference and motion throughout the material kingdoms . . . In its ceaseless progression and journeyings the atom becomes imbued with the virtues and powers of each degree or kingdom it traverses . . . all are privileged to possess the virtues existent in these kingdoms and to reflect the attributes of their organisms . . . From this point of view and perception pantheism is a truth, for every atom in the universe possesses or reflects all the virtues of life, the manifestation of which is effected through change and transformation.'

Thence the elemental atom is the guarantor of '. . . the intrinsic oneness of all phenomena . . .', wherefore '. . . all phenomena of material being are fundamentally one' and 'each phenomenon is the expression in degree of all other phenomena. The difference is one of successive transferences and the period of time involved in evolutionary process', wherefore 'all things are involved in all things',[119] the universe is 'one laboratory of might under one natural system and one universal law',[120] and 'the origin of all material life is one and its termination is likewise one'.[121]

The above words by 'Abdu'l-Bahá give a general view of His atomic conception. The following remarks are added in the hope that they will prove useful in the attempt to draw a parallel between that conception and some of the conclusions of modern science.

---

117. ibid. pp.4, 207, 286, 255, 59, 58.
118. ibid. p.285.
119. ibid. pp.284–6, 349, 350, 349.
120. *Some Answered Questions*, p.182.
121. *Promulgation*, p.350.

(i) 'Abdu'l-Bahá says that the universe is formed by indivisible particles which He refers to as 'elemental atoms': atom, in its etymological meaning as something that cannot be split; elemental, as simple, primal, fundamental. Modern scientists say that the atom is 'the smallest material unit in which any chemical element can be divided'.[122] This is not the philosophical atom. In fact, since the last century, scientists have understood that such an atom is neither simple nor indivisible. It was Rutherford[123] who proposed the model of atomic structure which is today accepted by most scientists: 'a kind of microscopical planetary system',[124] where instead of the sun there is a central nucleus, and instead of the planets there are electrons.[125] Subsequent studies demonstrated that not even the nucleus is simple and indivisible: it is formed by neutrons and protons. Neutrons and protons, in their turn, are formed by other simpler particles: quarks. Today the smallest known material particles are quarks and leptons (neutrins and electrons) and modern physicists think that all the matter which is in the universe is formed by four systems of two couples of particles (a quark-up and a quark-down, from one side, and an electron and a neutrin, from the other). But no one knows yet whether these sub-atomic particles are really simple or whether they can be divided into simpler ones. Whether and when scientists will discover the elemental atom, we do not know. But they accept the idea of its existence.

(ii) The elemental atoms are simple. Since in the world of creation death means decomposition, the elemental atoms, being simple, cannot be decomposed and therefore are eternal. This concept, for the time being, has no parallel in science: scientists at the most state that known elemental particles are billions of years old.

(iii) 'Creation is the expression of motion. Motion is life. A moving object is a living object, whereas that which is motionless and inert is as dead . . .'[126] says 'Abdu'l-Bahá; and moreover: 'Absolute repose does not exist in nature':[127] atoms — fundamental components of creation — are themselves subject to a perpetual motion. Modern scientists confirm this concept: the old division of matter into animate and inanimate matter is obsolete, because it is clear

---

122. G. Vegni, 'Atomo', in *Enciclopedia della Scienza e della Tecnica*, II, p.373.
123. Ernest Rutherford of Nelson (1871–1937), New Zealander, Nobel Prize in 1906, well-known for his studies on the theory of radioactivity and the atomic structure.
124. E. Fermi, 'Atomo', in *Enciclopedia Italiana*, V, p.245.
125. We are reminded of the following words by 'Abdu'l-Bahá: 'The smallest atoms in the universe are similar to the greatest beings of the universe . . .' (*Some Answered Questions*, p.182.)
126. *Promulgation*, p.140.
127. *Paris Talks*, p.88.

that all matter, in its microscopic dimension, is in motion. The elemental particles, in fact, are subject to a rotatory movement, called spin. Moreover, they literally move from one kingdom of existence to the other.

(iv) Among the elemental atoms there is a sort of attraction which 'Abdu'l-Bahá calls 'attraction' or 'atomical affinity':[128] this attraction is the cause of the existence of all phenomenal reality. In fact, since all phenomenal beings are formed by elemental atoms, thence only if an affinity exists among these elemental atoms is the existence of phenomenal beings possible. 'Abdu'l-Bahá indicates in such affinity the simplest expression, on the physical plane, of the metaphysical reality of love[129] and says that this is one of the spiritual lessons man can learn from physical reality: 'Throughout all creation, in all kingdoms, this law is written: that love and affinity are the cause of life, and discord and separation are the cause of death.'[130] 'Abdu'l-Bahá says that this power of attraction among the elemental atoms is a bounty that God bestows upon material creation through the agency of the world of the Kingdom: it is therefore the simplest expression of spirit in the world of creation.

Scientists are well aware of the existence of this power of attraction among the constituent particles of matter. The elemental particles are subject to the spin movement and this same movement produces forces of mutual attraction, which are called nuclear interactions. These forces binding together the elemental particles are extremely strong. Scientists have learnt how to release a part of those forces and the consequences of this release are manifest in the disruptive explosions of the atom bomb (which should be more properly called the neutron bomb).

(v) Elemental atoms are totipotent, inasmuch as each atom, as it is goes through the mineral, vegetable, animal and human kingdoms of the world of creation, and through the myriad forms and organisms of phenomenal existence in each of those kingdoms, variously combining with other elemental atoms, 'not only becomes imbued with the powers and virtues of the kingdom it traverses, but also reflects the attributes and qualities of the forms and organisms of those kingdoms'. It follows that 'all [atoms] are privileged to possess the virtues existent in these kingdoms and to reflect the attributes of their organisms'. Therefore 'each elemental atom of the universe is possessed of a capacity to express all the

---

128. *Promulgation*, p.4.
129. 'Abdu'l-Bahá writes: *'Love is . . . the unique power that bindeth together the divers elements of this material world, the supreme magnetic force that directeth the movement of the spheres in the celestial realms.'* (*Selections*, p.27.)
130. *Promulgation*, p.207.

virtues of the universe'. This concept is evidently also upheld by modern scientists who — as has been already said — agree that every existent being in the universe is formed by quarks and leptons. 'Abdu'l-Bahá states that this particular aspect of the phenomenal world is a great lesson of unity and 'the true explanation of pantheism'. He explains that God is transcendent in His Essence and that no direct relation exists between Him and His creatures. The world of creation receives the gifts of God by emanation from the intermediate world of the Kingdom through the agency of the spirit, which moves it and guides it in its moving. Following a path whose course is determined by natural laws — the Will of God as expressed on the phenomenal plane — atoms combine and generate the various beings, which differ from each other in 'degree and receptivity'.[131] But the 'original matter' of the elemental atoms is one, and the spirit which moves it, and as it moves, enables it to assume different shapes, is one. Therefore the universe is like a single great 'laboratory'[132] or 'workshop'[133] where the same material and metaphysical components — the elemental atoms and spirit animating and guiding them — are present. This is the foundation of the 'intrinsic oneness of all phenomena',[134] of the total, eternal, mutual involvement of all existing realities, of the perfect reciprocity of phenomena. It is in the light of these concepts that the following words by 'Abdu'l-Bahá should be read: 'the smallest atoms in the universe are similar to the greatest beings of the universe.'[135]

(vi) The atomic theory also explains '. . . the conservation of energy and the infinitude of phenomena, the indestructibility of phenomena, changeless and immutable because life cannot be annihilated. The utmost is this: that the form, the outer image, throughout these changes and transformations, is dissolved. The realities of all phenomena are immutable and unchangeable.'[136]

A question seems left unanswered: are all the elemental atoms equal, or do they differ from each other? On the grounds of the principle that there is no repetition in nature, it would appear that

---

131. *Promulgation*, pp.285, 285–6, 285, 14.
132. *Some Answered Questions*, p.182.
133. 'Tablet to Dr. A. Forel' in *Bahá'í World*, XV, p.40.
134. *Promulgation*, p.349.
135. *Some Answered Questions*, p.182. The charm of such concepts has not escaped some modern scientists who, perceiving a similarity between the greatest and the smallest, advance a theory on the structure of the universe wherefore the universe could be an enormous adron and, viceversa, adrons could be considered as strong microuniverses. *See* E. Recami, 'Particelle elementari come microuniversi', in *Scienza e Tecnica* 79, pp.60, 64.
136. 'The Three Realities' in *Star of the West*, VII, p.119.

among them there might be a 'point of contact' and a 'point of distinction':[137] the former might be their substance, perhaps the 'original matter'[138] which is the origin and the point of unity of all sensible reality; the latter might be in relation to their degree and function in the scale of reality.

Evolution

The two concepts of creation as emanation, and of the atomic structure of the universe are the foundation of another very important concept in the Bahá'í view of the universe and life: evolution.

The creative plan of God

The world of creation, as an emanation from God, *'reflecteth His glory'*; it is a *'mirror'* where His *'image is reflected'*.[139] *'His sovereign and pervasive Will . . . called into being . . . creation'*, and *'the unique distinction and capacity to know Him and to love Him'* that *'He chose to confer upon man'* is the purpose wherefore He willed to create, in Bahá'u'lláh's words, *'the generating impulse and the primary purpose underlying the whole creation'*.[140] As a Creator, therefore, God has a plan: to enable 'original matter', emanating from the world of the Kingdom as a necessity of divine attributes, to reflect more and more faithfully His image, so that it may produce man who, through his capacity *'to know Him and to love Him'*, brings the process a step further, transferring it from a plane of unconscious necessity to a level of willing consciousness. This process, through which the totipotent elemental atoms are enabled to manifest their 'capacity to express all the virtues of the universe' 'through change and transformation' and 'progressive transference and motion throughout the material kingdoms',[141] is evolution.

'Abdu'l-Bahá writes: *'Every plan is in need of a power for its execution'*:[142] the power through which 'the creative plan of God' is executed is the spirit, which emanating from the world of the Kingdom, 'in itself is progressive'. 'Abdu'l-Bahá says: 'Motion is

---

137. *Promulgation*, p.67.
138. *Some Answered Questions*, p.138.
139. *Gleanings*, p.166. Bahá'u'lláh writes: '. . . *whatever is in the heavens and whatever is on the earth is a direct evidence of the revelation within it of the attributes and names of God . . . To a supreme degree is this true of man . . . for in him are potentially revealed all the attributes and names of God to a degree that no other created being hath excelled or surpassed.*' (*Kitáb-i-Íqán*, pp.100–101.)
140. *Gleanings*, pp.61, 65.
141. *Promulgation*, pp.286, 285.
142. Quoted in 'The Need of a Universal Program', in *Star of the West*, XIII, p.132.

life. A moving object is a living object, whereas that which is motionless and inert is as dead . . .'[143] Thence it is the spirit which keeps in motion the world of creation, so that '. . . nothing which exists remains in a state of repose . . . Everything is either growing or declining . . .'[144] and 'all creation is growing and evolving. It never ceases.'[145] Therefore evolution is 'the expression of spirit in the world of matter' or else 'progress of the spirit'.[146]

General features of the creative plan of God

The Bahá'í texts fully explain the general features of this majestic process.

(i) From the world of the Kingdom two realities emanate, as a necessity of God's attributes: the spirit, that is the intermediary between the world of the Kingdom and the world of creation, and 'original matter', formed by 'elemental atoms'.

(ii) Spirit has a twofold effect on 'original matter':

—— it sets in motion elemental atoms, starting the never-ending chain of the continuous transformations of 'original matter';

—— it guides matter in its movements and transformations, according to criteria which man is able to perceive as natural laws. These criteria execute in the matter the 'creative plan of God', enabling the totipotent atoms to express, through their assembling together, their capacity to mirror forth the manifold attributes of life, i.e. 'the powers and virtues of the kingdom [they] traverse[s] . . . and the attributes and qualities of the forms and organisms of those kingdoms'.[147]

(iii) The 'original matter' is therefore characterized by a perpetual motion.[148] 'Abdu'l-Bahá says that this motion is 'essential, that is,

---

143. *Promulgation*, pp.293, 101, 140.
144. *Some Answered Questions*, p.233.
145. 'Progress in Religion', in *Star of the West*, XIII, p.99.
146. *Paris Talks*, pp.90, 88.
147. *Promulgation*, pp.293, 285.
148. Regarding motion 'Abdu'l-Bahá says: 'There are different degrees of motion. There is a motion of transit, that is from place to place . . . Another kind is the motion of inherent growth, like that of man from the condition of childhood to the state of manhood . . . The third is the motion of condition – the sick man passes from the stage of sickness to the state of health. The fourth motion is that of the spirit. For instance, the child while in the mother's womb has all the potential qualities of the spirit, but those qualities begin to unfold little by little, as the child is born and grows and develops, finally manifesting all the attributes and the qualities of the spirit. The fifth is the motion of the intellect whereby the ignorant become wise . . . the carnally minded spiritual . . . the sixth motion is that of the eternal essence. That is to say, all phenomena either step from the arena of non-existence into the court of objectivity, or from existence into non-existence. Just as being in motion is the test of life, so being stationary is the test of death and when a moving object stops it retrogrades.' ('Abdu'l-Bahá, *on Divine Philosophy*, pp.120–21.)

natural',[149] because it is 'necessary to existence'. According to the 'intrinsic oneness of all phenomena',[150] the 'original matter' follows in its motion criteria which apply to all phenomena of existence.[151] (iv) These criteria can be summarized as a never-ending process of growth, which is similar — according to one of the metaphors suggested by 'Abdu'l-Bahá — to the development of a seed which slowly sprouts, then grows, until it brings forth a fruit which contains a new seed.

This process of growth is therefore characterized by the following elements:

────── it is 'gradual':[152] from a degree of lesser (least) perfection it reaches a degree of greater (greatest) perfection or fulfilment;[153]

────── it is cyclical: whenever a material being reaches its greatest possible perfection, 'the point which it cannot overpass',[154] it declines until it ceases to exist in its original condition, while in its stead, 'a new order and condition is established'; this order and condition in its turn undergoes a new process of growth. 'The circle of existence is the same circle: it returns',[155] says 'Abdu'l-Bahá.

────── it is relative: since the possible perfections each material being can achieve are infinite, it follows that the greatest perfection any being may have attained is always a relative perfection;

────── it is infinite: since in physical reality taken as a whole the possible perfections are infinite, it follows that the evolutionary process is endless.[156]

Evolution in the world of creation

In the world of creation we can therefore perceive the following essential features:
(i) 'for existence there is neither change nor transformation; exist-

---

149. *Some Answered Questions*, p.233.
150. *Promulgation*, p.131, 349.
151. The very interesting general systemic theory of evolution advanced by E. Laszlo seems to agree with this concept of evolution viewed as a single great plan involving the entire creation. Laszlo writes: 'Scientific evidence of the patterns traced by evolution in the physical universe, in the living world, and even in the world of history is growing rapidly. It is coalescing into the image of basic regularities that repeat and recur.' (*Evolution*, p.5.)
152. *Paris Talks*, p.88.
153. These concepts also seem to fit in the theory advanced by E. Laszlo, when he writes that in the process of evolution 'we find an increase in the level of organization' and 'can readily appreciate that the products of evolution are distributed on multiple hierarchical levels.' (*Evolution*, p.24.)
154. *Some Answered Questions*, p.230.
155. *Promulgation*, p.124, 220.
156. *See* above, pp.47.

ence is ever existence: it can never be translated into nonexistence';[157]

(ii) 'Creation is the expression of motion. Motion is life. A moving object is a living object, whereas that which is motionless and inert is as dead. All created forms are progressive in their planes, or kingdoms of existence, under the stimulus of the power or spirit of life. The universal energy is dynamic. Nothing is stationary in the material worlds of outer phenomena or in the inner world of intellect and consciousness';[158] therefore all created things undergo a never-ending evolution;

(iii) as created things evolve, they go through 'gradual stages or degrees', characterized by a 'specialized capacity'[159] to mirror forth the spirit;

(iv) at last, created things attain a 'degree, or stage of maturity',[160] which they 'cannot overpass';[161]

(v) 'after which a new order and condition is established'.[162]

In this context, the concepts of physical life and death have different meanings, depending on the context:

—— in the light of the atomic conception of the universe, life means composition and death decomposition. According to such a definition, therefore, death is but a transference from one condition of existence to another;

—— in the light of the concept of evolution, existence 'is gradation; a degree below a higher degree is considered as non-existence'.[163] In fact, if we consider a mineral, this is undoubtedly dead in comparison to a vegetable. But spirit is present also in the mineral: it is that movement which generates the power of attraction, which in its turn binds together its constituent particles. '*All beings are endowed with life*,'[164] writes 'Abdu'l-Bahá. However, the vegetable has the power of growth, which is absent in the mineral. And the animal is alive, when it is compared with the vegetable, whereas the vegetable is dead, if it is compared to the animal. For example, a human being affected by a deep coma because of a severe trauma is said to live a vegetative life, and by this it is meant that his life is quite different from a normal human life. In the Bahá'í texts the word *death* indicates also the condition

---

157. *Promulgation*, pp.88–9.
158. ibid. p.104.
159. ibid. pp.131, 160.
160. ibid. p.430.
161. *Some Answered Questions*, p.230.
162. *Promulgation*, p.124.
163. *Promulgation*, p.89.
164. 'Tablet to Dr. A. Forel', in *Bahá'í World*, XV, p.38.

of such a man who, while alive in his animal life, is nevertheless, since he is spiritually wholly unconscious, even as dead. Such is the meaning of the well-known words of the Gospel: 'Let the dead bury their dead'.[165] spiritually dead the former, physically dead the latter. 'Abdu'l-Bahá explains, moreover, that '. . . though the existence of beings in relation to the existence of God is an illusion, nevertheless, in the condition of being it has a real and certain existence.'[166] Therefore, the world is but a show, when it is compared to the world of the Kingdom; but, in itself, it is really existent. Therefore, the concept of life and death is a relative concept.

(vi) '. . . for the whole universe, whether for the heavens or for men, there are cycles of great events, of important facts and occurrences. When a cycle is ended, a new cycle begins';[167]

(vii) within each cycle, each phenomenal reality undergoes a process of transformation, as regards its perfection, but not as regards its state. Each reality can achieve endless and infinite perfections, without any change in its state. Everything, writes Bahá'u'lláh, *'according to its capacities, indicateth, and is expressive of, the knowledge of God'*,[168] and 'Abdu'l-Bahá says: 'In every station there is a specialized capacity', 'a degree of function and intelligence';[169]

(viii) *'The transformation of the innate substance is impossible'*,[170] writes 'Abdu'l-Bahá; He says moreover: '. . . the world of existence is dependent for its progress upon reformation; otherwise it will be as dead';[171] this reformation is realized through the spirit emanating from the world of the Kingdom. In 'Abdu'l-Bahá's words: 'The transformation depends upon divine bounty. The mineral progresses in its own world. But from the mineral to the vegetable it progresses only by divine bounty. Also transformation from the vegetable to the animal is God's plan. Of itself the transformation cannot take place.'[172] These statements are very subtle: they require deeper investigation and studies than those that have been done up to now. Evolution is within the kingdoms,[173] says 'Abdu'l-Bahá. Vegetable and animal spirits, being a part of creation, are sufficient

---

165. *Luke* 9:50.
166. *Some Answered Questions*, p.278.
167. ibid. p.160.
168. *Kitáb-i-Íqán*, p.102.
169. *Promulgation*, pp.160, 240.
170. *Selections*, p.61.
171. *Promulgation*, p.279.
172. Quoted in A. Kunz, 'Some Questions about science and religion', in *Star of the West*, XIII, p.143.
173. *Some Answered Questions*, p.230.

for the intrinsic changes of each phenomenal being to take place. But for the transformations from one kingdom to another, these natural powers are not enough: a power from a higher level must assist. This is the divine bounty, the power of the world of the Kingdom, that is, the spirit.

In fact, evolution within the kingdoms implies but the perfecting of potential qualities: the 'power of attraction' in the mineral kingdom, the 'power of growth' in the vegetable kingdom, the 'power of sense perception' in the animal kingdom. But the transition from one kingdom to another implies the appearance of a new capacity, which previously did not exist, even potentially. It is a real transformation of substance, which cannot come to pass by itself. Therefore, it is only the power of the world of the Kingdom which — belonging to a superior level — can realize this transformation. Such a concept is evident, particularly in the process of man's spiritual evolution.

And yet, evolution — whatever the level on which it is examined — is always moved by the powers of the spirit, because 'the power of growth' and the 'power of sense perception' are themselves expressions of the spirit. The only difference is that these two capacities are expressions of the spirit in its acting in the world of creation, whereas the powers bringing the elemental atoms to meet so that they may give birth to the creatures of the mineral, or vegetable, or animal, or human worlds are expressions of the spirit in its acting in the world of the Kingdom.[174]

(ix) Evolution is progress: between the simple, tiny elemental atom and the great man with his complex brain, there is a sequence of degrees of existence, one following the other in a growing complexity of structures and a growing capacity to express in the physical world the qualities of the metaphysical world of the Kingdom. This evolutionary process is a process of approaching God, inasmuch as the higher degrees of perfection are achieved by physical reality as it evolves according to the guiding rules given by the world of the Kingdom; Bahá'u'lláh mentions *'the Command of God which pervadeth all created things'*.[175] The more completely this reality expresses the

---

174. 'Abdu'l-Bahá writes: '*Know that spirit in general is divided in five sorts — the vegetable spirit, the animal spirit, the human spirit, the spirit of faith and the divine spirit of sanctity* . . .'; He then continues, saying that the vegetable, animal and human spirits '*are not reckoned as Spirit in the terminology of the Scriptures and the usage of the people of truth, inasmuch as the laws governing them are as the laws which govern all phenomenal being [i.e. all existences belonging to the phenomenal or the material universe, called 'the world of generation and corruption'], in respect to generation, corruption, production, change and reversion* . . .'. (*Tablets*, pp.115–6.)

175. *Tablets*, p.141.

spiritual qualities of the world of the Kingdom, the closer it approaches God. It is in such perspective that 'Abdu'l-Bahá says: 'Progress is the expression of spirit in the world of matter.'[176]

(x) 'Inequality in degree and capacity is a property of nature,'[177] says 'Abdu'l-Bahá; because of this property the world of matter is a world of multiplicity, of 'contradictions . . . opposites',[178] which arise from the comparisons among, and the coexistence of, physical realities which are fundamentally equal but belong to different degrees. In other words, 'each phenomenon is the expression in degree of all other phenomena. The difference is one of successive transference and the period of time involved in the evolutionary process'. It is clear then that in the phenomenal world all things are fundamentally one and the difference among single realities is but 'one of degrees and receptivity'.[179]

In conclusion, the process of evolution can be viewed as that process through which those perfections which were engraved within each created being when it was brought into existence find an ever more complete expression, until that being reaches an apex called maturity. 'Abdu'l-Bahá says: 'All beings, whether large or small, were created perfect and complete from the first, but their perfections appear in them by degrees . . . .'.[180] Each created being possesses in itself — like a seed — potential perfections. Evolution is that process through which those perfections manifest themselves. What that created being will become depends, on the one hand, on its potential endowments; on the other, on the natural laws which start, move and guide its development; and finally on many external circumstances which interact with it, influencing its possibility of expressing those same perfections it was imbued with at its creation.

Evolution in the four kingdoms of the world of creation

If we examine the physical universe and its evolution in the light of these concepts, we will understand that the four kingdoms of the world of creation — mineral, vegetable, animal and human — are even as four different fruits arrived at maturity on the same tree (the world of creation) in different times; the lapse of time which must pass before maturity is attained is proportionate to the complexity of the structure of that kingdom. This metaphor is

---

176. *Paris Talks*, p.90.
177. *Promulgation*, p.132.
178. *Paris Talks*, p.90.
179. *Promulgation*, pp.349, 14.
180. *Some Answered Questions*, p.199.

offered by 'Abdu'l-Bahá in His talks, in order to explain that the four kingdoms, mutually dependent as they are, nevertheless do not stem from one another.[181]

The four kingdoms of creation are different from each other, inasmuch as their component material elements are organized in different ways and therefore express at different levels and degrees the spirit — the divine bounties emanating from the world of the Kingdom and pervading the whole creation. 'Each kingdom is receiving the light and bounty of the eternal Sun according to its capacity', says 'Abdu'l-Bahá; and moreover: 'In each kingdom we find the same virtues manifesting themselves more fully, proving that the reality has been transferred from a lower to a higher form and kingdom of being', which is possible because 'the atoms of the material elements are transferable from one form of existence to another, from one degree and kingdom to another, lower or higher'.[182]

'Abdu'l-Bahá dwells upon the details of the differences among these four kingdoms:

(i) The mineral kingdom has the capacity to manifest the spirit as 'power of attraction' and this is 'the only expression of love the stone can manifest'.[183]

(ii) The vegetable kingdom has the capacity to manifest the spirit as 'power of growth' or in other words as 'power of absorption from the earth';[184] in fact vegetables can absorb from the earth and the atmosphere what they need for preservation, reproduction and regulation — the three typical activities of living systems. This power, in 'Abdu'l-Bahá's words, 'results from the combination of elements and the mingling of substances by the decree of the Supreme God, and from the influence, the effect, the connection, of other existences. When these substances and elements are separated from each other, the power of growth also ceaseth to exist': this power is therefore viewed in the Bahá'í texts not as a mystical entity, but as a natural power and it is compared by 'Abdu'l-Bahá with the 'electric force'.[185]

(iii) The animal kingdom has the capacity to manifest the spirit as 'power of sense perception', a power that confers on the animals 'emotions and sensibilities', 'intelligence',[186] 'voluntary

---

181. See *Some Answered Questions*, p.199.
182. *Promulgation*, pp.173, 88, 87.
183. *Promulgation*, p.268.
184. ibid.
185. *Some Answered Questions*, p.143.
186. *Promulgation*, pp.29, 268, 17.

movements'[187] and 'memory'.[188] Also this power is viewed as a natural power, bound to vanish when the elements whose composition was conducive to its appearance in the physical plane are separated from each other, even as 'when the oil is finished and the wick consumed'[189] the light fades away.

(iv) the human kingdom has the capacity to manifest the spirit as 'intellect' or 'conscious intelligence', 'conscious reflection', 'intellectual investigation'.[190] Referring to human spirit, 'Abdu'l-Bahá says that, unlike the mineral, vegetable and animal spirits which belong to the world of creation and therefore have a beginning and an end, human spirit belongs to another degree. In fact, 'the body of man is . . . the most perfect existence'.[191] He likens it to a mirror and the human spirit to the sun; when the mirror is broken, the sun nevertheless remains; likewise the human spirit, which is of the world of the Kingdom, has no end. The comprehension of such a concept requires a more detailed analysis, which will be presented in the following chapters.

If we intended to draw a graphic representation of the evolutionary processes going on throughout the universe, we should not draw a staircase, but a tree: from the root (mineral kingdom) three branches grow (vegetable, animal and human kingdoms); from these three branches other branches and twigs grow (genuses, species, etc.) and so on.[192] Thus starting from the farthest branch we could follow from one branch to the other a path through which we could reach the root; all these branches are the successive transformations that branch (or that creature) underwent in its morphology, starting from the root, until it took on its present form.

Evolution according to Plotinus, in the Bahá'í texts

'Abdu'l-Bahá also explains evolution in Plotinian terms. The world of the Kingdom is the first emanation from God, 'Supreme Centre';[193] from this Centre begins the first arc of existence, the

---

187. *Some Answered Questions*, p.3.
188. *Promulgation*, p.240.
189. *Some Answered Questions*, p.143.
190. *Promulgation*, pp.49, 51, 17, 31.
191. *Some Answered Questions*, pp.143-4.
192. In this connection 'Abdu'l-Bahá says: 'The world is like a tree; the mineral kingdom is like the root; the vegetable kingdom is like the branches; the animal kingdom is like the blossoms; and man is like unto the fruit of that tree. The tree is but for its fruit. If the gardener did not expect fruit, he would never plant trees. In the same way everything is for man.' (quoted in G. Winterburn, *Table Talks with Abdul-Baha*, p.12.)
193. *Promulgation*, p.15.

arc of descent, the arc of material worlds: elemental atoms form the elements, which are the foundations of all material things: mineral, vegetable, animal. Man, who is possessed of all the qualities of the world of creation, i.e. 'a body which grows and which feels'[194] is 'the lowest point of the arc of descent',[195] or else the highest point of materiality. This process which, starting from the elemental atom, arrives at man, is termed 'beginning (literally: bringing forth)'[196] and man is its fruit. From man, who stands therefore opposite the 'Supreme Centre', begins the second arc of existence, the arc of ascent, the arc of the spiritual worlds. This arc comprises the spiritual degrees of existence and is termed 'progress (literally: producing something new)'.[196] This arc of ascent culminates in the world of the Kingdom (termed also First Mind, Primal Will, Word of God or Logos, Identity or Self or Soul of God). The circle of existence therefore has its beginning in the elemental atom, follows the arc of descent, with the degrees of material world – mineral, vegetable and animal kingdoms – and culminates in man. From man, who stands at the end of materiality and at the beginning of spirituality, the second arc of existence begins: it is the arc of ascent which, traversing the various degrees of the spiritual worlds such as the spirit of faith, the Holy Spirit, the Most Great Spirit, culminates in the Logos, which manifests itself in the world of creation as the Manifestation of God, Perfect Image of God, Perfect Man, perfect expression in the plane of the world of creation of all the qualities of the world of the Kingdom.

Evolution as an educative process

Evolution is described by Bahá'u'lláh as *'the revelation of the Name of God, the Educator'*. *'Behold,'* He writes, *'how in all things the evidences of such a revelation are manifest, how the betterment of all beings dependeth upon it. This education is of two kinds. The one is universal. Its influence pervadeth all things and sustaineth them. It is for this reason that God hath assumed the title, "Lord of all the worlds". The other is confined to them that have come under the shadow of this Name, and sought the shelter of this most mighty Revelation.'*[197] These words (which will be commented upon later on) point out the relation between the spiritual evolution each man undergoes through the efforts he exerts as he follows the guidance of the Revelation of God, and the evolution of the entire creation.

---

194. *Some Answered Questions*, p.235.
195. *Selections*, p.130.
196. *Some Answered Questions*, p.286.
197. *Gleanings*, p.190.

Evolution in the different planes of the world of existence

The evolutionary process can be studied in various perspectives. If we consider it in the world of being as a whole – the world of creation and the world of the Kingdom – this process should necessarily be viewed independently of its relation with time. In fact, in the world of the Kingdom time does not exist. The world of the Kingdom is coexistent and coeternal with God, to whom it is inferior though, because it depends on, and was created by, Him. In the level of the world of the Kingdom, beginning and end are one and the same thing, therefore any created being, viewed in that world, is simultaneously what it is – in the world of creation – in all phases of its evolution. Thus the world of creation could metaphorically be viewed as a magnificent fresco: each point in this fresco is an individual; groups of points, making together a detail of this fresco, are species; a group of details, forming a figure, is a kingdom of creation; groups of figures, forming a theme, are more kingdoms of creation, and so on. This metaphor enables us to understand how, in the plane of the world of the Kingdom, there is no transformation from individual to individual, from species to species, from kingdom to kingdom, because each of them has its own individuality and existence beside that of the others, though it comes into existence after the others, and forms with them the majestic fresco of the world of creation. It is in this perspective that 'Abdu'l-Bahá confirms the concept of 'conservation of species'[198] and of the absolute and complete distinction among the kingdoms of creation, and that He says: '. . . the original species of the genus do not change and alter, but the form, color, bulk will change and alter, or even progress'.[199] This statement parallels that law of evolution whereby '. . . all phenomena of being attain to a summit and degree of consummation, after which a new order and condition is established'.[200] Evolution is that progress whereby the potential qualities of the seed are transformed into the reality of the tree and its fruits: in the world of the Kingdom the seed is simultaneously tree and fruit; in the world of creation between the seed and the fruit there are many different stages, the stages of evolution.

At the level of the individual, evolution begins, for example, with the conception of a human being; it proceeds through successive stages (embryo, foetus, new-born baby, child, boy or

---

198. *Promulgation*, p. 359.
199. *Some Answered Questions*, p. 193.
200. *Promulgation*, p. 124.

girl, adolescent, young man or woman, mature individual, old individual); it brings forth its fruits during maturity (progeny and fruits of material and intellectual work); at last it ends in decomposition (death).

At the level of species, there is a phenomenal beginning, that is, whenever a species appears on the earth; an evolution through successive stages culminating in an apex of maturity; a stage of decline and at last its disappearance. Such phenomenon is fully proved by paleontological evidence (fossils) enabling scientists to study the evolutionary process of single species. A very well-known example is the evolution of dinosaurs. They appeared in the Triassic Period and attained an apex during the Jurassic and Cretaceous Periods, after which they disappeared.[201]

At the level of the world of creation viewed as a whole, the beginning of evolution can be traced in 'original matter' – the seed; its 'fruit'[202] is man, who – being the apex of physical evolution – is possessed of all the existing perfections of all the inferior grades. In fact, man has in himself the typical 'power of attraction' of the mineral kingdom; the 'power of growth' belonging to the vegetable kingdom; the 'power of sense perception', which is a distinctive feature of the animal kingdom. But besides all these powers, he has also the power of 'intellect', which belongs only to his kingdom. Therefore, man is the 'fruit' or the purpose of evolution.

This is the foundation of another important Bahá'í concept; how is it possible for the whole evolutionary process of the world of creation – infinite and eternal as a whole – to come to a close with such a powerless creature as physical man, who lives for a very few years on this earth and then dissolves in dust? Evolution is in itself a never-ending process: there must therefore be something else beyond physical man. The Bahá'í texts say that such a reality transcending physical man is the human soul, which – inasmuch as it has the capacity of intellectual and spiritual perception and is endowed with potential spiritual qualities – brings the evolutionary process a step forward from the world of creation to the world of the Kingdom.

Limitations of some modern concepts of evolution

Some evolutionists deny any unity, 'rationality' and finality in the evolutionary process.

---

201. 'Abdu'l-Bahá says: '. . . the species existing on this earth are phenomenal, for it is established that there was a time when these species did not exist on the surface of the earth.' (*Some Answered Questions*, p.151.)
202. *Some Answered Questions*, p.201.

(i) Regarding the progress in the physical world through evolution, this progress can be described in a Bahá'í perspective as a rising helicoidal motion. Each coil of the helicoid is a 'circle of existence'[203] with its beginning and its end. In the helicoid, the end of the coil always stands at a superior level to its beginning. In fact, just as any phenomenal reality, both individual and species, had a beginning, so it will also have an end, because any phenomenal reality, inasmuch as it is phenomenal, is limited in time and space. Therefore evolution, viewed in individuals and species, implies a stage of progress as well as a stage of regress, following that stage wherein that phenomenal being has attained its highest possible point of perfection, that is its maturity. Nevertheless, that individual, or that species, will be followed by other individuals, other species, which will bring his or its perfections a step forward. But they will do it on another level.

Evolution is therefore a very complex process. No wonder that because of such complexity it is so difficult to trace the specific conditions which have influenced the evolution of any given phenomenal reality. For example, it is an arduous task to discover why the earth has today such a shape, such component elements, geographical configuration, climate, vegetable and animal species, and man. It is up to men of science to investigate nature through their methods, so that they may unravel its mysteries. Bahá'í texts give a guidance which will prove useful as to the direction such studies could follow.

(ii) As for those which seem nature's mistakes, [204] its seemingly wrong choices, which are advanced as proof by those who deny its rationality and finality:

—— the universe and nature are perfect as a whole, but each individual being is manifestly imperfect. Therefore these mistakes are not a surprise.

—— some of these supposed mistakes in the evolutionary processes could be merely choices whose meaning is as yet undiscovered. It would be totally absurd for a man to claim a complete understanding of even phenomenal reality;

—— other supposed mistakes could be stages of regress of an individual or a species, when they have already yielded their fruit and are therefore inexorably declining towards the conclusion of their vital cycle.

---

203. *Promulgation*, p.220.
204. K. Lorenz writes: 'The mistakes and dead ends into which evolutionary processes can be lured by momentary advantages are everything except irrelevant to the continued existence of the lineage in question.' (*The Waning of Humaneness*, p.21.) Lorenz is one of those scientists who deny a teleological order in the universe.

(iii) To maintain that evolution is not just the outcome of chance, but is moved by an Intelligent Being Who guides it, does not belong — as the Bahá'í texts explain it — to the realms of tales and myth, but to the domains of reason. For the time being no one can demonstrate either hypothesis. To believe in the former or in the latter is therefore a matter of faith; but in this context too to have faith means that a hypothesis is true, because so it appears in the light of many other general ideas which, inasmuch as they are undoubtedly true and make this hypothesis probable and reliable, are the rational guarantors of a hypothesis, which is thus accepted in an act of faith.

In this regard, a suggestive anecdote is related by Guy Murchie 'about Charles Boyle, the fourth Earl of Orrery, who flourished in southern Ireland early in the eighteenth century — and of the theorem that bears his name. Having heard of Kepler's famous discovery of the laws of planetary motion and of Newton's recent work on gravitation, Lord Orrery had a working model of the solar system built inside his castle. It was an extraordinary dynamic and up-to-date piece of clockwork with orbital hoops and a brass sun in the center plus smaller globes representing Mercury, Venus, Earth, Mars, Jupiter and Saturn slowly revolving around it, even a moon circling the Earth and four little ones going around Jupiter.

'But it seems that Lord Orrery had an atheist friend who had an utterly materialistic outlook and thought of the universe as just an immense moving system of natural machinery that somehow coasts along, blindly but automatically maintaining itself without benefit of consciousness, mind or intelligence of any kind. So when the friend heard tell of Orrery's new and wonderful machine, he lost no time in going to the castle to see it. Entering the great hall where the model was in operation, the atheist's eyes widened with awe and the first question he asked Lord Orrery was: "Where did you get this magnificent thing? Who made it?"

'But Orrery, remembering previous arguments with the atheist about creation, surprised him by replying, "Nobody made it. It just happened".

' "How could that be?" retorted the atheist, "Surely these intricate gears and wheels couldn't create themselves. Who made them?"

'Lord Orrery stood his ground, insisting that his model of the solar system had just happened by itself. Meantime, the atheist worked himself into a state of hysterical frustration. Then at last, judging the time was ripe, Orrery let him have it. "Up to now", he declared, "I was testing you. Now I am going to offer you a bargain. I will promise to tell you truly who made my little sun and planets down here as soon as you tell me truly Who made the infinitely bigger, more wonderful and more beautiful real sun and planets up there in the heavens".

'The atheist turned a little pale and, for the first time, began to wonder whether the Universe could really have made itself, or possibly be running all this time automatically and unguided by the slightest twinge of intelligence. And this was the origin of the Orrery Theorem which says: "If the model of any natural system requires intelligence for its creation and its working, the real natural system requires at least as much intelligence for its own creation and working." '[205]

This anecdote is suggestive not so much for its persuasiveness, as for that subtle irony which is a distinctive feature of anyone who has attained a universal view of life and existence and consequently to a serenity which we think — because Bahá'u'lláh states it — to be man's birthright.[206] Any other outlook is conducive only to fruitless and unacceptable pessimism, or at most to agnosticism, which we accept only as a refuge where clever minds may withdraw when they do not meet or recognize anything worthy of their trust during their lives. But it is only a pause, a limbo whence they must sooner or later emerge to face with all its implications the inescapable task of finding an answer to the great existential questions of life, lest other forces prevail. Such forces, denying the transcendental worlds, deprive life of its meaning and human values of their pregnancy, and reduce man to being satisfied with considering himself an intelligent animal and thus becoming the most foolish of all living creatures — a creature who prefers to be even as his inferiors, who stupidly upholds and sanctions a society poisoned by competition and war. Whereas the concepts of the atom and of evolution, as explained in the Bahá'í texts, are in themselves a mighty trace of God in this phenomenal world, a trace which it is worthwhile following if that *'knowledge of God'*[207] in which all things begin is to be attained.

---

205. *The Seven Mysteries of Life*, p.611.
206. For an explanation of the concept that happiness is a human birthright *see* G. Townshend, *The Mission of Bahá'u'lláh*, pp.88 *passim*.
207. *Gleanings*, p.5.

4 The Wonders of Evolution

The concepts of creation, the atomic structure of the universe and the meaning and patterns of its never-ending transformations provide a wide-ranging foundation for other detailed explanations produced in the Bahá'í texts. These explanations, mostly offered in that metaphorical language which is typical of revelation, shed light on the entire course of the history of the universe, in other words the process of its evolution.

The origin of the universe

If the world of creation as a whole had no beginning and will have no end, if it is infinite, as well as its phenomena, is there any sense in discussing an origin of the universe? In the light of those statements, the origin of the universe seems rather a station than a precise time – a concept that has already been explained in Chapter 3. Here, we intend to present other Bahá'í concepts on this difficult topic and to compare them with modern scientific theories.

Bahá'u'lláh writes: '*The world of existence came into being through the heat generated from the interaction between the active force and that which is its recipient . . . Such as communicate the generating influence and such as receive its impact are indeed created through the irresistible Word of God . . .*'.[1] The explanation of this statement set forth by Bahá'u'lláh in His *Tablet of Wisdom* will require the extensive study and meditation of future Bahá'í scholars, who are more likely to be successful in their efforts than we can be today, as their understand-

---
1. *Tablets*, p. 140.

ing of the Bahá'í Revelation becomes wider and deeper. We take the liberty of writing but a few remarks about it.

It seems that through this general statement the origin of any created reality may be explained: an *'active force'*[1] communicates *'the generating influence'*[1] (for example a sperm fertilizes an ovum); a *'heat'* is generated (an energy is released through the fusion of the two gametes); a process of transformation is thus set in motion in the zygote, wherefore a new being will be formed (embryogenesis). If this statement is viewed as referred to the origin of the universe, the following could be one of its explanations: from the world of the Kingdom (*'the irresistible Word of God'*[1]) the spirit (*'the active force'*) and the original matter, composed of elemental atoms (*'its recipient'*), emanate; *'the generating influence'* of the spirit sets in motion the atoms composing the original matter, so that the evolutionary process starts.

This concept is somehow reminiscent of the big bang or great deflagration theory. According to this theory, which — as Melchiorri says — 'is but a rough approximation of what must have really happened at the beginning of time',[2] there has been for the universe a beginning when anything we see today was originated. At the beginning existed a primal nucleus — the proto-universe. It was composed of a proto-matter, and it supposedly had a diameter fifty times bigger than the diameter of the solar system, a density equal to 100 million times the density of water and extremely high temperatures, about 100 billion kelvin degrees. These physical characteristics — the great density as well as very high temperatures — caused a very fast initial expansion, almost a conflagration, which according to this theory should be considered as point zero in the scale of time. Such a tremendous phenomenon had two immediate effects: a gradual decrease of temperature, which one second after that explosion was ten billion kelvin degrees, a hundred seconds after, one billion kelvin degrees and so on; and a steady increase of the length of the radius of that huge globe.

The big bang occurred about fifteen billion years ago: immediately after, those transformations began through which such chemical elements as are known today were originated. The galaxies and the stars, as units in the structures of the universe and the galaxies respectively, were originated only three to four billion years ago.

2. F. Melchiorri and B. Olivo Melchiorri, 'Cosmologia del Big Bang', in *Scienza e Tecnica 80–82*, p.35. 'A theory formulated in the fifties by Russian physicist George G. Gamov in three short papers, almost three notes, published by *Physical Review*, the most prestigious American journal of physics.' (ibid.) Today, however, a series of successive big bangs, rather than a single big bang, is hypothesized.

This theory does not explain what was in existence before the proto-universe, nor whence and how it was originated, nor why it originally had those physical features; nor do the natural sciences and their methods seem fit to give answers to such questions.

Other scientists, through their mathematical processing of formulas describing proposed patterns of the universe, mathematically deduced that a condition must have existed whereby all the components of the universe were concentrated in a single geometrical point. Such an initial stage of 'mathematical singleness' is viewed as the beginning of the entire universe, 'a physical condition of extremely high density which cannot be described and should be viewed as beginning or creation . . .'.[3]

This deduction agrees with the following words uttered by 'Abdu'l-Bahá: '. . . there is no doubt that in the beginning the origin was one: the origin of all numbers is one and not two. Then it is evident that in the beginning matter was one . . .'.[4]

According to the Bahá'í teachings, therefore, the initial stage of creation is the stage of the 'original matter'. That matter is uniform, but not motionless, because the generating influence of the spirit (the Word or the Command of God) already pervades it, attracting it – by the power of love – towards motion, and guiding it – by the light of the intellect – towards a gradual perfecting process which enables it to acquire the growing capacities of reflecting and expressing the divine bounties of the spirit, continuously released from the world of the Kingdom. Thus the spirit increasingly appears in the original matter, as the original matter becomes specialized through the transformations it undergoes. The original matter may be viewed as the seed of the present universe: it potentially contains in itself all those things which today are actually in existence, as well as all those which will come into existence in the future. The history of the universe is but the succession of those material events through which the potentialities of that seed appeared in act. The original matter is somehow reminiscent of the proto-universe hypothesized in the big bang theory, out of which was created everything which exists today, or of the previously mentioned primal 'mathematical singleness'.

Evolution in the mineral kingdom

'Abdu'l-Bahá further explains the origin of the universe in the statement that: '. . . that one matter appeared in different aspects

---

3. L. Gratton, 'Cosmologia', in *Enciclopedia della Scienza e della Tecnica*, IV, p.338.
4. *Some Answered Questions*, p.181.

in each element. Thus various forms were produced, and these various aspects as they were produced became permanent, and each element was specialized. But this permanence was not definite, and did not attain realization and perfect existence until after a very long time'.[5]

This is the first stage in the evolution of the universe, a stage which scientists have studied and continue to study with the greatest attention. In the very instant of the initial big bang or big bangs, none of the systems of energy and matter we see today was in existence. However, the earliest particles — supposedly adrons (protons, neutrons and mesons) — appeared within a fraction of a second. Modern scientists can prove through demonstration based on radioactivity that in our galaxy chemical elements began to be produced very early on (between one hundred and one million years after the initial big bang). At that time the earliest atomic nuclei were formed through a process called nucleosynthesis which may be considered one of the earliest stages in the evolution of matter. The earliest nuclei to be formed were those of hydrogen and helium; in fact the former — being formed of a single proton — are the simplest known nuclei, whereas the latter are formed of two protons. It took billions of years for all the elements of the Mendeléev Table to come into existence. This theory agrees with a previously mentioned statement by 'Abdu'l-Bahá, that the specialization of the elements took 'a very long time'.

Another aspect of evolution in the mineral kingdom is the evolution of the terrestrial globe in particular and of all celestial bodies in general. 'Abdu'l-Bahá says in this regard: 'As each globe has a beginning, necessarily it has an end . . .', and particularly 'the earth hath not always existed'.[6] Such concepts are confirmed also by modern scientists, who are studying with great attention the evolutionary processes of the stars.

A question arises: how is it possible to understand 'Abdu'l-Bahá's statement that man 'has existed from all eternity', when He says as well that 'the earth hath not always existed'?[7] An explanation may be once again found in the following previously mentioned general concept: 'All beings, whether large or small, were created perfect and complete from the first, but their perfections appear in them by degrees'; and therefore, 'Similarly, the terrestrial globe from the beginning was created with all its elements, substances, minerals, atoms and organisms; but these only appeared by degrees:

5. ibid.
6. ibid. p.181, 151.
7. ibid. pp.195, 151.

The Wonders of Evolution

first the mineral, then the plant, afterward the animal, and finally man. But from the first these kind and species existed, but were underdeveloped in the terrestrial globe, and then appeared only gradually.'[8]

Living systems

As to what happened to the elements once they were formed and how all other creatures appeared, 'Abdu'l-Bahá says: 'Then these elements became composed, and organized and combined in infinite forms; or rather from the composition and combination of these elements innumerable beings appeared.'[9] In an early stage the elemental atoms combined so that they formed the smallest particles – supposedly quarks and leptons. Afterwards, quarks and leptons combined and formed neutrons, protons, etc. These, in their turn, combined and formed nuclei. Nuclei and electrons formed the elements. Those forces which keep the elemental particles together are called by scientists strong nuclear interactions. Elements, in their turn, are kept together by chemical affinity, whereby they combine and, as the evolutionary process develops, form chemical compounds characterized by a growing complexity.

Among those chemical elements which were formed through the combination of quarks and leptons, hydrogen, oxygen, carbon and nitrogen, as well as sulphur and phosphates, are of an extraordinary importance. They provide a substratum for those which traditional chemists would define as organic substances – organic, because they form those which were once called living organisms and today are more precisely termed living systems.

In the past the idea prevailed that the mineral kingdom on the one hand and the animal and vegetable kingdoms on the other were composed of totally different elements. Thus mineral, or inorganic, and vegetable and animal, or organic, substances were considered different from each other. However, today it is demonstrated that inorganic and organic substances differ from each other not because of the elements which compose them – which are the same – but because of the different properties taken on by those same components in the different kingdoms. These concepts agree with the following explanation by 'Abdu'l-Bahá: '. . . this perfection which is in all beings is caused by the creation of God from the composing elements, by their appropriate mingling and proportionate quantities, the mode of their composition, and the influence of other

8. ibid. p. 199.
9. ibid. p. 181.

beings.'[10] In other words, in the course of time, by virtue of the universal laws infused in the world of creation by the ordaining command of the Word of God, the elements bonded in such a way that matter, because of the qualities and quantities of its components and because of their appropriate mingling, the mode of their composition and their reciprocal influences, became specialized until the power of growth, typical of the vegetable kingdom, first appeared in it, followed in due time by the power of sense perception, typical of the animal kingdom.

In the light of these concepts, we may well agree with modern scientists who say that 'there is no extramaterial, nor mystical element in vital chemism' and that living systems are 'portions of matter which have a particular structure and organization, and as such are endowed with peculiar properties which, for the time being, may still be qualified as "vital" in the strict sense of the word'. After all, it is true that the composing elements of the so-called living matter may be found — identical — also in the mineral world. The difference between so-called living and inert matter is that 'in living matter chemical components have a particular structure, arrangement and distribution'. What is not true is that evolution, from the original matter of the proto-universe to man, is 'the fruit of trivial attempts of blind chance, which was merely assisted by time':[11] 'the universe is not created through the fortuitous concurrences of atoms; it is created by the good law which decrees that the tree brings forth certain definite fruits'.[12] And moreover, 'the transformation depends upon divine bounty. The mineral progresses in its own world. But from the mineral to the vegetable it progresses only by divine bounty. Also transformation from the vegetable to the animal is God's plan. Of itself the transformation cannot take place . . . .'.[13]

According to modern materialists, the whole evolutionary process occurred by virtue of the essential properties of matter and the casual meetings of subatomical particles which, owing to the extremely long times (billions of years) and the tremendous number of possibilities, brought the present universal order out of the initial chaos. It is something like unexpectedly winning a lottery. These concepts are undoubtedly at odds with the second thermodynamic law or principle of Carnot: 'order is improbable and disorder is probable'.[14] However, apart from this fact, this concept

10. ibid. p.178.
11. A. Delaunay, 'Vita', in *Enciclopedia della Scienza della Tecnica*, XII, p.673.
12. *Divine Philosophy*, p.136.
13. *See* above pp.60–61, nos(VII) and (VIII).
14. *See* W. S. Hatcher, 'The Unity of Religion and Science' in *World Order*, IX, pp.3, 22.

cannot be proved or falsified in the Popperian sense of the word. It is just a theory, upheld by its defenders because they believe in it in the light of their own personal experiences and general ideas, which make it credible and acceptable according to their judgement. Indeed their acceptance of such a theory is an act of faith.

According to the Bahá'í teachings, however, original matter, composed of elemental atoms, is – we repeat – only the phenomenal expression of a metaphysical reality: the world of the Kingdom which, through the agency of the spirit, animates, moves and guides it in a never-ending process of transformation. Through that process original matter is enabled to express with growing perfection in the physical level the qualities of that same metaphysical reality which moves it. The motion of elemental atoms is a phenomenal expression of the dynamism of the spirit, and the affinity which keeps atoms together is a phenomenal expression of the spiritual reality of love. Motion and affinity originate the evolutionary processes, giving birth to infinite growing beings which are strictly interdependent – inasmuch as they are part of the same organic universe. As these endless beings develop, they express in the universe an order and a harmony which are the physical manifestations of the order and the harmony of that same metaphysical world of the Kingdom which, through the agency of the spirit, incessantly moves and guides them. The great complexity of the phenomena of the world of creation prevents us from understanding all the existing interactions, from grasping all the rules of the game, rational as they are and expressive, in their rationality, of a Supreme Reason which sanctioned them, and of a human reason which has the capacity to perceive – in the laws of nature – the traces left by that Supreme Reason in the world of creation. Man, through his reason, understands the conditions of nature and, reproducing them, can also reproduce its phenomena. And supposing that the day comes when he learns how to shape in his laboratories a living system, he will undoubtedly do it according to a method that God Himself introduced into the world and that he has merely been able to grasp and reproduce.[15] God creates, man knows His creation; God creates the law, man discovers it through his reason and avails himself of it for his own purposes. But whereas the world of creation as a whole is as infinite and perfect as the Reason which shaped it, man is finite and limited in his understanding. Therefore he sometimes causes catastrophes, like the sorcerer's apprentice, through his senseless exploitation of his own discoveries. These concepts, like materialistic concepts, can be neither proved nor falsified; they are acceptable to anyone who

---

15. ibid.

considers them the most plausible assumption in the light of his own personal experiences and general ideas, in other words through an act of faith.

But perhaps, in the light of our previous arguments, it will be easier to rid the word faith of that stigma of superstition with which it has been branded up to now in the eyes of most people. Superstition is a blind faith, conflicting with things proved through sense perception, intellect and common sense. Not so a faith in an abstract conception, which in its abstraction cannot be proved or falsified in the Popperian sense of the word, but which nevertheless can be checked in the light of sensible and intellectual experience, of common sense and of its results in human life. Such a faith is a 'conscious knowledge', a certitude, because it agrees with an objectively observed reality, known through such criteria of knowledge as God Himself has bestowed upon man: sense perception, intellect, insight, Holy Writings.

The evolution of the elements up to the appearance of the earliest so-called living systems has been thoroughly investigated, but many questions remain as yet unanswered. The big bang occurred fifteen billion years ago. Chemical evolution, from nucleosynthesis to the appearance of the chemical elements of the Mendeléev Table, continued over billions of years. The earth was formed five billion years ago. The earliest living systems – bacteria, blue-green algae, preceded by the so-called pre-biotic systems, i.e. hydrocarbons, cyanide and their by-products – appeared 3.5 billion years ago. 'Abdu'l-Bahá says: '. . . life on this earth is very ancient. It is not one hundred thousand or two hundred thousand, or one million or two million years old; it is very ancient, and the ancient record and traces are entirely obliterated.'[16] It is not yet clear how all these things happened. But from that moment – 3.5 billion years ago – began the biological evolution of living systems, which culminated in the appearance of man.

Animals

Animals appeared on the earth about 800 million years ago. Since that time, the evolution of the animal kingdom has progressed from primal euchariotic cells to pongides through geological ages, producing many classes, subclasses, orders and species. In their eagerness to understand this evolutionary process, scientists have made much thorough research in the fields of comparative anatomy and embryology, both directly on living animals, and indirectly on

---

16. *Some Answered Questions*, p.160.

The Wonders of Evolution

fossil remains of extinct species, and have come to many interesting conclusions. Among these is the assumption, which many scientists uphold, that mankind is the highest animal species. The Bahá'í texts agree with most of the results of scientific research on evolution, but they do not accept the theory which considers man as a member of the highest animal species.

Bahá'í texts in fact distinguish between 'the world of nature' on the one hand, whose greatest representative is the animal, and the 'world of reason'[17] on the other, whose representative is man. They state moreover that these two worlds are fundamentally different from each other, so that they can be viewed as belonging to two totally different planes of existence.

'Abdu'l-Bahá says: '. . . the highest type of creation below is the animal, which is superior to all degrees of life except man.'[18] These words about the animals will be better understood once the qualities of the animals, as they are recorded in the Bahá'í texts, have been studied. The nature of the difference between man and animals, and the reasons why they are viewed as belonging to two separate kingdoms of the world of being will thus become apparent.

Qualities of the animals

Sense perception. This power, enabling animals to know sensible reality through the agency of their senses, is 'the lowest degree of perception'.[19] Moreover, *'in the animal world there is the sense of feeling'*:[20] and *'the feelings are one and the same'*, writes 'Abdu'l-Bahá, *'whether we inflict pain on man or on beast. There is no difference here whatever'.*[21]

Memory.[22] Animals have memory, says 'Abdu'l-Bahá, even stronger than man. Animals remember previous sensorial experiences. This

---

17. *Promulgation*, p.357.
18. ibid. p.303.
19. *Some Answered Questions*, p.217.
20. 'Tablet to Dr. A. Forel' in *Bahá'í World*, XV, p.38.
21. *Selections*, p.159.
22. 'Abdu'l-Bahá says: 'Briefly, in the powers which animals and men have in common, the animal is often the more powerful. For example, let us take the power of memory. If you carry a pigeon from here to a distant country, and there set it free, it will return, for it remembers the way. Take a dog from here to the centre of Asia, set him free and he will come back here and never once lose the road.' (*Some Answered Questions*, p.187.)
'Abdu'l-Bahá says: 'Man has memory; nature is without it.' (*Promulgation*, p.17. See also ibid. pp.81, 360.) This statement seems contradictory to the statement whereby the animal, which belongs to the world of nature, has memory. In this regard Shoghi Effendi wrote through his secretary '. . . when He says nature is devoid of memory He means memory as we have it, not the strange memory of inherited habits animals so strikingly possess.' (quoted in *Arohanui*, p.85.)

capacity is indispensable both for those genetically programmed behaviours we call instincts, and for their better adaptation to the environment, in view of enhancing the possibilities of survival.

Learning. It is well-known that animals have the capacity of learning. For one thing, they can learn from man, who often trains them in easy tasks. 'Abdu'l-Bahá says: '. . . we observe that animals which have undergone training in their sphere of limitation will progress and advance unmistakably, become more beautiful in appearance and increase in intelligence', and – excellent horseman as He was – He adds: '. . . how intelligent and knowing the Arabian horse has become through training, even how polite this horse has become through education.'[23] Moreover, animals can learn simple operations even by themselves, without any help from human beings. Recent studies on animal behaviour, made by zoologists and ethologists, have proved that animals have learnt certain behaviours in the course of their evolution which have become permanent in that species through cultural transference, i.e. not on account of genes, but by virtue of teaching and learning the processes. As early as 1960 Jane van Lawick-Goodall studied chimpanzees in Gombe Stream (Western Tanzania) Reserve. She observed how chimpanzees know how to shape wood rods (usually a twig is chosen and pruned) and to use them so that they may seize termites – their choicest food – inside termitaries. Whenever one of these rough utensils becomes useless (for instance because its tip bends) they try to repair it, breaking off the bent part. Moreover, they prepare primitive plugs using chewed leaves, and then they use them as instruments to draw water from hollows where it could not be otherwise reached. [24] Less evolved animals, as well, adopt and learn new behaviours. Many animals invent new techniques as an adaptation to changes in their environment. For example, in the American National Parks, grizzlies have learnt how to pierce tourists' tins so as to be able to eat the food inside.[25] In Japan's Koshima Islet, experimenters threw potatoes into the sea in front of macacoes. The macacoes jumped into the sea, picked them up and ate them. That was an occasion for the macacoes to taste salty potatoes, and they must have liked them better that way, for since then the monkeys always plunge their potatoes into the salty sea-water before eating them.[26] In Great Britain seagulls

23. *Promulgation*, p.77.
24. *See* J. Van Lawick-Goodall, 'The Behaviour of Free-Living Chimpanzees in the Gombe Stream Reserve', in *Animal Behaviour Monographs*, I, part 3, 1968.
25. *See* M. Jahoda, 'Uomini e orsi. Ma è possibile convivere?' in *Airone*, LI, p.71.
26. *See* M. Kawai, 'Newly acquired precultural behaviour in the natural troops of Japanese Monkeys at Koshima islet' in *Primates*, 1965, VI, pp.1–30.

acquired the habit of dropping the shells they had plucked out of the sea on the hard asphalt of a new coast road, with the clear intention of breaking them so that their content could be more easily eaten. This new habit of the seagull caused traffic difficulties: the asphalt, covered by molluscs, became slippery for the cars.

Voluntary movements.[27] Thanks to their instincts and memory of previous sensorial experience, animals can voluntarily move about with a view to survival, self-preservation, reproduction and the gratification of other instincts.

Natural emotions. Animals are genetically programmed in respect of certain so-called instinctive behaviours which are attended by emotions: rage, fear, affinity, etc. Such emotions and behaviours are intended for the survival of the individuals and the preservation of the species. In this light should also be viewed certain kinds of 'elemental attraction ... and selective affinity' which are very similar to such a feeling as is usually called love — for instance, couple bonds, parental bonds, group solidarity, attachment to human trainers, and last but not least such altruistic behaviours as the sacrifice of life for the sake of the offspring, or species survival. This is, says 'Abdu'l-Bahá, 'love manifest in the degree of the animal kingdom'.[28]

Being possessed of all these capacities, animals are undoubtedly possessed of a sort of abstract activity and reality, which might well be defined as mental. Nevertheless, such primordial ideality is curtailed because of the most typical animal features.

Animal limitations

(i) Animals 'have no power of abstract reasoning and intellectual ideals', remarks 'Abdu'l-Bahá; and elsewhere He adds that the animal 'cannot apprehend ideal realities ...' That is to say, 'the animal in its creation is a captive of the senses';[29]

(ii) Moreover, the animal has not 'the powers of ideation and conscious reflection which belong to man';[30]

(iii) 'The animal ... makes no distinction between man and itself,'[31] because it is not possessed of any self-consciousness, or

---

27. 'Abdu'l-Bahá says: '... there are no voluntary movements except those of animals and, above all, those of man.' (*Some Answered Questions*, p.3.) Elsewhere he says: 'The animal, in addition to existence and growth, hath the capacity of moving about, and the use of the faculties of the senses.' (*Paris Talks*, p.25.)
28. *Promulgation*, p.255.
29. ibid. pp.311, 357.
30. ibid. pp.172–3.
31. ibid. p.311.

possessed of any consciousness of its own body. The most 'clever' chimpanzee, in front of a mirror, does not recognize itself in the image reflected in the mirror.

(iv) Animals 'have no touch with the spiritual world and are without conception of God or the Holy Spirit'; they are 'utterly lacking spiritual susceptibilities, ignorant of divine religion and without knowledge of the Kingdom of God'; 'they have no knowledge of the Divine Prophets and Holy Books'; nor are they 'capable of apprehending the divine teachings';[32]

(v) Animals are deprived of the 'meditative faculty';[33]

(vi) 'They are deprived of that degree of intellect which can reason and discriminate between right and wrong, justice and injustice.'[34] Therefore, animals have not the capacity of distinguishing between good and evil, of establishing standards of values, but they react instinctively to each situation according to the peremptory requirements of individual survival and the preservation of species.

(vii) '. . . the animal is a captive of nature . . .' and '. . . acts in accordance with the requirements of nature, follows its own instincts and desires. Whatever its impulses and proclivities may be, it has the liberty to gratify them; yet it is a captive of nature. It cannot deviate in the least degree from the road nature has established.'[35]

These limitations have far-reaching consequences upon the life and development of animals:

(i) Their possibilities of progress are within the limits of the physical realm: 'Manifestly, the animal has been created for the life of this world. Its highest virtue is to express excellence in the material plane of existence. The animal is perfect when its body is healthy and its physical senses are whole', therefore, 'The world of nature is the kingdom of the animal. In its natural condition and plane of limitation the animal is perfect.'[36] But this same natural perfection is a great limitation as well: '. . . century by century and age by age man's intelligence grows and becomes keener, that of the animals remains the same',[37] and in fact, 'Man is progressive and nature is stationary.'[38]

---

32. ibid. pp.311, 177, 311, 61.
33. 'Abdu'l-Bahá says: 'You cannot apply the name "man" to any being void of this faculty of meditation; without it he would be a mere animal, lower than the beasts.'(*Paris Talks*, p.175.)
   34. *Promulgation*, p.352.
   35. ibid. pp.40, 177.
   36. ibid. pp.303, 311.
   37. *Paris Talks*, p.72.
   38. *Promulgation*. p.51.

(ii) Inasmuch as the animal is wholly unconscious of spiritual life, it 'has attained the fullest degree of physical felicity . . . This is the honor of the animal kingdom.'[39] As such, the animal is *'the embodiment of liberty and its symbol'*:[40] it is free in the gratification of its instincts. However, this same freedom is, in another respect, captivity: the servitude to those same instincts, or, in other words, to natural laws. 'In the world of nature we behold the living organisms in a ceaseless struggle for existence. Everywhere we are confronted by evidences of the physical survival of the fittest . . .'. Their ceaseless struggle for existence, 'their ignorance, sensuality and unbridled instincts and passions', and their accompanying succession of sorrows, cruelty, oppressions, deception, tyranny, ruthlessness and deprivation of 'spiritual enjoyment', are manifest evidence that 'the world of nature; (where the animal is the king) 'is inherently defective in cause and outcome'[41] when compared to the human world of reason with all its possibilities and potentialities.

From all these remarks on the nature of animals, it is clear that the fundamental difference between men and animals, that *quid* whose presence enabled man to evolve throughout the ages and whose absence kept animals stationary in their natural – and totally different from human – sphere, is not where it has mostly been looked for up to now. Animals too are possessed of a certain degree of intelligence and will, of a certain capacity of invention, of memory and of a limited capacity of material progress, of emotions and affinities. It is not these qualities that we should investigate in order to find a typically human *quid*. According to the Bahá'í teachings, this *quid* is man's capacity of becoming conscious of the reality of the superior world of the Kingdom and of mirroring forth its qualities in his individual as well as his social life: it is his soul.[42]

---

39. ibid. p.166.
40. *Gleanings*, p.335.
41. *Promulgation*, pp.400, 185. 'Abdu'l-Bahá says: 'His [man's] life is intended to be a life of spiritual enjoyment to which the animal can never attain. This enjoyment depends upon the acquisition of heavenly virtues.' (*Promulgation*, p.185.)
42. 'Abdu'l-Bahá writes: '*A human being is distinguished from an animal in a number of ways. First of all he is made in the image of God, in the likeness of the Supernal Light, even as the Torah says, "Let us make man in our image, after our likeness".*' (*Selections*, p.140.)

5 Man: The Fruit of Physical Evolution

In the Bahá'í texts we find very interesting statements on human nature: men '. . . are intelligent beings created in the realm of evolutionary growth',[1] suggesting that man is a part of that majestic evolutionary process which is the growth of the universe, and that intelligence is his distinguishing feature. Elsewhere it is said: 'God created all earthly things under a law of progression in material degree, but He has created man and endowed him with powers of advancement toward spiritual and transcendental kingdoms',[2] suggesting that man is subject to material evolution and that in him a new stage of the evolutionary process begins: that is, spiritual evolution. It is also said: 'Existence is like a tree, and man is the fruit',[3] suggesting that man is the highest point in the world of creation and the supreme purpose of it. It is said, moreover: 'Man is the noblest of the creatures',[4] suggesting that the noblest qualities of the world of being can be expressed in and through him. Man is 'the collective centre of spiritual as well as material forces',[5] suggesting that he is endowed with the perfections of both the material and the spiritual world. '. . . [M]an is endowed with the potentialities of divinity in his nature',[6] suggesting that he is possessed of potential spiritual qualities belonging to the divine

---

1. *Promulgation*, p.129.
2. ibid. p.302.
3. *Divine Philosophy*, p.105.
4. *Promulgation*, p.350.
5. ibid. p.303.
6. ibid. p.317.

world. Man is the 'temple of God, the image and likeness of the Lord',[7] suggesting that his spiritual and divine qualities are the image of God in him and that he is therefore the true 'temple of God'. And '... man is a creation intended for the reflection of divine virtues',[8] suggesting that the purpose of his creation is that his potential divine qualities may be expressed in act.

These concepts — the intelligence of man, his progress in the spiritual plane, the divine potentialities of his nature, the image of God in him, the spiritual purpose of his life — are undoubtedly a cause of great perplexity and an object of vehement argument in modern society. In this regard, the Bahá'í texts may offer many explanations, which will certainly prove enlightening.

When we study the evolutionary process from the elemental atom to man, we will see that man is the most perfect creature originating from that process of material evolution: man is the apex of the world of creation. 'Abdu'l-Bahá says: 'Man is the microcosm; and the infinite universe, the macrocosm. The mysteries of the greater world, or macrocosm, are expressed or revealed in the lesser world, the microcosm. The tree, so to speak, is the greater world and the seed, in its relation to the tree, is the lesser world. But the whole of the great tree is potentially latent and hidden in the little seed.'[9] Man is therefore possessed of the 'virtues'[10] of all the kingdoms of existence; he '... is the highest species because he is the possessor of the perfections of all the classes — that is, he has a body which grows and which feels'.[11]

When we study the phenomena of the world of creation, we will see how '... all phenomena of being attain to a summit and degree of consummation, after which a new order and condition is established'.[12] This concept applies also to the world of creation as a whole: man is the apex of the evolutionary process of the world of creation, its 'fruit', its 'degree of consummation'. But since the evolutionary process must necessarily go forward, in man 'a new order and condition' must appear, and such is that condition which Baha'í's call spiritual, others metaphysical.[13]

'Abdu'l-Bahá mentions — using a Plotinian expression — the 'circle of existence'.[14] From the elemental atom of the 'original

7. ibid. p.373.
8. ibid. p.303.
9. ibid. p.69.
10. *Paris Talks*, p.177.
11. *Some Answered Questions*, p.235.
12. *Promulgation*, p.124. *See* above, p.59.
13. One of the proofs of the immortality of the soul is founded upon this concept. *See* above pp.64, 67 and below pp.140–45.
14. *Promulgation*, p.220.

matter' to man, the first half of the circle ('bringing forth'[15]) is completed, characterized by the different stages of the mineral, vegetable and animal kingdoms. In man, the second half of the 'circle of existence' begins: the essence of man — which may also be called the soul or spirit of man — is, so to speak, the new elemental atom. In fact, the soul will in its turn undergo a further evolutionary process: its growth towards and in the metaphysical world of the Kingdom ('progress'[15]). Such a process cannot have an end, therefore the soul — whose growth has no end — is immortal.

Therefore, on the one hand, man is a part of the material or physical plane of existence, and thus summarizes in himself 'the mysteries of the greater world';[16] on the other, he is by virtue of his soul a part of the spiritual or metaphysical plane of existence.

'Abdu'l-Bahá explains that '. . . in the microcosm, or the little man, there are deposited three realities . . . an outward or physical reality . . . a second or higher reality which is the intellectual reality . . . a third reality . . . that is the spiritual reality'.[17] So in man there is a threefold reality: a first reality, an expression of the world of creation, related to the senses, common both to men and animals, subject to nature; a second reality, an expression of the world of the Kingdom, which is conscious and spiritual; and lastly an intermediate reality, typical of man, halfway between the other two. This threefold human reality or nature may be viewed also as a threefold (animal, human and spiritual) potentiality bestowed upon man.

* * *

Before describing these potentialities of human nature, it may be useful to mention the process through which they express themselves, a process that 'Abdu'l-Bahá calls 'demand and supply'.[18] Demand is the need for something which is necessary in view of a goal to be achieved, and a potentiality to be expressed. That demand is perceived as an unpleasant feeling of want and — inasmuch as it is unpleasant — represents a stimulus urging man to search out what will satisfy his want so that he may escape from his uneasiness. This is how man can profit from all those things God puts at his disposal and of which he is in need. On the physical plane of existence, his hunger is satisfied by food yielded from the earth. On the spiritual plane, his need for loftiness is satisfied

---

15. *Some Answered Questions*, pp. 183, 286.
16. *Promulgation*, p. 69. Bahá'u'lláh writes: *'Some have described him as the "lesser world", when, in reality, he should be regarded as the "greater world".'* (*Gleanings*, p. 340.)
17. 'The Three Realities' in *Star of the West*, VII, pp. 117–18.

through the divine bounties of the spirit. In other words, in man there are needs, or else the 'demand'; in the world of being there are the gifts of God fit to satisfy his needs, or else the 'supply'. The unpleasant feeling of want is what urges man to struggle so that he may reap those bounties God has put at his disposal. If a man's wants are to be satisfied he must be able to recognize them, and to reap the appropriate gifts copiously poured out by God for his sake throughout the universe. Whether the need is material, intellectual or spiritual, the process is the same.

Thus Bahá'u'lláh poetically explains the same concept: *'Out of the wastes of nothingness, with the clay of My command I made thee to appear, and have ordained for thy training every atom in existence and the essence of all created things. Thus, ere thou didst issue from thy mother's womb, I destined for thee two fountains of gleaming milk, eyes to watch over thee, and hearts to love thee. Out of My loving-kindness, 'neath the shade of My mercy I nurtured thee, and guarded thee by the essence of My grace and favour. And my purpose in all this was that thou mightest attain My everlasting dominion and become worthy of My invisible bestowals . . .'*[19]

His animal nature

The animal nature of man — *'that base and appetitive nature'*[20] writes Bahá'u'lláh, 'physical or animal degree of man',[21] says 'Abdu'l-Bahá — is on the one hand his body, on the other the abstract reality of his so-called 'natal self' with its 'natural emotions'.[22] It is that which Bahá'u'lláh describes as *'life of the flesh . . . common both to men and animals'*,[23] and which 'Abdu'l-Bahá identifies with the *'evil promptings of the human heart'*.[24]

That the body of man is similar to that of the animal is a manifest and well-known fact. Among the animals, apes are so similar to man that many consider him to be their close kin. 'Abdu'l-Bahá writes *'The physical body of man is like that of an animal'*,[25] and elsewhere He explains: man . . . 'cannot continue his existence without sleep, an exigency of nature; he must partake of food and drink, which nature demands and requires'.[26] In another context, He remarks that '. . . some animals with regard to the sense are

18. *Promulgation*, p.83.
19. *Hidden Words*, Persian no. 29.
20. *Gleanings*, p.161.
21. *Paris Talks*, p.96.
22. *Promulgation*, pp.310, 244.
23. *Kitáb-i-Íqán*, p.120.
24. *Selections*, p.256.
25. Quoted in 'Studies in Immortality', in *Star of the West*, XIV, p.37.
26. *Promulgation*, p.81.

more powerful than man',[27] as though He intended to emphazise the fact that human greatness is not due to a physical supremacy.

The 'natal self' too, with its 'natural emotions', is common both to man and animals. In fact, there are in man, as in animals, instinctive behaviours whose origin can be traced back to the world of nature. They can be viewed as 'programmes of action indicated by the genetic asset or . . . a precise sequence of chemical instructions contained in the genome'[28] which through biochemical and neuro-hormonal processes originate physiological activities and particular behaviours required, in a world dominated by the law of the struggle for existence, for certain physical goals to be achieved — preservation, reproduction and regulation. Such are those 'natural emotions' Bahá'u'lláh describes as *'vain and inordinate affections'*, *'covetous desires'*, and that are thus listed: *'self . . . desires . . . passions'*,[29] *'jealousy, greed, the struggle for survival, deception, hypocrisy, tyranny, oppression, disputes, strife, bloodshed, looting and pillaging'*,[30] and also 'attachment to the world, avarice, envy, love of luxury and comfort, haughtiness and self-desire,' as well as 'antagonism, hatred and selfish struggle for existence . . . jealousy, revenge, ferocity, cunning, hypocrisy, greed, injustice and tyranny'.[31]

'Abdu'l-Bahá considers 'natural emotions' as 'imperfections', refers to them as 'the imperfect attributes of the natal self', and likens them to a 'rust which deprives the heart of the bounties of God' and elsewhere to 'dust upon the mirror'.[32]

Whenever natural emotions are not appropriately guided, they lead man to be materialistic, selfish, an opposer of his fellow-men, a coward, a tyrant — in other words, a prisoner of the world of nature and therefore very similar to an animal, obscuring (even as a 'rust' or a veil of 'dust') the splendour of his spiritual reality. They lead him to comply with the demands of his own animal nature and to satisfy its needs, even though such an attitude may be detrimental to his superior, human and divine reality.

'Abdu'l-Bahá points out that in traditional Holy Writings 'this lower nature in man is symbolized as Satan', and explains that Satan is but 'the evil ego within us, not an evil personality outside':[33]

---

27. *Some Answered Questions*, p.217.
28. M. Piattelli Palmarini, 'Sui limiti della razionalità', in *Scienza e Tecnica* 75, p.180. 'Genome' is the collective term for all genes.
29. *Gleanings*, pp.323, 316–17.
30. *Selections*, p.206.
31. *Promulgation*, pp.244, 465.
32. ibid. pp.244, 465, 310, 244. Bahá'u'lláh describes them also as *'the dross and dust of earthly cares and limitations.'* (*Gleanings*, p.67.) As for the meaning of self, see below, pp.126, and no. 45.
33. *Promulgation*, pp.287. Bahá'u'lláh, in one of His Writings, refers to the natal self as *'satanic self'*. (*Seven Valleys*, p.11).

elsewhere He says: 'Satan, or whatever is interpreted as evil, refers to the lower nature in man. This baser nature is symbolized in various ways.'[34]

In the Bahá'í view, therefore, the animal nature of man is his body with its natal self. Such a nature expresses itself in genetically programmed behaviours intended, in man as in the animal, to satisfy physical needs so that he may provide for his own preservation, reproduction and regulation as an individual and as a species in a world ruled by natural laws. Therefore, the animal nature in itself is not 'evil'. Undoubtedly it is not evil in the animal. But inasmuch as man has also the capacity to express a superior nature — which his animal nature is inclined to ignore and to stifle — such a nature, relatively speaking, may be 'evil'.[35]

His human nature

Unique among all the creatures of the world, man has the capacity to throw off the yoke of nature. In the words of 'Abdu'l-Bahá: 'All created things are captives of nature and subject to its laws. They cannot transgress the control of these laws in one detail or particular. The infinite starry worlds and heavenly bodies are nature's obedient subjects. The earth and its myriad organisms, all minerals, plants and animals are thralls of its dominion. But man through the exercise of his scientific, intellectual power can rise out of his condition, can modify, change and control nature according to his own wishes and uses.'[36]

Man and the animal are, therefore, different, because in man there is a 'power different from any of those of the animals',[37] a power which is 'supernatural', '. . . a spirit with which God hath endowed him at creation', a power the Bahá'í texts refer to as human spirit, soul or — according to the terminology of those who are called by 'Abdu'l-Bahá Eastern philosophers — rational soul. This power expresses itself as intellect, reason, intelligence and, through the agency of the brain, as mind. This divine gift which distinguishes man from the animals is viewed as 'the most precious gift bestowed upon man by the Divine Bounty':[38] it is his human nature.

34. ibid. pp.294–5.
35. This concept falls under the Bahá'í concept of good and evil already referred to on p.46 and no. 84.
36. *Promulgation*, p.30. 'When 'Abdu'l-Bahá says man breaks the laws of nature, He means we shape nature to meet our own needs, as no animal does. Animals adapt themselves to better fit in with and benefit from their environment. But men both surmount and change environment.' (on behalf of Shoghi Effendi, in Shoghi Effendi, *Arohanui*, p.85.)
37. *Some Answered Questions*, p.187.
38. *Promulgation*, pp.49, 259, 41.

As human spirit manifests itself as the mind, it enables man 'to investigate reality', to 'perceive what is true'[39] and to understand 'the realities, the properties and the effects of the contingent beings':[40] 'the outcome of this intellectual endowment is science, which is especially characteristic of man.'[41]

Human spirit bestows upon man the knowledge of the material world; moreover '. . . *it discovers the innermost essence of all things and comprehends realities which cannot be seen*', and '. . . *discovers the realities of the things and understands universal principles*'.[42] 'Through its use man is able to arrive at ideal conclusions instead of being restricted to the mere plane of sense impressions . . . He acquires divine wisdom; he searches out the mysteries of creation; he witnesses the radiance of omnipotence . . .' Thus, human spirit enables man 'to investigate the ideals of the Kingdom and attain a knowledge which is denied the animal in its limitation'[43] and therefore somehow enables him 'to get in touch with those kingdoms'.[44] It is by virtue of his human spirit that '. . . man is always turned toward the heights, and his aspiration is lofty'; that 'he always desires to reach a greater world than the world in which he is, and to mount to a higher sphere than that in which he is. The love of exaltation is one of the characteristics of man . . . What a difference between the human world and the world of the animal, between the elevation of man and the abasement of the animal, between the perfections of man and the ignorance of the animal . . .'.[45] In other words, according to the Bahá'í teachings, it is the human spirit that confers on man the knowledge of reality, both in the physical or natural world – and this is how science and technology develop – and in the metaphysical or spiritual world, enabling him to catch a glimpse of a superior plane of existence and thus kindling in him an eagerness to rise up to it – and this is how his religious susceptibility develops. However, it is both by his latent spiritual potentialities, representing the third aspect of his nature, or divine nature, and by the assistance of superior spiritual forces, that is, the spirit of faith and the Holy Spirit, that man is effectively enabled to rise up to the spiritual plane of existence.

39. ibid. p.291, 63.
40. *Some Answered Questions*, p.218.
41. *Promulgation*, p.29.
42. *Selections*, pp.46, 61–2.
43. *Promulgation*, pp.262–3.
44. *Paris Talks*, p.41.
45. *Some Answered Questions*, p.188.

His divine nature

In the Holy Scriptures it is written that man is created in the image and likeness of God; 'Abdu'l-Bahá explains that '. . . the image of the Merciful consists of the attributes of the heavenly Kingdom',[46] and *'betokeneth all the qualities of perfection whose lights, emanating from the Sun of Truth, illumine the realities of men, and are among the perfect attributes that lie within wisdom and knowledge.'*[47] This is the divine nature of man, that is, the power of expressing in the material plane of existence the divine attributes of the world of the Kingdom.

The human spirit enables man both to know spiritual reality, and to express that reality during his earthly life. Such power of understanding, on the one hand, confers upon man his *'unique capacity of knowing* [God] *and of reflecting the greatness of His glory'*,[48] his 'powers of advancement toward spiritual and transcendent kingdoms', his 'capacity to attain human virtues', his capacity 'to witness the effulgence of the Sun of Reality, reflect the spirit of the Kingdom'[49]; and, on the other, imbues him with a 'love of exaltation'.[50] Therefore, 'Abdu'l-Bahá says: 'This endowment [the power of understanding] is the most praiseworthy power of man, for through its employment and exercise the betterment of the human race is accomplished, the development of the virtues of mankind is made possible and the spirit and mysteries of God become manifest.'[51] In this sense, 'Abdu'l-Bahá says also that the intelligence of man is 'the intermediary between his body and his spirit',[52] because through his intelligence man is enabled to manifest in himself — born of matter and therefore alive in the material plane — a different reality, born of the spirit (whose qualities it manifests as spiritual perceptions and divine virtues) and alive in the spiritual plane. This is 'the potentiality of divinity' with which he 'is endowed' 'in his nature':[53] i.e. his divine nature.

Man is therefore bound to feel a strong tension within himself between his animal and divine nature. On the one hand, he feels in thrall to a heavy and overbearing physical reality which conveys to him in the form of very unpleasant feelings any individual

---

46. *Promulgation*, p.335. 'And God said, Let us make man in our image, after our likeness.' (*Genesis* 1:26.)
47. *Selections*, p.140.
48. *Gleanings*, p.77.
49. *Promulgation*, pp.302, 378, 328.
50. *Some Answered Questions*, p.188.
51. *Promulgation*, p.31.
52. *Paris Talks*, p.96.
53. *Promulgation*, p.317.

diminution (that is, 'passion'), and which demands to be satisfied (that is, 'desire') — very often with awkward urgency and, if unchecked, at any cost.[54] This is the animal within each man; it is (as has already been said) not only his body, but also that nucleus of 'natural emotions' arising from his 'natal self', abstract when compared to the body, but certainly dependent on and conditioned by the body, because its foundations are undoubtedly to be found in the brain. This is man's animal nature. On the other hand, he also feels something within himself which urges him to make efforts (which are mostly small and weak at the beginning, but which, if he perseveres and complies with them, become stronger, more effective and somehow gratifying) aimed at bending his own body and natal self towards diverse and only initially wearying directions of love, peace and selflessness. This is man's divine nature. Therefore, there exist in him both a strong disposition to subordinate to his natal self the entire universe, and an opposite need to love his fellow-men, a tension between the urgency of taking and the need of giving, between self-protection and self-sacrifice, between the attraction toward sensible reality (which is felt with great immediacy) and toward an ideal reality (which is felt, if not with the same immediacy, certainly with great pregnancy), between hate and love, war and peace. 'Not in any other of the species in the world of existence is there such a difference, contrast, contradiction and opposition as in the species of man.'[55]

The power of understanding, which is typical of human nature, is the instrument capable of acting as an intermediary between these two poles. Whenever man avails himself of it in order to comply with the extremely lively needs of his body and natal self, his life is ruled by the *'satanic self'*,[56] 'the evil ego', the 'lower nature', 'Satan', as Judaic, Christian and Muslim Holy Texts, in a quasi-mythical allusion, call it. In that case he remains a captive of the 'world of nature' to which he is bound by his body; and he is like an animal, because his 'natural emotions'[57] — *'the evil promptings of the human heart'*[58] — prevail and he therefore manifests mainly animal qualities. The Scriptures say that such a man is dead; and indeed he is alive in the physical level, but in the spiritual plane still his life has really no beginning, because he has not yet

---

54. ibid. p.184.
55. *Some Answered Questions*, p.236.
56. *Seven Valleys*, p.11.
57. *Promulgation*, pp.287, 357, 244.
58. *Selections*, p.256.

begun to express the potential virtues of the world of the Kingdom which have been infused in him.[59]

On the contrary, whenever, through his power of understanding enlightened by the divine guidance of Revelation, he takes hold of the natural emotions of his natal self with the intention of using them so that the virtues of his divine nature may emerge, he begins to live in the spiritual plane; that is, he acquires a new personal dimension which is divine because it belongs to a world which transcends and enlightens physical reality. This is the beginning of a real transformation, to which the Bahá'í texts refer as 'spiritual progress'[60] and the Gospels as 'second birth':[61] the first time man is born into the world of nature once he has been conceived; the second time, he is born into the world of the spirit as he becomes conscious of the qualities or virtues of the world of the Kingdom and manifests them in his life.[62] In this sense 'Abdu'l-Bahá says that 'man is dual in his aspect' or that he has been given a 'dual endowment'.[63]

Human greatness and limitations

The prevailing opinion today is that the power of understanding, the greatest endowment of man, is a sufficient guarantee and instrument for human life, and that man does not need anything else for his progress. Nevertheless, a closer examination of human life clearly reveals that the human power of understanding is quite limited and, unaided, cannot guarantee anything, not even an absolutely objective knowledge.

---

59. In this regard, 'Abdu'l-Bahá writes: '. . . *as is clearly indicated in the Gospel where it says: "Let the dead bury their dead"* . . . *inasmuch as he who would bury these dead was alive with the vegetative, animal and rational human soul, yet did Christ – to whom be glory! – declare such dead and devoid of life, in that this person was devoid of the Spirit of Faith which is of the Kingdom of God.*' (*Tablets*, p.116.)

60. *Promulgation*, p.142.

61. See John 3:1–8.

62. These concepts explain the great difference between animals and men. 'Abdu'l-Bahá says: 'The physical body of man is like that of the animal, the only difference being on the level of consciousness.' (quoted in 'Studies in Immortality', in *Star of the West*, XIV, p.37.) In fact, if the highest perfection for animals is happiness and well-being through the physical perception of the material world, for man the highest perfection is in the knowledge of reality, on the one hand, and in 'the attainment of the supreme virtues of humanity through descent of the heavenly bestowals' (*Promulgation*, p.4), 'the honour allotted to man' (ibid. p.166) on the other. In this sense 'Abdu'l-Bahá confirms the concepts of 'the philosophers of the East – such as Plato, Aristotle and the Persians', who 'divide the world of existence or phenomena of life into two general categories or kingdoms: one the animal kingdom, or world of nature, the other the human kingdom, or world of reason.' (ibid. pp.356–7.)

63. ibid. p.324.

The narrowness of human understanding is manifest even in its most distinguished fruit, 'material science'.[64] In fact, this power of understanding leads man, through the experience of his sensory and rational perception, to a quite accurate knowledge of phenomenal reality. Nevertheless, whenever the meaning and the value of certain truths are to be understood and more comprehensive perspectives are to be achieved, or unifying theories formulated, the power of understanding very often misses the mark, as will become manifest when the history of science is studied. How many theories were first considered indisputable, and then, after further and deeper studies, proved to be false, and were discarded!

The limitations of human understanding become evident, even in the eyes of its most passionate advocates, whenever the applications and uses of science are considered. In this respect the power of understanding appears inadequate, because science requires, in its applications and uses, standards of value or criteria establishing what is good and what is bad, what is better and what is worse. In this respect, the power of understanding cannot assist us. Hans Schaefer says: '. . . Science is basically restricted to a cognitive sphere, which means that science can oblige people to focus their intellectual faculties on truth, but is unable in itself to provide a basis for action which is generally acceptable and therefore obligatory.'[65] Man is prevented by the limitations of his power of understanding and by his often blinding selfishness from achieving by himself a comprehensive and adequate perspective of reality, fit to guide him toward a good use of those same means science puts at his disposal. If this were not the case, we would not stand today – in this century which is undoubtedly illumined by the light of intellect – on the verge of an ecological catastrophe. In this respect man is in need of support: the support of a Unifying Intellect which may both show to him a standard of universal values to be followed for the good of individuals and society, and explain to him the meaning of that standard, thus motivating him in his adherence to it.

These meanings and motivations – history shows this fact and man can understand it – are always to be found in a transcendental reality. But in the face of such transcendental reality man is very limited in his powers. Guided and restricted in his understanding by his own sensory perception, which can bias him grievously, he is handicapped in grasping the spiritual or metaphysical realities of the transcendental world. And if he can hardly achieve a compre-

---

64. ibid. p.138.
65. Quoted in U. Schaefer, *The Imperishable Dominion*, pp.81–2.

hensive understanding of sensible reality, it is almost impossible for him to achieve a comprehensive understanding of spiritual or metaphysical reality. In this respect, man is in dire need of a *'Universal Mind'*[66] which may explain to him, in conformity with his powers of understanding, the nature of spirit and of his transcendental, spiritual reality, which may enable him to understand his position in the great 'creative plan of God',[67] the purpose of his existence, the direction of his development, the process of his growth, the laws governing his existence. Deprived of such transcendental guidance, man, through his powers of understanding, progresses at most on a merely intellectual and material plane. This is the case with the contemporary Western world, where the human power of understanding, free of the fetters of past superstitions and at long last used in freedom, has made so many useful discoveries. A civilization was born, to which 'Abdu'l-Bahá refers as 'material',[68] and which, on the one hand, is conducive to wellbeing and progress, but, on the other, is laden with potential and actual dangers for all mankind, inasmuch as it is wholly neglectful of the spiritual truths of transcendental reality and of such values as find their foundation in that world.

Last but not least, man is able through his power of understanding to recognize 'the imperfect attributes of the natal self' as well as 'the supreme virtue of humanity',[69] but he is not possessed of such forces as are required so that the former may be mastered and the latter achieved. Such forces do not belong to him, but they are at his disposal, if he is able to seize and use them, through his observance of such prescriptions as Revelation alone bestows upon him. Such are those *'confirmations of the Kingdom'* as have been mentioned by 'Abdu'l-Bahá, such is that *'dynamic power'* which is indispensable for *'every great cause'* to find *'visible expression'* in this world, i.e. the *'power of the Word of God'*.[70] Without these confirmations there is no possible transformation for man. Bahá'u'lláh writes: *'These energies . . . lie . . . latent within him [man], even as the flame is hidden within the candle and the rays of light are potentially present in the lamp. The radiance of these energies may be obscured by worldly desires even as the light of the sun can be concealed beneath the dust and dross which cover the mirror. Neither the candle nor the lamp can be lighted through their own unaided efforts, nor can it ever be possible for the mirror to free itself from its dross.'*[71]

66. *Selections*, p.256.
67. *Promulgation*, p.293.
68. ibid. p.11.
69. ibid. pp.310, 4.
70. quoted in *Peace* (comp.) p.13.
71. *Gleanings*, p.66.

We have thus said that man is in need of a superior guidance which may assist him in his scientific efforts, in advancing comprehensive views of reality, in elaborating standards of values, in discovering and understanding metaphysical reality and motivations for his struggle against the natural emotions of his natal self — a guidance which may bestow upon him the required forces and energies so that he may conquer in himself the binding power of nature and manifest that wonderful reality which is potentially hidden within him, i.e. his 'divine' nature: in other words, so that he may achieve that 'spiritual progress' 'Abdu'l-Bahá describes in the following words: 'spiritual progress is through the breaths of the Holy Spirit and is the awakening of the conscious soul of man to perceive the reality of Divinity.'[72]

His evolution and his divine nature

The appearance of his divine nature is a real and substantial transformation. Such a transformation, like any other, requires a motive and executive power. Whenever a mineral substance undergoes a transformation in its state, a contribution of energy is required. For example, whenever a liquid must be transformed into a gas, i.e. when it must be brought to its boiling point, a contribution of heat is required. That a seed may germinate, a contribution of energy is required in the form of heat, water and nourishing substances, otherwise that seed will not germinate. In fact, any physical work requires a contribution of energy. 'Abdu'l-Bahá writes: *'Every plan is in need of a power for its execution.'*[73] If man wants to rise above his animal nature and manifest his latent divine or spiritual nature, he is in need of a power.

---

72. *Promulgation*, pp.465, 142. When in the fifties, in the definitely materialistic aim of boosting the sales of consumer goods in the United States, the motivations of human behaviour were first studied so that they might be exploited in the production of advertising material, researchers discovered that only in a few cases were the motives of human behaviour rational; on the contrary, it was mostly determined by what psychologists call the unconscious or subconscious and which, in the Bahá'í view and in this context, may be defined as the natural emotions of the natal self. It is clear that these emotions are not the expression of the best or noblest side of man. No wonder that a man who follows them almost blindly finds himself today in such an intricate personal and social situation. It would appear, then, that in this modern world man is in need of a new scale of values appropriate to his new situation, inasmuch as the old values have been mostly criticized and rejected. This new scale should be one that anyone may understand and feel the urgency and the need of concentrating his energies upon it, thus finding a motivation in his struggle to give his spiritual qualities priority over his natural emotions. Human behaviour will then become more adequate to both individual and social progress. This is one of the most important goals of the Bahá'í Faith, as it has been of every other religion, at least in their early stages.

73. Quoted in 'The Need of a Universal Program', in *Star of the West*, XIII, p.132.

For a more complete understanding of such a process and of the character of the forces assisting man in his spiritual growth, it will be useful to recall the general principles of evolution in the world of creation.[74] The process of evolution develops in the universe because the elemental atoms, moved and guided by the impulse of the omnipresent command of the Word of God, become combined and separated according to such laws as have been introduced therein by that same Word. As atoms become associated, they acquire the capacity of manifesting in the plane of sensible reality such spiritual attributes of the world of the Kingdom as cohesion, growth, sense perception, intellectual perception. In man an analogous process takes place: as man, moved by forces of the spirit emanating from the Word of God, follows a course indicated by the command of that same Word, he acquires ever-increasing capacities and mirrors forth more and more perfectly, in the physical world, such spiritual qualities as are typical of his degree. 'Abdu'l-Bahá explains this event thus: *'Verily, I say unto you that the gifts of thy Lord are encircling thee in a similar way as the spirit encircles the body at the beginning of the amalgamation of the elements and natures in the womb: the power of the spirit begins to appear in the body gradually and successively according to the preparation and capacity to receive that everlasting abundance.'*[75] This *'power of the spirit'* first appears in man as power of cohesion, then as power of growth, then as sense perception, then as intellectual perception and finally as spiritual perception and collective expression of the ideal virtues of the world of the Kingdom.

The sensible and the human world, however, differ from each other in degree: in the sensible world there is no consciousness, nor volition, nor ideation, nor reflection nor conscious intelligence,[76]

---

74. In this regard 'Abdu'l-Bahá says: 'The world of humanity cannot advance through the mere physical powers and intellectual attainments; nay, rather, the Holy Spirit is essential. The divine Father must assist the human world to attain maturity. The body of man is in need of physical and mental energy, but his spirit requires the life and fortification of the Holy Spirit. Without its protection and quickening, the human world would be extinguished.'(*Promulgation*, p.182.) He says moreover: 'Bahá'u'lláh has announced that no matter how far the world of humanity may advance in material civilization, it is nevertheless in need of spiritual virtues and the bounties of God. The spirit of man is not illumined and quickened through material sources. It is not resuscitated by investigating phenomena of the world of matter. The spirit of man is in need of the protection of the Holy Spirit. Just as he advances by progressive stages from the mere physical world of being into the intellectual realm, so must he develop upward in moral attributes and spiritual graces. In the process of this attainment he is ever in need of the bestowals of the Holy Spirit.' (ibid. p.288.)
75. In *Bahá'í World Faith*, p.367.
76. See *Promulgation*, pp.17, 30, 54, 58, 61, 80, 90–91, 172, 178, 241, 332, 357, 417.

all of which do exist in man. Therefore, whereas in the sensible reality the evolution and the consequent appearance of the qualities of the spirit are a necessary and inescapable consequence of natural laws and forces infused in the reality of things by the Divine Command, such is not the case with man. Through his power of understanding, man can understand both the process and the laws of his spiritual growth. Moreover, by virtue of his power of will, he can also make voluntary and conscious efforts to comply with this process and in his observance of its laws. It is thus that he can 'overcome the laws and phenomena of nature'.[77] In other words, the evolutionary process of human growth is characterized by the fact that man has the power of understanding the process of his own growth and of promoting it through a willing and conscious effort. Therefore, whereas the realities of the sensible world profit by the bounties of the spirit through a process which does not imply knowledge, attraction or volition, and is therefore necessary, human beings profit by those bounties through a process characterized by three stages: 'knowledge, volition and action'.[78] The spiritual transformation of man requires therefore an intermediary of the spirit, manifesting itself on the plane of human life, so that

---

77. ibid. p.353.

78. In this context it is easier to understand the concepts of fate, predestination and will expounded by 'Abdu'l-Bahá: *'Fate and predestination consist in the necessary and indispensable relationships which exist in the realities of things. These relationships have been placed in the realities of existent beings through the power of creation and every incident is a consequence of the necessary relationship. For example, God hath created a relation between the sun and the terrestrial globe, that the rays of the sun should shine and the soil should yield. This relationship constitutes predestination, and the manifestation thereof in the plane of existence is fate. Will is the active force which controlleth these relationships and these incidents.'* (*Selections*, p.198.)

79. Bahá'u'lláh writes: '. . . *is not the object of every Revelation to effect a transformation in the whole character of mankind, a transformation that shall manifest itself both outwardly and inwardly, that shall affect both its inner life and external conditions? For if the character of mankind be not changed, the futility of God's universal Manifestations would be apparent.*' (*Kitáb-i-Íqán*, p.241.) And 'Abdu'l-Bahá explains: 'There is a point in which the philosophers and the prophets differ. The philosophers make education the test of knowledge, holding that any man who receives sufficient education can attain a state of perfection. That is to say, man possesses the potentiality for every kind of progress and education enables him to bring this into the court of objectivity.

'The prophets say that something else is necessary. It is true that education transforms the desert into a rose garden, the virgin forest into an orchard, saplings into trees, and single flowers into double and treble flowers, but there is a fundamental difference in man. You can know ten children of one country, in the same school, under the same master, treated and fed in the same way. One of these children may make great progress, others may remain stationary. In the innate nature there are differences of memory, perception and intelligence. There is a superior, a middle and an inferior degree which correspond to the difference in the fundamental states of creation. While recognizing the influence of education we must also become acquainted with the innate disposition.

'The prophets are sent to educate this innate quality in humanity.' (*Divine Philosophy*, pp.103–40.)

man may recognize it, love it and freely follow its directives. The Bahá'í texts call such an intermediary 'Manifestation of God.'[79]

The Manifestation of God is a '. . . *subtle . . . mysterious and ethereal Being*',[80] a Perfect Man, manifesting and revealing to the eyes of mankind as much of the world of the Kingdom as mankind is able to understand and as it is in need of for its own spiritual progress. At the same time, He bestows upon mankind such forces as are required for that progress to take place. Therefore, the Manifestation of God puts at the disposal of mankind the creative forces of the world of the Kingdom, so that men may recognize them and, willingly and freely exposing themselves to their influence, benefit from them. This concept is fundamental in all revealed religions, and a central theme in the Bahá'í Faith: it will be briefly discussed in the following pages.

In this regard, Shoghi Effendi wrote through his secretary: 'With the appearance of every Revelation a new insight is created in man and this in turn expresses itself in the growth of science.' (quoted in *The Light of Divine Guidance*, II, p.21.) In other words, it is necessary that the substance of man (character, inborn disposition, insight) is perfected, so that he may progress.

80. *Gleanings*, p.66.

6 The Perfect Man: The Manifestation of God

The discussion of such a deep and important topic deserves a more complete study than ours. However, we shall do our best to set forth in the following pages some fundamental concepts.[1]

The Manifestation of God in the history of mankind

From a historical point of view, the Manifestations of God are a small number of famous personages, whose existence is sometimes questioned, but whose traces are so evident in human history that no unbiased observer can fail to acknowledge them. They are the founders of the great revealed religions:[2] Abraham, Moses, Jesus, Muhammad, Buddha, Krishna, Zoroaster and, more recently, the Báb and Bahá'u'lláh.

We will now study these extraordinary personages in their common historical aspects, so that we may understand them in a theological and philosophical perspective. They are men of the most dissimilar social backgrounds: princes such as Buddha and Bahá'u'lláh, priests like Zoroaster, merchants such as Muhammad and the Báb, craftsmen like Jesus, courtiers such as Moses. None of them attended any school, or availed himself of worldly power. They announced to their fellow-men a message in the name of a Creator

---

1. Regarding the concept of the Manifestation of God *see* J. R. Cole, 'The Concept of Manifestation in the Bahá'í Writings', in *Bahá'í Studies*, IX; and A. Bausani, 'La Nascita di Bahá'u'lláh,' in *Opinioni Bahá'í*, VIII, no. 4, p.3.
2. For a deeper study of this topic *see* J. Mahmudi, 'The Institutionalization of Religion', in *World Order*, XI, no. 1, pp.16–25.

The Manifestation of God

God Whose mouthpiece they proclaimed themselves. Their message has always been indicative of the importance of rising above certain limitations which they referred to as earthly, so that an ethical-theoretical goal, which they referred to as spiritual, might be attained. They have thus urged mankind to accept hardship and renunciation so that these goals may be achieved, and promised as a reward or as a chastisement life or death of the spirit respectively.

In the beginning, a mere handful of God-intoxicated disciples follow this new Master, giving rise to a scandal among the right-thinkers, observant of the traditional rules — such a scandal as to raise storms of persecution against the Manifestation and His followers. However, despite their often violent deaths (e.g. Jesus and the Báb) and the murder of many of their early followers (martyrs) their ideas, which are at first strongly opposed, eventually, as they show their power of renewal, transform society and usher in a new civilization.

Their teachings therefore, unlike the teachings of philosophers, conquer mankind through their intrinsic power and, when they are put into practice, prove themselves fruitful and give birth to flourishing civilizations. No civilization, including modern Western civilization, is known that was not born through such a process.[3]

However, in the course of time these teachings lose their effectiveness amongst men and according to the universal law of evolution, having yielded their fruit they decline and die. It is then that a new Manifestation appears announcing a new message and new teachings so that mankind may achieve a new spiritual life. The cycle of the ages — an expression of the never-ending 'circle of existence'[4] — proceeds in its eternal motion even in the case of historical religions, which like any other phenomenal reality are born, grow, yield their fruit, decline and die.

These personages are fundamentally different from the great heroes of history. They are characterized by two distinctive features: (i) Their teachings, set forth by words and mostly in the form of one or more holy texts, represent the essence of such spiritual laws as are fit for mankind in its specific stage of growth. In fact, when mankind complies with them, its spiritual, intellectual and social progress is realized. They are the 'science of reality', says 'Abdu'l-Bahá, 'the greatest bestowal of God'; and He adds: '. . . the sphere of the divine teachings is boundless . . . without the teachings of

---

3. Regarding the topic of the birth of civilizations, *see* 'Abdu'l-Bahá, *Selections*, pp.283–4.
4. *Promulgation*, p.220.

God the world of humanity is like the animal kingdom', which anyhow 'is not capable of apprehending them'. In fact, these teachings 'are the bestowals specialized for man', 'above all other source of instruction and development for man', 'the basis of all civilization and progress in the history of mankind',[5] *'a power above and beyond the powers of nature'*, *'a power'* that can *'change this black darkness into light.'*[6]

(ii) Their spiritual power, which they bestow upon anyone who of his own free will and consciously identifies himself with those teachings, is that force through which man can be transformed into a creature endowed with the spiritual virtues of the world of the Kingdom and capable of great spiritual attainments in the world.

Their threefold reality

What is this power that enables them to bestow upon mankind such teachings and spiritual forces? The Bahá'í texts maintain that they convey to mankind *'the revelation of the Soul of God'*,[7] in other words they are the visible expression of the spiritual reality of the world of the Kingdom.[8] This spiritual reality, the First Emanation of the Divine Reality, is reflected in the human reality of these personages like the sun is reflected in a perfect mirror. They are therefore characterized by a threefold reality:

Material: that is, their bodies, which – like all human bodies – are bound to be born, to grow up, to develop and die.

Human: that is, their souls, their individualities. In this regard Bahá'u'lláh writes: *'Every one of them is a mirror of God . . . All else besides them are to be regarded as mirrors capable of reflecting the glory of these Manifestations Who are themselves the Primary Mirrors of the Divine Being . . .'*. He writes moreover that the soul of the Manifestation of God is *'a pure and stainless Soul'*[9] and 'Abdu'l-Bahá explains that it is 'a perfect soul', 'like a mirror wherein the Sun of Reality is reflected . . . a perfect expression of the Sun'.[10]

When the soul of the Manifestation is compared to God, it is like a perfect mirror reflecting the divine rays; when it is compared to mankind, that soul occupies a quite different position. 'Abdu'l-Bahá says: '. . . the individual reality of the Manifestation of God

---

5. ibid. pp.297, 61, 361.
6. *Selections*, p.53.
7. *Gleanings*, p.160.
8. The world of the Kingdom is called also First Mind, Primal Will, Word of God or Logos, Identity, Self or Soul of God. *See* above, pp.35–6.
9. *Gleanings*, pp.74, 66.
10. *Promulgation*, p.173.

is a holy reality, and for that reason it is sanctified and, in that which concerns its nature and quality, is distinguished from all other things . . .'.[11] In this context, He likens this perfect soul to the sun, which is the direct source of its shining rays, and human souls to the moon, which merely reflects those rays.

These souls are different from human souls also in another respect: 'The Prophets are pre-existent. The soul or spirit of the individual comes into being with the conception of the physical body. The Prophets, unlike us, are pre-existent. The soul of Christ existed in the spiritual world before His birth in this world. We cannot imagine what that world is like, so words are inadequate to picture His state of being . . .'.[12]

Also the Manifestations of God have a 'rational soul, which is the human reality', or 'human spirit', says 'Abdu'l-Bahá, and they '. . . share it with all mankind'. However, He explains that the degree of perception typical of the Manifestations of God is not the same rational perception which is typical of human souls, but a 'universal divine mind' transcending human knowledge, in that it is 'a conscious power, not a power of investigation and of research'. Such power 'is the special attribute of the Holy Manifestations and of the Dawning-Places of Prophethood; a ray of this light falls upon the mirrors of the hearts of the righteous'.[13] Therefore human knowledge is but the reflection of a ray, when compared to such a sun as is the knowledge of the Manifestation of God.

Moreover, in the station of their individualities 'the Divine Manifestations are so many different mirrors, because they have a special individuality . . . It is clear that the reality of Christ is different from that of Moses.' Nevertheless 'that which is reflected in the mirrors is the one sun', therefore it is easy to understand how, though the Manifestations of God differ from each other in many respects, yet they are essentially one and the same.

Divine: that is, the Word of God, the Logos. This reality has neither a beginning nor an end; it is eternal, yet it is inferior to God, because it was created by Him. '. . . this third state is alone partaken of by the divine messengers, although great saints have attained extraordinary pre-eminence and reflect the splendour of the sun,' says 'Abdu'l-Bahá.

These three aspects of the reality of the Manifestation of God are

---

11. *Some Answered Questions*, p.154.
12. On behalf of Shoghi Effendi in *Bahá'í News*, Supplement, no. 112, June 1967.
13. *Some Answered Questions*, pp.151, 208, 151, 218.
14. ibid. p.155.
15. *Divine Philosophy*, p.56.

described by 'Abdu'l-Bahá through the following metaphor: their material nature is as a niche, their human nature is as the lamp within the niche, their divine nature as the light which emanates from the lamp.[16]

Therefore, since the Manifestations of God are endowed with a 'divine universal mind', they know the essence of things, and not just their attributes. Their knowledge of the essence of things is likened by 'Abdu'l-Bahá to the self-consciousness of human beings: 'it is a conscious power, not a power of investigation and of research',[17] He says. As they are endowed with such perfect knowledge-consciousness of the world, they know also 'the essential connection which proceeds from the realities of things',[18] which 'Abdu'l-Bahá defines as 'nature' in its meaning of the will of God. Therefore they can convey to mankind as much of their knowledge as mankind can profit from in its specific time and circumstances, a knowledge which may well be defined as 'science of reality'.[19]

As to their spiritual power, it is an emanation of the world of the Kingdom whose Manifestation they are. In fact, Bahá'u'lláh writes that they are *'the vehicle for the transmission of the Grace of the Divinity itself'*;[20] and 'Abdu'l-Bahá explains: 'The greatest power of the Holy Spirit exists in the Divine Manifestations of the Truth. Through the power of the Spirit the Heavenly Teaching has been brought into the world of humanity . . . everlasting life has come to the children of men . . . the Divine Glory has shone from East to West and . . . will the divine virtues of humanity become manifest.'[21]

The Essence of God and the Manifestations of God

The relation between the Essence of God and the Manifestations of God falls within the concept of emanation which has been explained in the second chapter of this book. The Essence of God is sanctified above anything else. Its active attributes shine in the world of the Kingdom and appear in the human world through the Manifestations of God. Therefore, the Manifestations are not incarnations of God,[22] nor do they manifest His Essence, from which they are far

16. Bahá'u'lláh writes that they occupy a *'double station'*, divine and human (See Bahá'u'lláh, Gleanings, p.66) and have a *'twofold nature'*, *'the physical . . . and the spiritual.'* (ibid. pp.66–7.)
17. *Some Answered Questions*, p.218.
18. ibid. p.158.
19. *Promulgation*, p.297.
20. *Gleanings*, pp.67–8.
21. *Paris Talks*, p.87.
22. Bahá'u'lláh writes: '*Know thou of a certainty that the Unseen can in no wise incarnate His Essence and reveal it unto men. He is, and hath been, immensely exalted beyond all that can*

The Manifestation of God

remote.[23] They are an emanation of God — His First Emanation. 'Abdu'l-Bahá explains that they '. . . are as mirrors which have acquired illumination from the Sun of Truth, but the Sun does not descend from its high zenith and does not effect entrance within the mirror. In truth, this mirror has attained complete polish and purity until the utmost capacity of reflection has been developed in it; therefore, the Sun of Reality with its fullest effulgence and splendour is revealed therein.'[24]

The Manifestation of God is, therefore, the visible expression of that same spirit which creates, moves and guides the entire universe and which manifests itself in a Being who expresses man's material, human and divine natures in their perfection, so that mankind may freely recognize Him and of his own free will submit to his laws, thus undergoing — by virtue of those spiritual forces the Manifestation bestows — such a transformation as is the essence of human spiritual growth or progress.

Though the Manifestations of God are powerful and yield absolute power over mankind, yet they are wholly submitted to God and have no will of their own. Bahá'u'lláh refers to Himself as *'but a leaf which the winds of the Will of Thy Lord . . . have stirred'*.[25] And elsewhere He describes His Own station thus: *'This station is the station in which one dieth to himself and liveth in God. Divinity, whenever I mention it, indicateth My complete and absolute self-effacement. This is the station in which I have no control over mine own weal or woe, nor over my life nor over my resurrection.'*[26] The lives of the Manifestations of God — beset as they are with trials and hardships — are the evidence of their utmost submission to the will of God. Endowed with the power of omnipotence as they are, they

---

either be recounted or perceived . . . . He Who is everlastingly hidden from the eyes of men can never be known except through His Manifestation, and His Manifestation can adduce no greater proof of the truth of His Mission than the proof of His own Person.' (Gleanings, p.49.) He writes, moreover: 'However, let none construe these utterances to be anthropomorphism, nor see in them the descent of the worlds of God into the grades of the creatures, nor should they lead thy Eminence to such assumptions. For God is, in His Essence, holy above ascent and descent, entrance and exit; He hath through all eternity been free of the attributes of human creatures and ever will remain so. No man hath ever known Him; no soul hath ever found the pathway to His Being.' (Seven Valleys, pp.22–3.)

23. In this regard Bahá'u'lláh writes: 'Ten thousand Prophets, each a Moses, are thunderstruck upon the Sinai of their search at God's forbidding voice, "Thou shall never behold Me!"; whilst a myriad of Messengers, each as great as Jesus, stand dismayed upon their heavenly thrones by the interdiction: "Mine Essence thou shall never apprehend!".' And moreover: 'When I contemplate, O My God, the relationship that bindeth Me to Thee, I am moved to proclaim to all created things "verily, I am God": and when I consider my own self, lo, I find it coarser than clay.' (Bahá'u'lláh, in Shoghi Effendi, The World Order of Bahá'u'lláh, p.113.)
24. *Promulgation*, p.114.
25. *Proclamation*, p.57.
26. *Epistle*, p.41.

accept a life of humility, giving the highest and purest example of such voluntary submission unto the will of God as is their foremost teaching.

Their names

In the Bahá'í texts the Manifestations of God are given several names:

(i) Prophet, that is, one who speaks in the name of God;

(ii) Messenger, representative or apostle of God, that is one who is sent by God into the world so that he may bestow upon mankind the divine bounties of the world of the Kingdom;

(iii) Word of God, inasmuch as the Manifestations of God have the capacity of giving perfect expression to the spiritual meanings of reality, whereas human beings, limited as they are, have not such a capacity and therefore are referred to as *'letters'*;[27]

(iv) Sun of Truth or of Reality. In relation to the world of mankind they are like the sun in relation to the earth. They are the only source of life, enlightenment and growth for mankind, as the sun for the earth. Bahá'u'lláh writes: '... *if for one moment the tide of His mercy and grace were to be withheld from the world, it would completely perish,*'[28] and 'Abdu'l-Bahá explains: 'The outer sun is a sign or symbol of the inner and ideal Sun of Truth, the Word of God ... a function of the sun is the revelation of the mysteries and creative purposes hidden within the phenomenal world.' This Sun 'gives forth the light of religion and bestows the life of the spirit, imbues humanity with archetypal virtues and confers eternal splendors'; 'its lights are the lights of reality';[29]

(v) Perfect Man. The Manifestation of God is perfect in comparison with other men. Bahá'u'lláh writes: '*Upon the inmost reality of each*

---

27. *Gleanings*, p.196. 'Abdu'l-Bahá says: 'By the "word" we mean that creation with its infinite forms is like unto letters and the individual members of humanity are likewise like unto letters. A letter individually has no meaning, no independent significance, but the station of Christ is the station of the word. That is why Christ is the "word" – a complete significance. The universal bestowal of divinity is manifest in Christ. It is obvious that the evolution of other souls is approximate, or only a part of the whole, but the perfections of the Christ are universal, or the whole. The reality of Christ is the collective centre of all the independent virtues and infinite significances.' (*Divine Philosophy*, p.144.)

28. *Gleanings*, p.68.

29. *Promulgation*, pp.74, 94. The locution Sun of Reality or of Truth is often used to indicate the world of the Kingdom in its essence. 'Abdu'l-Bahá writes: '... *the Sun of Truth dwelleth in a sky to which no soul hath any access, and which no mind can reach, and He is far beyond the comprehension of all creatures. Yet the Holy Manifestations of God are even as a looking-glass, burnished and without stain, which gathereth streams of light out of that Sun, and then scattereth the glory over the rest of creation. In that polished surface, the Sun with all its majesty standeth clearly revealed.*' (*Selections*, p.50.)

and every created thing He hath shed the light of one of His names, and made it a recipient of the glory of one of His attributes. Upon the reality of man, however, He hath focused the radiance of all of His names and attributes, and made it a mirror of His own Self.' In the metaphor presented by Bahá'u'lláh, the Manifestations of God, in comparison with other men, are *'the Primary Mirrors'*.[30]

(vi) Divine Physician. Bahá'u'lláh writes: *'Regard the world as the human body which, though at its creation whole and perfect, hath been afflicted, through various causes, with grave disorders and maladies . . .'*; the Manifestation of God is that *'skilled . . . all-powerful and inspired Physician'* who gives the *'remedy'* fit for its *'healing'*.[31] In the same vein, 'Abdu'l-Bahá explains: *'Every divine Manifestation is the very life of the world, and the skilled physician of each ailing soul. The world of man is sick, and that competent Physician knoweth the cure, arising as He doth with teachings, counsels and admonishments that are the remedy for every pain, the healing balm to every wound.'*[32]

In the Bahá'í texts the Manifestations of God are also given many other names which describe their attributes: a deeper study of such a topic is beyond the scope of this book.[33]

Relations between the Manifestations of God

In the Bahá'í texts, the Manifestations of God are viewed in their mutual relations in two different perspectives:

The station of unity, that is *'of pure abstraction and essential unity'*:[34] in this station *'they all have but one purpose: their secret is the same secret'*,[35] writes Bahá'u'lláh. Therefore, at the times of their Dispensation[36] each one of them is the depository of the *'Most Great Infallibility'*[37] and *'to none is given the right to question His authority'*;

---

30. *Gleanings*, pp. 65, 74.
31. *Proclamation*, pp. 67–8.
32. *Selections*, p. 59.
33. For a meditation on the names of the Manifestations of God *see* R. Rabbani, *The Desire of the World*. She writes: 'We can now come to a selection from the passages of Bahá'u'lláh's writings which might be defined as the essence of theology, which consists for the most part of the titles of God and the titles of Bahá'u'lláh Himself.' (ibid. p. 163.) She then proceeds with that which she describes as a 'not complete . . . nevertheless a comprehensive and impressive selection of the gem-like metaphors and phrases He has used' to convey such a difficult concept, and which may be suggested as an effective starting-point in studying and meditating upon this important theme.
34. *Kitáb-i-Íqán*, p. 152.
35. *Gleanings*, p. 78.
36. 'Dispensation' is intended as a religious system as a stage in a progressive revelation.
37. *Tablets*, p. 108. Bahá'u'lláh writes: *'Know that the term "infallibility" hath numerous meanings and divers stations. In one sense it is applicable to One Whom God hath made immune*

whosoever does so deprives himself of any possibility of spiritual growth, like a tree shut out from the sun. In this respect, *'Whoso maketh the slightest possible difference between their persons, their words, their messages, their acts and manners, hath indeed disbelieved in God,'*[38] writes Bahá'u'lláh.

The station of distinction. Bahá'u'lláh writes: *'Each and every one of them hath been the Bearer of a distinct Message'*, of a *'divinely revealed Book'*, and has shown forth special qualities. In this station, therefore, they are different from each other. According to the Bahá'í texts, in fact, divine revelation through the Manifestations of God is an eternal phenomenon. Bahá'u'lláh writes: '. . . *the Manifestations of His Divine glory and the Day Springs of eternal holiness have been sent down from time immemorial, and been commissioned to summon mankind to the one true God. That the names of some of them are forgotten and the record of their lives lost is to be attributed to the disturbances and changes that have overtaken the world.'*[39] And 'Abdu'l-Bahá explains: '. . . the Kingdom of God is an ancient sovereignty . . . it is not an accidental sovereignty . . .' and therefore there have always been Manifestations of God coming to mankind. '. . . [T]here have been many holy Manifestations of God. One thousand years ago, two hundred thousand years ago, one million years ago, the bounty of God was flowing, the radiance of God was shining, the dominion of God was existing.'[40] The Manifestations of God come one after the other, each one of them representing a different stage in a progressive phenomenon. The Bahá'í texts explain that the law of evolution operates also in the succession of the Manifestations of God amongst men. In the divine revelation, there are evolutionary cycles whereby a fruit appears, through successive stages, from a seed. Each of the Manifestations of God is a stage in this process that Bahá'u'lláh calls *'the chain of successive Revelations'* and the teachings they bring are progressive. In this regard Bahá'u'lláh writes: *'Know of a certainty that in every Dispensation the light of Divine Revelation hath been vouchsafed unto men in direct proportion to their spiritual capacity'*; and moreover: *'Should the Word be allowed to release*

---

from error. Similarly it is applied to every soul whom God hath guarded against sin, transgression, rebellion, impiety, disbelief and the like. However, the Most Great Infallibility is confined to One Whose station is immeasurably exalted beyond ordinances or prohibitions and is sanctified from errors and omissions. Indeed He is a Light which is not followed by darkness and a Truth not overtaken by error. Were He to pronounce water to be wine or heaven to be earth or light to be fire, He speaketh the truth and no doubt would there be about it; and unto none is given the right to question His authority or to say why or wherefore.' (ibid. p.108.)

38. *Gleanings*, pp.87, 59–60.
39. ibid. pp.79, 74, 174.
40. *Promulgation*, p.463.

suddenly all the energies latent within it, no man could sustain the weight of so mighty a Revelation.' Elsewhere He writes: '*Their Revelation may be likened unto the light of the moon that sheddeth its radiance upon the earth. Though every time it appeareth, it revealeth a fresh measure of its brightness, yet its inherent splendour can never diminish, nor can its light suffer extinction.*'[41]

'Abdu'l-Bahá likens progressive revelation to human spirit appearing with different powers in the embryo, the newborn baby, and so on through the various stages of human life, or to the spirit of growth which is present in the seed but manifests itself in different ways in leaves and fruits; He says: '. . . revelation is progressive and continuous. It never ceases. It is necessary that the reality of Divinity with all its perfections and attributes should become resplendent in the human world.'[42]

Revelations come into the world one after the other, even as springtimes follow one another, year after year. 'Abdu'l-Bahá develops the metaphor of the Sun of Reality as the Manifestation of God and says: 'The coming of a Manifestation of God is the season of spiritual spring'; and elsewhere: '. . . just as the solar cycle has its four seasons, the cycle of the Sun of Reality has its distinct and successive periods.' These periods can be compared respectively to springtime, when the new spiritual era begins; to summertime, when the civilization ushered in by the Manifestation of God has attained its greatest flourishing; to autumn, when its fruits are gathered, but at the same time its decline begins; and to winter, when there is 'the death and disappearance of the divine growth and extinction of the light and love of God', whereas only 'dogmas and blind imitations' remain. At that time '. . . again the cycle begins and a new springtime appears'.[43]

'Abdu'l-Bahá explains the same concept in different words: '*From the days of Adam until today, the religions of God have been made manifest, one following the other, and each one of them fulfilled its due function, revived mankind, and provided education and enlightenment. They freed the people from the darkness of the world of nature and ushered them into the brightness of the Kingdom. As each succeeding Faith and Law became revealed, it remained for some centuries a richly fruitful tree and to it was committed the happiness of humankind. However, as the centuries rolled by, it aged, it flourished no more and put forth no fruit, wherefore was it then made young again.*'[44] Elsewhere thus He explains

---

41. *Gleanings*, pp.74, 87, 76–7, 79.
42. *Promulgation*, p.378.
43. ibid. pp.54, 95, 363, 95.
44. *Selections*, pp.51–2.

the origin of materialism: 'When the sun sets, it is the time for bats to fly. They come forth because they are creatures of the night. When the light of religion becomes darkened, the materialists appear. They are the bats of the night. The decline of religion is their time of activity; they seek the shadows when the world is darkened and clouds have spread over it.'[45] Through these explanations the reasons may be understood why the progress of civilizations cannot be described as a continuous ascending line, but rather as a discontinuous ascending line. E. Laszlo acutely writes: 'The historical record . . . gives good reasons to believe that societies . . . do not change at all times and in small increments. Rather, the mode of change appears saltatory and intermittent . . . progressive yet discontinuous . . .'[46] These periods of transformation may be compared to that which the Bahá'í texts call *'Day of God'*[47] or, through a metaphor, 'the season of the spiritual springtime', that is, 'the coming of a Manifestation of God.'[48]

The periods of stagnation are the phases of religious decline, of the triumph of fanaticism which in its turn is the direct cause of the victory of materialistic forces, who find their origin and the confirmation of their life theories in the mistakes perpetrated by the followers of religions. After all, the judgement pronounced by Karl Marx against religion refers to religious phenomena studied during their spiritual winter.[49]

Nevertheless, notwithstanding the differences between them, all the Manifestations of God manifest all the names and attributes of God. *'They only differ'*, writes Bahá'u'lláh, *'in the intensity of their revelation and the comparative potency of their light.'*[50] The Bahá'í texts are very emphatic on this point: whoever does not believe in the oneness of the Manifestations of God does not believe in the oneness of God.

Their purposes

The Manifestations of God have a twofold purpose: to promote the spiritual growth of individuals and to further the progress of society.

(i) Promoting the spiritual growth of individuals: 'Abdu'l-Bahá says, 'God hath sent forth the Prophets for the purpose of

---

45. *Promulgation*, pp.179–80.
46. *Evolution*, pp.101, 105.
47. *Gleanings*, p.11.
48. *Promulgation*, p.54.
49. For a deeper discussion of this concept, see G. Nash, *The Phoenix and the Ashes*, p.104. As to the comparison between materialists and bats, see above p.16 and no.80.
50. *Gleanings*, p.48.

The Manifestation of God

quickening the soul of man into higher and divine recognitions'; 'to train the souls of humanity and free them from the thralldom of natural instincts and physical tendencies';[51] 'to teach and enlighten man, to explain to him the mystery of the Power of the Holy Spirit; to enable him to reflect the light, and so, in his turn, to be the source of guidance to others';[52] and, in the words of Bahá'u'lláh, *'to lay bare those gems that lie hidden within the mine of their true and inmost selves'*. In this sense, Bahá'u'lláh compares the revelation to the mythical elixir: the former changes copper into gold, the latter transforms the animal nature of man into a divine nature.[53] Bahá'u'lláh writes concisely that the purpose of the Manifestations of God is *'to endue all men with righteousness and understanding, so that peace and tranquillity may be firmly established amongst them'*.[54] And 'Abdu'l-Bahá says: '. . . the wisdom of the Manifestations of God is directed toward the establishing of the bond of a love which is indissoluble.'[55]

(ii) The first purpose fulfils also the second: furthering the progress of society or, in the words of Bahá'u'lláh, *'to carry forward an ever-advancing civilization'*,[56] or, in the words of 'Abdu'l-Bahá, '. . . unifying humanity and establishing universal peace'. In this sense 'Abdu'l-Bahá says also: 'The Prophets have founded divine civilization.'[57]

Therefore, the Manifestations of God are the great Educators of mankind, which is in need of them because 'the world of existence is but a jungle of disorder and confusion, a state of nature producing nothing but fruitless, useless trees'.[58] They are sometimes likened to 'the heart [of] the body of the universe . . . Through his spiritual faculty he receives the teachings and bounties of the Almighty God and then imparts them to the world through material means in which he shares with other men'.[59]

As their religions have a twofold purpose, two aspects can be identified in them: 'one, the essential or fundamental, the other, the material or accidental. The first aspect . . . concerns the ethical development and spiritual progress of mankind, the awakening of potential human susceptibilities and the descent of the divine

---

51. *Promulgation*, p.310.
52. *Paris Talks*, p.61.
53. *Gleanings*, p.287. *See* also ibid. p.200.
54. ibid. p.225.
55. *Promulgation*, p.344.
56. *Gleanings*, p.215.
57. *Promulgation*, pp.97, 375.
58. ibid. p.466.
59. Mírzá Abu'l-Faḍl, 'The Heart', in *Star of the West*, X, p.115.

bestowals. These ordinances are changeless, essential, eternal. The second function . . . deals with material conditions, the laws of human intercourse and social regulation. These are subject to change and transformation in accordance with the time, place and condition.'[60]

In the light of all these qualities and functions, we may well understand the following exalted words Bahá'u'lláh wrote describing the Manifestation of God: *'It is God's supreme testimony, the clearest evidence of His truth, the sign of His consummate bounty, the token of His all-encompassing mercy, the proof of His most loving providence, the symbol of His most perfect grace.'*[61] We understand also why it is so vitally important for men to recognize the Manifestation and to submit wholeheartedly to his guidance.

Their proofs

Through what signs is mankind enabled to identify these Perfect Men, these Unique Teachers? Thus Bahá'u'lláh answers such an important question: *'The first and foremost testimony establishing His truth is His own Self. Next to this testimony is His Revelation. For whoso faileth to recognize either the one or the other He hath established the words He hath revealed as proofs of His reality and truth. This is, verily, an evidence of His tender mercy unto men. He hath endowed every soul with the capacity to recognize the signs of God.'*[62]

Thus 'Abdu'l-Bahá explains this important issue: 'One of the proofs is through the fulfilment of former prophecies, the second proofs are the creative words and phrases which salute the hearts of humanity, the third are their deeds and the fourth are their

---

60. *Promulgation*, pp.97–8. In this regard, 'Abdu'l-Bahá says also: 'Each one of the divine religions has established two kinds of ordinances: the essential and the accidental. The essential ordinances rest upon the firm, unchanging, eternal foundations of the Word itself. They concern spiritualities, seek to stabilize morals, awaken intuitive susceptibilities, reveal the knowledge of God and inculcate the love of all mankind. The accidental laws concern the administration of outer human actions and relations, establishing rules and regulations requisite for the world of bodies and their control. These are ever subject to change and supersedure according to exigencies of time, place and condition. For example, during the time of Moses . . . divorce was sanctioned and polygamy allowable to a certain extent . . . Briefly, the foundation of the divine religions is one eternal foundation, but the laws for temporary conditions and exigencies are subject to change. Therefore, by adherence to these temporary laws, blindly following and imitating ancestral forms, difference and divergence have arisen among followers of the various religions, resulting in disunion, strife and hatred. Blind imitations and dogmatic observances are conducive to alienation and disagreement; they lead to bloodshed and destruction of the foundations of humanity. Therefore, the religionists of the world must lay aside these imitations and investigate the essential foundation of reality itself, which is not subject to change or transformation. This is the divine means of agreement and unification.' (*Promulgation*, pp.338–9.)
61. *Gleanings*, p.195.
62. ibid. pp.105–6.

teachings.' 'Abdu'l-Bahá does not seem to attach great importance to prophecies, very difficult to interpret and very easy to refute. He does not ascribe a great value to their miracles, 'convincing to a limited number only'.[63] He attaches the greatest importance to their deeds, to their teachings and to the power of their words. Regarding their deeds, 'Abdu'l-Bahá writes: '. . . *the Divine Educator must teach by word and also by deed, thus revealing to all the straight pathway of truth*'. Among their deeds He mentions particularly their '*strength and endurance*'[64] under tests and trials. Regarding their teachings and the power of their words, He says: 'The proof of the validity of a Manifestation of God is the penetration and potency of His Word, the cultivation of heavenly attributes in the lives and hearts of His followers and the bestowal of divine education upon the world of humanity. This is absolute proof. The world is a school in which there must be Teachers of the Word of God.' Elsewhere He says: 'If we wish to discover whether anyone of these Souls or Messengers was in reality a Prophet of God, we must investigate the facts surrounding His life and history, and the first point of our investigation will be the education He bestowed upon mankind.' And moreover: 'It is evident, then, that the proofs of the validity and inspiration of a Prophet of God are the deeds of beneficent accomplishment and greatness emanating from Him. If He proves to be instrumental in the elevation and betterment of mankind, He is undoubtedly a valid and heavenly Messenger.' And finally: 'The essential requirement and qualification of Prophethood is the training and the guidance of the people.'[65]

This transformation produced by virtue of the influence exercised by the Manifestation of God upon His followers is such that some of them go as far as to offer their lives, rather than recant their faith: these are the martyrs, the pride of all revealed religions.[66]

History, therefore, is once more the tribunal which will judge, by demonstrating his meanness, anyone who may unduly lay claim to prophethood, whereas the fruits manifest in the lives of the followers of any true divine Messenger and in the character of the civilization he has ushered in are clear evidence of his truth. When Christ was asked by His disciples how they could distinguish the false from the true prophet, He answered: 'Ye shall know them by their fruits. Do men gather grapes of thorns, or figs of thistles?'[67]

---

63. *Divine Philosophy*, pp.39–40.
64. *Selections*, p.56.
65. *Promulgation*, pp.341, 364, 366, 411.
66. For an explanation of the meaning of martyrdom *see Kitáb-i-Íqán*, pp.221–8, and *Gleanings*, pp.179–83.
67. *Matt.* 7:16–17.

Denial

The Manifestations of God are seemingly as frail creatures as any human being, even wholly deprived of any worldly power; and yet they are the bearers of teachings which are really 'iconoclastic'[68] in their disruptive influence on time-honoured traditions, traditions which in the long run have mostly turned into prejudices. No wonder, then, that they have always been rejected and persecuted by their contemporaries, or that at the beginning it is so difficult for most people to accept their teachings and recognize their station. On the other hand, that is part of the rules of the game of human spiritual growth. It is a process that rests upon a free and conscious choice between a concrete and alluring sensible reality, and a difficultly perceived and appreciated spiritual reality. In fact, how could such a choice be free, and such a process achieve its educational purpose, if the signs of the Manifestations of God were evident and attractive to human eyes, i.e. to that same animal nature that must be conquered and overcome? Or if those signs were easily grasped by human minds, which are requested to independently put themselves at the service of the Manifestation? It is the human soul's attraction towards the world of the Kingdom that, despite all else, must be the guide of human beings, so that they may overcome any obstacle raised by the natal self with its natural emotions, and by the mind itself through the prejudices it may easily fall prey to, and may recognize the shining reality of the Manifestation of God.

---

68. *Promulgation*, p.154. See also *Kitáb-i-Íqán*, pp.4 *passim* and *Gleanings*, pp.56–9.

7 Striving Towards Perfection: Dynamics of Human Transformation

The method

Everything is perfectly arranged: man stands at the end of imperfection (i.e. he is the fruit of the world of creation and is possessed of all its qualities) and at the beginning of perfection (i.e. he is potentially possessed of the capacity for all the spiritual qualities of the world of the Kingdom). The instrument through which he can set in motion and operate the process whereby his divine potentialities will be manifested is his power of understanding, typical of human nature. Man can avail himself of his power of understanding so that he may recognize the Manifestation of God, who manifests, within the reach of human beings, the spiritual qualities and the creative forces of the world of the Kingdom, and who in doing so bestows upon mankind two great bounties:
(i) A set of teachings and laws representing a reflection of the great laws and truths of the world of the Kingdom; whoever adheres to these teachings and observes these laws will have concrete results in his own life: personal excellence and collective progress.
(ii) The forces required for man on the one hand to conquer in himself such material qualities as belong to his animal nature and hamper his transformation, and on the other to both manifest the qualities of his divine nature and achieve a deeper comprehension of the Revelation. 'This quickening spirit emanates spontaneously from the Sun of Truth',[1] says 'Abdu'l-Bahá. These two great

1. *Promulgation*, p.59.

bounties are often referred to, in the Bahá'í texts, as the bounty of the Holy Spirit[2] and the spirit of faith.[3]

The Manifestation of God thus reveals to mankind the path and the method of its transformation, and at the same time puts at its disposal the powers — if mankind is but willing to reap them — through which this transformation may occur. Mankind can obtain such powers only through its willing compliance with the method prescribed by the Manifestation.[4]

The transformation of man from his animal nature to his divine nature — or spiritual progress — is the highest evolutionary stage attained upon the earth by one who is born from the composition of elemental atoms and who has successively traversed, in the course of long ages, the mineral, vegetable and animal kingdoms. Recognizing the Manifestation of God is therefore 'the first step in the path of God, but the distance of the way is great . . .'[5] Since this

---

2. 'Abdu'l-Bahá says that the 'Holy Spirit is the energizing factor in the life of a man' because 'whosoever receives this power is able to influence all those with whom he comes into contact', whereas 'the greatest philosophers without this Spirit are powerless'. (*Paris Talks*, p.165.) The Holy Spirit is the 'mediator between God and His creatures', (*Some Answered Questions*, p.145), '. . . the mediator of the Holy Light from the Sun of Reality which it gives to the sanctified realities.' (ibid. p.145.) The Holy Spirit in fact conveys the spiritual knowledge of reality, mostly through the Utterances and the written Revelation of the Manifestation of God.

3. 'Abdu'l-Bahá says that the spirit of faith is that 'power which makes the earthly man heavenly, and the imperfect man perfect. It makes the impure to be pure, the silent eloquent; it purifies and sanctifies those made captive by carnal desires, it makes the ignorant wise.' (*Some Answered Questions*, pp.144–5.) It 'comes from the breath of the Holy Spirit'. (ibid. p.144.) He writes also: '*But the Spirit of Faith which is of the Kingdom (of God) consists of the all-comprehending Grace and the perfect attainment . . .*' (*Tablets*, p.116.)

4. In various circumstances, 'Abdu'l-Bahá refers to a supreme gift conferred by God on man: the intellect which He says to be 'the most precious gift bestowed upon man by the Divine Beauty'. (*Paris Talks*, p.41.) *See* above, p.89; '*the attainment unto His unfailing guidance*' (quoted in *Bahá'í Education*, (comp.), p.12), which he says to be '*the most precious of gifts*' (ibid.); the individuality, as 'capacity of attaining human virtues' (*Promulgation*, p.378), which He says to be 'the greatest bestowal of God to man' (ibid.); and 'spirituality' (*Paris Talks*, p.112), viewed as 'the awakening of the conscious soul of man to perceive the reality of Divinity' (*Promulgation*, p.142) and made possible only through 'the breaths of the Holy Spirit' (ibid. p.142), which He says to be 'the greatest of God's gifts' (*Paris Talks*, p.112.)

If we make a deeper study of those 'precious gifts', we will discover that man knows through his intellect; through the '*attainment unto His unfailing guidance*', he directs his own understanding towards such goals as God Himself indicates to him; through his 'individuality', he expresses in his life, in the form of spirituality, the results of his turning towards the guidance of God.

'Abdu'l-Bahá concisely expounds these concepts in the following words: 'The greatest bestowal of God in the world of humanity is religion, for assuredly the divine teachings of religion are above all other sources of instruction and development to man. Religion confers upon man eternal life and guides his footsteps in the world of mortality. It opens the doors of unending happiness and bestows everlasting honour upon the human kingdom.' (*Promulgation*. p.361.).

5. 'Abdu'l-Bahá, quoted in 'Join the Army of Peace', in *Star of the West*, XIII, p.113.

transformation is a process of growth, it complies with the laws of evolution in the same way as any other process of this kind: it is gradual and may be compared to the growth of a 'seed',[6] which, cultivated by the farmer, germinates, grows and yields its fruits by virtue of the energy poured out by the sun, and of the mineral substances absorbed from the air and the soil — thus expressing its potential qualities. This is one of the metaphors 'Abdu'l-Bahá suggests in order to explain the dynamics of spiritual transformation.[7] Other metaphors are as follows: a stone which must be cleared from 'the dust and dross of this world' so that it may mirror forth the light of the sun; a 'sterile soil' which must be laboriously tilled so that it may become fertile and yield its fruits. One of the most suggestive amongst these metaphors is that of light. 'Abdu'l-Bahá refers to God as 'Supreme . . . Centre of Light' and says: 'the more we turn to this Centre of Light, the greater will be our capacity'. And moreover: '. . . spiritual advancement may be likened to the light of the early dawn. Although this dawn light is dim and pale, a wise man who views the march of the sunrise at its very beginning can foretell the ascendancy of the sun in its full glory and effulgence. He knows for a certainty that it is the beginning of its manifestation and that later it will assume great power and potency.'[8] He likens moreover *'the brilliant realities and sanctified spirits . . . to a shining crescent . . . {This crescent},'* He writes, *'has one face turned toward the Sun of Truth, and another face opposite to the contingent world. The journey of this crescent in the heaven of the universe ends in (becoming) full moon. That is, the face of it which is turned toward the divine world becomes also opposite to the contingent world, and by this, both its merciful and spiritual, as well as contingent perfections become complete.'*[9] Finally, He describes this process as a process of approaching God and He adds: 'nearness is likeness',[10] because 'the Prophets teach us that the only way to approach God is by characterizing ourselves with the attributes of divinity'.[11] Such can (and must) be this likeness that one's existence may become 'non-existence', 'for when the ray,' 'Abdu'l-Bahá writes, 'returneth to the sun, it is wiped out, and when the drop cometh to the sea, it vanisheth and when the true lover finds his Beloved, he yieldeth up his soul'.[11]

6. *Promulgation*, p.91.
7. See *Promulgation*, pp.16, 21, 131, 420, 451.
8. ibid. pp.14, 148, 15, 131.
9. *Tablets*, pp.108–9.
10. *Promulgation*, p.148.
11. *Divine Philosophy*, pp.93, 76.

Prerequisites of human transformation

The Bahá'í texts offer so much advice and so many admonitions concerning the prerequisites of human transformation that it would be impossible to list them all. Besides, there would be the risk of making arid and cold that which — written in the peerless, metaphoric language typical of revelation — has the capacity not only to make the concepts clear to any searching mind, but also to awaken in receptive hearts such feelings whereby the inherent obstacles of this process may be overcome. We will therefore content ourselves with discussing just a few of the topics which seem both vital and easier to understand and set forth.

Voluntary submission to the will of God

Three are '*the most holy words*' prescribed by God for human souls when they are brought to existence, as prerequisites for the quickening of their inherent divine potentialities: '*Prefer not your own will to Mine, never desire that which I have not desired for you, and approach Me not with lifeless hearts, defiled with worldly desires and cravings.*'[12] These words are expressive of that voluntary and conscious '*submission to*' the '*command*' or will of God which — accepted for the sake of His love and abundantly exemplified in the lives of the Manifestations of God, who have always willingly accepted any affliction in the fulfilment of their missions — is conducive to detachment from '*worldly desires and cravings*' and to the attainment of the 'nearness of God'.

Purity

'Abdu'l-Bahá says, 'Nearness to God is dependent upon the purity of the heart and exhilaration of the spirit through the glad tidings of the Kingdom.' In this context, it seems that 'pure' is anyone possessed — either because he never lost it or because he regained it — of such inborn susceptibility as enables him, on the one hand, to rejoice in his inmost heart at that which satisfies the demands of his divine nature, drawing his soul closer to the world of the Kingdom, and, on the other, to suffer because of that which draws his soul far away from that same spiritual world. A pure soul, therefore, is strongly attracted towards the words and the teachings of the Manifestation of God, in that they are the expressions of the

---

12. *Hidden Words*, Persian no. 19. Bahá'u'lláh writes: '*Walk in My statutes for love of Me.*' (*Hidden Words*, Arabic, no. 38.)

13. See 'Abdu'l-Bahá, *Selections*, pp. 146–50. 'Purity will be studied in Chapter 8. *See* below pp. 162–3.

Striving Towards Perfection

world of the Kingdom (such is the 'exhilaration of the spirit through the glad tidings of the Kingdom'[14]). As that pure soul follows this attraction, it will advance along the path of its search for the Kingdom.

Endeavour

Any pure and attracted person who is seeking the world of the Kingdom should be 'lofty in endeavour'; in fact, 'as long as he lacks susceptibility to divine influences, he is incapable of reflecting the light and assimilating its benefits' and therefore 'he must seek capacity and develop readiness'. This is the path of spiritual perfection, through which two capacities may be achieved: on the one hand, 'capacity, susceptibility and worthiness that [he] may hear the call of the glad tidings of the Kingdom', i.e. the capacity of understanding the teachings of the Manifestation, on the other, the 'susceptibility to the divine influences,' so that he may 'reflect the light and assimilate its benefits',[15] i.e. the capacity of expressing the divine virtues in his life. It is certainly not a quick and sudden transformation; on the contrary, it is often a slow and troublesome change, made possible through constant endeavour in one's effort to rise above one's inherent animal nature, as well as through such generous divine bounties as are the teachings of the Manifestation and the forces of the Holy Spirit and of the spirit of faith.

Directions of human endeavour

When we study the Bahá'í texts, we will immediately find certain vital prerequisites a man should meet if he is to progress along the path of spirituality:
(i) The first prerequisite is *'the knowledge of God'*, i.e. the recognition of the Manifestation of God. In the absence of such a prerequisite, spiritual life is sorely crippled: *'his cry shall not be heard by God'*,[16] sounds the dramatic warning uttered by Bahá'u'lláh.
(ii) The second prerequisite is *'steadfastness in His love'* and *'in His Cause'*. Whoever aims at the gift of such *'steadfastness'*,[17] should recognize that *'He [God] shall not be asked of His doings'*. In other words, he should recognize the infallibility of the Manifestation of God and fulfil the duty of surrendering to His will. Through such

---

14. *Promulgation*, p.147.
15. ibid. pp.186, 148, 149, 148.
16. *Gleanings*, pp.5, 293. See *Kitáb-i-Íqán*, pp.139 passim.
17. *Gleanings*, pp.289, 290.

recognition he will be delivered *'from all manner of doubt and perplexity'*[18] and will attain a condition which is referred to as *'knowledge'*.[19]

Whoever wants to attain the bounty of such steadfastness is also recommended to meditate upon the words of the Manifestation, so that he may grasp their inner meanings and draw from their creative forces.

(iii) The third prerequisite is strict observance of certain prescribed commandments:[20] daily prayer, daily reading of and pondering upon the Holy Writings, so that the truths enshrined within them may be discovered; mirroring forth the moral and spiritual teachings of the Manifestation in everyday life; teaching the Faith with the twofold purpose of assisting other souls so that they may find their way towards God and of contributing to bringing about the unity of mankind in the world.[21]

The special meaning of the Revealed Word

Prayer and the perusal of the Holy Texts are an instrument of spiritual progress because the words revealed by the Manifestations of God have a special meaning, as has been previously explained. In fact, the Manifestations of God translate their own direct knowledge of the world of the Kingdom and of the world of creation into words which are within the reach of human understanding — words which they convey to mankind through their utterances and writings. It is clear, therefore, that such words are a vital link between mankind and the world of the Kingdom.

The messages of the Manifestations of God are worded quite differently from those of ordinary human beings. The Manifestations mostly avail themselves of metaphors, because in so doing they can convey spiritual truths which could not be described through such univocal language as is rightly required and usually used in scientific activity. The topic of the literary style of the Bahá'í texts is beyond our scope.[22] It is enough here to quote an

---

18. *Kitáb-i-Aqdas*, in *Synopsis*, pp. 25, 26.
19. *Seven Valleys*, p. 11.
20. Bahá'u'lláh writes: '*The beginning of all things is the knowledge of God, and the end of all things is strict observance of whatsoever hath been sent down from the empyrean of the Divine Will that pervadeth all that is in the heavens and on the earth.*' (*Gleanings*, p. 5.) See also ibid. pp. 289–90.
21. These laws are set forth in the *Kitáb-i-Aqdas*. See *The Importance of Prayer, Meditation and the Devotional Attitude*, (comp.), p. 3.
Regarding the topic of teaching, A. Taherzadeh wrote in October 1982 an important letter: 'Notes on the Bahá'í Concept of Spirituality', in *New Day*, May–June 1984.
22. See *Kitáb-i-Íqán*, pp. 3 passim; *Some Answered Questions*, pp. 83–6; *Promulgation*, p. 149. See also A. Bausani, 'Some Aspects of the Bahá'í Expressive Style', in *World Order*, XIII, no. 2, p. 36; John S. Hatcher, 'The Metaphorical Nature of Material Reality', in *Bahá'í Studies*, III; A. Taherzadeh, *The Revelation of Bahá'u'lláh*, vol. I, pp. 18–44.

important statement by 'Abdu'l-Bahá explaining how the comprehension of such metaphors is always gradual and adequate to the spiritual capacities and susceptibilities of the audience: 'Consider how the parable makes attainment dependent upon capacity. Unless capacity is developed, the summons of the Kingdom cannot reach the ear, the light of the Sun of Truth will not be observed, and the fragrances of the rose garden of inner significance will be lost.'[23]

Through prayer – whose daily practice is recommended in the Bahá'í texts, using those numerous prayers which, revealed as they are by the Manifestation of God, are perfectly worded – a goal is pursued which, as a man advances in his spiritual growth, rises from an invocation aimed at obtaining satisfaction of a material need, to a supplication for aid so that a spiritual gift may be obtained, to the expression of feelings of contrition for a past transgression, to feelings of personal helplessness, to an anthem of praise and thanksgiving to God for His abundantly bestowed bounties, to the contemplation of His manifest Beauty in the world of creation and in one's own innermost being.[24] The Bahá'í texts explain, moreover, that true prayer, like any other activity of human thought, cannot remain in the plane of thought only but should be translated into actions, otherwise it is utterly useless.

Therefore, the devout reading or chanting of the specially revealed prayers of the Manifestations of God is a means through which such spiritual forces may be obtained as are required to attain the spiritual goals that those prayers recommend and that are being eagerly pursued.

Meditation on the Holy Writings is very similar to prayer in its meaning. Through this important practice a deeper understanding of the truths enshrined within those same words may be achieved, so that they may be mirrored forth in daily life.

Finally, through the perusal of the Holy Writings (a practice which implies a mental activity aiming at understanding their contents) a deeper knowledge of the Writings and the Teachings may be obtained so that they may be practised and taught more easily.

Serving mankind

Teaching the Faith is viewed in the Bahá'í texts as '*the most*

---

23. *Promulgation*, p.149.
24. On the topic of prayer *see The Importance of Prayer, Meditation and the Devotional Attitude*, (comp.); Amatu'l-Bahá Rúhíyyih K͟hánum, 'The Prayers of Bahá'u'lláh', in *Bahá'í World*, IX, p.792; R. Rabbani, *The Desire of the World*, pp.104–153; W. & M. Hellaby, *Prayer: A Bahá'í Approach*; R. Moffett, *Du'á: On Wings of Prayer*; G. A. Shook, *Mysticism, Science and Revelation*, pp.82–107.

meritorious of all deeds'.[25] Many important spiritual purposes are fulfilled through this activity:

(i) First of all, teaching the Faith is viewed as an activity aiming at drawing a soul closer to God and thus to itself. If the Manifestations of God mirror forth all the attributes of God, if they are the source of all the bounties vouchsafed by God unto mankind, there is no higher goal for a man to aim for than recognizing them and being exposed to their quickening influence. Could any other greater gift be bestowed upon a soul than assisting it in recognizing such an exalted Being?

(ii) Secondly, whoever recognizes the Manifestation of God will immediately put himself at the service of His primal purpose: to realize the unity of mankind. Therefore, when the followers of Bahá'u'lláh teach the Faith they fulfil another of the duties prescribed by Him: to devote all their energies to the attainment of the unity of mankind.

(iii) Finally, 'Abdu'l-Bahá writes: '. . . *in spiritual training it is impossible for an imperfect one to perfect another, or train another, unless he first conquer his own self and desire, and become purified from selfish iniquities in order to become capable of Merciful Splendours*'.[26] Indeed, when we study the Bahá'í texts on the topic of teaching, we come to understand that this vital task requires wisdom, tolerance, kindness, patience, tact, moderation, love, sincerity, consistency, a good character and holy deeds, courage, dignity, humility, modesty and many other virtues. Therefore, while the spiritual seeker strains every nerve so that he may befittingly deliver the Message, he finds a training ground and a strong motivation for the inner improvement he is aiming at and a good opportunity to practise in his life those same spiritual truths he is attracted to.

However, the Bahá'í texts suggest many other deeds of service to humanity. They offer two kinds of directives: on the one hand they recommend, through exhortations and admonitions, those virtues which should be acquired so that mankind may be befittingly served; on the other they offer practical instructions in view of such service. The former inculcate a standard of behaviour and kindle in the hearts a yearning to rise up to those heights; the latter outline those practical steps through which the standards recommended may be realized.

An inspiring epitome of the former is the following exhortation addressed by Bahá'u'lláh to one of His sons, to which Rúḥíyyih

---

25. *Gleanings*, p.278.
26. Quoted in 'Become Lamp of the True One', in *Star of the West*, IX, p.162.

Rabbani refers as 'the most succinct and perfect guide to what should constitute the character of a true human being':[27]

'*Be generous in prosperity, and thankful in adversity. Be worthy of the trust of thy neighbour, and look upon him with a bright and friendly face. Be a treasure to the poor, an admonisher to the rich, an answerer of the cry of the needy, a preserver of the sanctity of thy pledge. Be fair in thy judgement, and guarded in thy speech. Be unjust to no man, and show all meekness to all men. Be as a lamp unto them that walk in darkness, a joy to the sorrowful, a sea for the thirsty, a haven for the distressed, an upholder and defender of the victim of oppression. Let integrity and uprightness distinguish all thine acts. Be a home for the stranger, a balm to the suffering, a tower of strength to the fugitive. Be eyes to the blind, and a guiding light unto the feet of the erring. Be an ornament to the countenance of truth, a crown to the brow of fidelity, a pillar of the temple of righteousness, a breath of life to the body of mankind, an ensign of the hosts of justice, a luminary above the horizon of virtue, a dew to the soil of the human heart, an ark on the ocean of knowledge, a sun in the heaven of bounty, a gem on the diadem of wisdom, a shining light in the firmament of thy generation, a fruit upon the tree of humility.*'[28]

Many passages in the Bahá'í texts offer practical counsels. The directions suggested, the examples proposed and the situations provided for are so various that any seeker is immediately faced by a difficulty he must learn to overcome. As this new era is characterized by the spiritual maturity of mankind, decisions and choices are always left to the responsibility of individuals. Whoever looks in the Bahá'í texts for precise and binding recipes, a sort of casuistry to comply with in the various specific circumstances of life, will be disappointed. The Bahá'í texts establish only a few fundamental and universal principles, and it is on this ground that everyone must learn how to manage his own life in full consciousness and freedom. It is the duty of everyone to identify each time, in his own specific and peculiar condition, the best decision to take so that the sought-after '*good pleasure of* [the] *Beloved*'[29] may be obtained. The best thing to do is to identify the 'spiritual principles or what some call human values',[30] because on that ground solutions for any personal or social problem may be found. When these are identified, then the context should be raised 'to the level of principle, as distinct from pure pragmatism'.[30] Here lies the secret of such a life in the service of mankind as is an indispensable prerequisite of spiritual progress.

27. R. Rabbani, *The Desire of the World*, p.47.
28. *Epistle*, p.93.
29. *Kitáb-i-Íqán*, p.129.
30. The Universal House of Justice, *The Promise of World Peace*, p.14.

It would be impossible to enumerate all the practical counsels offered by the Bahá'í texts for the different circumstances of our daily lives. Such a comprehensive view may be conceived and such intimate feelings may be kindled only from an open-minded and thorough perusal of the Holy Writings. Whether within the family, or in the sphere of studies or job, in the socio-political field or in interpersonal relationships, a spiritual seeker will never lose sight of his goal, which is the world of the Kingdom. Whenever he happens to act, he will strive so that he may show forth those qualities of the world of the Kingdom he is seeking for and discovering in his own inner self. These qualities are indeed both 'means'[31] for the entrance into that spiritual Kingdom and *qualifications of the divinely enlightened souls*',[32] who have already attained to it. And in the course of his efforts, he will not waste his time in metaphysical hairsplitting or in strange occult practices. Bahá'u'lláh writes: '*Averse is God from putting aught into effect except through its (material) means*', and moreover He says that '*God hath made the achievement of everything conditional upon material means.*'[33] And when an inquirer asked of 'Abdu'l-Bahá, what is the relationship between material means and prayer, He answered:

'*Prayer is like the spirit and material means are like the human hand. The spirit operateth through the instrumentality of the hand. Although the one True God is the All-Provider, it is the earth which is the means to supply sustenance . . . but when sustenance is decreed it becometh available, whatever the means may be. When man refuseth to use material means, he is like a thirsty one who seeketh to quench his thirst through means other than water or other liquids. The Almighty Lord is the provider of water, and its maker, and hath decreed that it be used to quench man's thirst, but its use is dependent upon His Will. If it should not be in conformity with His Will, man is afflicted with a thirst which the oceans cannot quench.*'[34]

The Bahá'í texts clearly recommend that human goals be achieved through such instruments as the world itself offers. Therefore, scientific discoveries can and must be employed. Many passages in the Bahá'í texts will be starting points for the most acute minds, in their endeavours to promote science – psychology, sociology, anthropology, medicine and others – for the benefit of mankind in its pursuance of physical, intellectual and spiritual progress, both individual and collective.

31. *Promulgation*, p.226.
32. 'Abdu'l-Bahá, *Tablets*, p.459.
33. Quoted in *Ḥuqúqu'lláh*, nos. 32, 33.
34. Quoted in *The Importance of Prayer*, (comp.), p.9.

Striving Towards Perfection

Means of entrance into the Kingdom

'Abdu'l-Bahá mentions in one of His talks seven 'means' that should be achieved for the purpose of spiritual transformation. These 'means' are: '. . . the knowledge of God . . . the love of God . . . faith . . . philanthropic deeds . . . self-sacrifice . . . severance from this world . . . sanctity and holiness'.[35] He says elsewhere: 'Entrance into the Kingdom is through the love of God, through detachment, through holiness and chastity, through truthfulness, purity, steadfastness, faithfulness and the sacrifice of life.'[36]

Qualifications of the enlightened souls

'Abdu'l-Bahá enumerates, in one of His writings, *'seven qualifications of the divinely enlightened souls:*

'Knowledge. Man must attain the knowledge of God.

'Faith.

'Steadfastness.

'Truthfulness. Truthfulness is the foundation of all the virtues of the world of humanity. Without truthfulness, progress and success in all the worlds of God are impossible for a soul. When this holy attribute is established in man, all the divine qualities will also become realized.

'Uprightness. And this is one of the greatest divine attainments.

'Fidelity. This is also a beautiful trait of the heavenly man.

'Evanescence or humility. That is to say, man must become evanescent in God. He must forget his own selfish conditions that he may thus arise to the station of sacrifice . . . When he attains to this station, the confirmations of the Holy Spirit will surely reach him.'[37]

It is clear that the 'means' for 'entrance into the Kingdom' and for spiritual transformation more or less coincide with such 'qualifications of the divinely enlightened souls' as are the fruits of the process of spiritual transformation. It would therefore seem a vicious circle: these means are required for 'entrance into the Kingdom'[38] and for spiritual transformation; at the same time they are themselves 'merciful gifts'[39] i.e. the fruits of the process. However, what is up to the seeker is his choice between the world of creation and the world of the Kingdom; this is the first step. 'Knock, and the door shall be opened to you'[40] re-echoes the comforting warning uttered by Christ. 'And whoso maketh efforts

---

35. *Promulgation*, p.226.
36. *Some Answered Questions*, p.459.
37. *Tablets*, p.459.
38. *Some Answered Questions*, pp.242, 459.
39. *Promulgation*, p.226.
40. *Matt* 7:7.

for Us, in Our ways will We guide them',[41] says the Qur'án. '...He, verily, will aid every one that aideth Him, and will remember every one that remembereth Him,'[42] writes Bahá'u'lláh; and moreover: 'He is the prayer-hearing, prayer-answering God.'[43] For the very reason that the world of the Kingdom is being sought; that the attraction towards that spiritual Kingdom has been preferred to the attraction towards the world of nature; that the required steps are being taken so that such an attraction may be favoured — steps which are mostly practical and by no means mysterious — for all those reasons, 'merciful gifts . . . and powers' are received as a reward. As those efforts continue, they are rewarded through a more bountiful outpouring of those same 'gifts' and an increasing rate of spiritual growth. At the beginning, that growth is slow and painful, but when the method has been learnt through action, progress will be faster and easier, supported as it is by those 'merciful gifts' (which 'Abdu'l-Bahá also describes as 'powers . . . [or] forces . . .') though which spiritual progress is promoted.[44]

Obstacles to human transformation

The Bahá'í texts mention some important obstacles in the path of spirituality: these are the self or self-centredness, estrangement, malice, envy, backbiting, excess of words.

Self or self-centredness[45]

'Abdu'l-Bahá writes: '*self-love . . . is a strange trait and the means for the destruction of many important souls in the world. If a man be imbued*

---

41. *Qur'án* 29:69.
42. Quoted in Shoghi Effendi, *Advent*, p.64.
43. *Bahá'í Prayers*, p.86.
44. *Promulgation*, p.226. As to the topic of spiritual progress, *see* W. S. Hatcher, 'The Concept of Spirituality', in *Bahá'í Studies*, XI, p.22.
   He writes also: 'As in the case with any new discipline, so it is with learning spiritual growth. Our first steps are painfully self-conscious and hesitant . . . Yet, as we pursue the process, we become more adept at it . . . the rate of progress increases as we go along because we are not only making progress but also perfecting our skill at making progress.' (ibid. p.2.)
45. The Bahá'í texts refer to the self as a 'veil' shutting out man from truth. Bahá'u'lláh writes: '*Tear asunder, in My Name, the veils that have grievously blinded your vision . . . Suffer not yourselves to be wrapt in the dense veils of your selfish desires . . .*' (*Gleanings*, p.143.) And moreover: '*Burn away, wholly for the sake of the Well-Beloved, the veil of self with the flame of the undying Fire . . .*' (ibid. p.316.) In the *Kitáb-i-Íqán* He quotes two Islamic traditions: '*Knowledge is the most grievous veil between man and his Creator*' (p.69), and '*The most grievous of all veils is the veil of knowledge*' (p.188): from these words it would appear that whenever human intellect is subjected to the natal self with its natural emotions, it produces such knowledge as may well be defined as '*satanic*' (ibid. p.69), because it is conducive to '*arrogance, vainglory and conceit*'. (ibid.) Elsewhere He mentions '*the wrappings of illusion*'. (*Seven Valleys*, p.24.) Other metaphors describing the

Striving Towards Perfection

with all qualities but be selfish, all the other virtues will fade or pass away and eventually he will grow worse.'[46] He writes moreover: '. . . there is no veil more obstructive than the self, and however tenuous that veil may be, at the last it will completely shut a person out, and deprive him of his portion of eternal grace.' And He wrote to two enquirers: 'Do all you can to become wholly weary of self, and bind yourselves to that Countenance of Splendours: and once ye have reached such heights of servitude, ye will find, gathered within your shadow, all created things. This is boundless grace: this is the life that dieth not . . . .'*[47] He refers moreover to *'the rust of egotism'* and tells of *'. . . the subtlety of the ego of man. It is the Tempter (the subtle serpent of the mind) and the poor soul not entirely emancipated from its suggestions is deceived until entirely severed from all save God.'*[48]

Whereas attraction towards the world of the Kingdom is the first step in the process of spiritual growth, self-centredness is exactly the opposite. It is attraction towards the natal self, the animal nature in man belonging to that same plane of existence which must be consciously and of one's own free-will overcome so that the divine world of the Kingdom may be attained. Self-centredness leads a man to put his powers of understanding at the service of his own natal self, expressing and developing its obscure attributes: such a man will thus yield to his own *'lusts and corrupt inclinations'* and will be numbered among *'the lost'*. Conversely, whoever is attracted to the world of the Kingdom yearns after its qualities. In fact, 'nearness is likeness', and 'nearness to God necessitates sacrifice of the self'.[49] A selfish man is inclined to consider himself 'a little

---

self are: a *'cage'* (*Hidden Words*, Persian no. 38), a *'prison'* (ibid. Persian nos. 39 and 40), *'fire'* (ibid. Persian no. 66), *'dust'* (ibid. Persian no. 69), *'mire'* (*Epistle*, p. 131), *'the spotting of self'* upon *'the mirror of the heart'* (*Selections*, p. 182), *'. . . the Tempter (the subtle serpent of the mind . . .'* ('Abdu'l-Bahá, quoted in a letter dated 4 August 1977 written on behalf of the Universal House of Justice to an individual believer.)

As to the meaning of the word 'self' in the Bahá'í texts, Shoghi Effendi wrote through his secretary the following explanation: '. . . self has really two meanings, or is used in two senses, in the Bahá'í writings; one is self, the identity of the individual created by God. This is the self mentioned in such passages as "he hath known God who have known himself" etc. The other self is the ego, the dark, animalistic heritage each one of us has, the lower nature that can develop into a monster of selfishness, brutality, lust and so on.' (quoted in *Living the Life* (comp.), p. 28.)

46. *Tablets*, p. 136.
47. *Selections*, pp. 182, 76–7.
48. *Gleanings*, p. 297.
49. *Promulgation*, p. 148. 'Abdu'l-Bahá says moreover: 'The prophets teach us that the only way to approach God is by characterizing ourselves with the attributes of divinity.' (*Divine Philosophy*, p. 93.)

He writes moreover that the process of approaching God implies a progressive expansion of a man's concerns, so that he will gradually forget his own self and think of his family, his tribe, his country, his race and at last of all mankind. (*See* below, p. 201.) Therefore 'Abdu'l-Bahá recommends universality; He says: *'Every universal cause is divine and every particular one is temporal.'* (*Selections*, pp. 68–9.)

better than, a little superior to, the rest'; 'Abdu'l-Bahá says that such a man 'is in a dangerous position'.[50]

Our self is therefore our real enemy, and 'Life is a constant struggle, not only against forces around us, but above all against our own "ego" '.[51] However, '. . . the complete and entire elimination of the ego would imply perfection, which man can never completely attain. But the ego can and should ever-increasingly be subordinated to the enlightened soul of man. This is what spiritual progress implies.'[52]

Estrangement

Estrangement is a kind of self-centredness. 'Abdu'l-Bahá says: 'When the souls become separated and selfish, the divine bounties do not descend, and the lights of the Supreme Concourse are no longer reflected even though the bodies meet together.'[53] Quoting the Qur'án, He writes: ' "*Verily, God loveth those who, as though they were a solid wall, do battle for His Cause in serried lines!*" . . . *meaning crowded and pressed together, one locked to the next, each supporting his fellows*,'[54] because cooperation is the mainspring of civilization; whoever is not willing to cooperate with his fellow-men is opposing the progress of civilization in the world, which is one of the fundamental purposes of human life.

Malice

Bahá'u'lláh writes: '. . . *malice is a grievous malady which depriveth man from recognizing the Great Being, and debarreth him from the splendours of the sun of certitude. We pray and hope that through the grace and mercy of God He may remove this mighty obstacle.*' In the concept of malice an inclination to transgression is implied, a propensity to act wickedly, to harm people, to indulge in vice, sustained by a conscious will, an inner gratification, a capacity of dissimulation, a customary wont.[55] This attitude is exactly the opposite of such sincere submission to the laws and such purity of heart as are the

---

50. Quoted in *Bahá'u'lláh and the New Era*, p.84.
51. Shoghi Effendi, quoted in *Principles of Bahá'í Administration*, p.87.
52. On behalf of Shoghi Effendi, quoted in *Living the Life* (comp.), pp.17–18.
53. *Promulgation*, p.4.
54. *Selections*, p.260.
55. *Epistle*, p.96. S. Battaglia explains the meaning of the world malice thus: 'Natural or acquired (and mostly practised through cunning dissimulation and wicked satisfaction, until it becomes customary) inclination toward transgression of moral and religious laws, through perverse actions, conducive to harm and suffering for others or by indulging in vices and perversions.' (*Il Grande Dizionario della Lingua Italiana*, vol. IX, p.158.)

indispensable prerequisites of anyone who is struggling for his own spiritual transformation.

Envy

Bahá'u'lláh writes: '*Know, verily, the heart wherein the least remnant of envy yet lingers, shall never attain My everlasting dominion, nor inhale the sweet savours of holiness breathing from my Kingdom of sanctity.*'[56] In fact envy – characterized as it is by regret and resentment when faced with the happiness, the well-being, the prosperity of other people – is the negation of that love 'Abdu'l-Bahá thus refers to: 'Until love takes possession of the heart, no other divine bounty can be revealed in it.' 'Abdu'l-Bahá says elsewhere that one of the most important reasons why Judas Iscariot betrayed Jesus was because he was envious of Peter the Apostle being so highly considered by Christ.[57]

Backbiting

Bahá'u'lláh writes: '*. . . backbiting quencheth the light of the heart, and extinguisheth the life of the soul*' and forbids it specifically in His great Book of Laws.[58] How could a society be united whose members, far from being mutually sincere and frank, indulge in backbiting, proving themselves disloyal towards each other? Since backbiting is conducive to disunity, it is a highly prejudicial deed to both individuals and society.

Exceeding in words

Bahá'u'lláh writes: '*he whose words exceed his deeds, know verily his death is better than his life*'.[59] The glory of a man and the beginning

---

56. *Hidden Words*, Persian no.6.
57. *Promulgation*, p.15. Regarding Judas Iscariot and his envy, 'Abdu'l-Bahá writes: '*Such is the outcome of envy, the chief reason why men turn aside from the Straight Path.*' (*Selections*, p.163.)
58. *Kitáb-i-Íqán*, p.193. See *Gleanings*, p.164; *Synopsis and Codification of the Kitáb-i-Aqdas*, pp.47, xxii. In this regard, 'Abdu'l-Bahá writes: '*If any soul speak ill of an absent one, the only result will clearly be this: he will dampen the zeal of the friends and tend to make them indifferent. For backbiting is divisive, it is the leading cause among the friends of a disposition to withdraw. If any individual should speak ill of one who is absent, it is incumbent on his hearers, in a spiritual and friendly manner, to stop him, and say in effect: would this detraction serve any useful purpose? Would it please the Blessed Beauty, contribute to the lasting honour of the friends, promote the holy Faith, support the Covenant, or be of any possible benefit to any soul? No, never! On the contrary, it would make the dust to settle so thickly on the heart that the ears would hear no more, and the eyes would no longer behold the light of truth.*

'*If, however, a person setteth about speaking well of another, opening his lips to praise another, he will touch an answering chord in his hearers and they will be stirred up by the breathings of God . . .*' ('Abdu'l-Bahá, *Selections*, pp.230–31.)
59. *Tablets*, p.156.

of his spiritual life is in his deeds. Good words, in this respect, are only an obstacle, because, when they are not translated into actions, they imply hypocrisy, cowardliness and boastfulness.

* * *

The concept is now very clear: the prerequisite of spiritual progress is the attainment of the bounties of the Holy Spirit through the knowledge and the love of the Manifestation of God, and the observance of the laws of His Revelation. Such a condition is realized whenever a man submits his own will to that of the Manifestation, forgets his own little self and circles around the Self of God, i.e. His Manifestation. Whosoever gravitates towards his own self, and does not love his fellow men, and does not act righteously, and keeps aloof from society, will not achieve such spiritual forces as are required for his own spiritual transformation. He will be like a vessel whose sails are stricken, or upwind: that vessel will toil along and sooner or later capsize.

Meanings of sorrow and sacrifice

The process of spiritual growth requires detachment from the natal self and the turning to the Self of God, i.e. His Manifestation. This is the meaning of sacrifice which implies – at least in its initial phases – suffering. Bahá'u'lláh writes: *'The companions of all who adore Thee are the tears they shed, and the comforters of such as seek Thee are the groans they utter, and the food of them who haste to meet Thee is the fragments of their broken hearts.'*[60] And yet, most people are put to the test because of human suffering in general or of their own afflictions in particular, and some of them reach the point of denying the existence of a merciful and just God. But the Bahá'í texts abundantly enlighten the manifold meanings of human sufferings, explaining that they are a vital and essential aspect of life and that it is impossible to avoid them.

Meanings of sorrow

An instrument of human perfection. First of all, 'Grief and sorrow do not come to us by chance,' says 'Abdu'l-Bahá, 'they are sent to us by the Divine Mercy for our own perfecting,'[61] therefore they are adequate to our capacity ('. . . *God hath never burdened any soul beyond its power* . . .'[62] echo the reassuring words written by

---

60. *Epistle*, p.95.
61. *Paris Talks*, p.50.
62. *Gleanings*, pp.106–7.

Bahá'u'lláh). 'Men who suffer not, attain no perfection,'[63] says 'Abdu'l-Bahá. Moreover He writes: '*Unless one accept suffering, undergo trials and endure vicissitudes, he will reap no reward nor will he attain success and prosperity.*'[64] Then He explains: '*Were it not for tests, genuine gold could not be distinguished from the counterfeit. Were it not for tests, the courageous could not be known from the coward. Were it not for the tests, the people of faithfulness could not be known from those of selfishness . . . As the servants and the handmaidens of the Merciful stand firmly and persevere, the good seed will soon grow in the field and bear the fruit of blessing. Then will spirituality and fragrance prevail and joy and rejoicing come from the Heavenly Sphere, sorrows and toil shall be forgotten and eternal peace and rest appear.*'[65] Therefore, the first meaning of grief and sorrow is to put men to the test as to the purity of their intentions, the sincerity of their love, the genuineness of their attraction towards the world the Kingdom. Until these requirements are met, no seeker will be able to welcome the fire of trials, in other words, to forget his own natal self which with its natural emotions is the mainspring of such grief,[66] and to fix his gaze upon the intended goal: the Self of God in His Manifestation.

An instrument of self-knowledge. The less a man is aware of his own weakness, the more such tests are needed. 'Abdu'l-Bahá says: 'Tests are a means by which a soul is measured as to its fitness, and proven out by its own acts. God knows its fitness beforehand, and also his unpreparedness, but man, with an ego, would not believe himself unfit unless proof were given him. Consequently his susceptibility to evil is proven to him when he falls into the tests, and the tests are continued until the soul realizes its own unfitness, then remorse and regret tend to root out the weakness. The same test comes again in greater degree, until it is shown that a former weakness has become a strength, and the power to overcome evil has been established.'[67] Therefore, a second meaning of grief is that it helps us to understand ourselves: our faults, so that we may overcome them, and our talents, so that we may make use of them.

An instrument of detachment from the world of creation. 'Abdu'l-Bahá writes: '*All calamities and afflictions have been created for man so that*

---

63. *Paris Talks*, p. 51.
64. Quoted in M. M. Rabb, 'The Divine Art of Living', in *Star of the West*, VIII, p. 240.
65. Quoted in 'Extracts from Tablets from Abdul-Bahá to Mrs Isabella D. Brittingham', in *Star of the West*, XIV, p. 353.
66. 'Abdu'l-Bahá says: '. . . all the sorrow and the grief that exist come from the world of matter – the spiritual world bestows only the joy!' (*Paris Talks*, p. 110.)
67. 'The Worst Enemies of the Cause are in the Cause', in *Star of the West*, VI, p. 45.

he may spurn this mortal world – a world to which he is much attached. When he experienceth severe trials and hardships, then his nature will recoil and he will desire the eternal realm – a realm which is sanctified from all afflictions and calamities. Such is the case with the man who is wise. He shall never drink from a cup which is at the end distasteful, but, on the contrary, he will seek the cup of pure and limpid water. He will not taste the honey that is mixed with poison.'[68] This is a third meaning of grief and sorrow: to show that the world of the Kingdom is superior to the world of creation; from the former we receive only joy, from the latter we draw but ephemeral and apparent joys, and in reality mostly trials and tests.

Meanings of sacrifice

However, if grief and sorrow are to play their educational role, the station of sacrifice must be attained. The concept of sacrifice – whose etymological meaning is *sacrum facere*, i.e. to make holy deeds – is clearly explained in the Bahá'í texts.

Conquering the natal self. '*With reference to what is meant by an individual becoming entirely forgetful of self: the intent is that he should rise up and sacrifice himself in the true sense, that is, he should obliterate the promptings of the human conditions, and rid himself of such characteristics as are worthy of blame and constitute the gloomy darkness of this life on earth – not that he should allow his physical health to deteriorate and his body to become infirm.*'

'Abdu'l-Bahá writes moreover: '*This is the true sacrifice: the offering of oneself, even as did Christ, as a ransom for the life of the world.*' And elsewhere: '. . . *this plane of sacrifice is the realm of dying to the self, that the radiance of the living God may then shine forth. The martyr's field is the place of detachment from self, that the anthems of eternity may be upraised.*' And moreover, describing sacrifice, He writes: '. . . *he* [man] *must renounce his own self . . . he must renounce his inordinate desires, his selfish purposes and the promptings of his human self, and seek out the holy breathings of the spirit, and follow the yearnings of his higher self, and immerse himself in the sea of sacrifice, with his heart fixed upon the beauty of the All-Glorious.*'[69]

Self-sacrifice for a universal cause. This twofold meaning of sacrifice, as self-sacrifice for a good and universal cause and as the giving up of the natal self, is thus explained by 'Abdu'l-Bahá in one of His writings: '*The moth is a sacrifice to the candle. The spring of water is a sacrifice to the thirsty one. The sincere lover is a sacrifice to the beloved.*

---

68. *Selections*, p.239.
69. ibid. pp.180, 65, 76, 207.

One must wholly forget himself . . . He must seek the pleasure of the True One, desire the face of the True One, and walk in the path of the True One: he must become intoxicated with His cup, resigned in His hand and close his eyes to life and living . . . This is the first station of sacrifice.'[70]

Attaining the qualities of the world of the Kingdom. '*The second station of sacrifice: Man must become severed from the human world; be delivered from the darkness of this world; the illumination of mercifulness must shine and radiate in him, the nether world become as non-existent and the Kingdom become manifest.*' 'Abdu'l-Bahá suggests the metaphor of a piece of iron: as it becomes hot, it loses its own qualities – '*blackness, coldness and solidity*' – and becomes soft, red-hot, luminous as fire.

'*Likewise, when souls are released from the fetters of the world, the imperfections of mankind and animalistic darkness and have stepped into the realm of detachment, have partaken from the outpouring of the Placeless and have acquired lordly perfections, they are the "ransomed ones" of the Sun of Truth, who are hastening to the altar of heart and soul.*'[71] In this sense, sacrifice is a process of purification, and purification – in the words of the Báb – '. . . *is regarded as the most acceptable means for attaining nearness unto God and as the most meritorious of all deeds*'.[72]

Human transformation as spiritual progress

Briefly, 'Abdu'l-Bahá says that a man should not '. . . follow his own natural impulse but govern his action by the light of Their [the Manifestations'] precept and example . . .', and that '. . . he should do that which is found to be praiseworthy by the standard of reason and judgment of intellect, even though it be opposed to his natural human inclination'.[73]

'Abdu'l-Bahá refers to this transformation of man from his animal to his spiritual nature as 'development of the spiritual nature in man' or else as 'spiritual progress', and He says that 'spiritual progress is through the breaths of the Holy Spirit and is the awakening of the conscious soul of man to perceive the reality of Divinity'. As this transformation draws man closer to God, it is an essentially mystical process; however, it develops only by virtue of an active daily endeavour in the world and not through escaping from it. Thus 'Abdu'l-Bahá describes this path of service every man should tread, if he is to achieve his cherished goal: '. . . nearness

---

70. *Tablets*, p.354.
71. ibid.
72. *Selections*, p.98.
73. *Promulgation*, p.40.

to God is possible through devotion to Him, through entrance into the Kingdom and service to humanity: it is attained by unity with mankind and through loving-kindness to all; it is dependent upon investigation of truth, acquisition of praiseworthy virtues, service in the cause of universal peace and personal sanctification. In a word, nearness to God necessitates sacrifice of self, severance and the giving up of all to Him.'[74] Only when man is thus transformed does he quicken the world.

Spirituality as love in action

'Abdu'l-Bahá says: 'Spirituality . . . is love in action.'[75] This statement may well be considered the epitome of all the concepts we have been expounding on the dynamics of the transformation of man: the first step of this transformation is the recognition of the Manifestation of God; the second one is the love of God, i.e. of His Manifestation. This love is an irresistible attraction towards the perfections of the world of the Kingdom, mirrored forth into the world by the Manifestation of God; this love leads its prey to a conscious and willing submission to the laws revealed by the Manifestation. In this regard Bahá'u'lláh writes: '*Walk in My statutes for love of Me*,'[76] and 'Abdu'l-Bahá says: '. . . the first principle of the divine teaching . . . is love.'[77]

In the Bahá'í texts, love is described as the prime motor of the process of transformation: God is the '*magnet*' and the soul is the iron which is attracted closer and closer to it. Love is also described as a '*fire*'[78] capable of burning away '*the veils of the satanic self*',[79] thus bestowing upon the soul the bounty of the inner vision and of the 'likeness'[80] to God. As man, attracted by the magnetic force of the love of God, comes closer to Him, he burns away at the fire of this love the imperfect attributes of his natal self and more vividly mirrors forth into the world the attributes of Divinity. This process is painful and only in the 'insanity' of his love towards God is man willing to accept it; it is '*the dying from self*',[81] at first laden with anguish and sufferings, but ultimately conducive – as it is the cause of his 'second birth' or 'his release from the captivity of nature'[82] – to infinite joy.

74. ibid. pp.60, 142, 148.
75. Quoted in 'Join the Army of Peace' in *Star of the West*, XIII, p.112.
76. *Hidden Words*, Arabic no.38.
77. *Promulgation*, p.8.
78. *Selections*, p.191.
79. Bahá'u'lláh, *Seven Valleys*, p.11.
80. *Promulgation*, p.148.
81. *Seven Valleys*, p.36.
82. *Promulgation*, pp.304, 305.

The second birth

To summarize what has been said: the body and the natal self with its natural emotions belong to the physical plane of creation: they come from the world of creation and they return to it when at the time of physical death the bonds of affinity between the component elemental atoms come to an end, as soon as the connection soul-body is broken off.

In the body there is a very delicate and perfect instrument: the nervous system, which was created so that the power of understanding vouchsafed unto human spirits might be expressed in the physical plane of existence.[83] This power of understanding is very important, because it can discover the mysteries of the physical universe and, when it is guided and confirmed by the Manifestation of God, it can grasp the reality of the transcendental world. When the power of understanding is enlightened, guided and confirmed by the Manifestation of God, it enables man to express his divine nature in the world through the instrumentality of his body. This divine nature is his 'divine aspect or spiritual nature', 'the potentiality of divinity', or else the 'potential power to attain . . . likeness to God', 'the image or likeness of God . . . the world of exemplars constituting the heavenly body of man', 'the most noble of phenomena . . . the meeting between man and God . . . the animus of human life and collective centre of all human virtues';[84] '. . . a celestial power which is infinite as regards the intellectual as well as the physical realms . . . [a] power . . . conferred upon man through the breath of the Holy Spirit . . . an eternal reality, an indestructible reality . . .'[85]

It is this reality 'which belongs to the divine kingdom . . . [that] delivers man from the material world' and is '. . . the power which enables man to escape from the world of nature'.[86]

When this divine reality prevails upon the animal reality, the natural emotions of the natal self — which are expressions of the world of nature whence the body is born — give way to divine virtues and the inner vision appears, a power of spiritual perception

---

83. 'Abdu'l-Bahá says: 'Reason has its seat in the brain.' (*Divine Philosophy*, p.92.) Thus we might even — almost paradoxically — accept the statement pronounced by materialistic philosopher Cabanis, who maintained that 'thought is a secretion of the brain' (Cabanis, *Rapport du physique et du moral de l'homme*), as long as the soul is intended as the promoter of those secretions.
   Regarding the concept of mind, *see* above pp.4–5, and below pp.156–7, 218 and no. 69.
84. *Promulgation*, pp.41, 317, 302, 464, 239.
85. 'The Three Realities', in *Star of the West*, VII, p.118.
86. ibid.

which cannot be found in any other of the living beings of the world.

The forces required for this transformation – from natural emotions to divine virtues, from sense perception to intellectual and inner perception – are not inherent in man, who is possessed only of their potentialities. These forces are bestowed upon him through the spirit of faith and the Holy Spirit. These spirits are emanations of the world of the Kingdom and therefore man can attain unto them whenever – out of his love towards the Divine Reality – he of his own free-will and consciously surrenders his own will to the Will of the Manifestation of God, Who manifests in the human plane the Reality of the world of the Kingdom.

This mystical concept is indeed extremely rational and practical when viewed within the context of the evolutionary concept of reality set forth in the Bahá'í texts. Just as the power of growth typical of the vegetable kingdom appears whenever the elemental atoms composing matter properly combine by virtue of the power of cohesion and in conformity with natural law, and its appearance occurs because those elemental atoms have become arranged according to a certain order whereby they have acquired the capacity of growth, so the qualities of the spirit of faith and of the Holy Spirit appear within man whenever he has acquired the capacity for them, inasmuch as he has created an order within himself according to the laws revealed by the Manifestation of God and which he has observed of his own free-will. It is as though man metaphorically orders his inner being in such a way as to acquire the capacity to reflect those spiritual qualities. The process of evolutionary growth is therefore the same both in the world of creation and within the soul of man. The active forces are those of the spirit. But the level of the process is quite different: it is a conscious and voluntary process in the world of the soul; an unconscious and involuntary process in the world of creation. Both are educational processes: universal, the latter; individual, the former.

Through such growth certain vital purposes are achieved:
(i) '. . . witness[ing] the effulgence of the Sun of Reality . . . behold[ing] the manifest evidences of the reality of Divinity, comprehend[ing] irrefutable proofs of the immortality of the soul.'[87]
(ii) '. . . the attainment of the supreme virtues of humanity through the descent of the heavenly bestowals', which 'Abdu'l-Bahá says is both 'the honour allotted to man' and 'the greatest bestowal of God to man'.[88]

---

87. *Promulgation*, p.328.
88. ibid. pp.4, 166, 378.

(iii) '. . . reflect[ing] the spirit of the Kingdom . . . liv[ing] in conscious at-one-ment with the eternal world and becom[ing] quickened and awake with the life and the love of God'.[89]

When a man is thus transformed, 'there is no created being more heroic, more undaunted' than he, because he has attained 'the highest development of man': 'his entrance into the divine Kingdom'. Herein lies his glory: '. . . in the knowledge of God, spiritual susceptibilities, attainment to transcendent powers and the bounties of the Holy Spirit . . . in being informed of the teachings of God'.[90]

In this stage, his spirit 'receives illumination from the light of God and reflects it to the whole universe'; his reality is 'a radiant light in the world of creation, a source of life and the agency of constructiveness in the infinite fields of existence'; 'the cause of the illumination of this world'; it is '. . . as the spirit of this world, for just as the animus of life quickens the physical human body, so the body of the world will receive its vivification through the animating virtue of the sanctified spirit of man'.[91] He thus fulfils the purpose of his creation: 'to irradiate the Divine light and to illumine the world by his words, action and life'.[92]

Such a creature is certainly a man and not a 'perfect animal', because he has fully acquired those qualities which distinguish him from animals, and which 'Abdu'l-Bahá thus enumerates: 'intellectual attainment, spiritual perception, the acquisition of virtues, capacity to receive the bestowals of Divinity, lordly bounty and emanations of heavenly mercy'. He has thus attained that stage 'Christ has interpreted . . . as the second birth' and 'Abdu'l-Bahá defines as 'spiritual progress'[93] or 'spirituality'.[94]

---

89. ibid. p.328.
90. ibid. pp.264, 335, 312.
91. ibid. pp.264, 352, 239, 330–1.
92. *Paris Talks*, p.113.
93. *Promulgation*, pp.304, 332, 142.
94. *Paris Talks*, p.112.

8 The Soul: The Reality of Man

'Man – the true man – is the soul . . .', says 'Abdu'l-Bahá. However, there is no more difficult theme to deal with, nor more elusive reality to know. Its existence is even denied by many who think man to be merely a body and his mind just an outcome of his brain. For the soul is a spiritual, metaphysical reality which cannot be perceived through the senses, and therefore eludes anyone who relies only upon sensory and intellectual perception. 'Abdu'l-Bahá remarks: 'If we wish to deny anything that is not sensible, then we must deny the realities which unquestionably exist . . . The power of attraction is not sensible, though it certainly exists. From what do we affirm these existences? From their signs . . .'. And He points out how in man there are 'signs, powers and perfections'[2] from which it may be inferred that a spiritual reality exists in him which is unique in the world of creation, i.e. the soul or spirit of man.

Rational proofs of its existence and immortality

The Bahá'í teachings uphold the existence and the immortality of the soul and produce many rational proofs demonstrating these concepts. A short, incomplete list of such proofs is offered as follows.

---

1. *Paris Talks*, p.85. Bahá'u'lláh writes: '. . . *true life is not the life of the flesh but the life of the spirit. For the life of the flesh is common both to men and animals, whereas the life of the spirit is possessed only by the pure in heart who have quaffed from the ocean of faith and partaken of the fruit of certitude. This life knoweth no death and this existence is crowned by immortality.*' (*Kitáb-i-Íqán*, p.120.)
2. *Some Answered Questions*, pp.189–90.

The Soul: The Reality of Man

Proofs of its existence

Human rational faculty.
(i) A proof from which the existence in man can be inferred of a particular power which is absent in the world of nature, is that man is capable of escaping the rule of nature and of surpassing all the animals of the earth. As far as we know, man is the only creature who has been capable of creating a civilization and of establishing his rule in the world. This capacity is not due to his physical qualities, because 'In the physical powers and sense . . . man and animals are partners. In fact, the animal is often superior to men in sense perception.'[3] On the contrary, it depends on that very particular power man is possessed of, which is called soul or spirit of man.

(ii) The same argument is set forth also in other words:

Man is possessed of qualities (consciousness, volition, ideation, conscious reflection and intelligence), which are absent in nature.[4]

'If we accept the supposition that man is but a part of nature, we are confronted by an illogical statement, for this is equivalent to claiming that a part may be endowed with qualities which are absent in the whole.'

'The truth is that God has given to man certain powers which are supernatural.'[5]

Inner perception. The fact that man is possessed of the power of knowing and seeing without instruments or organs, as is for example the case when he sleeps, is mentioned by 'Abdu'l-Bahá as further evidence of the existence of the soul: '. . . how many times it happens that a question that one cannot solve in the world of wakefulness is solved in the world of dreams. In wakefulness, the eye sees only for a short distance, but in dream he who is in the East sees the West. Awake he sees the present; in sleep he sees the future.'[6]

Human inner reality. A further proof of the existence of the soul is that a reality exists within man which is independent from the

---

3. *Promulgation*, p.241.
4. See *Some Answered Questions*, pp.185–190; *Promulgation*, pp.17, 30, 54, 58, 61, 80, 90, 172, 178, 241–2, 332, 357, 417. See above p.97 and no. 76.
5. *Promulgation*, p.17. See ibid. p.360.
6. *Some Answered Questions*, p.17. As to the meanings of dreams, Shoghi Effendi wrote through his secretary: 'That truth is often imparted through dreams no one who is familiar with history, especially religious history, can doubt. At the same time dreams and visions are always coloured and influenced more or less by the mind of the dreamer and we must beware of attaching too much importance to them.' (Quoted in *Bahá'í Institutions* (comp.), p.107.)

body, a reality which he consults: 'When you wish to reflect upon or consider a matter', says 'Abdu'l-Bahá, 'you consult something within you. You say, shall I do it, or shall I not do it? Is it better to make this journey or to abandon it? Whom do you consult? Who is within you deciding this question? Surely there is a distinct power, an intelligent ego.[7] Were it not distinct from your ego, you would not be consulting it. It is greater than the faculty of thought. It is your spirit which teaches you, which advises and decides upon matters.'[8]

* * *

The Bahá'í texts uphold not only the existence, but also the immortality of the soul. Created as an individual entity at the moment of conception, the soul has a beginning, but it has no end. In fact, '. . . the individual realities of mankind, when spiritually born, are emanations from the reality of Divinity . . . and inasmuch as eternality is a property of Divinity, this emanation is everlasting.'[9] Elsewhere He explains: '. . . the world of things is the world of imperfection in comparison with that of man, and the world of man is the world of perfection in comparison with that of things. When imperfections reach the station of perfection, they become eternal (i.e. in the kingdom of man, where alone the Spirit manifests immortality).'[10]

In the Bahá'í texts many proofs are advanced demonstrating and explaining this concept. A preliminary short list of these proofs is offered here. These proofs will be divided, in conformity with the classical philosophical canons, into metaphysical proofs (i.e. founded upon the attributes of the soul) and moral proofs (i.e. founded upon the purpose of its existence).

Metaphysical proofs of its immortality

On the grounds of movement: 'We have seen that movement', says 'Abdu'l-Bahá, 'is essential to existence; nothing that hath life is without motion . . . it must either ascend or descend. But with the human soul, there is no decline. Its only movement is towards perfection; growth and progress alone constitute the motion of the soul.

'Divine perfection is infinite, therefore the progress of the soul

---

7. As to the meaning of the words of self or ego, *see* above, pp.126–7 and no. 45.
8. *Promulgation*, p.242. *See* ibid. pp.242–3, 464.
9. ibid. p.59.
10. *Some Answered Questions*, p.152.

The Soul: The Reality of Man

is also infinite . . . When the body dies the soul lives on. All the differing degrees of created physical beings are limited, but the soul is limitless!'[11]

On the grounds of the soul defined as substance:
(i) 'The realities of all phenomena,' says 'Abdu'l-Bahá, 'are immutable and unchangeable. Extinction or mortality is nothing but the transformation of pictures and images. But the reality back of these images is eternal.'[12] Thence since the soul is not a form, but reality or substance, it is immortal.
(ii) '. . . the human body', says moreover 'Abdu'l-Bahá, 'has one form. In its composition it has been transferred from one form to another but never possesses two forms at the same time. For example, it has existed in the elemental substances of the mineral kingdom. From the mineral kingdom, it hath traversed the vegetable kingdom and its constituent substances; from the vegetable kingdom it has risen by evolution into the kingdom of the animal and from thence attained the kingdom of man. After its disintegration and decomposition it will return again to the mineral kingdom, leaving its human form and taking a new form unto itself. During these progressions one form succeeds another, but at no time does the body possess more than one.

'This spirit of man, however, can manifest itself in all forms at the same time . . . the form of the physical body of man must be destroyed and abandoned before it can assume or take unto itself another. Mortality, therefore, means transference from one form to another . . . But the human spirit in itself contains all these forms, shapes and figures. It is not possible to break or destroy one form so that it may transfer itself into another. As an evidence of this, at the present moment in the human spirit you have the shape of a square and the figure of a triangle. Simultaneously also you can conceive a hexagonal form. All these can be conceived at the same moment in the human spirit, and not one of them needs to be destroyed or broken in order that the spirit of man may be transferred to another. There is no annihilation, no destruction; therefore, the human spirit is immortal because it is not transferred from one body into another body.'[13]
(iii) '. . . the soul has no place in space,' says 'Abdu'l-Bahá. 'Space

---

11. *Paris Talks*, p.89. This argument, supporting immortality of the soul on the ground of its motion, seems similar to an argument set forth by Plato in his *Phaedrus*.
12. 'The Three Realities' in *Star of the West* VII, p.119. This argument may be paralleled by an argument set forth by Plato in His *Phaedo*, stating that the soul is immortal because it is not an accident, but a substance.
13. *Promulgation*, p.307. *See* ibid. pp.242, 306. This argument may be brought back to argument no.(i) immediately above.

is a quality of material things and that which is not material does not partake of space. The soul, like the intellect, is an abstraction. Intelligence does not partake of the quality of space, though it is related to man's brain. The intellect resides there, but not materially. Search in the brain, you will not find the intellect. In the same way, though the soul is a resident of the body, it is not to be found in the body.'[14] 'If the spirit of man — He says moreover — belonged to the elemental existence, the eye could see it, the ear hear it, the hand touch. As long as these five senses cannot perceive it, the proof is unquestioned that it does not belong to the elemental world, and therefore, is beyond death or mortality, which are inseparable from that material realm of existence. If being is not subject to the limitation of material life, it is not subject to mortality.'[15]

(iv) '. . . the spirit is not affected by . . . changes or transformations' of the body, says 'Abdu'l-Bahá. 'The body of man becomes lean or fat; it is afflicted with disease, suffers mutilation; perhaps the eyes become blind, the ears deaf; but none of these imperfections and failings afflict the spirit. The spirit of man remains in the same condition, unchanged. A man is blinded, but his spirit continues the same. He loses his hearing, his hand is cut off, his foot amputated, but his spirit remains the same. He becomes lethargic, he is afflicted with apoplexy; but there is no difference, change or alteration in his spirit. This is proof that death is only destruction of the body, while the spirit remains immortal, eternal.'[16] 'Abdu'l-Bahá mentions also the example of sleep, ' . . . when all the physical faculties are in abeyance and the soul travels in all realms seeing, hearing, speaking, so when the physical body is decomposed, the soul is not affected'.[17]

On the grounds of the soul being simple, as a substance: 'The soul is not a combination of elements', says 'Abdu'l-Bahá, 'it is not composed of many atoms, it is of one indivisible substance and therefore eternal. It is wholly extraneous to the order of physical creation: it is immortal.'[18] In fact, '. . . according to natural philosophy it is an assured fact that single or simple elements are indestructible', because death means decomposition of a composed being into its

---

14. *Divine Philosophy*, p.124.
15. *Promulgation*, p.308. See p.308. This argument may be brought back to argument no.(i).
16. *Promulgation*, pp.417, 308.
17. See *Divine Philosophy*, p.124; *Some Answered Questions*, p.229; *Promulgation*, p.308. This argument may be brought back to argument no.(i).
18. *Paris Talks*, p.91.

component simple elements. But simple elements cannot subdivide, and therefore they are eternal. 'Abdu'l-Bahá remarks: 'If an elementary substance is possessed of immortality, how can the human spirit or reality, which is wholly above combination and composition, be destroyed?'[19]

On the grounds of the presence of truth within the soul: 'Reflect', says 'Abdu'l-Bahá, 'that no effect, no trace, no influence remains of any being after its members are dispersed and its elements are decomposed, whether it be a mineral, a vegetable, or an animal. There is only the human reality and the spirit of man which, after the disintegration of the members, the dispersing of the particles, and the destruction of the composition, persists and continues to act and to have power.'[20] Therefore, 'the traces of the Spirit of Jesus Christ, the influence of His Divine Teaching . . . the Sacred Writings (with ever the same Teaching) prove the continuity of the spirit', whose traces they are, because 'anything which does not exist, can, of course, give no sign of its existence'.[21]

On the grounds of its natural aspiration for immortality: 'The very fact that our spiritual instinct, surely never given in vain, prompts us to pray for the welfare of those, our loved ones, who have passed out of the material world: does it not bear witness to the continuance of their existence?'[22]

On the grounds of the idea of mortality: '. . . the idea of mortality presupposes the existence of immortality – for if there were no Life Eternal, there would be no way of measuring the life of this world.'[23]

Moral proofs of its immortality

As a requirement of human moral life:
(i) 'Abdu'l-Bahá writes: *'The consummation of this limitless universe, with all its grandeur and glory hath been man himself, who in this world*

---

19. *Promulgation*, p.260. See ibid. pp.260, 306, 415; *Paris Talks*, p.91. This argument seems similar to the arguments set forth by Plato in his *Phaedo* and by St Thomas Aquinas in his *Summa Contra Gentiles*, when they declare that the soul is immortal because it is 'simple'.
20. *Some Answered Questions*, p.225.
21. *Paris Talks*, p.91. See *Some Answered Questions*, p.225; *Promulgation*, pp.307–8; *Paris Talks*, p.91. This argument seems similar to the argument produced by Plato in his *Menon*, by Augustine in His *Soliloquia* and by St Thomas Aquinas in his *Summa Contra Gentiles*, when they say that the presence of truth in the soul is a warrant for its immortality.
22. *Paris Talks*, p.93. St Thomas Aquinas mentions this argument as a *signum* (as something that seemingly reveals something else) in his *Summa Theologica*.
23. ibid. p.93. See *Paris Talks*, p.93.

of being toileth and suffereth for a time, with diverse ills and pains, and ultimately disintegrates, leaving no trace and no fruit after him. Were it so, there is no doubt that this infinite universe with all its perfections has ended in sham and delusion with no result, no fruit, no permanence and no effect. It would be utterly without meaning . . . this Great Workshop with all its power, its bewildering magnificence and endless perfections, cannot eventually come to naught. That still another life should exist is thus certain . . .'[24] And in one of His talks he explains '. . . the world of existence does not culminate here. If this were so, existence itself would be sterile. There are many worlds of light. For even as the plant imagines life ends with itself and has no knowledge of our existence, so the materially-minded man has no knowledge of other worlds of consciousness.'[25]

(ii) 'The immortality of the spirit', says moreover 'Abdu'l-Bahá, 'is mentioned in the Holy Books; it is the fundamental basis of the divine religions. Now the punishments and rewards are said to be of two kinds: first, the rewards and punishments of this life; second, those of the other world.'[26] And He adds: 'We read in the sacred writings that "all good works are found again". Now, if the soul did not survive, this also would mean nothing.'[27]

On the grounds of consensus gentium:
(i) 'In all religions', says 'Abdu'l-Bahá, 'the belief exists that the soul survives the death of the body. Intercessions are sent up for the beloved dead, prayers are said for the forgiveness of their sins. If the soul perished with the body all this would have no meaning . . . If it were not possible for the soul to advance toward perfection after it had been released from the body, of what avail are all these loving prayers of devotion?'[28]

(ii) Bahá'u'lláh writes: '*How could such Souls [the Manifestations of God] have consented to surrender unto their enemies if they believed all the worlds of God to have been reduced to this earthly life?*'[29] And 'Abdu'l-Bahá says: 'If the spirit were not immortal, how could the Manifestations of God endure such terrible trials?'[30] And moreover: 'Were

---

24. 'Tablet to Dr. A. Forel', in *Bahá'í World*, XV, p.40. See 'Abdu'l-Bahá, *Selections*, pp.184–5; *Paris Talks*, p.92; *Divine Philosophy*, p.119.
25. *Divine Philosophy*, p.119.
26. *Some Answered Questions*, p.223.
27. *Paris Talks*, pp.89–90. See ibid. p.93. As to this argument, upholding the immortality of the soul as 'a requirement of human moral life', N. Abbagnano writes: 'This argument was not successful in ancient times; it has rather proved the reason (very often hidden) why philosophers were lead to seek out other arguments proving the immortality of the soul.' (*Dizionario di Filosofia*, p.471.)
28. *Paris Talks*, p.89. It is the ancient, recurring argument called *consensus gentium* (general consent), set forth by Cicero in his *Tusculanae Disputationes*.
29. *Gleanings*, p.158.
30. *Paris Talks*, p.93.

there nothing after death, Christ would have not accepted the cross; the prophets of all time would not have sacrificed their lives.'[31]

From the above quotations it clearly appears that most of the rational proofs of the existence and immortality of the soul mentioned by 'Abdu'l-Bahá in His writings and talks may be found in the writings of the great philosophers. However, He comes to the conclusion that these proofs, like rational proofs of the existence of God, are neither indispensable nor fundamental to the understanding of human reality. 'This is a rational proof which we are giving, so that the wise may weigh it in the balance of reason and justice. But if the human spirit will rejoice and be attracted to the Kingdom of God, if the inner sight becomes opened, and the spiritual hearing strengthened, and the spiritual feelings predominant, he will see the immortality of the spirit as clearly as he sees the sun, and the glad tidings and the signs of God will encompass him.'[32] Once again, we find a warning in the Bahá'í texts not to be satisfied with a merely rational investigation of reality, but to make use of all those cognitive means we have been given by God. Only thus shall we discover our own reality, the most luminous trace of God we can find in the universe: the soul of man.

What is the soul?

Bahá'u'lláh writes: '. . . *the human soul is, in its essence . . . a mystery among His mysteries*', and moreover: '*Wert thou to ponder in thine heart, from now until the end that hath no end, and with all the concentrated intelligence and undertaking which the greatest minds have attained in the past or will attain in the future, this divinely ordained and subtle Reality, this sign of the revelation of the All-Abiding, All-Glorious God, thou wilt fail to comprehend its mystery or to appraise its virtue*'; and then He adds: '*This confession of helplessness which mature contemplation must eventually impel every mind to make is in itself the acme of human understanding, and marketh the culmination of man's development.*'[33] Thus, it is impossible to comprehend the soul.

'Abdu'l-Bahá explains the reasons why the soul cannot be comprehended:
(i) 'Be it known that to know the reality of the essence of the soul of man is impossible, for, in order to know a thing, one must comprehend it, and since a thing cannot comprehend itself, to know one's self in substance or essence is impossible . . .'[34]

---

31. *Divine Philosophy*, p. 119. The argument of the *consensus* becomes more pregnant when that *consensus* is not given by common people, but by such authorities as the Manifestations of God.
32. *Some Answered Questions*, pp. 115–16.
33. *Gleanings*, pp. 160, 182.
34. 'Survival and Salvation', in *Star of the West*, VII, p. 190.

(ii) 'Man discerns only manifestations, or attributes, of objects, while the identity, or reality, of them remains hidden',[35] thence how could a man know his own soul, which is his own innermost essence?

As it is impossible to comprehend the soul, so it is impossible to give its exact definition. However, in the Bahá'í texts many statements may be found describing the soul, statements which may assist us in grasping some of its aspects.

(i) The soul is 'the reality of man',[36] says 'Abdu'l-Bahá; or else 'the substance'[37] of man; and also 'a pure and unknown essence',[38] and, finally, the 'inner reality'.[39] He writes that '. . . *the body has to die, when its light has come to an end. Therefore, of what importance is it?*',[40] suggesting that the true man is the soul and undoubtedly the body is of minor importance.

(ii) '. . . man has a soul in which dwells the divine spirit',[41] suggesting that the soul belongs to the divine world.

(iii) 'As to the soul,' writes Bahá'u'lláh, '. . . *it is sent forth by the Word of God*';[42] and 'Abdu'l-Bahá says that the soul is 'a spirit with which God has endowed him [man] at creation';[43] it is '. . . a depository, emanating from the light of the Ancient Entity – God',[44] 'It is a divine bounty. It is the effulgence of the Sun of Reality',[45] suggesting that the soul is a spiritual entity created by God through emanation.

(iv) 'Abdu'l-Bahá writes that the soul is '*the intermediary between the Supreme Concourse and the lower concourse*',[46] suggesting that the soul acts as a link between the world of creation and the world of the Kingdom.

(v) He says moreover that the soul is '. . . *the medium of the spiritual life*',[47] '. . . the heavenly body, the ethereal form which corres-

---

35. *Promulgation*, p.421.
36. 'Survival and Salvation', in *Star of the West*, VII, p.190.
37. *Some Answered Questions*, p.239. It seems that 'Abdu'l-Bahá gives to the word 'substance', in this statement, the Aristotelian meaning: that which necessarily is what it is.
38. 'Survival and Salvation', in *Star of the West*, VII, p.190. Essence, in this statement, seems accepted in its meaning of 'necessary essence', i.e. 'substance'.
39. *Promulgation*, p.464.
40. Quoted in M. M. Rabb, 'The Divine Art of Living', in *Star of the West*, VII, p.151.
41. *Paris Talks*, p.25.
42. Quoted in 'Studies in Immortality', in *Star of the West*, XIV, p.8.
43. *Promulgation*, p.60.
44. 'Survival and Salvation', in *Star of the West*, VII, p.190.
45. *Promulgation*, p.60.
46. *Tablets*, p.611.
47. ibid. p.591.

ponds to this body',[48] suggesting that man belongs, by virtue of his soul, to the spiritual world, whose life he can live.

(vi) He also says that the soul is 'the conscious reality', 'the heavenly gift of consciousness', suggesting that consciousness is the most important among the qualities of the soul which appear in this world.[49]

(vii) In the soul, Bahá'u'lláh writes, *'are potentially revealed all the attributes and names of God'*,[50] and 'Abdu'l-Bahá says that it is a 'collective reality', 'the collective centre of all human virtues', 'the world of exemplars',[51] suggesting that the soul has the capacity of expressing all the divine attributes, or exemplars.

(viii) The soul is *'the harbinger that proclaimeth the reality of all the worlds of God'*, writes Bahá'u'lláh, a *'. . . sign of the revelation of the Divine Being',*[52] and 'Abdu'l-Bahá says that the soul is 'sign[s] and trace[s] of the divine bounty', suggesting that the soul — 'collective centre'[53] of all the divine attributes as it is — is a proof of the existence of God.

(ix) Bahá'u'lláh mentions an Islamic tradition which says: '. . . *the soul . . . is divine and celestial. It is a divine energy, a substance, simple, and self-subsistent.*'[54] And 'Abdu'l-Bahá writes: *'The spirit . . . is a single essence, fine and delicate, incorporeal, everlasting and of God.'*[55]

The above-mentioned concepts could be thus summarized: from

---

48. *Promulgation*, pp.464–5. The word 'form' here refers to an immaterial reality; it is not therefore used — it seems — in its Aristotelian meaning of 'substance of things which are possessed of matter', but in its Scholastic meaning of 'necessary essence, or substantial principle which characterizes a being and determines its specific nature'. (See N. Abbagnano, *Dizionario di Filosofia*, pp.145–7.)

49. *Promulgation*, pp.465, 258. The Bahá'í texts attach the greatest importance to human consciousness; however, consciousness is viewed as one of the divine qualities of human soul and not as its essence, such as in the case of certain modern philosophers. In the Bahá'í texts, the greatest importance is attached also to love and will.

50. *Kitáb-i-Íqán*, p.101.

51. *Promulgation*, pp.418, 239, 464.
For an interesting discussion of this topic see W. S. Hatcher, 'The Concept of Spirituality', in *Bahá'í Studies*, XI, pp.19–23. He says: 'A close examination of the psychology of the spiritual growth process as presented in the Bahá'í writings indicates that the proper and harmonious functioning of our basic spiritual capacities depends on recognizing a hierarchical relationship among them. At the apex of this hierarchy is the knowing capacity.' And he supports his statement quoting passages from the Bahá'í texts. Then he writes: 'In the above passages and in many others not quoted, the hierarchical ordering of spiritual faculties is the same: Knowledge leads to love which generates the courage to act (i.e. faith) which forms the basis of the intention to act (i.e. motive and good will) which in turn leads to action itself (i.e. good deeds). Of course, the knowledge which starts this psycho-spiritual chain reaction is not just any kind of knowledge, but the knowledge of God which is equivalent to true self-knowledge.' (ibid. pp.19–20.)

52. *Gleanings*, pp.160, 191.

53. *Promulgation*, pp.286, 239.

54. *Epistle*, p.12.

55. *Selections*, p.167.

God the world of the Kingdom emanates; from the world of the Kingdom the spirit emanates; the spirit manifests itself in different realities which differ from each other in the degree they occupy in the world of being. The soul of man is one of these realities. Therefore, the relation of the soul to God '. . . is similar to that of the ray to the sun – the effect to the primal cause'.[56] It is similar to the relation between God and any other of His creatures. But whereas the other creatures reflect only one of the attributes of Divinity, the soul of man reflects them all. 'Abdu'l-Bahá explains that '. . . for each name, each attribute, each perfection which we affirm of God there exists a sign in man'.[57] For this reason the soul of man – a sign of God – is said to be the 'collective reality', the centre where 'the perfections of God, the divine virtues are reflected or revealed', where God has engraved 'the mysteries of the divine Kingdom'.[58] The soul is a ray of the divine Sun of Reality: though it does not partake in the essence of the sun, it is however possessed of all its attributes, first among them consciousness.

Its individuality

The spiritual reality of the soul is individual. In other words the soul is characterized by potential endowments and qualities – metaphorically described by Bahá'u'lláh as *'gems that lie hidden within the mine of their* [man's] *true and inmost selves'*[59] – which, taken as a whole, are unique, inimitable and infinite. In the words of 'Abdu'l-Bahá, as 'there are no repetitions in nature', so each man 'differs in natal capacity and intrinsic intellectual endowment'.[60] Moreover, as the attributes of God are infinite, so, in the words of Bahá'u'lláh *'the favours vouchsafed by Him unto mankind have been, and will ever remain, limitless in their range'*.[61] In other words, as 'Abdu'l-Bahá says, '. . . the virtues of humanity and the possibilities of human advancement are boundless'.[62]

The soul *'is not susceptible of any change'* in *'its original state or character'*,[63] writes Bahá'u'lláh, whereas 'Abdu'l-Bahá says that it

56. 'Survival and Salvation', in *Star of the West*, VII, p.190.
57. *Some Answered Questions*, p.196.
58. *Promulgation*, pp.418, 69, 303.
59. *Gleanings*, p.160.
60. *Promulgation*, pp.285, 84. Bahá'u'lláh writes that for every man God *'poureth forth'* a *'share of the flood of grace'* and then He adds: *'Let none, therefore consider the largeness or smallness of the receptacle. The portion of some might lie in the palm of a man's hand, the portion of others might fill a cup, and of others even a gallon-measure.'* (*Gleanings*, p.8.) Elsewhere He writes: *'Unto each one hath been prescribed a pre-ordained measure . . .'* (ibid. p.149.)
61. *Gleanings*, p.194.
62. *Promulgation*, p.377.
63. *Gleanings*, p.160.

The Soul: The Reality of Man

'. . . is the natural God-given personality . . . the inner aspect of man which is not subject to change'. Its characteristics are 'divine attributes, invisible in the rest of creation'. These attributes 'are divine in origin . . . they are emanations of the Father. They are the significance of his names and attributes, the direct rays of which illuminate the very essence of these qualifications.'[64] Since individuality 'consists of the attributes of the heavenly Kingdom', it is 'the image of the Merciful': 'Therefore, it is said that man has been created in the image and likeness of God.'[65]

Individualities differ from each other and thus there is 'a difference in the intrinsic or natal capacity of individuals', as well as a 'difference in degree of capacity . . . among human souls'.[66] From the explanations of the difference among human souls given by 'Abdu'l-Bahá we may understand that there is no soul who is not possessed of its own, however limited, excellence. '. . . although divine creation is purely good', He says, 'yet the varieties of natural qualities in man come from the difference of degree; all are excellent, but they are more or less so, according to the degree.'[67] Because of these varieties of natural qualities, 'each human creature has individual endowment, power and responsibility in the creative plan of God'. No wonder therefore that individuality – viewed as 'capacity to attain human virtues' – is considered by 'Abdu'l-Bahá 'the greatest bestowal of God to man':[68] in fact it is because of this endowment that man is the apex of creation.

'Abdu'l-Bahá writes that the spirit of man '. . . *is like unto the light which is potential and in the candle and gets inflamed with the fire of the love of God, then streams its light in the stage of visibility*'.[69] In this sense He says that '. . . the human reality may be compared to a seed . . . the merciful God, our Creator, has deposited within human realities certain latent and potential virtues. Through education and culture these virtues deposited by the loving God will become apparent in human reality, even as the unfoldment of the tree from within the germinating seed.'[70] Therefore a man should endeavour, while he lives on this earth, to manifest the divine qualities enshrined in his soul, of whose individuality they are a

---

64. *Divine Philosophy*, p.127.
65. *Promulgation*, pp.335, 70.
66. ibid. pp.85, 24.
67. *Some Answered Questions*, p.212.
68. *Promulgation*, pp.293, 378.
69. 'Recent Tablets to Bahais in America, in *Star of the West*, II, p.58. Bahá'u'lláh writes: '*All that which ye potentially possess can, however, be manifested only as a result of your own volition.*' (*Gleanings*, p.149.)
70. *Promulgation*, p.70.

part, in the form of knowledge, feelings, deeds and words. In the process of such growth and endeavour '. . . his individuality which is divine and heavenly should be his guide'.[71] This is the real self-realization.[72]

Its dual nature

'The essence of man', writes Bahá'u'lláh, *'is hidden in his individuality which must appear through the polish of education. This is man's glory, and all else which depends upon other things is not a part of man himself.'*[73] That which thus appears of a man's individuality is called personality. Personality, says 'Abdu'l-Bahá, '. . . is the result of acquired arts, sciences and virtues with which man is decorated' and '. . . is obtained through the conscious effort of man by training and education'. Human personality, He says moreover, '. . . has no element of permanence. It is a slightly changeable quality in man which can be turned in either direction. For if he acquire praiseworthy virtues, these strengthen the individuality of man and call forth his hidden forces; but if he acquire defects, the beauty and simplicity of the individuality will be lost and its God-given qualities will be stifled in the foul atmosphere of self.'[74]

The same concept is repeatedly explained in the Bahá'í texts; for instance, Bahá'u'lláh writes: '. . . *the soul hath two wings. If it flieth in the air of the love and will of God, it will be attributed to the Merciful: but if it flieth in the atmosphere of desire, it will be attributed to satan — may God protect us and you against it . . . And if it is kindled by the fire of the love of God, it will be a pleasing and tranquil soul: but if it be kindled by desire, it is a passionate soul.'*[75] And moreover: *'If it be faithful to God, it will reflect His light, and will, eventually, return unto Him. If it fail, however, in its allegiance to its Creator, it will become a victim to self and passion, and will, in the end, sink in their depths.'*[76]

'Abdu'l-Bahá writes: '. . . *soul is the intermediary between the Supreme Concourse and the lower concourse. It (the soul) hath two phases — the higher aspireth to the kingdom of El-Abhá and the lights of the mind shine forth from that horizon upon its higher sphere. The other side inclineth to the lower concourse of the material world, and its lowest phase is enveloped in the darkness of ignorance.'* He writes moreover: *'There is a*

---

71. *Divine Philosophy*, p.129.
72. As to the topic of self-realization, see W. S., Hatcher, 'The Concept of Spirituality', in *Bahá'í Studies*, XI. See moreover D. C. Jordan, *Becoming Your True Self: The Meaning of Deepening*.
73. 'The Federation of the World', in *Star of the West*, XIV, p.297.
74. *Divine Philosophy*, pp.127, 128.
75. Quoted in 'Studies of Immortality', in *Star of the West*, XIV, p.8.
76. *Gleanings*, p.159.

human spirit and a divine spirit, the latter arising through knowledge and belief in God. The human spirit is superior to the body and struggles with it for control of the soul: when it succeeds, the soul becomes heavenly; when the body obtains control, the soul becomes degraded.'[77]

'Abdu'l-Bahá says: '. . . the human personality appears in two aspects: the image or likeness of God and the aspect of Satan. The human reality stands between these two: the divine and the satanic.'[78] He says moreover: 'As long as man is a captive of habit, pursuing the dictates of self and desire, he is vanquished and defeated. This passionate personal ego takes the reins from his hands, crowds out the qualities of the divine ego, and changes him into an animal, a creature unable to judge good from evil, or to distinguish light from darkness. He becomes blind to divine attributes, for this acquired individuality, the result of an evil routine of thought, becomes the dominant note of his life.'[79] And He writes: *'In short, man is endowed with two natures: one tendeth towards moral sublimity and intellectual perfection, while the other turneth to bestial degradation and carnal imperfections.'*[80]

It is clear therefore that the soul, in the process of developing its individuality in this world, is subject to the influences of two realities which are equally active upon it: its divine nature, urging the soul to develop its potential spiritual qualities typical of the world of the Kingdom: and its material or animal nature, leading the soul to indulge in the natural emotions of its natal self and thus to lower itself from the spiritual kingdom whence it comes to an inferior, animal level, to which the body belongs and into which it allures the soul.

Therefore man, guided by '. . . his individuality which is divine and heavenly' develops a personality 'through the conscious effort . . . by training and education'. Thus 'capacity' appears in him 'in accordance with striving and sincerity'.[81]

This process of growth has been described in previous chapters. Bounties or powers of the soul, required for that process to unfold, will be described in the following pages.

---

77. *Tablets*, p.611.
78. *Promulgation*, p.464.
79. *Divine Philosophy*, p.130.
80. *Selections*, p.288.
81. *Divine Philosophy*, pp.129, 128, 114. 'Abdu'l-Bahá says: 'He [man] has the innate character, the inherited character, and the acquired character which is gained by education.

'With regard to innate character, although the divine creation is purely good, yet the varieties of natural qualities in man come from the difference of degree; all are excellent, but they are more or less so, according to the degree . . .

'The variety of inherited qualities comes from strength and weakness of constitution

The oneness of the spirit

Bahá'u'lláh writes: '*Say, that spirit, mind, soul, hearing and sight are one, but differ through differing causes. In the case of man, for instance, ye see that by which man understands, moves, speaks, hears, and sees: all of these are through the power of his God in him, but they each one are different, according to the difference of their cause. Verily, this is indeed the truth.*

'*For example, if all these faculties are turned to that which causes hearing, then hearing and its results become manifest, and if they are turned to that which causes sight, another activity and another result will appear: if turned to the brain, head, etc., the manifestations of mind and soul will appear.*'[82]

He writes, moreover: '*Consider the rational faculty with which God hath endowed the essence of man. Examine thine own self, and behold how thy motion and stillness, thy will and purpose, thy sight and hearing, thy sense of smell and power of speech, and whatever else is related to, or transcendeth, thy physical senses or spiritual perceptions, all proceed from, and owe their existence to, this same faculty.*'[83]

And 'Abdu'l-Bahá explains: 'It is the same reality which is given different names, according to the different conditions wherein it is manifested. Because of its relation to matter and the phenomenal world when it governs the physical functions of the body, it is called the human soul; when it manifests itself as the thinker, the comprehender, it is called the mind. And when it soars into the atmosphere of God, and travels in the spiritual world, it becomes designated as spirit.'[84]

These words enable us to understand the fundamental oneness of the spirit, beyond the multiplicity of its expressions. The instruments of the soul (or spirit of man) should not, therefore, be viewed as independent entities, but as different aspects of the same reality in its different functions.

— that is to say, when the two parents are weak, the children will be weak; if they are strong, the children will be robust . . .

'But the difference of the qualities with regard to culture is very great, for education has great influence . . . Education has a universal influence, and the differences caused by it are very great.' (*Some Answered Questions*, pp.212–4.)

Therefore, in the Bahá'í view, individual characters depend on the interaction of these three factors and on the efforts exerted so that those God-given qualities (innate character and inherited qualities) may be mirrored forth in the plane of concrete reality, under the particular circumstances allotted by God Himself (characters acquired from education). Since these efforts are conscious and voluntary, (*see* above pp.96–9, 135–7 and below pp.169–71), each individual is responsible for his own personality under his own particular circumstances.

82. Quoted in 'Studies in Immortality', *Star of the West*, XIV, p.8.
83. *Gleanings*, p.164.
84. 'Survival and Salvation', in *Star of the West*, VII, p.190.

Soul and body

The relation between body and soul is explained in many passages of the Bahá'í texts. 'Abdu'l-Bahá says that '... this essence or soul of man because of its innate purity and its connection with the unseen Ancient Entity is old as regards time, but new as regards individuality'. The soul therefore – as regards its individuality – has a beginning at the time of fertilization. In that circumstance, the zygote or fertilized ovum which potentially contains in itself a future human being becomes as 'a mirror'[85] reflecting into the world of creation the 'effulgences' of that 'spirit' 'emanated from the reality of Divinity',[86] i.e. the soul. Elsewhere it is said that the zygote is like 'a magnet ... for the spirit' which 'will become manifest in [it] with all its perfections'.[87] This event is part of the great 'creative plan of God':[88] matter – in its evolution and transformations – acquires different capacities of expressing in the world of creation the spiritual realities of the world of the Kingdom. In the stage of human zygote, matter acquires the capacity of manifesting the spirit of man.

Explaining the relation between soul and body, Bahá'u'lláh uses the metaphor of the sun (the soul) and the earth (the body),[89] whereas 'Abdu'l-Bahá adduces other examples. He says that '... the human spirit does not enter into the physical body, nay, rather, it has some "attachment" (to it). This "attachment" is like that of the mirror and the sun.'[90]

Other examples He mentions are: '... the body is a mere garment utilized by the spirit', and moreover: 'The spirit, or human soul, is the rider; and the body is only the steed.'[91] In other words, on the one hand, the soul is mirrored forth from the body and, on the other, it utilizes the body as an instrument through which its qualities may be expressed. 'Abdu'l-Bahá says: 'The soul acts in the physical world with the help of the body.'[92]

Therefore '... the soul is the intermediary between the body and spirit ...',[93] and *'The soul is a link between body and spirit. It*

---

85. *Some Answered Questions*, p.144.
86. *Promulgation*, p.59.
87. *Some Answered Questions*, p.201.
88. *Promulgation*, p.293.
89. Bahá'u'lláh writes: *'The soul of man should be likened unto this sun, and all things on earth should be regarded as his body ... The soul of man is the sun by which the body is illumined, and from which it draweth its sustenance, and should be so regarded.'* (*Gleanings*, pp.154–5.)
90. Quoted in 'Studies in Immortality', in *Star of the West*, XIV, p.37.
91. *Promulgation*, pp.259, 416.
92. *Divine Philosophy*, p.123.
93. *Paris Talks*, p.98.

receives bounties and virtues from the spirit and gives them to the body, just as the outer senses carry that which they receive from the outer world to the inner senses, in order that (these impressions) may be deposited in the memory and, through his various powers, may be utilized by man.'[94]

Though the soul is closely related to the body, nevertheless it is independent of it. *'That a sick person'*, writes Bahá'u'lláh, *'showeth signs of weakness is due to the hindrances that interpose themselves between his soul and his body, for the soul itself remaineth unaffected by any bodily ailments.'* The body, on the contrary, is strictly dependent on the soul: *'So closely are they* [the senses] *related unto it* [the rational faculty]*'*, writes Bahá'u'lláh, *'that if in less than the twinkling of an eye its relationship to the human body be severed, each and every one of these senses will cease immediately to exercise its functions and will be deprived of the power to manifest the evidences of its activity.'*[95]

The body therefore is but a machine functioning thanks to the *'bounties'*[96] the soul receives from the world of the Kingdom and continuously bestows upon it ('It is the soul . . .', says 'Abdu'l-Bahá, 'that directs a man's faculties, that governs his humanity'[97]) and at the same time it is an instrument through which the soul expresses itself in the world of creation.

Its bounties or powers[98]

'Abdu'l-Bahá writes: '. . . *the soul hath limitless manifestations of its own'*[99] and therefore it is impossible to describe all those *'bounties'*[100] the soul bestows upon the body; in other words the powers it manifests in the world of creation. However, when the Bahá'í texts are studied, the most important of these bounties and powers may be understood.

The soul as coordinator and motor of the body

'. . . *the various organs and members, the parts and elements, that constitute the body of man, though at variance, are yet all connected one with the other by that all-unifying agency known as the human soul, that causeth them to function in perfect harmony and with absolute regularity'*,[101] writes 'Abdu'l-Bahá. And moreover: 'the mind force —

---

94. *Tablets*, p.611.
95. *Gleanings*, pp.154, 164.
96. *Tablets*, p.611.
97. *Paris Talks*, p.86.
98. *See also* H. A. Weil, *Closer than your Life Vein*, pp.42–70.
99. 'Tablet to Dr. A. Forel', in *Bahá'í World*, XV, p.38.
100. *Tablets*, p.611.
101. ibid. pp.39–40.

whether we call it pre-existent or contingent — doth direct and coordinate all the members of the human body, seeing to it that each part or member duly performeth its own special function.'[102] And He says: 'It is the soul . . . that directs a man's faculties, that governs its humanity.'[103]

He says moreover that the mediator between the soul and the body is the *'sympathetic nerve'*[104] — to which He refers also as 'common faculty'[105] — and regarding which He writes: '[it] *is connected with both. It phenomena shall be perfect when its spiritual and physical relations are normal.*'[106]

The body is therefore an instrument through which the soul materializes itself, and which the soul utilizes so that its allotted purposes in the world may be accomplished. 'Abdu'l-Bahá says: 'The attainment of any object is conditioned upon knowledge, volition and action. Unless these three conditions are forthcoming, there is no execution or accomplishment.'[107] Since human life bears its fruits only when it is spent in the pursuance of the God-given goal of human souls *'to know Him and to love Him'*,[108] it may be useful to describe the main powers of the soul through which the three conditions of knowledge, volition and action are realized in human life, i.e. the powers of knowing, loving and willing.[109]

Knowledge

Each human cognitive process is realized through the soul. 'Abdu'l-Bahá states clearly that the soul can know 'through instruments and organs'[110] and without them.[111] The instruments which the soul utilizes so that it may know are the senses, through which 'sense perception' is realised; and the brain — through which the 'reasonable perception' or 'intellection'[112] is realised. The soul can also

---

102. *Selections*, p.48.
103. *Paris Talks*, p.86.
104. *Tablets*, p.309.
105. *Some Answered Questions*, p.210.
106. This concept deserves further discussion and study in the light of the concept of the spiritual nature of man. Then many aspects of human behaviour and neurosis will be better understood, and more effective ways of curing and preventing the so-called psychosomatic diseases will be discovered. *See* H. B. Danesh, 'Health and Healing', in *World Order*, III, no.3, p.15.
107. *Promulgation*, p.157.
108. *Gleanings*, p.65.
109. *See Some Answered Questions*, pp.300–305. For an interesting exposition of these three fundamental spiritual powers of man, *see* W. S. Hatcher, 'The Concept of Spirituality', in *Bahá'í Studies*, XI, pp.19–23.
 As to these attributes — knowledge, love and will — as expressed in the act of creation, *see* above pp.36–7.
110. *Some Answered Questions*, p.227.
111. *See Some Answered Questions*, p.227; *Promulgation*, pp.86, 90; *Paris Talks*, p.86.
112. *Promulgation*, pp.357, 417.

know directly 'without instruments and organs':[113] this is 'insight, the power of inner perception',[114] or 'intuitive knowledge'.[115]

Sense perception. It is shared by men and animals and one of its purposes is *'to separate the beneficial from whatever causeth harm'*.[116] In the animal it is the typical expression of the spirit at that level. In men, it is one of those expressions of the animal spirit. However, in men the typical expression of spirit is the 'reasonable perception'.[117]

Bahá'u'lláh writes: '. . , *if all these faculties* [the faculties of the spirit] *are turned to that which causes hearing, then hearing and its results become manifest, and if they are turned to that which causes sight, another activity and another result will appear; if turned to the brain, head, etc., the manifestations of mind and soul will appear . . .'*.[118] And 'Abdu'l-Bahá explains: '[the body] is only the medium of the grossest sensations',[119] and elsewhere He says: 'It is not the body which feels pain or trouble, but the soul . . . though the body is the cause of that trouble.'[120] He writes moreover that *'feelings'* in men and animals *'are one and the same'*.[121] But it seems that though 'sense perception' is shared by men and animals, yet in men it has a different meaning and importance: in fact — though it is undoubtedly produced through the body — yet it is immediately elaborated by the soul through its power of 'reasonable perception' through which it becomes conscious.

'Reasonable perception' or *'intellection'*.[122] 'Abdu'l-Bahá writes: '. . . *the human spirit is an all-encompassing power that exerteth its dominion over the inner essences of all created things, uncovering the well kept mysteries of the phenomenal world.'* Through this power, He adds, man *'. . . graspeth universal ideas and layeth bare the secrets of creation'* as well as *'abstract and universal ideas'*.[123] He explains that this kind of knowledge is possible because of certain powers of the soul expressing themselves through the agency of the brain. In fact, among *'the inherent properties of the soul'* there are those to which He refers as *'mental faculties'*[124] or 'spiritual powers': imagination,

---

113. *Some Answered Questions*, p.227.
114. *Promulgation*, p.325.
115. *Some Answered Questions*, p.157.
116. *Selections*, p.155.
117. *Promulgation*, p.357.
118. Quoted in 'Studies in Immortality', in *Star of the West*, XIV, p.8.
119. *Promulgation*, p.417.
120. Quoted in M. M. Rabb, 'The Divine Art of Living', in *Star of the West*, VIII, p.230.
121. *Selections*, p.159.
122. *Promulgation*, pp.357, 417.
123. *Selections*, pp.170.
124. 'Tablet to Dr. A. Forel', in *Bahá'í World*, XV, p.38.

thought, comprehension, memory, common faculty.[125] He says that they are properties of the soul *as the radiation of light is the essential property of the sun*',[126] and that they find their expression in the world of creation through the instrument of the brain. This '... *action of the soul's power*'[127] expressed through the brain is called mind. The mind, says 'Abdu'l-Bahá, 'is the power of the human spirit. Spirit is the lamp; mind is the light which shines from the lamp. Spirit is the tree, and the mind is the fruit.'[128] Mind is strictly dependent on the brain, where 'Abdu'l-Bahá says it 'has its seat':[129] *'For the mind to manifest itself, the human body must be whole: and a sound mind cannot be but in a sound body.'* Because mind depends on the brain, it is *'circumscribed'*.[130] In fact mind comprehends through senses: without them it cannot function.

'Abdu'l-Bahá explains the process of intellection. Senses perceive material reality and convey their perceptions to the brain. In the brain, perceptions are conveyed through the common sense to the mind; the mind in its turn elaborates them through its mental faculties, i.e. imagination, thought, comprehension and memory. Thus *'The mind comprehendeth the abstract by the aid of the concrete.'*[130]

'Abdu'l-Bahá writes that '... *the human spirit is an all-encompassing power that exerteth its dominion over the inner essences of all created things, uncovering the well kept mysteries of the phenomenal world.*

'The divine spirit, however, doth unveil divine realities and universal mysteries that lie within the spiritual world.' Therefore the mind — assisted by the *'divine spirit'*[131] or 'spirit of faith'[132] — enables man to know also the reality of the spiritual world. This knowledge of the spiritual world is confirmed and strengthened through the soul's direct knowledge, its 'inner perception or insight'.[133]

'Inner perception or insight'[134] or *'intuitive knowledge'*.[135] The Bahá'í texts very often refer to inner eye and vision, inner ear and hearing, as well as inner mind,[136] and 'Abdu'l-Bahá very often mentions

---

125. *Some Answered Questions*, p.210.
126. 'Tablet to Dr. A. Forel', in *Bahá'í World*, xv, p.38.
127. *Tablets*, p.611.
128. *Some Answered Questions*, p.209.
129. *Divine Philosophy*, p.92.
130. 'Tablet to Dr. A. Forel', in *Bahá'í World*, xv, p.38.
131. *Selections*, p.170.
132. *Some Answered Questions*, p.208.
133. *Promulgation*, p.325.
134. ibid.
135. *Some Answered Questions*, p.157.
136. 'Abdu'l-Bahá says: 'He has given us material gifts and spiritual graces, outer sight to view the lights of the sun and inner vision by which we may perceive the glory of God. He has designed the outer ear to enjoy the melodies of sound and the inner hearing wherewith we may hear the voice of our Creator.' (*Promulgation*, p.90.)

two instruments — mind and heart — as factors of spiritual progress.¹³⁷ Mind has been previously discussed. The heart might be viewed as that kind of knowledge the soul achieves without instruments and organs. This kind of knowledge is immediate, independent of any physical instrument, reflection or reasoning, and leads man directly to the 'knowledge of being'.¹³⁸ It is insight or intuition.¹³⁹

In the Bahá'í view, this cognitive capacity is not bestowed only upon the chosen ones, through God knows what occult, mystical and magical arts. It is a power shared by all mankind; but today it is atrophied because it is very seldom used. In fact 'Abdu'l-Bahá says: '. . . if the spiritual qualities of the soul, open to the breath of the Divine Spirit, are never used, they become atrophied, enfeebled, and at last incapable . . .'¹⁴⁰ Very few people make a deliberate, conscious and methodical use of their insight. Most of its fruits are reaped without an awareness of their origin. Contrary to this pattern, the Bahá'í texts prescribe a systematic use of this extraordinary cognitive power, and point to meditation as the specific practice through which this power may be both used and developed. Such is the importance attached in the Bahá'í texts to meditation, that 'Abdu'l-Bahá says: 'You cannot apply the name "man" to any being void of this faculty of meditation; without it he would be a mere animal, lower than the beasts.'¹⁴¹

But it is primarily the spiritual progress resulting from the choice made by the soul of turning towards the world of the Kingdom and its endeavours in facing the necessary sacrifices while it perseveres in that choice, that quicken such intuitive powers as will be useful in daily life. 'Abdu'l-Bahá writes: *'The human spirit possesseth wondrous powers, but it should be reinforced by the Holy Spirit . . . Then will that human spirit uncover realities, and unravel mysteries.'* And elsewhere He writes: *'The divine spirit . . . doth unveil divine realities.'*¹⁴² He writes moreover: *'I now assure thee . . . that if thy*

---

137. See *Promulgation*, pp. 187, 270. 'Abdu'l-Bahá writes moreover: '. . . *the sight of the heart is illumined. It discerneth and discovereth the divine Kingdom. It is everlasting and eternal.*' (*Selections*, pp. 37–8.)

For a preliminary study of the knowledge of the heart, *see* J. McLean, 'The Knowledge of God: An Essay on Bahá'í Epistemology', in *World Order*, XII, no. 3, p. 3; A. Bausani, 'Cuore, cervello, mistica, religione', in *Opinioni Bahá'í*, II, no. 1, p. 5.

The word intuition has its etymology in the locution *intus ire*, to go inside. It suggests therefore a kind of knowledge which goes beyond the surface, or the qualities of things, reaching to the core, or essence. Insight means to see inside.

138. *Some Answered Questions*, p. 157.
139. For the concept of insight, *see* above pp. 4–5, 135–6, 139–40.
140. *Paris Talks*, p. 97.
141. ibid. p. 175. As to the concept of meditation, *see* above pp. 120, 121.
142. *Selections*, pp. 160, 164.

mind become empty and pure from every mention and thought and thy heart attracted wholly to the Kingdom of God, forget all else besides God and come in communion with the Spirit of God, then the Holy Spirit will assist thee with a power which will enable thee to penetrate all things, and a Dazzling Spark which enlightens all sides, a Brilliant Flame in the zenith of the heaven, will teach thee that which thou dost not know of the facts of the universe and of the divine doctrine.'[143]

We may thus epitomize some of the most important functions of this power of the human soul:[144]

(i) Since it is a source of thought, it strengthens the mind and promotes creativity.

(ii) It assists man in his moral choices, helping him in understanding the spiritual principles relevant to any issue to be faced and solved.

(iii) It assists man in understanding the true nature of his own or another's individuality, behind the veil of personality; thus it assists man in loving himself and others, showing to him the sign of God in man.

(iv) It assists man in comprehending the Revealed Words, whereas mind often leads to a superficial understanding and may sometimes even be an obstacle, particularly when it falls a prey to prejudice.

(v) It assists man in consultation, because it draws him closer to truth and helps him in understanding and loving his fellow-men.

'Abdu'l-Bahá explains that insight and mind cannot function simultaneously. 'The sign of the intellect is contemplation', He says, 'and the sign of contemplation is silence.'[145] 'Abdu'l-Bahá therefore indirectly recommends that the importunate mind be silenced from time to time, so that in that inner silence the voice of the spirit may be heard.[146]

Self-consciousness. Man, unique among the creatures on the earth, is self-conscious. Such is the importance of this divine bestowal that 'Abdu'l-Bahá says that 'the spiritual faculty' is 'the heavenly gift of consciousness'. This extraordinary power of the soul bestows upon man the capacity of 'conscious reflection', 'conscious ideation', 'conscious intelligence', 'consciousness'. 'Abdu'l-Bahá says: 'God has created such a conscious spirit within him [man] that he is the most wonderful of all contingent beings.'[147]

---

143. *Tablets*, p.706.
144. See H. Weil, *Closer Than Your Life Vein*, pp.48–55.
145. *Paris Talks*, p.174.
146. 'Abdu'l-Bahá delivered a very interesting speech on the topic of intuition, which is recorded in the collection of His French talks. See *Paris Talks*, pp.173–6.
147. *Promulgation*, pp.258, 17, 58, 51, 178.

Consciousness distinguishes man from animals, since animals cannot have such self-image as he has.[148] This concept set forth by 'Abdu'l-Bahá is shared by modern scientists. It is well known that when a chimpanzee, which is the most evolved among the primates, sees its own image reflected in a mirror, it does not understand that it is its own image. At most it looks behind the mirror, searching there for another animal. In fact the animal is not possessed of the capacity of memorizing the image of its own body and therefore it cannot know itself as an individual.

Thanks to this power, men know and are conscious of their knowledge. Sense perception, reasonable perception of material reality achieved through the mental faculties of the soul, intellectual perception of 'the Divine reality of things',[149] inner perception or insight and any other human activity (emotions and feelings, attraction and attachment, volition and endeavour) are, one and all, conscious activities.

The Bahá'í texts say that this consciousness has been bestowed upon man so that certain important purposes may be achieved:

(i) 'to investigate and discover the truth' 'for himself'; to 'perceive what is true'; arriving at 'valid conclusions' and 'at the verities of existence';[150]

(ii) to 'safeguard and protect himself';[151]

(iii) to apprehend 'the divine teachings';[152]

(iv) to arrive at 'the choice of good or evil';[153]

(v) to free himself 'from all the fetters of self';[154]

(vi) 'to render effective the will of God and give it material station';[155]

(vii) to acquire and manifest '. . . the bounties of God, that he may establish the kingdom of God among men and attain to happiness in both worlds, the visible and invisible'.[155]

Love

Love is another fundamental characteristic of the soul. Bahá'u'lláh

---

148. See *Promulgation*, pp.17, 30, 58, 61, 173, 177, 241, 332. As to the differences between men and animals, *see* above pp.63–4.

149. *Paris Talks*, p.85.

150. *Promulgation*, pp.291, 293, 63, 312–3, 316. Bahá'u'lláh writes: '*This gift giveth man the power to discern the truth in all things.*' (*Gleanings*, p.94).

151. *Promulgation*, p.48.

152. ibid. p.61.

153. *Some Answered Questions*, p.250. Bahá'u'lláh writes: '*This gift [consciousness] . . . leadeth him to that which is right.*' (*Gleanings*, p.194).

154. *Divine Philosophy*, p.117.

155. 'Abdu'l-Bahá, quoted in M. M. Rabb, 'The Divine Art of Living', in *Star of the West*, VII, p.161.

writes: '*I have breathed within thee a breath of My own Spirit, that thou mayest be My lover*',[156] suggesting that this capacity of loving, typical of man, is one of the divine qualities shining within him. In the Bahá'í texts love is described as an eternal, marvellous, irresistible, all-pervading force which is 'the cause of the existence of all phenomena'.[157] Creation is the outcome of 'the love of God towards the Self or Identity of God':[158] this love shines forth in the various levels of existence – in different degrees according to their respective capacities – in conformity with a single, universal law enunciated thus by 'Abdu'l-Bahá: '*the whole attracteth the part, and in the circle, the centre is the pivot of the compasses*', with its corollary: '*. . . any movement animated by love moveth from the periphery to the centre.*' In the mineral kingdom we see the affinity among the elemental atoms to which 'Abdu'l-Bahá refers as: '*the unique power that bindeth together the diverse elements of this material world*'; we see moreover '*the supreme magnetic force that directeth the movements of the spheres in the celestial realms*';[159] in the animal kingdom we find 'certain affiliation and fellowship . . . and selective affinity'[160] typical of that kingdom. In the human kingdom we see that man, being possessed of an animal nature belonging to the world of creation, is attracted towards that world; while, being possessed of a divine nature belonging to the world of the Kingdom, he is also attracted towards that Kingdom.[161] The human soul therefore is subject to such typical tension (previously mentioned) as arises from the divergent attractions towards those two different kingdoms of existence. At first the human soul hesitates and is doubtful in its choice between material reality or the world of creation, and divine reality or the world of the Kingdom. When the soul chooses the love of the divine reality, its spiritual growth begins. Thus, the soul arises to a superior degree of reality and loves both the world of the Kingdom and the world of creation. But if the soul chooses the world of creation, which is an inferior degree, it will ignore the world of the Kingdom, which is a superior degree.

The most important characteristics of this capacity of loving typical of man are described in the Bahá'í texts.

The capacity of feeling joy and pain. Love is always attended by feelings of joy and pain: pain whenever the loved one is far away,

---

156. *Hidden Words*, Persian, no.19.
157. *Promulgation*, p.255.
158. *Paris Talks*, p.180.
159. *Selections*, pp.63, 189, 35.
160. *Promulgation*, p.255.
161. 'Abdu'l-Bahá says also that men are possessed of '. . . spiritual instinct, surely never given in vain'. (*Paris Talks*, p.90.)

joy whenever the loved one is close.[162] This important capacity of feeling joy and pain is typical of the soul: 'It is not the body which feels pain or trouble', says 'Abdu'l-Bahá, 'but the soul . . . though the body is the cause of that trouble',[163] and He adds: 'If we are caused joy or pain by a friend . . . it is the soul that is affected.'[164] This capacity of feeling joy and pain is very important for the soul. 'Abdu'l-Bahá says: 'It is the nature of man to find enjoyment in that which is gratifying to his senses,' and moreover: 'God originally endowed man with an individuality which enjoyed that which was beneficial. . . .'. Joy and pain are therefore for man's protection, so that he may not draw close to that which harms him or escape from that which profits him. However, '. . . man through his evil habits changes this creation and transforms the divine illumination into satanic darkness'.[165] And moreover, He writes: '. . . *every individual is born holy and pure, and only thereafter may become defiled.*'[166] We understand now why purity is such an important human quality: when a man is impure, his capacity of judgement is undoubtedly impaired; when he is pure, he is able to turn towards that which profits him.

Purity of heart is inborn in man. 'The hearts of all children are of the utmost purity', says 'Abdu'l-Bahá, and therefore they are 'near to God'. He says moreover: 'They are mirrors upon which no dust has fallen.' Yet the original purity of children is because of their weakness. In the course of their lives, their purity may be strengthened 'through the power of intelligence . . . through the great power of reason and of understanding', so that when those children grow to manhood they become 'pure . . . simple . . . sincere'.[167] These qualities enable them to be aware of their truest

---

162. This process is one of the expressions of a fundamental condition in the world of existence: the previously mentioned process of 'demand' and 'supply' (*Promulgation*, p.83) which in man, a conscious being, expresses itself as the process of joy and pain. See above, pp.86–7.

From the cognitive sphere we have thus come to the affective sphere. First, man knows and understands reality. Then he feels the attraction towards reality and becomes conscious of his own relation to it: he feels attracted to or rejected by it; he loves or hates it; he receives from it joy or pain. The soul is originally attracted towards such aspects of reality as it is in need of. Such a need is felt by the soul as a pain, which continues until the need is satisfied.

This capacity is expressed in the human body as sensitivity to pain, one of the most important instruments for the protection of physical integrity. Congenital agnosia to pain is a very dangerous condition: anyone affected by it may be horribly mutilated without being aware of it.

163. Quoted in M. M. Rabb, 'The Divine Art of Living', in *Star of the West*, VIII, p.230.
164. *Paris Talks*, p.65.
165. *Divine Philosophy*, pp.129–30.
166. *Selections*, p.190.
167. *Promulgation*, p.53.

The Soul: The Reality of Man

human needs, which are their spiritual needs, above their less noble, material instincts which may draw them far away from their true spiritual reality. But sometimes those children are enticed by their natal selves with their natural emotions. In this case their purity is lost and, 'Abdu'l-Bahá says, their souls may fall prey to 'selfish disorders, intellectual maladies, spiritual sicknesses',[168] so that they go so far as to love harmful things and to hate beneficial things. The soul is, in a sense, subject as regards its purity to a phenomenon of addiction, i.e. it may easily fall into bad habits. It is like the nose, which at first smells any odour, but after a prolonged exposition to an odour, it no longer perceives it.[169] Such is the condition of impurity. Man must therefore be possessed of the capacity and of the ability to distinguish between harmful and beneficent things, to avoid harmful things lest he get accustomed to them and stop feeling such repugnance for them as is caused by the trouble those same things originally give him. Purity is closely connected with that human faculty *'which deterreth him from, and guardeth him against, whatever is unworthy or unseemly, and which is known as his sense of shame'*.[170] In this regard 'Abdu'l-Bahá writes: *'It is clear . . . that the emergence of this natural sense of human dignity and honour is the result of education'*, *'one of the bounties deriving from the instructions of the Prophets of God'*.[171] The Manifestation of God, in fact, reveals to man how he should behave in his life in view of his own material, mental and spiritual progress. His sense of shame is trained at the school of religion, where man is taught how to satisfy his inborn — animal, human and spiritual — needs, in view of a harmonious and balanced growth of all his potentialities. It seems therefore to be a potential human capacity, a part of his individuality, which will grow and become manifest only through training.

The power of love. Love is described in the Bahá'í texts as an amazing power, 'the most wonderful, the greatest of all living powers'.[172] Love very often works independently of the power of reason. Bahá'u'lláh writes: '. . . *the lover hath no desire save union with his beloved.*' In his eagerness to reach his goal, the lover ignores any other thing, and is capable of any insanity: '. . . *when the fire of love*

---

168. ibid. pp.204–5.
169. Bahá'u'lláh writes, alluding to the prevailing irreligion of our times: *'In this day the tastes of men have changed, and their power of perception hath altered. The contrary winds of the world, and its colours, have provoked a cold, and deprived men's nostrils of the sweet savours of Revelation.'* (Bahá'u'lláh, quoted in Shoghi Effendi, *Promised Day*, p.119.)
170. *Tablets*, p.63.
171. *Secret of Divine Civilization*, pp.97–8.
172. *Paris Talks*, p.179.

is ablaze', Bahá'u'lláh writes, *'it burneth to ashes the harvest of reason.'*[173] The Bahá'í texts very often describe love through metaphors drawn from the experience of human love between a man and a woman. This passion may therefore be viewed as a metaphor of the highest expression of love which a man may experience: the unselfish, total love towards the Absolute, i.e. God Himself. The object of love is important, as regards its results in daily life. In fact, the consequence of such insanity will be either destructive or constructive depending on whether its object is beneficent or maleficent. It is one thing to eat healthy food which gives strength and energy to the body, and another to become poisoned by a venomous draught.

Love and knowledge. 'Abdu'l-Bahá says: 'When reality envelops the soul of man, love is possible,'[174] and He explains: *'When man's soul is rarified and cleansed, spiritual links are established, and from these bonds sensations felt by the heart are produced. The human heart resembleth a mirror. When this is purified human hearts are attuned and reflect one another, and thus spiritual emotions are generated.'*[175]

Knowledge assists man in choosing the object of his love: the closer to reality this knowledge is, the closer to the Absolute is the object of love, and the nobler are the deeds produced through his will.

Love and courage. Bahá'u'lláh writes: *'Love is a light that never dwelleth in a heart possessed by fear'*; and moreover: *'A lover feareth nothing and no harm can come nigh him.'* The logic of love would have the lover ready to do anything that he may reach his beloved, even to offer *'a hundred lives'*. Therefore Bahá'u'lláh writes: *'The steed of this Valley [of love] is pain.'* This pain is caused not only by separation from the beloved, but also because love *'seeth life in death'*: in the reunion with the beloved the lover longs for total annihilation, and is there any greater pain than the dying to oneself? In the path of the spiritual search the lover is ready to give up the attributes of his natal self that he may take on the divine qualities. For this purpose, *'at every step he throweth a thousand heads at the feet of the beloved'*.[176]

The growth of love. The capacity of loving — as any other reality within man — is a potential capacity, bound to develop. This growth is a gradual change of the object of love, from the love of

---

173. *Seven Valleys*, pp.8, 10.
174. *Promulgation*, p.234.
175. *Selections*, p.108.
176. *Seven Valleys*, pp.55, 9.

the natal self to the love of greater and more universal realities, until it focuses upon the Self of God, the Logos.

Man is endowed with dynamics, attributes and capacities which assist him in developing his own capacity of loving: the dynamics of joy and pain, the attribute of purity, the capacity of knowing reality, and thus of somehow choosing the object of his love. But none of these endowments will prove sufficient to preserve the soul from the destruction ensuing from a love whose object is unworthy. Divine assistance is needed. *'Wouldst thou the mind should not entrap thee? Teach it the science of the love of God'*, writes Bahá'u'lláh. And 'Abdu'l-Bahá explains that this science is religion, suggesting that man should always adhere to such laws of the Universal Mind as are expounded by the Manifestation of God, so that he may not be deceived by his own mind, in its proposing objects of love. Bahá'u'lláh writes moreover: *'The lover's teacher is the Loved One's beauty: His face their lesson and their only book'*,[177] suggesting that the world of creation is a marvellous school of the love of God, if man only learns how to look at it.

Will

Knowledge, as self-consciousness, and love, as awareness of such feelings as are generated from attraction, qualify choice, or will. Will, therefore, seems to be the choice of a satisfying attraction or, in other words, the choice of the object of love. This choice is made by the soul. The soul is confined within the condition of 'servitude',[178] and of powerlessness, yet it has been endowed by God with the bounty of free will or free choice. *'The essence of all power is God's'*,[179] writes Bahá'u'lláh; and moreover: *'Know, also, that the life of man is from the Spirit and to turn indeed is from the soul.'*[180] And also: *'All that which ye potentially possess can, however, be manifested only as a result of your own volition'*,[181] suggesting that the soul is free to manifest either its divine nature or its animal nature. 'Abdu'l-Bahá says: '. . . in the choice of good and bad actions he [man] is free, and he commits them according to his own will.'[182] And moreover: 'God, himself, cannot compel the soul to become spiritual; the exercise of a free human will is necessary.'[183]

---

177. ibid. pp.49, 53.
178. *Some Answered Questions*, p.230.
179. *Gleanings*, p.341.
180. Quoted in 'Studies in Immortality', in *Star of the West*, XIV, p.8.
181. *Gleanings*, p.149.
182. *Some Answered Questions*, p.248.
183. Quoted in J. M. Grundy, *Ten Days in the Light of 'Akká*, p.6.

Explaining this particular human condition, 'Abdu'l-Bahá says: '... this condition is like that of a ship which is moved by the power of the wind or steam; if this power ceases, the ship cannot move at all. Nevertheless, the rudder of the ship turns it to either side, and the power of the steam moves it in the desired direction ... in all the action or inaction of man, he receives power from the help of God; but the choice of good or evil belongs to the man himself.'[184] The soul therefore may '*turn*', or make its choice of inner and outer attitude, according to such attraction as it feels and to its understanding of that attraction. The choice of the world of creation — which in man expresses itself as animal nature — is the easiest choice, because it does not imply any change, any transition from an inferior to a superior stage. On the contrary, the choice of the world of the Kingdom — which in man expresses itself as divine nature — is a difficult choice, at least at the beginning, because it implies an awareness of a remote reality, a change, a transition from an inferior to a superior stage: it is the second birth or spiritual progress.

In the Bahá'í texts, human freedom is viewed as a moral liberty of choosing between the attraction towards the world of nature and the attraction towards the world of the Kingdom, between love of the natal self and love of the Self of God. Most of the facts and circumstances of human life belong to a process which eludes the command of human will. They may be viewed as expressions of the will of God. Therefore, whosoever rebels against them somehow rebels against the will of God Himself. Man's dignity and freedom lie in his striving to mirror forth the qualities of the world of the Kingdom in such particular circumstances as are his lot. In fact, these circumstances are both an outcome of his choices and of a chain of events which do not depend on him. He may try to modify those facts and circumstances in his life which do not mirror forth the world of the Kingdom, so that they may do it. On the other hand, he may rebel against the will of God in several ways. One of the most widespread kinds of rebellion in the Western world is the attitude of changing pain into despair. Pain cannot be avoided. Whenever acutely-felt needs cannot be satisfied, or realities encountered in which the light of the world of the Kingdom is too dimly reflected, any soul feels pain. Rebellion occurs whenever a soul dwells unduly upon such unpleasant aspects of life, whenever it indulges in its painful feelings, whenever it does not show those concrete and positive attitudes through which that need may be

---

184. *Some Answered Questions*, pp. 249–50.

satisfied, that dim light may become more brilliant. In fact, God has willed joy and high aims for us. '*I will no longer be sorrowful and grieved. I will be a happy and joyful being . . . I will no longer be full of anxiety, nor will I let trouble harass me. I will not dwell on the unpleasant things of life*',[185] is the promise 'Abdu'l-Bahá exhorts us to make in one of His prayers. And elsewhere He gives the following advice to an inquirer: '*Then better for thee to bow down thy head in submission, and put thy trust in the All-Merciful Lord.*'[186]

It is clear that human choice, or the exercise of the 'power of will',[187] depend on both attraction (or love) and knowledge. Man chooses what he knows will satisfy such needs as he is aware of, because he feels them as pain. That is why 'Abdu'l-Bahá writes: '*Regarding the "two wings" of the soul: These signify wings of ascent. One is the wing of knowledge, the other of faith, as this is the means of the ascent of the human soul to the lofty station of divine perfections.*'[188] And elsewhere He says that faith is: 'love that flows from man to God . . . attraction to the Divine, enkindlement . . .'[189]

Knowledge, therefore, is but the first step into the path of spiritual progress. Through his knowledge man becomes, on the one hand, conscious of his needs, and, on the other, aware of the means through which those needs may be satisfied. Having attained such consciousness and awareness, he will be ready to make his choice by the agency of his will. His heart will be ready to choose its 'attachment',[190] an attachment that may be called in this context love. Will, in this context, is the choice of the object of attachment or of love. Only at this point will he be ready to act, and his action will thus be guided by a faith which is both '*conscious knowledge*'[191] and 'love'.[192]

Action

If knowledge, love and will are to be conducive to action, an effort is requested from the soul. Bahá'u'lláh writes: '*Success or failure, gain or loss must, therefore, depend upon man's exertions.*' And moreover: '*The greater the effort exerted . . . the more faithfully will it* [the soul] *be made to reflect the glory of the names and attributes of God.*'[193] And

185. *Bahá'í Prayers*, pp.80–81.
186. *Selections*, p.51.
187. *Promulgation*, p.83.
188. *Tablets*, p.178.
189. *Paris Talks*, p.180.
190. *Divine Philosophy*, p.133. 'Abdu'l-Bahá says: . . . the heart must have some attachment.' (ibid.)
191. *Tablets*, p.549.
192. *Paris Talks*, p.180.
193. *Gleanings*, pp.81, 262.

'Abdu'l-Bahá says: 'we must strive with energies of heart, soul and mind to develop and manifest the perfections and virtues latent within the realities of the phenomenal world.'[194] And moreover: 'Capacity is in accordance with striving and sincerity.'[195]

Therefore, the soul leads the body to act in the world of creation on the grounds of its understanding of reality and of the attraction it has decided to follow, prompted in this decision by its sometimes vague feeling that its needs will be satisfied thereby. Any action implies a change of a previous condition, and therefore requires an effort. The soul is possessed of the required qualities for its efforts to be successful: steadfastness, perseverance, firmness, courage and many other qualities of the soul which are indispensable for any action.[196] 'Abdu'l-Bahá writes: '. . . *the soul hath limitless manifestations of its own.*'[197] In fact, the powers of knowledge, love and will are three great categories of qualities expressed by the soul in accomplishing the purpose of its creation. In each of these three categories, many qualities may be recognized. These qualities are reflections of the divine qualities of the world of the Kingdom, and constitute potential endowments at the disposal of any human soul in its endeavour of approaching, step by step, the goal of its existence: to return conscious into that world of the Kingdom whence it came forth unconscious.

Moreover as knowledge, love and will are closely interrelated, so knowledge, will and action – being their outcome – should be viewed not as three successive and independent steps of a linear process, whose reciprocal relations are univocal cause-effect relations. They should rather be viewed in the light of the concept of unity and of the evolution of reality set forth in the Bahá'í texts. They are the outcome of three aspects of a single reality, the soul, and therefore they interact. Sometimes in the sight of God there is no difference between intention and action: '*Every act ye meditate is as clear to Him as is that act when already accomplished,*'[198] writes Bahá'u'lláh. Knowledge and love influence will, and will is

---

194. *Promulgation*, pp.90–1.
195. *Divine Philosophy*, p.114.
196. It is vitally important that the soul act in conformity with what it understands and its chosen attraction. Bahá'u'lláh writes: '*The first and foremost duty prescribed unto men, next to the recognition of Him Who is the Eternal Truth, is the duty of steadfastness in His Cause.*' (*Gleanings*, p.290.) In this regard 'Abdu'l-Bahá wrote, praising a group of believers: '[they] *remain steadfast under all conditions, neither at the first sign of trouble do their footsteps slip. They are not changeable, playing fast and loose with some project and soon giving it up. They do not, for some trivial reason, fail in enthusiasm and zeal, their interest gone. No, in all they do they are stable, rock solid and staunch.*' (*Selections*, p.219.)
197. 'Tablet to Dr. A. Forel', in *Bahá'í World*, XV, p.38.
198. *Gleanings*, p.150.

conducive to action. But each one of them is influenced as well by the other. Knowledge is no longer the same once will has been fulfilled, through the impulse of love, in an action. Any action confirms or denies cognitive or volitional-effective data through a dynamic which is very similar to biological feed-back.[199]

Moreover, knowledge, love and will are so strictly interrelated that divided from one another they lose their meaning. An unconscious and involuntary action is not the same as a conscious and a voluntary one.[200] Whenever knowledge, love and will are not translated into actions, they lose importance. The cognitive, affective, volitional and practical aspects of human reality are therefore closely interrelated and, depending on the circumstances, they confirm or deny one another.

The dynamics of the choice

Such are the reasons and the dynamics of the choice. The following steps are required, so that the choice may be properly directed:
(i) Whenever the cognitive powers are properly used, knowledge of reality is achieved.
(ii) Knowledge of reality fosters the soul's 'attraction to the Divine', which, in the words of 'Abdu'l-Bahá, is faith, in its meaning of 'the love that flows from man to God'.[201]
(iii) Faith is realized as *'conscious knowledge and the practice of good deeds'*[202] whenever the attraction to the world of the Kingdom is favoured.
(iv) The attraction to the world of the Kingdom and the conscious knowledge of reality are conducive to the willing acceptance of any consequence ensuing for the soul from its efforts to become attracted towards the world of the Kingdom. This is the real meaning of sacrifice.
(v) All these conditions (knowledge, love and will as expressed through action) attract 'the power of the Holy Spirit',[203] which in its turn transforms the nature of man and draws out of him his potential divine virtues, or in other words his capacities.
(vi) As man's divine virtues emerge, he becomes more and more

---

199. Feed-back or retroaction is a process through which in a given system, if A influences B, any variation produced by A in B in its turn modifies A in its acting upon B.
200. For an explanation of this concept, see *Some Answered Questions*, pp.300–305. See above pp.72–3, 155.
201. *Paris Talks*, p.180.
202. *Tablets*, p.459.
203. *Paris Talks*, p.85.

fit to reach his spiritual goal, and the process of his spiritual growth becomes more and more easy and speedy.

Now it is clear that knowledge, love and will are not enough for a man to produce concrete and positive results through his actions. 'Abdu'l-Bahá writes: '... *every great Cause in this world of existence findeth visible expression through three means: first, intention; second, confirmation; third, action.*' Therefore a confirmation is required so that intention may be translated into action. In the same text, He explains that '*confirmation*' means '*the confirmations of the Kingdom*', '*a Dynamic power*', '*the power of the Word of God*':[204] in other words the assistance of the Holy Spirit.

The Bahá'í texts say that if we are to receive such a confirmation, we should — out of pure love — orientate our choices and efforts according to the prescriptions of the Manifestations, that is towards the world of the Kingdom. Only thus will such divine virtues be achieved as are both means for the entrance into the Kingdom and qualifications of the enlightened souls, i.e. fruits of spiritual progress.

Whenever, on the contrary, a man decides that he will not follow the guidance of the Manifestation of God, either because he does not know it, or because, although he knows it, he has nevertheless preferred to turn his back on reality and to rely upon his own fancies, the process will follow a quite different course. Mostly, a man decides that he will favour his attraction towards the world of nature whenever he has used his cognitive powers improperly and has thus not understood the greater importance of the world of the Kingdom when compared to the world of creation. 'Abdu'l-Bahá writes in this regard: '... *some souls are ignorant, they must be educated; some are sick, they must be healed; some are still of tender age, they must be helped to attain maturity, and the utmost kindness must be shown to them.*'[205] This concept is reminiscent of the 'Socratic identification of science and virtue'.[206] On the grounds of this fundamental mistake, such a man places his *faith* — which is both knowledge and love — in an unworthy reality and his deeds will mirror forth the qualities of that same reality. Those deeds, therefore, will not be conducive to love, unity and cooperation, but will manifest the law of self-centredness and of the struggle for existence with the survival of the fittest, typical of the world of creation or nature. Thus his love will not be attraction towards the world of

---

204. Quoted in *Peace* (comp.), p.13.
205. *Selections*, p.28.
206. N. Abbagnano, *Storia della Filosofia*, p.70. This Socratic concept is expounded in Plato's *Protagoras*.

the Kingdom, but only attachment, i.e. bondage to the material reality in which he was created so that he might become detached from it. As there is no spiritual love within him, neither will there be any willing acceptance of pain and suffering, whose meaning he has not understood. To him such pain will be both retribution for a wrong choice, and an encouragement to change his ways. Since such a man makes no sacrifice, the power of the Holy Spirit will not be attracted and none of the divine virtues enshrined in his inner reality will become manifest. He will sink deeper and deeper into the world of creation, at whose service he will have put his own mind, 'God's greatest gift to man';[207] *'daily [will] he strut abroad with the characteristic of a wild beast'*, be it *'a ferocious tiger'*, or *'a creeping, venomous viper'* and will become *'viler than the most fierce of savage creatures'*.[208]

In this condition, the qualities of the world of nature will emerge in that man: cruelty, ruthlessness, aggression, selfishness, as well as fear, anguish, anxieties, agony, cares; and he will not be able to escape them. He will experience the hell of his *'insistent self'*, with its *'evil promptings'* and *'carnal desires'*.[209] His spiritual progress will stop. Of such men Christ said: '. . . *let the dead bury their dead*,'[210] and Bahá'u'lláh wrote that they abide in *'the abode of dust'* or in the *'plane of heedlessness'*.[211] Until they abandon such behaviour, they will not reach the goal intended for men: knowing their own true being, which is divine, through the realization of divine virtues.

The choice is thus a dynamic process, rich in negative and positive feed-backs. But each forward step will lead to higher levels of knowledge, will and action.

The soul as the mirror of human choice[212]

The results of the choice are manifest in the soul, which will mirror forth either the natural emotions of its natal self, i.e. the darksome world of nature, or its spiritual feelings and divine virtues, i.e. the

---

207. *Paris Talks*, p.41.
208. *Selections*, p.288.
209. ibid. pp.242, 205.
210. *Matt.* 8:22. The same concept is explained also in a famous Islamic tradition, mentioned by Bahá'u'lláh in His *Kitáb-i-Íqán*: '. . . *two of the people of Kúfih went to 'Alí, the Commander of the Faithful. One owned a house and wished to sell it; the other was to be the purchaser. They had agreed that this transaction should be effected and the contract be written with the knowledge of 'Alí. He, the exponent of the law of God, addressing the scribe, said: "Write thou: A dead man hath brought from another dead man a house. That house is bounded by four limits. One extendeth toward the tomb, the other to the vault of the grave, the third to the Sirát, the fourth to either Paradise or hell"*.' (p.119.)
211. *Seven Valleys*, pp.4, 5.
212. See H. A. Weil, *Closer than your Life Vein*, pp.58–60.

luminous world of the Kingdom, depending on whether the attraction towards the former or the latter has been chosen. Between these two extremes there are indeed many intermediate degrees, closer to one or to the other end depending on the spiritual progress achieved, and which are actually expressed by human beings in their daily lives. 'Abdu'l-Bahá writes: *'The souls of the believers, at the time when they first become manifest in the world of the body, are equal, and each is sanctified and pure. In this world, however, they will begin to differ one from the other, some achieving the highest stations, some a middle one, others remaining at the lowest stage of being.'*[213]

The bounties of the spirit, reflected within the soul, become visible in the world of creation – through the instrumentality of the body – as spiritual knowledge, feelings, deeds and words.

Spiritual knowledge.[214] Bahá'u'lláh writes: '. . . *keenness of understanding is due to keenness of vision.*'[215] And 'Abdu'l-Bahá writes to an inquirer: *'Verily, it* [the Holy Spirit] *is the shining morning and the rosy dawn which will impart unto thee the lights, reveal the mysteries and make thee competent in science, and through it the pictures of the Supreme World will be printed in thy heart and the facts of the secrets of the Kingdom of God will shine before thee.'*[216] Elsewhere He writes: *'Once a soul becometh holy in all things, purified, sanctified, the gates of the knowledge of God will open wide before his eyes.'*[217] It is the Holy Spirit that bestows the bounty of knowledge. The Holy Spirit opens the inner eye and therefore confers a deeper comprehension of both the material and spiritual worlds.

Moreover, spiritual perception and virtues are closely interrelated, because whoever shows forth any virtue will have an experience of it, and therefore will know it. It follows that any virtuous man has a deeper spiritual understanding of the world of the Kingdom to which his own virtues belong.

Spiritual feelings. Spiritual feelings are virtues of the world of the Kingdom reflected in human hearts. Whosoever is adorned therewith will not need words or deeds to manifest them. They are part of his individuality and personality. They radiate from him, as a light from its source. Of these men the Báb, quoting the Qur'án, said: *'On that day will We set a seal upon their mouths; yet shall their*

---

213. *Selections*, p.171.
214. Bahá'u'lláh mentions in His *Kitáb-i-Íqán* a divine knowledge and a Satanic knowledge. See above p.13 and no. 64.
215. *Tablets*, p.35.
216. ibid. p.706.
217. *Selections*, p.191.

hands speak unto Us, and their feet shall bear witness to that which they shall have done.'[218]

Joy is one of the most typical feelings of spiritual men. Bahá'u'lláh writes: '*Whoso keepest the commandments of God shall attain everlasting felicity.*'[219] And 'Abdu'l-Bahá says: 'Afflictions and troubles are due to the state of not being content with what God hath ordained for you. If one submits himself to God, he is happy.'[220] And moreover: 'The most great, peerless gift of God to the world of humanity is happiness born of love — they are the twin sisters of the superman; one is the complement of the other.'[221] But He says also: 'Although the bestowal is great and the grace is glorious, yet, capacity and readiness are requisite. Without capacity and readiness, the divine bestowal will not become manifest and evident . . . Therefore we must obtain capacity in order that the signs of the mercy of the Lord may become revealed. We must endeavour to make the soil of the hearts free from these useless weeds and sanctified from the thorns of useless thoughts in order that the cloud of Mercy may bestow its power upon it.' Therefore, only a sacrifice met for the sake of love will deliver man from the natural emotions of his natal self, will confer upon him 'capacity and readiness',[222] and will enable him to achieve true happiness. Happiness is a 'spiritual state',[223] and is '. . . dependent upon the susceptibilities of the heart and the attitude of the mind'.[224] He writes: '*As to material happiness, it never exists: nay, it is but imagination, an image reflected in mirrors, a spectre and shadow . . . It is something, which but slightly removes one's afflictions . . . All the material blessings . . . bestow no delight on the mind, nor pleasure to the soul: nay, they furnish only the bodily wants . . .*

'*As to spiritual happiness, this is the true basis of the life of man, because life is created for happiness, not for sorrow; for pleasure, not for grief . . . This great blessing and precious gift is obtained by man only through the guidance of God.*'

He writes also that spiritual happiness is '. . . *light . . . glad-tidings . . . the Kingdom . . . life . . . the fundamental basis from which man*

---

218. Nabíl-i-A'zam, *The Dawn-Breakers*, p.92.
219. *Gleanings*, p.289.
220. Quoted in M. M. Rabb, 'The Divine Art of Living', in *Star of the West*, VII, p.187.
221. Quoted in 'A Fortune That Bestows Eternal Happiness', in *Star of the West*, XIII, p.103.
222. Quoted in 'Capacity and Spiritual Revelation', in *Star of the West*, XIII, p.214.
223. Quoted in 'A Fortune That Bestows Eternal Happiness', in *Star of the West*, XIII, p.103.
224. Quoted in 'From the Unpublished Diary of Ahmad Sohrab', in *Star of the West*, XIII, p.153.

is created, worlds are originated, the contingent beings have existence and the world of God appears like unto the appearance of the sun at mid-day. This happiness is but the love of God', whereas sorrow is 'darkness . . . disappointment . . . the earthly world . . . non existence'. *'Were it not for this happiness'*, He adds, *'the world of existence would not have been created.'*[225] This condition of *'spiritual enjoyment'* is of such importance that He mentions it among the peculiar traits of man 'to which the animal can never attain', because it 'depends from the acquisition of heavenly virtues'[226] animals are debarred from.

Spiritual deeds. Spiritual deeds are in the Bahá'í view of life those actions which, suggested by love, promote the unity of mankind, through a well-pondered voluntary action. Whether they are humble actions in the modest sphere of a limited personal existence or great deeds relevant to the well-being of the whole of mankind, their meaning is always the same: 'to render effective the will of God and give it material station.'[227] In fact, God's will for today is that the divine attribute of unity may become manifest in the world and that a society of unity and peace may be created. Such deeds are well-pleasing to God because when they are weighed 'in the scales of divine teachings',[228] they comply with them. This topic has been previously discussed.

Spiritual words. As to spiritual words, 'Abdu'l-Bahá says: 'The heart is like a box, and language is the key.' Then He adds: '. . . the function of language is to portray the mysteries and secrets of human hearts.'[229]

Words may be thus viewed under two aspects:
(i) Words are the key to open the 'boxes' of the hearts;
(ii) Words portray the mysteries and secrets of human hearts.

The Bahá'í texts recommend certain conditions, so that words may be properly used as unique and powerful means of communication.

First, Bahá'u'lláh attaches the greatest importance to words: '. . . *the impression which each word maketh is clearly evident and perceptible . . . One word may be likened unto fire, another unto light, and the influence which both exert is manifest in the world . . . One word is like unto springtime causing the tender saplings of the rose-garden of*

---

225. Quoted in M. M. Rabb, 'The Divine Art of Living', in *Star of the West*, VII, p.163.
226. *Promulgation*, p.185.
227. Quoted in M. M. Rabb, 'The Divine Art of Living', in *Star of the West*, VII, p.161.
228. *Divine Philosophy*, p.98.
229. *Promulgation*, p.60.

knowledge to become verdant and flourishing, while another word is even as a deadly poison,'[230] He writes. And elsewhere: '. . . the tongue is a smouldering fire, and excess of speech a deadly poison.'[231] Numerous are His counsels we should follow, if our words are to *'possess penetrating power'* whereby they may *'exert* [their] *influence.'* He recommends *'hearts which are detached and pure . . . spirit . . . pure and heart stainless'*, so that words may be possessed of *'penetrating power'*. He recommends moreover *'tact and wisdom'*, so that *'moderation'* may be achieved, as well as *'leniency and forbearance'*.[232]

The Bahá'í texts recommend that, once the use of words is perfected, they should be devoted to the fostering of unity and peace in the world. This purpose may be achieved in two fundamental ways: teaching the Faith and consultation.

(i) *Teaching the Faith*. The best use of words in such a world of unity and peace as Bahá'u'lláh wants mankind to build, is for the opening of *'the city of the human heart'*,[233] or for causing *'the bushes to be enkindled and the call "Verily, there is no God but Me, the Almighty, the Unconstrained" to be raised therefrom'*,[234] i.e. for the kindling in human hearts of love of the Manifestation of God.

(ii) *Consultation*. The proper use of words represents moreover one of the fundamental elements of that method of confrontation of ideas and deliberation Bahá'u'lláh describes as an expression of *'the maturity of the gift of understanding'*, one of the *'two luminaries'* enlightening the *'heaven of divine wisdom'* and which He recommends as a unique instrument of *'welfare'* and *'well-being'*, as *'a cause of awareness and awakening'*,[235] i.e. the method of consultation.

Consultation is recommended not only as an effective method of finding solutions to personal and interpersonal problems, but is also

---

230. *Tablets*, p.173.
231. *Kitáb-i-Íqán*, p.193.
232. *Tablets*, pp.188–9, 173.
233. *Gleanings*, p.304.
234. *Tablets*, p.143.
235. Quoted in *The Heaven of Divine Wisdom* (comp.), pp.5, 1, 5. For a discussion of the topic of consultation see *The Heaven of Divine Wisdom. A Compilation*; J. E. Kolstoe, *Consultation: A Universal Lamp of Guidance*.

The main characteristics of consultation are thus epitomized in a recent paper written by Dr. H. B. Danesh:

'a) The main goal of consultation is to increase the level of unity, harmony and understanding among the participants . . .

'b) The most important objective of consultation is to act with justice so that the rights of every person affected by the decision are safeguarded . . .

'c) The most essential tools for consultation are frankness and openness, on the one hand, and mutual respect and trust, on the other . . .

'd) All ideas, once expressed in the course of consultation, become the property of the communicating group and not of the individual who initially expressed the idea.' (H. B. Danesh, 'Conflict-free Conflict Resolution', Unpublished.)

prescribed for the administration of public affairs. Issues of social life find a better solution whenever groups of specially elected or appointed people meet in consultation. Consultation will be well conducted and will produce good results only when certain simple technical rules are observed, and whenever the hearts of those consulting (where the required words for any exchange of ideas during consultation find their origin) are well advanced in their spiritual progress. Without these prerequisites, consultation will not be optimal, it will be more difficult to find solutions, and it will be more likely that those solutions may be wrong. Nevertheless consultation, however imperfect it may be, is in itself a means of spiritual perfecting, because any effort aimed at achieving a harmonious view of an issue is in itself an effort towards spiritualization. Consultation is therefore recommended also as an instrument of personal and collective spiritual progress. We may now well understand why the spiritualization of mankind is required for any real improvement of the political and social conditions of the world.

* * *

Spiritual knowledge, feelings, deeds and words are therefore an expression of the qualities of the soul – knowledge, love and will – manifested in the world of creation through the instrumentality of the body. The Perfect Man, the Manifestation of God, in His perfect consciousness of inner and outer reality, realizes a perfect unity and harmony between these expressions of His reality. Imperfect man, in his almost total ignorance of reality, realizes disharmony and conflict and creates difficulties for himself and for others. Spiritual progress implies a growing consciousness of inner and outer reality and a more and more bountiful confirmation of the spirit and therefore an increasing harmony between knowledge, feelings, deeds and words.

The journey of the soul

'Abdu'l-Bahá says: '. . . the human spirit is a Divine Trust, and it must traverse all conditions, for its passage and movements through the conditions of existence will be the means of its acquiring perfections . . . when the human spirit passes through the conditions of existence, it will become the possessor of each degree and station.'[236] Human life is therefore a 'journey', a 'pilgrimage' of the soul, the 'journey back to God', and 'the

---

236. *Some Answered Questions*, p.200.

The Soul: The Reality of Man

pathway of life is the road which leads to divine knowledge and attainment',[237] whereas '*every atom in existence and the essence of all created things*' have been ordained by God for man's '*training*'.[238]

Preexistent as an undifferentiated potentiality in the divine world of the Kingdom, the human soul appears as a potentially self-conscious individuality in the world of creation at the moment of conception. The purpose of its journey through the mineral, vegetable, animal and human kingdom is for the soul to make the experience and to acquire the qualities of those kingdoms, so that it may go back adorned with consciousness and will into that world of the Kingdom whence it departed unconscious, and whose attraction it has always felt, albeit obscurely and dimly.

It is the pen of a poet that assists us in expressing the feelings of this human condition: the mystical pen of Rumi, that tells of the consuming yearning of the soul in its remembrance of that world of the Kingdom whence it departed and from which it feels so remote:

> Listen to the reed how it tells a tale, complaining
>   of separations –
> Saying, 'Ever since I was parted from the reed-bed, my
>   lament hath caused man and woman to moan.
> I want a bosom torn by severance, that I may unfold
>   (to such a one) the pain of love-desire.
> Every one who is left far from his source wishes back
>   the time when he was united with it.
> In every company I uttered my wailful notes. I consorted
>   with the unhappy and with them that rejoice.[239]

It is once again his pen which suggests a prayer – mentioned by Bahá'u'lláh Himself in His *Four Valleys* – to be raised up to God, that He may assist our souls in their quest:

> O Lord! O Thou Whose bounty granteth wishes
> I stand before Thee, all save Thee forgetting.
> Grant that the mote of knowledge in my spirit
> Escape desire and the lowly clay;
> Grant that Thine ancient gift, this drop of wisdom,
> Merge with Thy mighty sea.[240]

That same inspired pen thus described – after a toilsome journey

---

237. *Promulgation*, pp. 294, 336, 294.
238. Bahá'u'lláh, *Hidden Words*, Persian, no. 29.
239. Quoted in R. A. Nicholson, *Selected Poems from the Divan Shamsi Tabrizi*, p. 5.
240. *Seven Valleys*, p. 54.

through endless times and spaces — the enraptured amazement of self-annihilation and of the vision of God in the innermost heart:

> Cross and Christians, from end to end
> I surveyed; He was not on the Cross.
> I went to the idol-temple, to the ancient pagoda;
> No trace was visible there.
> I went to the mountains of Herat and Candahar;
> I looked: He was not in that hill-and-dale.
> With set purpose I fared to the summit of Mount Qaf;
> In that place was only the 'Anqa's habitation.
> I bent the reins of search to the Ka'ba;
> He was not in that resort of old and young.
> I questioned Ibn Sina of his state;
> He was not in Ibn Sina's range.
> I fared towards the scene of *'two bow-length distance'*;
> He was not in that exalted court.
> And I gazed into my own heart;
> There I saw Him; He was nowhere else.
> Save pure-souled Shamsi Tabriz
> None ever was drunken and intoxicated and distraught.[241]

---

241. Quoted in Nicholson, *Selected Poems*, pp. 71–3.

9 Human Evolution

Since man is the outcome of the evolution of the world of creation, he himself is subject — as any other created thing — to that 'law of progression'[1] whereby any creature appears as a seed, then develops through successive degrees until it attains maturity and yields its fruit.

Human evolution may be studied in two different perspectives: individual and collective evolution,[2] and should be considered in the light of the three aspects of human nature: material, intellectual, and spiritual.[3]

Individual evolution

The characteristics of this process have been previously examined. We will now summarize them, dwelling only upon certain aspects, so that a more comprehensive view may be obtained.

Material evolution

Material evolution has its beginning in the fertilization of the ovum

---

1. *Promulgation*, p.302.
2. 'Abdu'l-Bahá says: 'Just as he [man] advances by progressive stages from the mere physical world of being into the intellectual realm, so must he develop upward in moral attributes and spiritual graces. In the process of this attainment he is ever in need of the bestowals of the Holy Spirit.' (*Promulgation*, p.288.)
3. E. Laszlo says: 'Scientific evidence of the patterns traced by evolution in the physical universe, in the living world, and even in the world of history is growing rapidly. It is coalescing into the image of basic regularities that repeat and recur. It is now possible to search out these regularities and obtain a glimpse of the fundamental nature of evolution — of the evolution of the cosmos as a whole, including the living world and the world of human social history . . . We can now begin to make sense of the confusing tangle of facts and events that make up the history of human societies and understand the most basic laws of change and transformation.' (*Evolution*, pp.5–6.)

and its conclusion in the death of the body. It is the object of study of biological sciences: embryology, anatomy, physiology, auxology, gerontology.

Since the material evolution of individual beings is an expression of that 'law of progression' to which all created things are subject, it is no wonder that the stages a human embryo goes through while it develops in its mother's womb are very similar to such stages as humanity has collectively traversed during its development on the earth. 'Abdu'l-Bahá says: '. . . the development and growth of man on this earth, until he reached his present perfection, resembles the growth and development of the embryo in the womb of the mother . . . .'[4]

Intellectual evolution

Intellectual evolution is a gradual process characterized by '. . . periods, or stages, each of which is marked by certain conditions peculiar to itself'; '. . . in the human kingdom', says 'Abdu'l-Bahá, 'man reaches maturity when the lights of intelligence have their greatest power and development.'[5]

The age of intellectual maturity is of the greatest importance in the life of a man. It is that age when he begins to make use of his – by that time ready – intellect, so that its assigned functions may be carried out: knowing outer and inner reality and assisting in the process of spiritual fulfilment.

Bahá'u'lláh writes: '. . . *man should know his own self and recognize that which leadeth unto loftiness or lowliness, glory or abasement, wealth or poverty.*' Therefore He recommends the power of understanding to be used first as an instrument through which, on the one hand, the Divine Law and, on the other, individual capacity of responding to that same Law may become known. And He adds immediately after: '*Having attained the stage of fulfilment and reached his maturity, man standeth in need of wealth, and such wealth as he acquireth through the crafts and professions is commendable and praiseworthy in the estimation of men of wisdom . . . .*'[6] Therefore He also recommends the power of understanding to be used not only for purely inner, but also for outer – personal and social – purposes.

Bahá'u'lláh writes moreover: '. . . *keenness of understanding is due to keenness of vision*',[6] while 'Abdu'l-Bahá says: '. . . *a sound mind*

---

4. *Some Answered Questions*, p.183. This concept is reminiscent of the famous statement by E. H. Haeckel: 'Ontogenesis summarizes phylogenesis.' (*Generelle Morphologie der Organismen.*)
5. *Promulgation*, p.438.
6. *Tablets*, p.35.

cannot be but in a sound body',[7] pointing out how closely interrelated are intellectual, spiritual and material developments.

Spiritual evolution

Spiritual evolution is a deliberate and conscious process whereby spiritual qualities bestowed upon human souls in the form of 'individuality'[8] develop and become manifest as spiritual knowledge, words, feelings and actions, characterized by their being conducive to unity in the world. It is that process the Holy Gospels refer to as 'second birth'[9] and the Bahá'í texts as 'spiritual progress',[10] or 'spirituality'.[11]

Spiritual progress is the highest evolution man undergoes; it is the purpose of his creation; the reason why he is called 'fruit'[12] of existence. In fact, material evolution is fulfilled in him and a new order and condition appear, through which the evolutionary process goes further, i.e. the spiritual order and condition.

In the spiritual plane, evolution moves forward indefinitely, because in that plane evolution is the acquiring of the ideal and divine virtues of the world of the Kingdom. Now, since a man will never be able to attain perfection as regards those divine qualities, then it follows that this evolutionary process is infinite and eternal. 'Abdu'l-Bahá says: '. . . the virtues of humanity and the possibilities of human advancement are boundless. There is no end for them, and whatever be the degree to which humanity may attain, there are always degrees beyond . . . There is a consummation for everything except virtues . . .'.[13] Virtues are gifts bestowed by God; if we say that they are limited, we say that God is limited. Moreover, to say that a man could attain perfection in even one of these virtues is tantamount to saying that he could attain God's perfection. This argument is among the rational proofs of the immortality of the soul, as has been previously expounded.

* * *

Though individual human evolution proceeds on three different levels, yet it is a single process. Moreover, these three aspects of human evolution are very similar in character. For example, if we

---

7. 'Tablet to Dr. A. Forel' in *Bahá'í World*, xv, p.38.
8. *Divine Philosophy*, p.127.
9. *John* 3:1–8.
10. *Promulgation*, p.142.
11. *Paris Talks*, p.112.
12. *Divine Philosophy*, p.105.
13. *Promulgation*, p.377.

carefully investigate material and intellectual development, we will see that it is characterized by successive detachments or separations from previous situations, which become obsolete as a consequence of growth. When a newborn baby comes out of its mother's womb, it must detach itself from the placenta, which during the time before its birth has been for it an indispensable means of life. Afterwards it must detach itself from its mother's breast, which after its birth and for a certain time has been its primary source of food. Once the child has become detached from its mother's breast it must, as it grows, detach itself from mother herself, who for a time has been its great protector, so that it may proceed in its mastery of its world. Afterwards, it must detach itself from many other situations, both physical and mental, which are useful at a certain stage of its growth, but which become useless and even dangerous as it attains higher levels of maturity. Bahá'u'lláh writes: *'If ye be seekers after this life and the vanities thereof, ye should have sought them while ye were still enclosed in your mothers' wombs, for at that time ye were continually approaching them, should ye but perceive it. Ye have, on the other hand, ever since ye were born and attained maturity, been all the while receding from the world and drawing closer to dust.'*[14]

As material life is the embryo's goal and the embryo prepares for it during those thirty-eight weeks it passes in its mother's womb, so life in the world of the Kingdom is man's goal while he lives on the earth and he must prepare for it. Those successive detachments typical of the evolutionary processes he undergoes during his earthly life may therefore be viewed as a prelude to the final detachment, the entrance into the Kingdom beyond death; and as metaphors of the spiritual virtue of detachment, i.e. the choice of attraction towards the world of the Kingdom at the expense of the attraction towards the world of creation.

Human education

The concept of men as 'intelligent beings created in the realm of evolutionary growth'[15] or creatures possessed of the capacity of material, intellectual and spiritual growth, is the foundation of Bahá'í pedagogy.

It would be useless to search in the Bahá'í texts for 'a definite and detailed educational system': we could not find it. In fact, '. . . the teachings of Bahá'u'lláh and 'Abdu'l-Bahá . . . simply offer certain basic principles and set forth a number of teaching ideals

---

14. *Gleanings*, p.127.
15. *Promulgation*, p.129.

that should guide future Bahá'í educationalists in their efforts to formulate an adequate teaching curriculum, which would be in full harmony with the spirit of the Bahá'í Teachings, and would thus meet the requirements and needs of the modern age.'[16]

'Abdu'l-Bahá writes: '. . . *education cannot alter the inner essence of a man, but it doth exert tremendous influence, and with this power it can bring forth from the individual whatever perfections and capacities are deposited within him.*'[17] Education is, therefore, intended as that process through which potential individual qualities are gradually brought forth. From this point of view, the entire evolutionary process is an educational process. Bahá'u'lláh writes: '*Consider, for instance, the revelation of the light of the Name of God, the Educator. Behold, how in all things the evidences of such revelation are manifest, how the betterment of all beings dependeth upon it. This education is of two kinds. The one is universal. Its influence pervadeth all things and sustaineth them. It is for this reason that God hath assumed the title, "Lord of all the worlds". The other is confined to them that have come under the shadow of this Name, and sought the shelter of this most mighty Revelation.*'[18]

This evolutionary-educational process, stretching from the atom to Perfect Man, is ultimately the best pedagogical pattern. As that universal process of evolution of the world of existence proceeds along three lines – material, intellectual and spiritual – and consists in the gradual appearance of the qualities of the world of the Kingdom, so human education must proceed simultaneously along the same lines and must aim at assisting individuals to manifest their peculiar potential qualities. Thus 'Abdu'l-Bahá concisely explains, in one of His Tablets, the criteria of such education: '*All humankind are as children in a school, and the Dawning-Points of Light, the Sources of divine revelation, are the teachers, wondrous and without peer. In the school of realities they educate these sons and daughters, according to teachings from God, and foster them in the bosom of grace, so that they may develop along every line, show forth the excellent gifts and blessings of the Lord, and combine human perfections; that they may advance in all aspects of human endeavour, whether outward or inward, hidden or visible, material or spiritual, until they make of this mortal world a wide-spread mirror, to reflect that other world that dieth not.*'[19]

It is the Manifestation of God who bestows upon men whatever they need for their education. Human educators should aim at

---

16. Letter on behalf of Shoghi Effendi, quoted in *Bahá'í Education* (comp.), p.70.
17. *Selections*, p.132.
18. *Gleanings*, pp.189–90.
19. Quoted in *Bahá'í Education* (comp.), p.30.

drawing from His teachings a pedagogical system whereby individuals may be assisted in manifesting in act their God-given material, intellectual and spiritual potentialities.[20]

In the light of these concepts, every human being is viewed as a *'mine rich in gems of inestimable value'*,[21] inimitable, unique, and as such to be considered with the greatest respect from the very beginning of his existence, as soon as the ovum is fertilized. Bahá'u'lláh writes: *'Man is even as steel, the essence of which is hidden: through admonition and explanation, good counsel and education, that essence will be brought to light. If, however, he be allowed to remain in his original condition, the corrosion of lusts and appetites will effectively destroy him.'*[22] And elsewhere: *'Education can, alone, cause it [the mine of human hearts] to reveal its treasures and enable mankind to benefit therefrom.'*[23] No wonder therefore that the principle of universal compulsory education is one of the Bahá'í principles.

Bahá'u'lláh writes: *'Unto every father hath been enjoined the instruction of his sons and daughters in the art of reading and writing and in all that hath been laid down in the Holy Tablet. He that putteth away that which is commanded unto him, the Trustees are then to take from him that which is required for their instruction, if he be wealthy, and if not the matter devolveth upon the House of Justice.'*[24]

Such is the importance attached in the Bahá'í texts to the education of children, that in the Bahá'í view most of the problems afflicting modern society will not be solved until this vital prerequisite is properly met.[25]

Material education. As to material education, Bahá'í texts give a few fundamental principles about hygiene and health which modern medical scholars and students would do well to peruse and develop. In fact, the Bahá'í texts pay the greatest attention to the problem

---

20. This pedagogical concept implies that man is potentially capable of learning and that his educators should merely assist him in making a good use of his own qualities, so that he may find his own solutions and answers to his manifold problems, in the awareness that absolute Truth is far beyond the reach of man. See above pp.8–9. As such, this pedagogical concept is reminiscent of the ancient Socratic maieutic method.
21. *Gleanings*, p.260.
22. Quoted in *Bahá'í Education* (comp.) p.3.
23. *Gleanings*, p.260.
24. *Kitáb-i-Aqdas*, in *Synopsis*, p.15. 'Abdu'l-Bahá says: '. . . universal education is a universal law.' (*Promulgation*, p.300.) He writes moreover: *'If the parents are able to provide the expenses of this education, it is well, otherwise the community must provide the means for the teaching of that child.'* (*Selections*, p.304.)
25. This concept is explained in its manifold aspects by the Universal House of Justice (see above p.20, n.92) in its weighty *The Promise of the World Peace*, addressed 'To the People of the World' in 1985.

of prevention, which is today an object of general interest,[26] and propose many ideas on this topic.

(i) The idea that the body, as the temple of the soul, should be kept away from anything that may cause *'repugnance'*[27] is the foundation of hygiene, to which Bahá'u'lláh attaches the greatest importance.[28] 'Abdu'l-Bahá explains some aspects of cleanliness and purity in one of His most well-known Tablets, where He writes: *'First in a human being's way of life must be purity, then freshness, cleanliness, and independence of spirit.'* Then He adds: *'And although bodily cleanliness is a physical thing, it hath, nevertheless, a powerful influence on the life of the spirit.'*[29] And He explains this concept through a comparison between bodily cleanliness and music which, though it is mere sound, may yet stir deep feelings within human hearts.[30]

(ii) The recommendation of moderation in daily living is another fundamental factor in preserving good health. *'. . . the temperance and moderation of a natural way of life'* enable man to preserve that *'state of equilibrium'* whereby *'whatever is relished will be beneficial to health'*.[31]

(iii) The injunction to abstain from every habit-forming substance

---

26. The idea that medical science should prevent, rather than cure disease, is not new in the history of medicine. Yet general interest began to focus upon it only after the International Conference on Primary Health Care held at Alma Ata on 6–12 September 1978. During that Conference a new definition of health was worded, as 'a condition of complete physical, mental and social well-being', and not merely as 'absence of sickness and disease'; it was stated moreover that 'the promotion and protection of human health is a *conditio sine qua non* for a sustained economical and social progress.'

27. The Báb writes: *'God loveth those who are pure. Naught in the Bayán and in the sight of God is more loved than purity and immaculate cleanliness . . .'* (*Selections*, p.80.) And moreover: *'As this physical frame is the throne of the inner temple, whatever occurs to the former is felt by the latter. In reality that which takes delight in joy or is saddened by pain is the inner temple of the body, not the body itself. Since this physical body is the throne whereon the inner temple is established, God hath ordained that the body be preserved to the extent possible, so that nothing that causeth repugnance may be experienced.'* (ibid. p.95.)

28. Bahá'u'lláh sets forth in the *Kitáb-i-Aqdas*, His great Book of Laws, certain specific commandments concerning hygiene and health. He prescribes to His followers *'to be the essence of cleanliness'*. (*Synopsis*, p.51.) Moreover He sets forth laws concerning personal and environmental hygiene and the treatment of sickness and disease. Other counsels on this topic are given in many other of His Writings.

29. This Tablet by 'Abdu'l-Bahá is known among the Bahá'ís as the *Tablet of Purity*. See *Selections*, pp.146–50.

30. 'Abdu'l-Bahá writes: *'It is even as a voice wondrously sweet, or a melody played: although sounds are but vibrations in the air which affect the ear's auditory nerve, and these vibrations are but chance phenomena carried along through the air, even so, see how they move the heart. A wondrous melody is wings for the spirit, and maketh the soul to tremble for joy. The purport is that physical cleanliness doth also exert its effect upon the human soul.'* (*Selections*, p.147.)

31. *Selections*, pp.153, 155.

(not only drugs, but also alcohol[32]) as well as the exhortation to abstain from smoking[33] are other important factors of material education.

(iv) The recommendation of the pursuit of spiritual growth is another factor of physical health. Spiritual growth enables man to guide his emotions — and among these also sexual emotions — instead of repressing them or yielding to them, and is thus conducive to a feeling of spiritual joy, which is an important factor of physical health.[34]

(v) The injunction of bearing fruits in life through useful work contributes to that feeling of personal fulfilment which is indispensable for a healthy life. Bahá'u'lláh writes: '. . . *when occupied with work one is less likely to dwell on the unpleasant aspects of life.*'[35]

In the Bahá'í texts, human work is released from the divine curse mentioned in the Book of Genesis: 'cursed is the ground for thy sake; in sorrow shalt thou eat of it all the days of thy life; . . . in

---

32. The Bahá'í laws strictly forbid the consumption of habit-making drugs and inebriating drinks: 'As to opium, it is foul and accursed . . . For opium fasteneth on the soul, so that the user's conscience dieth, his mind is blotted away, his perceptions are eroded. It turneth the living into the dead. It quencheth the natural heat. No greater harm can be conceived than that which opium inflicteth.' (*Selections*, pp.144–5.) He writes moreover: '. . .This wicked hashish extinguisheth the mind, freezeth the spirit, petrifieth the soul, wasteth the body and leaveth man frustrated and lost.' ('Abdu'l-Bahá, quoted in a letter addressed by the Universal House of Justice to the National Spiritual Assembly of the Bahá'ís of the United States, 6 October 1967.) As to alcohol, Bahá'u'lláh writes in His *Kitáb-i-Aqdas*: 'It is forbidden for an intelligent person to drink that which depriveth him of his intelligence; it behoveth him to engage in that which is worthy of man, not in the act of every heedless doubter.'

33. The Bahá'í texts do not explicitly forbid smoking, but they discourage it. In this regard, 'Abdu'l-Bahá writes: '[smoking] *is dirty, smelly, offensive – an evil habit, and one the harmfulness of which gradually becometh apparent to all. Every qualified physician hath ruled – and this hath also been proven by tests – that one of the components of tobacco is a deadly poison, and that the smoker is vulnerable to many and various diseases. This is why smoking hath been plainly set forth as repugnant from the standpoint of hygiene . . . smoking is deprecated, abhorrent, filthy in the extreme, and, albeit by degrees, highly injurious to health. It is also a waste of money and time, and maketh the user a prey to a noxious addiction . . . this habit is therefore censured by both reason and experience, and renouncing it will bring relief and peace of mind to all men. Furthermore, this will make it possible to have a fresh mouth and unstained fingers, and hair that is free of a foul and repellent smell. On receipt of this missive, the friends will surely, by whatever means and even over a period of time, forsake this pernicious habit. Such is my hope.*' (*Selections*, pp.147–8.)

34. 'Abdu'l-Bahá says: 'Joy gives us wings! In times of joy our strength is more vital, our intellect keener, and our understanding less clouded. We seem better able to cope with the world and to find our sphere of usefulness. But when sadness visits us we become weak, our strength leaves us, our comprehension is dim, and our intelligence veiled. The actualities of life seem to elude our grasp, the eyes of our spirits fail to discover the sacred mysteries, and we become even as dead beings.' (*Paris Talks*, pp. 109–10.)
Many passages in the Bahá'í texts set forth similar concepts: joy promotes good health, sadness and grief are harmful. Spiritual progress is conducive to true joy (*see above*, pp.161–2) as well as to physical health.

35. *Tablets*, p.175.

the sweat of thy face shalt thou eat bread'.³⁶ Bahá'u'lláh writes: *'We have graciously exalted your engagement in such work to the rank of worship unto God, the True One . . . When anyone occupieth himself in a craft or trade, such occupation itself is regarded in the estimation of God as an act of worship; and this is naught but a token of His infinite and all-pervasive bounty.'*³⁷

(vi) Collective commitment to the task of creating and preserving a healthy and balanced civilization in the world will contribute to such a social environment as will favour the healthy development of human beings.³⁸ Moreover, love of God and the vision of the world as a garden to cultivate and beautify, imply an effort to protect and improve the natural environment, which will undoubtedly be to the advantage of the physical health of mankind.³⁹

(viii) The recommendation that girls should study *'whatever will nurture the health of the body and its physical soundness, and how to guard their children from disease'*⁴⁰ contributes to the promotion of the awareness of the necessity of preventive medicine and to the acquisition of the ability to practise it.

Intellectual education. In the Bahá'í texts intellectual education is viewed as a fundamental and inescapable aspect of human life. Parents – or in their absence or incapacity, society itself – have the sacred duty of assuring that each human being not only knows how to read and write, but also how to carry out useful work.⁴¹ Thus

36. *Genesis* 3:17–9.
37. *Tablets*, p.26.
38. The Universal House of Justice in its *Promise of World Peace* points out the main practical goals to achieve so that '. . . a social system at once progressive and peaceful, dynamic and harmonious, a system giving free play to individual creativity and initiative but based on cooperation and reciprocity' (p.3) may be created, a system that is, however, considered as utopian by most contemporary thinkers in their rather pessimistic view of mankind.
39. For a discussion of the Bahá'í concepts about nature and the environment, see *The Bahá'í Statement on Nature and Environment* issued by the Office of Public Information of the Bahá'í International Community in October 1987 when the Bahá'ís joined the Network on Conservation and Religion of the World Wide Fund for Nature (WWF). See also A. L. Dahl, *Perspective on Nature and the Environment*.
40. *Selections*, p.124. For a discussion of the Bahá'í teachings about health and healing *see Health and Healing: Some Aspects. A Compilation*; H. B. Danesh, 'Health and Healing', in *World Order*, XIII, no.3, p.15; E. Zohoori (comp.) *The Throne of the Inner Temple*.
41. 'Abdu'l-Bahá writes: *'In this new and wondrous Cause, the advancement of all branches of knowledge is a fixed and vital principle, and the friends, one and all, are obliged to make every effort toward this end, so that . . . every child, according to his need, will receive his share of the sciences and arts – until not even a single peasant's child will be found who is completely devoid of schooling.'* (quoted in *Bahá'í Education* (comp.), p.39.) He says moreover: *'In addition to this widespread education each child must be taught a profession, art or trade, so that every member of the community will be enabled to earn his own livelihood.'* (*Divine Philosophy*, p.79.)

every individual will be independent and his special potentialities will not be lost to society. Moreover, individuals are enabled through intellectual education to avail themselves of all those bounties, whether natural products or fruits of human ingeniousness, which God has bestowed upon the world of creation for the benefit of mankind.

According to the Bahá'í texts, intellectual education should inculcate certain fundamental concepts of vital importance for the creation of a true international culture:
(i) free and unfettered search after truth;
(ii) freedom from every kind of prejudice, be it racial, religious, national, social, cultural or any other kind;
(iii) the oneness of mankind;
(iv) the oneness of religion;
(v) harmony between science and religion, reason and faith, so that superstition and materialism, both conducive to prejudice and conflict, may disappear from the world;
(vi) an auxiliary international language, so that communication may be greatly improved, even among people of very distant countries.

Spiritual education. By spiritual education is meant that kind of education which, on the one hand, enables man to understand his own spiritual nature and to learn the dynamics of its development so that once maturity has been attained he may automatically foster his own spiritual growth, and, on the other hand, which trains him from his early childhood so that he may manifest in his life the qualities of the world of the Kingdom and not the traits of the world of creation.

Spiritual education should begin early if this twofold purpose is to be achieved. It is recommended that spiritual laws be taught in early childhood,[42] that at the same time feelings conducive to the desire to observe these laws be inspired in the hearts of children,[43]

---

42. As to the necessity of giving children an early spiritual education, 'Abdu'l-Bahá writes: '*A child is as a young plant: it will grow in whatever way you train it. If you rear it to be truthful, and kind, and righteous, it will grow straight, it will be fresh and tender, and will flourish. But if not, then from the faulty training it will grow bent, and stay awry, and there will be no hope of changing it.*' (quoted in *Bahá'í Education* (comp.), p.47.) He writes moreover: '*It is extremely difficult to teach the individual and refine his character once puberty is passed. By then, as experience has shown, even if every effort be exerted to modify some tendency of his, it all availeth nothing . . . Therefore it is in early childhood that a firm foundation must be laid. While the branch is green and tender, it can easily be made straight.*' (ibid. p.24.)

43. 'Abdu'l-Bahá writes: '*The individual must be educated to such a high degree that he would rather have his throat cut than tell a lie, and would think it easier to be slashed with a sword or pierced with a spear than to utter calumny or be carried away by wrath.*' (quoted in *Bahá'í Education*, p.24.)

and that the habit of such attitudes be inculcated in them. Two inner attitudes seem of vital importance in the attainment of these goals: 'love of reality'[44] and love of God. Through the former man is spurred towards that knowledge of reality that enables him to escape from the self-deception of blind imitation. Through the latter, not only does he accept the sacrifice required in the path of spiritual progress, but as well he attains to a joy born of the inner experience of the qualities of the world of the Kingdom, a joy by which he is motivated in his actions. Thus man makes progress in all the three fundamental aspects of his reality: knowledge, love and will. The secret of his equilibrium and serenity lies in such harmonious growth.

When a child is given material, intellectual and spiritual education in the light of the teachings of the Manifestation of God, he will be assisted to fulfil the purpose of his creation, within the limits of his personal endowments and particular circumstances. This is one of the most important aspects of such a unitary, balanced and harmonious concept of human life as emerges from the Bahá'í texts. This education is also the most important means through which the long-cherished ideal of the oneness of mankind will be realized. In other words, this education both proposes the goal of unity, and also assists every individual in acquiring the instruments (qualities and capacities) required to attain it and the eagerness to do so. Finally, it improves individual behaviour and thus creates an optimal social environment within which any individual potentiality may become manifest.[45]

The evolution of mankind

'Abdu'l-Bahá says: 'the body politic may be likened to the human organism.' And moreover: 'the world of humanity may be likened to the individual man himself.'[46] This analogy between the individual and the collectivity extends to the development of humanity. As individual human beings grow to maturity from zygotes or fertilized human ova, traversing successive stages of development in the three aspects − physical, intellectual and spiritual − of their reality, so mankind itself evolves through successive stages of development in its physical, intellectual and spiritual nature.[47]

44. *Promulgation*, p.49.
45. For a concise discussion of this topic *see* J. Savi, *The Child and Spiritual Life in the Family: A Bahá'í Perspective*.
46. *Promulgation*, pp.98, 202.
47. In this regard 'Abdu'l-Bahá writes: *'The suckling babe passes through various physical stages, growing and developing at every stage, until his body reacheth the age of maturity. Having*

Material evolution

If we study the evolution of life on the earth, we will recognize a thread through which we could go back in time and discover the ancestors of mankind, material entities quite different in their material attributes from present human beings. However, each of these ancestors was a potential human being, because present human beings derive (albeit after a very long time) from them, and not from other creatures, however similar they may be. Therefore 'Abdu'l-Bahá says: 'When we were in the mineral kingdom, although we were endowed with certain gifts and powers, they were not to be compared with the blessings of the human kingdom.' Those ancient stages are stages of immaturity and preparation. He says: 'In the world of existence man has traversed successive degrees until he has attained the human kingdom. In each degree of his progression he has developed capacity for advancement to the next station and condition. While in the kingdom of the mineral, he was attaining the capacity for promotion into the degrees of the vegetable. In the kingdom of the vegetable he underwent preparation for the world of the animal, and from thence he has come onward to the human degree, or kingdom. Throughout this journey of progression he has ever and always been potentially man.'[48]

Thus 'Abdu'l-Bahá explains that man has always been in existence, as regards his spiritual reality. His evolution was and is a continuous, although not uniform, process through which his potentialities have been gradually becoming manifest and continue to do so. And yet he was not always in existence, as regards his physical reality, in the shape we see today: in this respect he has undergone successive transformations. However, since his physical reality is temporary, whereas his spiritual reality is lasting, the latter is undoubtedly of much greater importance than the former. Therefore we could say that man, as regards his more important spiritual reality, has always been in existence, independently of all

---

arrived at this stage it acquireth the capacity to manifest spiritual and intellectual perfections. The lights of comprehension, intelligence and knowledge become perceptible in it and the powers of its soul unfold. Similarly, in the contingent world, the human species hath undergone progressive physical changes and, by a slow process, hath scaled the ladder of civilization, realizing in itself the wonders, excellencies and gifts of humanity in their most glorious form, until it gained the capacity to express the splendours of spiritual perfections and divine ideals and became capable of hearkening to the call of God. Then at last the call of the Kingdom was raised, the spiritual virtues and perfections were revealed, the Sun of Reality dawned, and the teachings of the Most Great Peace, of the oneness of the world of humanity and of the universality of men were promoted.' (*Selections*, pp.285–6.) In these words most of the concepts which will be explained in the following pages are beautifully summarized.

48. *Promulgation*, pp.90, 225.

those changes his physical body has undergone throughout the ages on the earth. This is a confutation of the theory whereby man is a descendant of the animals and belongs to the animal kingdom. Though 'Abdu'l-Bahá pursues this confutation through persuasive arguments, yet He does not deny that in past ages the human body was quite different from what it is today. The most important arguments of 'Abdu'l-Bahá's refutation are summarized here:[49]
(i) The universe is and ever has been free from imperfection;
man is the apex of the world of creation;
if man was not always in existence in the world, then
there was a time when the world of creation was imperfect;
therefore man has always been in existence.[50]

The same argument is set forth also in other words: if the purpose of the universe is that the divine perfections may appear in the world, and if these divine perfections have their highest expression in the universe through man, then it is impossible for man not to have always been in existence, for in that case creation would have been imperfect, and God himself would be imperfect. Man is here intended – says 'Abdu'l-Bahá – as the Perfect Man, the Manifestation of God.[51]

(ii) Every creature owes its own perfections to five factors regarding its component elements: their quality, their proportionate quantities, their mutual balance, the mode and method of their combination, their mutual influence. To all this the influence and action of different beings should be added. Whenever the same conditions are realized, the ensuing creature is the same. Therefore, man was always man. '. . . [W]hen these existing elements', says 'Abdu'l-Bahá, 'are gathered together according to the natural order, and with perfect strength, they become a magnet for the spirit; and the spirit will become manifest in them with all its perfections.' Thus, according to the different characteristics of these five factors, from

---

49. See *Promulgation*, pp.225–6, 355–61; *Some Answered Questions*, pp.176–199. Thus Shoghi Effendi wrote through his secretary on this important topic: 'We cannot prove man was always man for this is a fundamental doctrine, but it is based on the assertion that nothing can exceed its own potentialities, that everything, a stone, a tree, an animal and a human being existed in plan, potentially, from the very "beginning" of creation. We don't believe man has always had the form of man, but rather that from the outset he was going to evolve into the human form and species and not be a haphazard branch of the ape family.

'You see our whole approach to each matter is based on the belief that God sends us divinely inspired Educators; what they tell us is fundamentally true, what science tells us today is true, tomorrow may be entirely changed to better explain a new set of facts.' (quoted in *Arohanui*, p.85).

50. See *Some Answered Questions*, pp.177–8.
51. See ibid. pp.195–7.

the combination of the elements a mineral, a vegetable, an animal or a human being will respectively come into existence.[52]

(iii) 'Abdu'l-Bahá says that undoubtedly: '. . . man at a time was an inmate of the sea, at another period an invertebrate, then a vertebrate and finally a human being standing erect'. Therefore, when we see vestiges of disappeared organs in him, this means only that his previous shape was different from his present one and that his outward appearance has changed. But just as a human embryo is a human being from the very beginning, though it is quite different in its aspect from an adult human being, so also primitive man was a man from the beginning.[53]

(iv) Human discoveries and inventions cannot be the outcome of faculties shared by men and animals. In fact, animals are very often possessed of superior physical capacities in comparison with man. Therefore, '. . . if there were not in man a power different from any of those of the animals, the latter would be superior to man in inventions and the comprehension of realities.' From this argument it becomes clear that man is endowed with something which makes him totally different from animals.[54]

(v) Animals appeared on the earth before man because their constitution is simpler. Therefore a shorter lapse of time was required for them to be framed in the laboratory of nature. It is only a temporal priority. Men and animals are like the fruits of the same tree; they attain maturity at different times, but more recent men do not come from more ancient animals.[55]

(vi) Certain traces of organs in the human body are considered as a proof of its animal descent. However those vestiges could be organs whose function is as yet unknown, just as with many other things in the universe.[56] Moreover, we know with certainty that human organs have undergone great changes in the course of evolution.[57]

In conclusion: modern scientists consider man in his physical nature, and uphold that in ancient ages he was an animal. There is a semblance of truth in their assumption, provided man be viewed only in his physical aspects. But if we say that men are 'intelligent beings created in the realm of evolutionary growth'[58] and if we remember that 'in the beginning of his [man's] formation

---

52. ibid. p.201. *See* ibid, pp.178–9.
53. *Promulgation*, p.359. *See* ibid. pp.358–9; *Some Answered Questions*, pp.182–4.
54. ibid. p.187. *See Promulgation*, pp.359–60; *Some Answered Questions*, pp.187–8.
55. *See Some Answered Questions*, p.192.
56. *See* ibid.
57. *See* ibid. p.184.
58. *Promulgation*, p.129.

the mind and spirit also existed, but they were hidden; later they were manifested',[59] a conclusion may be arrived at agreeing both with scientific theories and the explanations given by 'Abdu'l-Bahá. Man has undergone material, intellectual and spiritual evolution; in the course of his evolution his shape and behaviour have changed; but potentially he was always a man, even when his typical human quality — the power of understanding — was as yet undeveloped. As in the zygote the adult man is potentially existent, so '. . . in the protoplasm, man is man', says 'Abdu'l-Bahá; even in the 'mineral' man already exists.[60]

Intellectual evolution

According to recent paleontological discoveries, the first expressions of human intellect are the primitive lithic industries (choppers and chopping tools) dating back three million years. Australopithecus may have been responsible for that important step. They appeared about five million years ago and disappeared after four million years, and are considered hominids and not human beings.

Man used his mind first — as may be easily understood — for exploring and knowing material reality; food, shelter, protection against natural phenomena, ways of living in common with his fellow-beings, were his earliest cares.

The earliest signs from which we may infer that man had begun to investigate spiritual reality are much more recent: they could be the earliest remnants of the cult of the dead, which started sporadically about 75,000 years ago, and became a usual practice 35,000 years later. But when and how the concept of a spiritual and transcendent reality was first conceived by a human being is likely to remain a hidden secret.

In the light of what has been said about man in previous chapters, man could be described as a creature which knows how to produce tools (because he knows, and knows how to modify, material reality) and leaves behind traces of cult (because he is, albeit dimly, aware of spiritual reality and modifies his own behaviour in consequence). After all, it is a question of definition: are human zygotes men or not? And what are embryos and foetuses? And newborn babies, children, adolescents? Is man only an adult human being at the age of his full psycho-physical maturity? Then what shall we say of a spiritually immature man? Is that a man? Undoubtedly, the Manifestation of God alone is a Perfect Man,

---

59. *Some Answered Questions*, p.184.
60. *Promulgation*, pp.359, 225. *See* ibid. p.225.

since He manifests the whole perfection of the Self of God, i.e. the image of God he has in Himself. Yet whoever has been potentially endowed with this image is also man, no matter how much of that potentiality has become actuality within him. As the zygote is man from the very beginning, because a man and not, for instance, a chimpanzee will issue forth from it, so also man is 'the protoplasm' and the 'mineral' from which a man, as we see him today, will be born in the course of long ages.

'Abdu'l-Bahá says: 'The important factor in human improvement is the mind . . . otherwise, no result will be attained from betterment of the mere physical structure.'[61] This idea is shared by most modern paleontologists when they say that culture, an outcome of human intellect, is the reason for man's supremacy over other living creatures. F. Facchini says: 'Evolutionary history teaches that man's success on the earth is mostly due to his culture . . .'[62]

Up to now intellectual development has not been homogeneous in the different parts of the world. There was a time when different species of hominids and men coexisted on the earth: Australopithecus and Homo habilis, Homo habilis and Homo erectus, Homo erectus and Homo sapiens. Even today we see in the world men of many different levels of intellectual development: men of cybernetics and computer science live on the same planet as so-called primitive people: Australian Arandas, African Pygmies, Guyanan Wai-wais, Burnei Keniahs, whose intellectual development is of a different level.

One of the most typical and promising traits of our present age is the concrete and real possibility that such differences may disappear. Technological tools are available, the cultural drive is present everywhere in the world. Many knowledgeable, assenting and enlightened human beings are striving towards such a goal. Though it is mostly viewed as difficult and remote, yet groups of people all over the world – among them the Bahá'ís – already see how this long-cherished hope may be realized, and propose and promote actions so that it may come about.[63]

That the human mind has been used only from recent times is undoubtedly an encouraging fact. Human history and pre-history,

---

61. ibid. p.278.
62. F. Facchini, *Il Cammino dell'Evoluzione Umana*, p.229.
63. The Universal House of Justice states in its *Promise of World Peace* that the existence of the Bahá'í community is 'another evidence that humanity can live as one global society, equal to whatever challenges its coming of age may entail', and presents it as a 'model for study' to all those who are interested in the solutions the Bahá'í community is advancing and practising. (p.24.)

during which we know that mind has been used, is in fact very short — a few thousand years — in comparison to the millions of years of human evolution. Therefore it is to be hoped that intellectual evolution will produce great results in human individual and social behaviour. At present, modern society is founded upon the struggle for existence with the sometimes metaphorical but all-too-often, alas, literal survival of the fittest. Human society thus still resembles an animal society, and is quite remote from a true human society, which should be founded upon such cooperation as intellect demonstrates and humanity requires.

The intellectual development of humanity is conducive to the flourishing of that aspect of civilization 'Abdu'l-Bahá calls material. In fact, as man develops in his intellect, he investigates material reality. Material science is produced, and that is conducive to 'material progress' and 'material civilization'.[64] This aspect of civilization 'ensures the happiness of the human world', says 'Abdu'l-Bahá; however 'alone [it] will not satisfy' because 'its benefits are limited to the world of matter', whereas man is not a mere material being, but primarily a spiritual being. 'Abdu'l-Bahá says moreover: '. . . although material advancement furthers good purposes in life, at the same time it serves evil ends' and 'in material civilization good and evil advance together and maintain the same pace'. Material civilization can both build 'schools and colleges, hospitals, philanthropic institutions, scientific academies and temples of philosophy' and also produce 'means and weapons for human destruction'.

The divine or spiritual civilization deriving from spiritual progress is the indispensable prerequisite of a happy human life. 'Abdu'l-Bahá says: 'For man two wings are necessary. One wing is physical power and material civilization; the other is spiritual power and divine civilization. With one wing only, flight is impossible. Two wings are essential.' He says moreover: 'material civilization is like unto the lamp, while spiritual civilization is the light in that lamp . . . material civilization is like unto a beautiful body, and spiritual civilization is like unto the spirit of life.'[65] According to the Bahá'í texts, mankind is today well advanced in

---

64. *Promulgation*, pp.142, 101. 'Abdu'l-Bahá says: 'Progress is of two kinds: material and spiritual. The former is attained through observation of the surrounding existence and constitutes the foundation of civilization. Spiritual progress is through the breaths of the Holy Spirit and is the awakening of the conscious soul of man to perceive the reality of Divinity. Spiritual progress ensures the happiness and eternal continuance of the soul. The Prophets of God have founded the laws of divine civilization.' (ibid. p.142.)

65. *Promulgation*, pp.142, 101, 109, 12, 11.

the field of material civilization, and the flourishing of a divine civilization which will enlighten the whole world is at hand.

Spiritual evolution

Spiritual evolution becomes manifest in human history as an increasing capacity of man to manifest his divine qualities through his knowledge, actions, feelings and words. 'Abdu'l-Bahá says: '... that the splendour of the Sun of Reality may be revealed fully in human hearts as in a mirror ... This is the true evolution and progress of humanity.'[66]

'The chain of successive Revelations'[67] has been guiding (and continues to guide) man towards an ever deeper understanding of spiritual reality and a more and more perfect moral capacity. From the concept of the existence of God and the awareness of good and evil taught by Adam, to the concept of the 'unity of God'[68] taught by Abraham, who – in 'Abdu'l-Bahá's words – was *'the Founder of Monotheism'*;[69] from the concept of the due observance of the 'law of God' which Moses 'founded' to 'the attainment of supreme human virtues through love'[70] suggested by Christ, to the union of a people and the founding of a nation upon the divine law[71] taught by Muhammad, man, guided by these 'agents of one civilizing process'[72] has passed through various phases in his knowledge of spiritual reality and in his manifesting of it through his actions and undertakings. We are just now emerging from a vision of spiritual reality which could be described as mythological – 'we see through a glass, darkly'[73] said St Paul – and after a quite defective expression of spiritual truth, we now stand on the threshold of an era when – as Christ said to His disciples – the Holy Spirit is leading mankind 'into all truth'.[74] This Gospel statement is certainly difficult to understand. However, it would appear that a man who has attained his physical maturity and who has learnt how to avail himself of his mind will face the issue of spirituality in a totally new way when compared with the past.

66. ibid. p.59.
67. Bahá'u'lláh, *Gleanings*, p.74.
68. 'Abdu'l-Bahá, *Some Answered Questions*, p.13.
69. *Selections*, p.55.
70. *Promulgation*, pp.406, 5.
71. See *Some Answered Questions*, pp.18–24; *Promulgation*, pp.117, 128, 346–7, 367–8, 401.
72. The Universal House of Justice, *Promise*, p.7.
73. I *Cor*. 13:12. For an explanation of this verse by St Paul, *see Promulgation*, pp.11–3.
74. *John* 16:13.

Therefore, 'Abdu'l-Bahá joyously announces: 'Development and progression imply gradual stages or degrees . . . Now is the beginning of the manifestation of spiritual power'; [now the world of humanity] is approaching maturity';[75] and moreover: '. . . *The Manifestation of the Most Great Name* [Bahá'u'lláh] . . . *was an expression of the coming of age, the maturing of man's inmost reality in the world of being.*'[76] Human mind has been prepared and trained throughout the ages; today at last it is ready to attain a deeper knowledge of the mysteries of transcendency and the spiritual laws of the universe. Therefore, man is at long last ready to take into his hands the reins of his own spiritual development, by conforming himself to those means and methods which have been previously mentioned. 'It is like the birth from the animal kingdom into the kingdom of man', says 'Abdu'l-Bahá. These words remind us of the stupendous revolutions through which man gradually emerged from an animal way of living and became the creature he is today: upright position, speech, the discovery of fire, the production of the earliest tools, agriculture, the earliest societies, etc. No wonder that the Bahá'í texts foresee, beyond the immediate dark horizons, a luminous future for mankind on the earth. 'This time of the world', says 'Abdu'l-Bahá, 'may be likened to the equinoctial in the annual cycle . . . this is the spring season of God.' Therefore, the incoming age will be such as mankind 'will realize an immeasurable progress upward', and 'spiritual effulgences will overcome the physical, so that divine susceptibilities will overpower material intelligence . . . .'.[77]

The spiritual development of mankind is conducive to the development of divine civilization, whose real founders are the Prophets. 'Abdu'l-Bahá says: 'Their mission is the education and advancement of the world of humanity. They are the real Teachers and Educators, the universal Instructors of mankind'. 'Mankind receives the bounties of material civilization as well as divine civilization from the heavenly Prophets. The capacity for achieving extraordinary and praiseworthy progress is bestowed by Them through the breaths of the Holy Spirit, and heavenly civilization is not possible of attainment or accomplishment otherwise.'[78] This capacity of educating mankind is the foremost proof through which the Manifestations of God may be distinguished from the great heroes of history. Historians will therefore have to re-read the

---

75. *Promulgation*, pp.131, 38.
76. *Selections*, p.56.
77. *Promulgation*, pp.305, 38, 131.
78. *Promulgation*, pp.364, 375.

annals of the peoples of the world in the light of this important concept. It will thus become manifest that there is no civilization which is not founded upon a Divine Revelation. Up to now the Manifestations of God exerted their influence upon a single people or small groups of peoples. That is why so many civilizations and cultures exist in the world. Today, thanks to the preliminary work done by the ancient 'preliminary Manifestations',[79] mankind has attained its maturity, so that a global teaching may be understood, and a world civilization may be established. This will certainly not signal the end of the spiritual evolution of mankind. This evolution will continue throughout the ages, propelled by the teachings of many other future Manifestations.[80]

In the course of history, material and spiritual civilization advanced at the same rate and not one after the other, or the one in opposition to the other. Each civilization manifested in different degree one or the other aspect, depending upon the circumstances and the intellectual and spiritual maturity attained within its sphere of influence. Today, our civilization is characterized by a great material and intellectual development and a quite poor spiritual development. A dangerous disharmony has resulted and the whole world is affected by its consequences. This disharmony will be corrected only when mankind makes sufficient progress in its spiritual nature also.

The future civilization – whose model, methods and ways are clearly set forth in the Bahá'í texts – will be the civilization of a mature mankind. Its progress will therefore be infinite. 'Abdu'l-Bahá says: 'There is no limitation to the spirit of man, for spirit in itself is progressive, and if the divine civilization be established, the spirit of man will advance. Every developed susceptibility will increase the effectiveness of man. Discoveries of the real will become more and more possible, and the influence of divine guidance will be increasingly recognized. All this is conducive to the divine form of civilization.'[81]

---

79. Shoghi Effendi, *World Order of Bahá'u'lláh*, p.166. For a preliminary study of this topic, *see* G. Townshend, *Christ and Bahá'u'lláh*.

80. In this regard Shoghi Effendi wrote: 'It should also be borne in mind that, great as is the power manifested by this Revelation and however vast the range of the Dispensation its Author has inaugurated, it emphatically repudiates the claim to be regarded as the final revelation of God's will and purpose for mankind. To hold such a conception of its character and functions would be tantamount to a betrayal of its cause and denial of its truth. It must necessarily conflict with the fundamental principle which constitutes the bedrock of Bahá'í belief, the principle that religious truth is not absolute, but relative, that Divine Revelation is orderly, continuous and progressive and not spasmodic or final.' (*The World Order of Bahá'u'lláh*, p.115.)

81. *Promulgation*, p.101.

Human Evolution

Contemporaneousness of material, intellectual and spiritual evolutionary processes

Though the evolutionary processes of mankind develop along three different lines, material, intellectual and spiritual, yet they are a single process, whose stages coincide to a certain extent. Simpler capacities appear earlier: more complex capacities appear at a more advanced stage of development. Therefore material evolution begins earlier. A special bodily structure is formed. This structure is conducive to certain material behaviours, and these in their turn are conducive to the expression of certain intellectual and spiritual qualities. Going back to the origin of man – seven to eight million years ago, according to paleontologists – the upright position released forelimbs from locomotion and left them at man's disposal so that he could use them for the manipulation of objects. These activities in their turn were the cause of the quantitative and qualitative development of encephalic structures, which thus became fit for an early expression of the mental faculties of the soul. It was about three million years ago that man began to produce handmade products. Through that activity, mental faculties developed. Mind was then trained: first, it knew material reality: then – undoubtedly directed by ancient Manifestations of God whose traces have been lost due to *'their extreme remoteness, as well as to the vast changes which the earth hath undergone since their time'*[82] – it became aware and began to study spiritual reality too. As mind continues to develop man is acquiring a wider and deeper inner perception of reality, and thus he is raising his aims toward transcendent goals of love and unity, order and peace.

Discontinuity of evolutionary process

Since the revelations of the Manifestations of God are the mainspring of human development, human progress has not been uniform, but discontinuous. On a diagram we should represent it not as an ascending and continuous line, but an ascending and broken one. In fact, in the course of human history periods characterized by great upheavals and innovations have been

---

82. *Gleanings*, p.172. Explaining the statement by Bahá'u'lláh that 'the universe hath neither beginning nor ending', 'Abdu'l-Bahá says: 'Briefly, there were many universal cycles preceding this one in which we are living. They were consummated, completed and their traces obliterated. The divine and creative purpose in them was the evolution of spiritual man, just as it is in this cycle. The circle of existence is the same circle; it returns. The tree of life has ever borne the same heavenly fruit.' (*Promulgation*, pp.220.)

followed by periods of fruition, and afterwards by periods of stagnation and even regression. 'Abdu'l-Bahá likens this evolutionary process to the succession of seasons in the course of the solar year: springtime is characterized by an outburst of life; in summer and autumn trees and plants grow and yield their fruits; in winter there is an apparent decay and stagnation of every form of life (trees shed their leaves, certain animals go into hibernation, once-flourishing vegetation withers and apparently dies). Modern scientists agree with this important concept as regards both biological and historical evolutionary process. As to biological evolution, F. Facchini writes: 'The concept of evolution implies that transformations are somehow gradual. However, today phases of acceleration and of slackening are generally accepted.'[83] As to historical evolution, E. Laszlo describes a 'discontinuous, non-linear mode of historical development.'[84]

Social evolution

The material, intellectual and spiritual development of mankind has always had important expressions within society. As man advances in his progress, he achieves a better understanding of the importance of socialization. 'Abdu'l-Bahá says: 'Some of the creatures of existence can live solitary and alone. A tree, for instance, may live without the assistance and cooperation of other trees. Some animals are isolated and lead a separate existence away from their kind. But this is impossible for man. In his life and being, cooperation and association are essential. Through association and meeting we find happiness and development, individual and collective.'[85]

Social development is a gradual process, as is any other kind of development. 'Abdu'l-Bahá says: '. . . there are periods and stages in the life of the aggregate world of humanity.' Since 'the body politic may be likened to the human organism', various stages may be distinguished in social evolution. 'Abdu'l-Bahá says: 'The world of humanity has, heretofore, been in the stage of infancy: now it is approaching maturity.' The characteristics of the various ages mankind has gone through during its social evolution reflect the grades of maturity of mankind. This maturity expresses itself in 'the collective expressions of unity' mankind is capable of attaining. In fact, as 'cooperation and association are essential'[86] for man, so

83. F. Facchini, *Il Cammino dell'Evoluzione Umana*, p.16.
84. E. Laszlo, *Evolution*, p.101.
85. *Promulgation*, p.35.
86. ibid. pp.86, 438, 98, 37–8, 190, 35.

his capacity of forming widening groups, including increasing numbers of increasingly different human beings, is the sign of his progressive social growth.[87] This concept is shared by some contemporary scholars. F. Facchini says: 'Evolutionary history shows that man's success is mainly due to his culture, through an increasing tension of communication and by virtue of widening unities whose importance should be stressed. Undoubtedly the onward march of mankind has been beset with competition and struggles, that may have been conducive to important turning-points.'[88]

'Abdu'l-Bahá writes: *'Every imperfect soul is self-centred and thinketh only of his own good. But as his thoughts expand a little he will begin to think of the welfare and comfort of his family. If his ideas still more widen, his concern will be the felicity of his fellow citizens: and if they still widen he will be thinking of the glory of his land and of his race. But when ideas and views reach the utmost degree of expansion and attain the stage of perfection, then will he be interested in the exaltation of humankind. He will then be the well-wisher of all men and the seeker of the weal and prosperity of all lands. This is indicative of perfection.'*[89]

Shoghi Effendi explains that human evolution '. . . has had its earliest beginnings in the birth of family life, its subsequent development in the achievement of tribal solidarity, leading in turn to the constitution of the city-state, and expanding later into the institution of independent and sovereign nations'.[90] But as 'now is the beginning of the manifestation of spiritual power', and mankind 'is approaching maturity',[91] so the highest possible level of co-operation and unity in the world – the unity of mankind – can be at last attained. This concept is not new: some consider it to be merely utopian, but its advent is predicted and its realization is promoted by the most enlightened minds. And it may well be foreseen that just as 'the spirit of a rising nationalism among the peoples liberated from the Napoleonic yoke', strongly opposed to as it was by 'the members of the Holy Alliance',[92] succeeded in conquering the whole of Europe, so likewise today, 'the process of nation building'[93] being completed, the concept of the unity of the

---

87. This is the expression of the gradual growth of the power of love, typical of man. For a deeper discussion of this concept, see H. B. Danesh, 'The Violence-Free Society: A Gift for Our Children', in *Bahá'í Studies*, VI, pp.20–21, 33–7.
88. F. Facchini, *Il Cammino dell'Evoluzione Umana*, p.229.
89. *Selections*, p.69.
90. *World Order of Bahá'u'lláh*, p.43.
91. *Promulgation*, pp.131, 37–8.
92. See *World Order of Bahá'u'lláh*, pp.44–5.
93. The Universal House of Justice, *Promise*, p.3.

nations, although strongly opposed by unrestrained nationalistic forces in the recent past decades and despite the fact that it is still today considered utopian, may become in a not distant future an operating reality for the good of all mankind. 'Brotherhood' is — in the words of 'Abdu'l-Bahá — 'potential . . . natal . . . intended in humanity'.[94] Therefore man, far from being 'incorrigibly selfish and aggressive'[95] as many think today, is possessed of the capacity of co-operation with his fellow-men, and such co-operation is the purpose of his creation.[96] Until mankind expresses such potential capacity, any real global progress will be unattainable.

This is why the Bahá'í texts exalt the greatness of this day which they call *'the Day of God'*, the day of the spiritual maturity of mankind. Bahá'u'lláh refers to it thus: *'The potentialities inherent in the station of man, the full measure of his destiny on earth, the innate excellence of his reality, must all be manifested in this Promised Day of God.'*[97]

An early social and organizational expression of this stage of maturity — which will be realized by degrees like any other process of growth in the world of being — might be the establishment of 'a social system at once progressive and peaceful, dynamic and harmonious, a system giving free play to individual creativity and initiative but based on co-operation and reciprocity'.[98] Such a society will undoubtedly ensure peace and justice and may therefore be viewed as an early stage of that advent of the Kingdom of God which was the promise of the ancient religions.[99]

---

94. *Promulgation*, p.129.
95. The Universal House of Justice, *Promise*, p.3.
96. F. Facchini writes: '. . . the process of human adaptation implies an increasing co-operation, in view of new social and economical requirements, and of impending dangers threatening the future of mankind and involving not merely single peoples, but the whole of mankind.

'This co-operation should not be intended only on an international level. It is a great movement that must come about among individuals, families, social strata, peoples. In this sense co-operation becomes an indispensable and indivisible value, and not a mere way of life.

'Unity for the future of mankind must traverse and develop through the manifold expressions and co-operative actions among human beings.' (F. Facchini, *Il Cammino dell'Evoluzione Umana*, p.229.)
97. *Gleanings*, p.340.
98. The Universal House of Justice, *Promise*, p.3.
99. Shoghi Effendi writes in this regard: 'His [Bahá'u'lláh's] mission is to proclaim that the ages of the infancy and of the childhood of the human race are past, that the convulsions associated with the present stage of its adolescence are slowly and painfully preparing it to attain the stage of manhood, and are heralding the approach of that Age of Ages when swords will be beaten into ploughshares, when the Kingdom promised by Jesus Christ will have been established, and the peace of the planet definitely and permanently ensured.' (*The Faith of Bahá'u'lláh*, p.3.)

Up to now, paleontology and history describe the evolution of mankind from Australopithecus to Homo habilis, to Homo erectus, to Homo sapiens: mankind has traversed in its collective growth the stages of physical, psycho-physical and intellectual maturity. This is the day of its spiritual maturity, and mankind is on the verge of its attainment. Spiritual maturity implies that man learn how to escape the yoke of nature in his social behaviour as well as in his individual life. Once, the crowd was viewed as a blind element, an easy prey of the lowest passions and of animal instincts. This view is true of an animal-like society founded upon the law of competition. It is to such a society that Konrad Lorenz refers when he writes: 'The Ten Commandments begin to lose their fundamental effectiveness when the anonymity of human society increases . . . The imagination of the human heart is not evil from youth onwards, humans are good enough for eleven-man societies, but not good enough to commit themselves for an anonymous, personally unknown member of a mass society . . .'[100]

In the Bahá'í view, man must be taught from his childhood the concept of the unity of mankind. A society will consequently appear in whose context the instincts – which in the Bahá'í texts are mostly referred to as natural emotions of the natal self – will be under the guidance of a spiritually enlightened intellect. Such a society will be founded upon co-operation and, in due time, upon love, and will therefore begin to mirror forth into the world the unity of the divine world of the Kingdom.

A crucial stage of human development has begun. In this stage the virtues of the spiritual world revealed by Christ, so that they might become manifest in the life of individuals and in personal relations, can and must become the rule even in social life. This is the stage of the spiritualization of society. Thus man fulfils the purpose of his creation: 'the attainment of the supreme virtues of humanity, through descent of the heavenly bestowals', 'so the body of the world will receive its vivification through the animating virtue of the sanctified spirit of man'.[101]

Evolution–creation drew forth from the chaos of original matter the ordered universe we know today, with its most exquisite fruit: man. Thanks to his characteristic and extraordinary power of understanding, and through the indispensable assistance and guidance of the Holy Spirit, man can mirror forth in the physical plane of existence the excellence of the world of the Kingdom. From the original chaos of an animal-like society, with its prevailing law

---

100. Lorenz, *The Waning of Humaneness*, pp.126–7.
101. *Promulgation*, pp.4, 331.

'*homo homini lupus*' theorized by Hobbes,[102] man through his efforts of voluntary and conscious submission to the enlightened divine guidance vouchsafed by the Manifestation of God creates a society where the natural emotions of the natal self are guided and harmonized by the qualities of the spirit, and thus equilibrium, beauty, love and creativity become manifest. It is impossible to imagine a higher stage in the material plane of existence. This stage is the apex of social evolution and a mighty sign of God, made manifest in this world of creation through human efforts guided by the Holy Spirit.

---

102. Hobbes, *Leviathan*, p. 13. This famous statement, taken from *Asinaria*, a comedy by Plautus (3rd–2nd century BC, the greatest of the Roman playwrights), was revived by Bacon (1561–1626) and Hobbes (1588–1679).

10 The World of the Kingdom

In our quest throughout the universe we have found traces of God made manifest according to the different capacities of the various kingdoms of the world of creation. These are the expressions of the world of the Kingdom in the creatures. In this sense, Bahá'u'lláh writes: *'Every created thing in the whole universe is but a door leading into His knowledge, a sign of His sovereignty, a revelation of His names, a symbol of His majesty, a token of His power, a means of admittance into His straight path . . .'*[1] These traces are of such great relevance to our purpose of 'comprehending the reality of things, as they exist',[2] that it seems opportune here to summarize them briefly, so as to focus on what we can understand about the world of the Kingdom.

The world of the Kingdom within the creatures

The traces of the world of the Kingdom become manifest in the world of creation in different ways and degrees, depending on the capacities of the creatures. The 'power of attraction' binding together the 'elemental atoms'[3] of 'original matter'[4] is but the simplest expression, in the material level, of the spiritual reality of love.

The 'perpetual motion' which moves those elemental atoms is the expression of the dynamism of the 'universal energy'.[5]

The 'law of progression'[6] and the perpetual evolution to which

1. *Gleanings*, p. 160.
2. *Some Answered Questions*, p. 221.
3. *Promulgation*, pp. 268, 284.
4. *Some Answered Questions*, p. 183.
5. *Promulgation*, pp. 284, 140.
6. ibid. p. 302.

all beings and the world of creation as a whole are subject are 'the expressions of spirit in the world of matter'[7] as progressiveness.

The 'power of growth'[8] typical of the vegetable world is a further expression of the progress typical of the world of the Kingdom.

The 'power of sense perception'[9] of the animal world is 'the lowest degree of perception'[10] and yet it is a glimmer of the knowledge of the world of the Kingdom.

Other traces of that supernal world are the continuity of creation, the infinity of the universe, the infinite variety and 'the absolute order and perfection'[11] of its phenomena, the oneness of its laws, the intimate relations among created things which are, therefore, a part of an organic unity and, last but not least, individuality – in the sense of uniqueness of phenomena – as a sign of the divine unity.

Nor are these all the traces of God within our reach. On the one hand, God has caused the world of creation to be an 'outer expression or fac-simile of the inner kingdom of the spirit'[12] and, on the other, He has bestowed upon man an extraordinary power which *'apprehends the spiritual . . . (and) sees the world of the Kingdom'*:[13] the power of knowing through his mind and insight. Therefore, whenever the world of creation is seen through the eye of the spirit, the world of the Kingdom will become manifest in each of the phenomena of existence. This is 'the metaphorical nature of material reality' which has been so keenly discussed by J. S. Hatcher.[14]

Since the world of creation is somehow a metaphor of the world of the Kingdom, it provides continuous and endless opportunities for reflecting upon and understanding spiritual reality. The Bahá'í texts, like all other Holy Scripture, are rich in metaphors offered by the Manifestations of God for our understanding of spiritual truth. Spiritual truth belongs to a plane of existence transcending the sense perception to which human beings are bound, and is therefore difficult to represent or understand. In the Bahá'í texts, the sun is at various times a metaphor of the Essence of God, or the Word of God, or spirit, or the Manifestation of God. Enlarging

---

7. *Paris Talks*, p.90.
8. *Some Answered Questions*, p.143.
9. *Promulgation*, p.29.
10. *Some Answered Questions*, p.217. See ibid. pp.217–9.
11. *Promulgation*, p.79.
12. ibid. p.270.
13. 'Abdu'l-Bahá, *Tablets*, p.604.
14. See J. S. Hatcher, 'The Metaphorical Nature of Material Reality', in *Bahá'í Studies* III, and *The Purpose of Physical Reality*. A metaphor is a figure of speech which 'relates to a certain object an image which evokes immediate impressions and feelings we experience in front of the object'. (A. Ghiselli and C. Casalgrande, *Lingua e Parola*, p.394.)

The World of the Kingdom

the metaphor, the succession of the four seasons as the sun makes its transit through the zodiacal stations is suggested to represent the evolutionary cycle of the great revealed religions.[15] The lunar cycle is suggested by 'Abdu'l-Bahá as a metaphor of the gradual spiritual growth of human beings.[16] The same concept is expressed through other metaphors as well: daylight increasing from dawn to noon,[17] or a germinating seed which grows and yields its fruit,[18] or the soil which must be cultivated if the seeds thrown upon it are to yield their fruit,[19] or a mirror which must be polished and

---

15. 'Abdu'l-Bahá says: '. . . just as the solar cycle has its four seasons, the cycle of the Sun of Reality has its distinct and successive periods. Each brings its vernal season or springtime. When the Sun of Reality returns to quicken the world of mankind, a divine bounty descends from the heaven of generosity. The realm of thoughts and ideas is set in motion and blessed with new life. Minds are developed, hopes brighten, aspirations become spiritual, the virtues of the human world appear with freshened power of growth, and the image and likeness of God become visible in man. It is the springtime of the inner world. After the spring, summer comes with its fullness and spiritual fruitage; autumn follows with its withering winds which chill the soul; the Sun seems to be going away, until at last the mantle of winter overspreads, and only faint traces of the effulgence of that divine sun remain. Just as the surface of the material world becomes dark and dreary, the soil dormant, the trees naked and bare, and no beauty or freshness remain to cheer the darkness and desolation, so the winter of the spiritual cycle witnesses the death and disappearance of divine growth and extinction of the light and love of God. But again, the cycle begins and a new springtime appears. In it, the former springtime has returned; the world is resuscitated, illumined and attains spirituality; religion is renewed and reorganized, hearts are turned unto God, and life is again bestowed upon man.' (*Promulgation*, pp.93–6.) *See* above, pp.38, n.40; 106, n.29.

16. 'Abdu'l-Bahá writes: '. . . *the brilliant realities and sanctified spirits are likened to a shining crescent. It has one face turned toward the Sun of Truth, and another face opposite to the contingent world. The journey of this crescent in the heaven of the universe ends in (becoming) a full moon. That is, that face of it which is turned toward the divine world becomes also opposite to the contingent world, and by this, both its merciful and spiritual, as well as contingent, perfections becomes complete.*' (*Tablets*, pp.108–9.) *See* above, p.117.

17. 'Abdu'l-Bahá says '. . . spiritual advancement may be likened to the light of the early dawn. Although this dawn light is dim and pale, a wise man who views the march of the sunrise at its very beginning can foretell the ascendancy of the sun in its full glory and effulgence. He knows, for a certainty, that it is the beginning of its manifestation and that later it will assume great power and potency.' (*Promulgation*, p.131.) *See* above, p.117.

18. 'Abdu'l-Bahá says: '. . . the human reality may be compared to a seed. If we sow the seed, a mighty tree appears from it. The virtues of the seed are revealed in the tree; it puts forth branches, leaves, blossoms, and produces fruits. All these virtues were hidden and potential in the seed. Through the blessing and bounty of cultivation these virtues become apparent. Similarly, the merciful God, our Creator, has deposited within human realities certain latent and potential virtues. Through education and culture these virtues deposited by the loving God became apparent in the human reality, even as the unfoldment of the tree from within the germinating seed.' (*Promulgation*, p.91.)

19. '. . . the human reality is like the soil. If no bounty of rain descends from the heaven upon the soil, if no heat of the sun penetrates, it will remain black, forbidding, unproductive; but when the moistening shower and the effulgent glow of the sun's rays fall upon it, beautiful and redolent flowers grow from its bosom. Similarly, the human spirit or reality of man, unless it becomes the recipient of the lights of the Kingdom, develops susceptibilities and consciously reflects the effulgence of God, will not be the manifestation of ideal bounties . . .' (*Promulgation*, p.330.) *See* above, p.117.

cleaned from dust if it is to mirror forth the light of the sun,[20] or a bird which, once its wings are grown, does not remain upon the earth, but wings its flight towards the sky.[21] Water is another metaphor suggesting the Word or the teachings of God:[22] *'rain-showers of divine mercy'* which *'cleanse the human heart'*,[23] or an *'ocean'* in whose waters men are invited to immerse themselves that they *'may unravel its secrets, and discover all the pearls of wisdom that lie hid in its depths'*,[24] or *'rivers'* which water *'the soil of hearts'*, drawing forth from them *'the tender herbs of wisdom and understanding'*.[25] The idea of a 'journey' or 'pilgrimage'[26] is suggested as a metaphor for human life.

The Bahá'í texts are an inexhaustible source of such metaphors, and thus a precious instrument through which we may be trained in our understanding of that correspondence between the material world (the world of creation) and the spiritual world (the world of the Kingdom) so that the ancient dualism between spirit and matter may find its solution. Thus will be healed the painful fracture in the heart of a man who wants to learn to express his divine nature in a plane of reality – material reality – which tends to dim it, but which should not for that reason be viewed as inherently evil. When material reality is illumined through its metaphorical – or educational – meaning, it will disclose to our eyes all its beauty, a beauty which is in itself a metaphor of the Divine beauty of its Creator. And when we discover in the world of creation His beauteous traces, we will at long last be no longer broken within ourselves – soul and body, as two enemies – and we will exclaim like Doctor Faustus: 'Stop, fleeting moment, you are

---

20. 'Abdu'l-Bahá says: 'The most important thing is to polish the mirrors of the hearts in order that they may become illumined and receptive of the divine light. One heart may possess the capacity of the polished mirror; another, be covered and obscured by the dust and dross of this world. Although the same Sun is shining upon both, in the mirror which is polished, pure and sanctified you may behold the Sun in all its fullness, glory and power, revealing its majesty and effulgence; but in the mirror which is rusted and obscured there is no capacity for reflection, although so far as the Sun itself is concerned it is shining thereon and is neither lessened nor deprived. Therefore, our duty lies in seeking to polish the mirrors of our hearts in order that we shall become reflectors of that light and recipient of the divine bounties which may be fully revealed through them.' (*Promulgation*, pp. 14–15.)

21. See ibid. pp. 294, 336. He writes moreover: '. . . *once a bird hath grown its wings, it remaineth on the ground no more, but soareth upward into high heaven – except for those birds that are tied by the leg, or those whose wings are broken, or mired down.*' (*Selections*, p. 58.)

22. Bahá'u'lláh often refers to the *'Water of Life'* (*Gleanings*, p. 213), as the teachings of the Manifestation of God which, even as water, quicken the soil of human hearts.

23. *Selections*, p. 146.

24. *Kitáb-i-Aqdas*, in *Synopsis*, p. 27.

25. *Gleanings*, p. 43.

26. *Promulgation*, pp. 294, 336.

The world of the Kingdom within man

beautiful.' And our Lucifer will be disappointed, because our love for this earthly life will not bind our soul to an inferior reality, but will be an instrument for its edification through that same life whose true meaning we will have at long last understood and learnt to love.

The world of the Kingdom within man

Among the numberless phenomena of creation, man is the creature intended to reflect the entire beauty of that world of the Kingdom to which his soul belongs.

From time immemorial the Manifestations of God have come into the world one after the other to guide man into the way of virtues, in order that man may give expression to them in this world more completely and perfectly. In His Sermon on the Mount[27] Jesus indicated the heights of spirituality a human being may attain. In His *Hidden Words*[28] and in many other of His Writings, Bahá'u'lláh – after almost two thousand years – renewed and broadened this pattern of spirituality, and at the same time announced that the day of human spiritual maturity has come.

This is an age when each human being gradually – the times being ripe – will manifest in himself, through his own efforts, the wonders of the world of the Kingdom, and these wonders will enlighten the world.

In this sense, a man may be viewed as the raw material from which an artist draws forth an inspiring work through his genius, inspiration and ability. Man can, metaphorically, be the artist or the creator of himself. If he avails himself of his God-given instruments[29] and of the '*gems*'[30] he has been endowed with, and if

---

27. See *Matt.* 5:1–48 and *Luke* 6:20–49. With such words does 'Abdu'l-Bahá pay tribute to the moral teachings of Jesus: '. . . *Jesus . . . founded the sacred Law and the foundation of moral character and complete spirituality and to those who believed in Him traced a special way of living which constitutes the highest way of acting on the earth.*' (*Secret of Divine Civilization*, p.82.)

28. These are the opening words of that precious collection of aphorisms: '*This is that which hath descended from the realm of glory, uttered by the tongue of power and might, and revealed unto the Prophets of old. We have taken the inner essence thereof and clothed it in the garment of brevity, as a token of grace unto the righteous, that they may stand faithful unto the Covenant of God, may fulfil in their lives His trust, and in the realm of the spirit obtain the gem of the Divine virtue.*' (*Hidden Words*, p.3.) A perusal of this booklet and the practice of the advice it offers therein will prove a sufficient means of the spiritual progress of anyone who will exert his efforts with purity of motive.

29. G. A. Eyford writes: 'Man must work on himself as he would upon a piece of art. His standards and criteria will be a blend of the aesthetic and the moral as he strives to achieve beauty, purity, virtue, goodness, unity, authenticity, and truth.' ('Aesthetics and Spiritual Education', in *World Order*, XIV, no.1, p.36.) For a better understanding of this concept, the perusal of the whole paper by G. A. Eyford is suggested.

30. *Gleanings*, p.260.

he consciously and willingly strives – out of his love of God – to observe the laws of revelation, then he will create in himself such incomparable harmony of spiritual feelings as will be conducive to his own happiness, to the edification of his fellow-men, and to collective progress. This is the meaning of the old tale of the Beast transformed into a handsome prince by Beauty out of her love, or of the ugly duckling which grows into a beautiful swan, or of that fine Japanese poem introduced to me by H. B. Danesh:

> I asked the almond tree
> 'Sister, speak me of God!'
> And the almond blossomed.

That such a goal of inner perfection, of fulfilment of the self, of active and constructive participation in collective progress should be attained through such a barren, hard and fatiguing path, which has apparently nothing in common with the light and joy of the goal it leads to, may seem strange, and even unjust and cruel.

St Teresa of Avila[31] said: 'I am not surprised, my Lord, that Thy friends are so few, if Thou dealest with them in such a way.' This path has been variously described in the Sacred Scriptures and in mystical writing. Jesus said: '. . . strait is the gate, and narrow is the way which leadeth unto life'.[32] Bahá'u'lláh poetically described it as the *'valley of love'*, but He said also that *'the steed of this valley is pain; and if there be no pain this journey will never end'*.[33] 'Abdu'l-Bahá mentions the *'stony path of God'*;[34] in one of His prayers He writes: *'This, Thy servant, hath advanced toward Thee, is passionately wandering in the desert of Thy love'*,[35] and describes Himself as *'this wanderer in the wilderness of God's love'*.[36] The modern mystic Thomas Merton mentions a 'night of the senses' preceding the contemplation of God, and describes a heavy 'journey through the desert' filled with 'aridness' and 'desolation'[37] leading to the vision of the Lord. In the sixteenth century, St John of the Cross mentions a 'night of sense and spirit' that 'the soul should first traverse, if it is to attain to the stage of perfection'.[38]

However, if man does not of his own free-will tread this path –

---

31. St Teresa of Avila or of Jesus (1515–1582), mystic, Spanish writer, reformer of the Carmelite Order together with the contemporary Spanish mystic St John of the Cross (1542–1591).
32. *Matt.* 7:14.
33. *Seven Valleys*, p.8.
34. *Selections*, p.226.
35. *Bahá'í Prayers*, p.82.
36. *Selections*, p.276.
37. *New Seeds of Contemplation*.
38. St John of the Cross, *Opere*, pp.350, 15.

the path of purification from the '*satanic self*'[39] — he will not be able to demonstrate through his deeds that he has chosen the attraction towards the world of the Kingdom and given up the ties binding him to the world of creation, and therefore he will not be able to acquire experience of that divine Kingdom.

Once again the words of a poet can assist us: the Persian mystic 'Attár, who conveys through his verses the eagerness of that inner yearning, a yearning which, supported by perseverance, endeavour and fortitude, urges man to painfully climb those heights beyond which an initially remote and unknown joy will be found in the nearness of God.

> Moths gathered in a fluttering throng one night
> To learn the truth about the candle's light,
> And they decided one of them should go
> To gather news of the elusive glow.
> One flew till in the distance he discerned
> A palace window where a candle burned —
> And went to nearer; back again he flew
> To tell the others what he thought he knew.
> The mentor of the moths dismissed his claim,
> Remarking: 'He knows nothing of the flame'.
> A moth more eager than the one before
> Set out and passed beyond the palace door.
> He hovered in the aura of the fire,
> A trembling blue of timorous desire,
> Then headed back to say how far he'd been,
> And how much he had undergone and seen.
> The mentor said: 'You do not bear the signs
> Of one who's fathomed how the candle shines.'
> Another moth flew out — his dizzy flight
> Turned to an ardent wooing of the light;
> He dipped and soared, and in his frenzied trance
> Both Self and fire were mingled by his dance —
> The flame engulfed his wing-tips, body, head;
> His being glowed a fierce translucent red;
> And when the mentor saw that sudden blaze,
> The moth's form lost within the glowing rays,
> He said: 'He knows, he knows the truth we seek,
> That hidden truth of which we cannot speak.'
> To go beyond all knowledge is to find
> That comprehension which eludes the mind,

---

39. *Seven Valleys*, p.11.

> And you can never gain the longed-for goal
> Until you first outsoar both flesh and soul;
> But should one part remain, a single hair
> Will drag you back and plunge you in despair —
> No creature's Self can be admitted here,
> Where all identity must disappear.[40]

It is obviously impossible to describe the infinite richness and variety of attributes, qualities, capacities and endowments which a man may express during his earthly life. As 'man is a creation intended for the reflection of [the] virtues'[41] of a perfect world of the Kingdom, so, if those virtues are infinite, the potentialities of human nature are infinite as well. In the Bahá'í texts there is a wealth of passages in which the infinite potentialities vouchsafed to man are described through exhortations, loving counsels, descriptions of inner realities or examples of spirituality. Some of the powers of the soul have been already discussed. Each of these powers is, so to speak, assisted by infinitely many spiritual virtues through which it may be brought into operation in daily life. In the sphere of direct or indirect knowledge there is consciousness, certitude, wisdom, eloquence, and also justice, equity and honesty. In the sphere of love there is attraction toward the Kingdom, love of God, charity, benevolence, selflessness, courtesy, kindness, loving-kindness, goodness, patience, tolerance, compassion and mercy; and moreover, there is brotherhood, friendship, respect, purity, chastity and holiness as well as harmony, trustworthiness, honesty, sincerity, truthfulness, equity, justice, faithfulness, loyalty, integrity, righteousness, frankness, humility, meekness, joy and radiance. In the sphere of will, there is tranquillity, moderation, temperance, freedom, fear of God, trust in God, resolution, steadfastness, fortitude, diligence, perseverance, patience, endurance, gratitude (even in troubles), spirit of sacrifice and courage. And these are not all the human possibilities. It is only a short and incomplete list of the potential qualities that a human being may concretely manifest in the world of creation, if he only makes an effort. This is the most luminous trace of the world of the Kingdom that a man may discover. However, at this point, personal endeavour is required; a living experience has to be obtained. Abstract knowledge of these 'exemplars'[42] will not be of

---

40. Farídu'd-Dín 'Attár (1117–1230). These verses are from his most famous poem, *antiqu't-Tayr* ('The Conference of the Birds'). See ibid. p.206.
41. *Promulgation*, pp.302–3.
42. *Promulgation*, p.464. The word exemplar (or archetype) is seemingly used by 'Abdu'l-Bahá, in this context, in its neo-platonic meaning of 'ideas [attributes] existing in the mind of God as models of created things'. (N. Abbagnano, *Dizionario di Filosofia*, p.65). See above, p.147.

much use. It is only through a direct perusal of, and meditation upon, the Sacred Words that minds may be enlightened, that the urge to fulfil them may be kindled in the hearts and the required forces bestowed. Thus may be attained a knowledge which, far from being abstract or merely intellectual, will be an inner experience, a way of being. And whoever attains that knowledge will, though he lives on the earth, indeed be getting closer to Paradise, which is reunion with God and His good-pleasure.[43] The meeting with God within human hearts is the core of the aim and purpose of the earthly journey: the soul learns, through deeds performed and feelings experienced upon the earth, the practice of virtues, and thus becomes aware of the virtues by its own experience. In this way man discovers 'the world of exemplars' within himself and, in so doing, he knows God, for those 'exemplars' are the reflections of His attributes. This is the meaning of the Islamic tradition mentioned by Bahá'u'lláh in His *Kitáb-i-Íqán*: 'He hath known God who knoweth himself.'[44] This tradition re-echoes the aphorism 'know thyself', attributed to Thales and engraved by Chilon of Sparta on the pediment of the famous Temple of Delphi. In past ages these words could be understood only by a few chosen ones; today they convey a truth that each human being in the world can understand and practise for himself.

The world of the Kingdom within society

As man comes to realize and know the world of the Kingdom within himself, he will manifest it in society as well. It is thus that civilization is born. Civilization itself – in its twofold aspect of material civilization with its offspring of science and technology, and of divine civilization, with its progressive stages as regards man's awareness of spiritual reality and the attainment of higher stages of cooperation and unity within society – is a sign and an expression of the world of the Kingdom in the world of creation. Civilization, on the one hand, manifests the bounties of knowledge and learning, prosperity and success; and, on the other, is conducive to 'complete attraction and affinity', 'unity and harmony', and 'eternal happiness, love and everlasting life'.[45]

Most people today fail to recognize these signs within society. Traversing a period of great disharmony between material civilization, which is well advanced, and spiritual civilization, which is

---

43. Bahá'u'lláh writes: ' *"Where is Paradise, and where is Hell?" Say: "The one is reunion with Me; the other is thine own self"*.' (*Tablets*, p.118.) The Báb writes: '*Paradise is attainment of His good-pleasure.*' (*Selections*, p.158.)
44. p.102.
45. *Promulgation*, pp.4, 9.

quite backward in comparison with its present potentialities, the majority of mankind consider divine civilization to be a mere utopia; while material civilization is thought to be the outcome of unaided human efforts, without God (Whose existence is mostly denied) having any part in it.[46] The Bahá'í view is quite different;[47] it will be for the history of future decades to demonstrate its soundness, as the driving forces of history, which are always spiritual, bring about a condition of political peace notwithstanding the present difficulties. Within the context of this political peace, the new spiritual civilization for which mankind is now ready will flourish in all its unfolding splendour.

According to the Bahá'í teachings, these possibilities and capacities of peace, cooperation and harmony which are slowly and painfully making their ways in the world are among the shining traces of the world of the Kingdom which spiritual seekers can see. Thus the contemporary flourishing of material civilization may be viewed not only in its material aspects of well-being and ease, nor only in its worst aspects of pollution, impoverishment of the planet's resources, unequal distribution of material wealth, and awesome possibilities of destruction, but also in its diametrically opposed possibilities of realizing, through the efforts of spiritually more mature individuals, such noble goals as the protection of the environment, the preservation of the resources, the promotion of economic equity, and the extension of an acceptable standard of life, of education, health and work to all human beings, as well as the furtherance of spiritual edification.[48] The material means are available. Only the will is missing, perhaps because most men still do not open their inner eyes and thus do not see the bounties of the world of the Kingdom lavished by an All-Bountiful God throughout His creation, nor do they understand that these

---

46. This concept is thus concisely set forth by the Universal House of Justice in its *Promise of World Peace*: '. . . religion and religious institutions have, for many decades, been viewed by increasing numbers of people as irrelevant to the major concerns of the modern world. In its place they have turned either to the hedonistic pursuit of material satisfactions or to the following of man-made ideologies designed to rescue society from the evident evils under which it groans.' (p.6.)

47. Bahá'u'lláh writes: '*Religion . . . is the chief instrument for the establishment of order in the world and of tranquillity amongst its peoples. The weakening of the pillars of religion hath strengthened the foolish and emboldened them and made them more arrogant . . . The greater the decline of religion, the more grievous the waywardness of the ungodly. This cannot but lead in the end to chaos and confusion.*' (*Tablets*, pp.63–4.)

48. The interested reader would do well to read *Call to the Nations*, a compilation of writings by Shoghi Effendi, published in 1977 by the Universal House of Justice. In this compilation, the most important Bahá'í texts dealing with these and other important issues are collected.

bounties may be either seized or ignored by us, His creatures, depending on our own free choice.

The world of the Kingdom as the world beyond

But man cannot be satisfied with knowing the world of the Kingdom only through its glimmerings in the creatures of the world and from the feelings he himself experiences in his heart. Man has always been eager to know what his condition will be when he somehow returns — after his physical death — into that world. The Bahá'í texts inform us that *'the nature of the soul after death can never be described, nor it is meet and permissible to reveal its whole character to the eyes of men.'*[49] Nevertheless, they refer to that world through metaphors, in order to permit us an understanding within the limits of our capacities, an understanding that can foster our attraction towards that reality.

It transcends time and space

The world of the Kingdom is often referred to by Bahá'u'lláh as the *'Placeless'*;[50] and 'Abdu'l-Bahá says that it is a kingdom of 'eternal life'[51] which *'transcends the life and limitations of this mortal sphere'*.[52] Thus, the world of the Kingdom cannot be explored and studied through the categories of time and space typical of our material universe.

When 'Abdu'l-Bahá was asked where the world of the Kingdom is, He answered: *'. . . the Kingdom of God . . . is within this world. The people of this world, however, are unaware of that world, and are even as the mineral and the vegetable that know nothing of the animal and the world of man.'* In fact, *'. . . the world of existence'*, He writes, *'is a single world, although its stations are various and distinct'*.[53] Therefore, we are already in the world of the Kingdom now, but we must become aware of this fact. And since it is the faculties of mind and insight which, under the guidance of Revelation, enable us to become aware of spiritual truth within material reality, these faculties must be trained and developed in order to acquire such important awareness.

---

49. *Gleanings*, p. 156.
50. *Hidden Words*, Persian no. 17. Bahá'u'lláh mentions in His *Hidden Words* 'the gates that open on the Placeless' (Persian no. 17), 'the realms of the Placeless' (Bahá'u'lláh, ibid. Persian no. 39), *the paradise of the Placeless* (Persian no. 39), as well as in His *Kitáb-i-Íqán*, 'the domain of the Placeless.' (p. 157.)
51. *Promulgation*, p. 226.
52. *Selections*, pp. 194–5.
53. ibid. pp. 194–5, 193.

But above all, it should be remembered that the world of the Kingdom is 'nearness to God', and that such a nearness can be attained during this earthly life through 'the attainment of the highest virtues of humanity'.[54] 'Abdu'l-Bahá writes: *'Those souls that, in this day, enter the divine kingdom and attain everlasting life, although materially dwelling on earth, yet in reality soar in the realm of heaven. Their bodies may linger on earth, but their spirits travel in the immensity of space. For as thoughts widen and become illumined, they acquire the power of flight and transport man to the Kingdom of God.'* Whosoever attains this stage will understand that '. . . *the Kingdom is the real world, and this nether place is only its shadow stretching out . . . images reflected in water*'.[55]

Metaphors of the world of the Kingdom in the Bahá'í texts

Although in its limited way the material world is only *'images reflected in water'*, it can yet permit us to conceive a metaphorical idea of the world beyond.

The Bahá'í texts metaphorically describe the world of the Kingdom as an earthly kingdom: *'the Realm of Immortality'*, *'the Realm of Glory'*, the *'Abhá Kingdom'*.[56] In this Kingdom, there is a *'Glorious Height'*[57] from which the Voice of God is speaking forth. Bahá'u'lláh describes moreover the *'Sacred and inviolable Sanctuary'* of God, 'the *'Celestial Pavilion'*, all metaphors that should be perused and deeply meditated upon to be understood. When Bahá'u'lláh describes that Kingdom, He depicts charming country scenery: *'rustling . . . leaves'*, a *'whispering breeze'*, *'flowing waters'*[58] all raising anthems of praise to God. In one of His prayers, He implores that He may drink *'from the sweet-scented streams of Thine eternity'*, *'taste the fruits'* of the *'tree of Thy Being'*. In that same prayer, He mentions refreshing *'crystal springs of Thy love'*, *'meadows of Thy nearness'*, where He asks that He may wander, as well as a *'fragrant breeze of Thy joy . . melodies of the dove of Thy oneness . . . [a] garden of Thine immortality'*.[59] In those places of spiritual delight *'Maids'* or *'Damsels'*[60] of Heaven as well as *'heavenly armies'*[61] dwelling in

---

54. *Promulgation*, p.304.
55. *Selections*, pp.202, 178.
56. *Gleanings*, pp.141, 301, 207.
57. Bahá'u'lláh, *Tablet of the Holy Marineer*.
58. *Gleanings*, pp.11–12, 31.
59. *Bahá'í Prayers*, pp.77–8.
60. Bahá'u'lláh, *Tablet of the Holy Marineer*.
61. 'Abdu'l-Bahá writes: 'By heavenly armies those souls are intended who are entirely freed from the human world, transformed into celestial spirits and have become divine angels. Such souls are the rays of the Sun of Reality . . . They are delivered from human qualities and the defects of the world of nature, and characterized with the characteristics of God, and are attracted with the fragrances of the Merciful.' (*Tablets of the Divine Plan*, p.47.)

'mansions of Eternity' within *'celestial chambers'*, *'illumine the heaven and all that is therein'* and perfume *'all things in the Land of Holiness and Grandeur'*.[62] This world is also described as *'oceans above of God'* whose *'billows of grace'* are surging over *'all mankind'*.[63]

These metaphors disclose the beauty and the greatness of that World, when compared to the limitations of this one, whose beauties are nevertheless a reflection of the beauties of the former. However, once again, only through a direct and personal perusal of the revealed Words and meditation upon them can a glimpse of the deep inner meanings of these metaphors be caught.

Qualities of the world of the Kingdom

The world of the Kingdom is, 'Abdu'l-Bahá says, 'the Kingdom of complete attraction and affinity', of 'real love', that love 'which exists between God and His servants, the love which binds together holy souls, not the love of physical bodies and organisms'; the world of the Kingdom is a world of 'light and reality . . . bliss and joy', of 'radiance . . . illumination', in comparison with the 'darkness and uncertainty' of this world. It is a world of 'absolute immortality, completeness and unchangeable being', in comparison to the 'separation [and] disintegration, which characterize the world of material existence'. It is a world of 'unlimited' virtues, whereas 'the virtues of the material world are limited'. It is 'a world of sanctity and radiance . . . of spirituality, faith, assurance, the knowledge and love of God . . . a world of lights . . . of love . . . of perfections . . . vivified by the breaths of the Holy Spirit', in comparison to this 'world of gloom . . . of defects . . . without enlightenment'.[64] In that world, the veils will be cleft asunder, *'verities will come to light, and all things unknown before will be made clear, and hidden truths be understood'*.[65] It 'is the realm of divine bestowals and the bounties of God. It is attainment of the highest virtues of humanity; it is nearness to God; it is capacity to receive the bounties of the ancient Lord', in the sense that in that world the closer the 'nearness to God' or the 'likeness unto' Him, the more perfectly will human potentialities be fulfilled. This unceasing progress which is typical of the world of the Kingdom is animated and guided by the Manifestation of God. 'In the inner world, the world of the Kingdom, the Sun of Reality is the Trainer and Educator of minds, souls and spirits. Were it not for the effulgent rays of the Sun of Reality, they would be deprived of

---

62. Bahá'u'lláh, *Tablet of the Holy Mariner*.
63. *Selections*, p.252.
64. *Promulgation*, pp.4, 9, 256, 47, 332, 47, 90, 205, 226, 332.
65. *Selections*, p.177.

growth and development; nay, rather, they would be nonexistent . . . the radiation of the light and heat of the Sun of Reality gives growth, education and evolution to minds, souls and spirits toward the station of perfection.'[66]

The body separates man from that world like a screen. 'Abdu'l-Bahá compares it to an *'interposed veil'* which must be metaphorically *'lifted away'* so that that *'world of perceptions and discoveries'* may be perceived. This will undoubtedly occur when the body dies. At that moment, man will hasten *'away from this mortal place into the kingdom of God, then he will be born in the spirit; then the eye of his perception will open, the ear of his soul will hearken, and all the truths of which he was ignorant before will be made plain and clear.'* However, this process may begin during physical life with that which is called second birth or spiritual progress.[67]

Human souls in the world of the Kingdom

'Abdu'l-Bahá, dwelling more specifically upon the condition of the soul after death, informs us that at the physical death when the body is decomposed, 'only consciousness . . . is left . . .'; He says, moreover: 'After death the condition is one which cannot be clearly explained in words. It is one of comprehension, understanding, which involves all other things – feeling, etc.' He also says: 'You will retain your individuality and will not be swallowed up in one vast spirit. Concerning the condition of the human soul after its ascension from the material world: the essence of the human soul is clarified from material substances and purified from the embodiment of physical things. It is exclusively luminous; it has no body; it is a dazzling pencil of light; it is a celestial orb of brightness.'[68] Therefore, if the body disappears, the mind, which depends on the body,[69] disappears as well; and when the mind disappears, animal and human nature will disappear too. There is no longer that tension between animal and divine nature typical of the earthly life of man, which has been called dual nature of the soul. The

---

66. *Promulgation*, pp.304, 148, 271.
67. *Selections*, pp.170, 149. To a seeker, lamenting her separation from Him, 'Abdu'l-Bahá wrote: *'We are all under the shade of the unicoloured pavilion of the world of humanity, but heedlessness forms a veil and an obstacle. When it is removed, the veil will be rent asunder and we shall see one another gathered up together and present.'* ('Tablets of Abdul-Baha Recently Revealed', in *Star of the West*, x, p.7.)
68. Quoted in 'Studies in Immortality', in *Star of the West* XIV, pp.37, 38.
69. In the Bahá'í texts the mind is described as the manifestation of the mental faculties of the soul through the agency of the brain. Since mind is not the only cognitive means at man's disposal, it follows that though man's intelligence (or reason, or intellect) is conditioned by his mind, yet it is not identical with it.
As to the concept of mind, *see* above, pp.156–7.

unremitting necessity of choosing between material and spiritual attraction, typical of this earthly life, disappears. The evolution of the soul will be a progressive and continuous 'approaching unto God',[70] the Supreme Centre of Attraction, through the agency of the bounties of the Sun of Reality, the Manifestation of God. Thus, in the world of the Kingdom, the Manifestation of God 'continues . . . to be our means of contact with the Almighty',[71] and whoever has learnt during his earthly life how to profit from His bounties, will profit from them all the more in the next one.

Bahá'u'lláh writes that in the world of the Kingdom, the soul '. . . *will assume the form that best befitteth its immortality*'.[72] And 'Abdu'l-Bahá explains that '. . . *in the other world the human reality doth not assume a physical form, rather doth it take on a heavenly form, made up of elements of that heavenly realm*',[73] and it remains 'in the degree of purity to which it has evolved during life in the physical body'.[74]

For man as an individual, then, earthly life is nothing but a preparation for the life beyond, when the soul will take the consequences or reap the fruits of its life in this world. Bahá'u'lláh writes: '*Every pure, every refined and sanctified soul will be endowed with tremendous power, and shall rejoice with exceeding gladness*'; in fact, '. . . *all men shall, after their physical death, estimate the worth of their deeds, and realize all that their hands have wrought*', and '. . . *the souls of the infidels . . . shall . . . be made aware of the good things that have escaped them*'[75] and will suffer.

It is evident that the souls occupy quite different stages in the world beyond according to 'what they acquire of virtues or vices in this world'.[76] 'Abdu'l-Bahá writes in this regard: '*Know that immortality belongs to such souls as have been imbued with the spirit of life. Beside them all the others are lifeless – they are dead, as Christ explained in the Gospel.*'[77]

---

70. *Paris Talks*, p.66.
71. Letter on behalf of Shoghi Effendi, quoted in *Dawn of a New Day*, p.67. Bahá'u'lláh, describing a '*true believer*', writes: '*his spirit will everlastingly circle round the Will of God*'. (*Gleanings*, p.141.)
72. *Gleanings*, p.157.
73. *Selections*, p.194.
74. *Paris Talks*, p.66.
75. *Gleanings*, pp.154, 171, 170.
76. *Some Answered Questions*, p.233.
77. *Selections*, p.189. Shoghi Effendi, explains some passages from the Writings of Bahá'u'lláh on the same subject in the following words written through his secretary: 'The word "perish" . . . does not mean that the human soul will cease to exist, but will be deprived of all spiritual capacity and understanding . . . by "everlasting life" is meant spiritual felicity, communion with the Divine Spirit.' (quoted in *Bahá'í Institutions* (comp.), p.115.)

However, this condition is not a static one. In fact '. . . nothing which exists', says 'Abdu'l-Bahá, 'remains in a state of repose', and '. . . as the spirit continues to develop after death, it necessarily progresses or declines; and in the other world to cease to progress is the same as to decline; but it never leaves its own condition, in which it continues to develop'.[78] Thus, the condition of the soul after physical death is certainly not stationary. The soul proceeds in the world of the Kingdom in its never-ending journey back to God.

In the world beyond, the progress of the soul is through the bounties of the Manifestations of God, as well as by intercession of other souls, both of souls who are still in the physical stage of their lives — as will be seen further on — and of souls who have ascended into the world of the Kingdom. 'Abdu'l-Bahá says: '. . . it is certain that those who are near the Divine Court are allowed to intercede, and this intercession is approved by God. But intercession in the other world is not like the intercession in this world. It is another thing, another reality, which cannot be expressed in words.'[79]

Relations between this world and the other

Bahá'u'lláh, further explaining the relation between this life and the other, writes: *'The world beyond is as different from this world as this world is different from that of the child while still in the womb of its mother.'*[80] Earthly life is described by 'Abdu'l-Bahá as *'the condition of a human being in the womb, where his eyes are veiled, and all things are hidden away from him. Once he is born out of the uterine world and entereth this life, he findeth it, with relation to that of the womb, to be a place of perceptions and discoveries, and he observeth all things through his outer eyes. In the same way, once he hath departed this life, he will behold in that world whatsoever was hidden from him here: but there he will look upon and comprehend all things with his inner eye . . .'*[81] According to this metaphor, just as whatever is needed for this world is acquired during intrauterine life even though some of those instruments are utterly useless inside the womb, so during this life such instruments are acquired as will prove indispensable in the world beyond, and which will be used to a certain extent in this life too.

'. . . [I]n this world', says 'Abdu'l-Bahá, 'he must prepare himself for the life beyond.' And then He enumerates all the

---

78. *Some Answered Questions*, p.233.
79. ibid. p.231.
80. *Gleanings*, p.157.
81. *Selections*, p.171.

qualities which man must equip himself with: 'sanctity and radiance . . . spirituality, faith, assurance, the knowledge and love of God . . . illumination . . . virtues or perfections . . . breaths of the Holy Spirit . . . everlasting life.'[82]

On the other hand, just as a bodily defect acquired in the womb may have far-reaching consequences upon the conditions of life once a person is born into this world, so a defect in one's spiritual evolution will exert its influence on the conditions of one's life in the world of the Kingdom. 'Abdu'l-Bahá explains the condition of a man at his physical death, in the light of this same metaphor: 'At first the infant finds it very difficult to reconcile itself to its new existence. It cries as if not wishing to be separated from its narrow abode and imagining that life is restricted to that limited space. It is reluctant to leave its home, but nature forces it into this world. Having come into its new condition it finds that it has passed from darkness into a sphere of radiance; from gloomy and restricted surroundings, it has been transferred to a spacious and delightful environment . . . and then it praises God for its release from the confinement of its former condition and attainment to the freedom of a new realm. This analogy expresses the relation of the temporal world to the life hereafter – the transition of the soul of man from darkness and uncertainty to the light and reality of the eternal Kingdom. At first, it is very difficult to welcome death, but after attaining its new conditions the soul is grateful, for it has been released from the bondage of the limited to enjoy the liberties of the unlimited. It has been freed from a world of sorrow, grief and trials to live in a world of unending bliss and joy. The phenomenal and physical have been abandoned in order that it may attain the opportunities of the ideal and spiritual.'[83]

A further metaphor suggested by 'Abdu'l-Bahá, in order to explain the relation between this earthly life and the life hereafter is that of a garden: *'It is as if'*, He writes, *'a kind gardener transferreth a fresh and tender shrub from a confined place to a wide open area. This transfer is not the cause of the withering, the lessening or the destruction of that shrub: no, on the contrary, it maketh it grow and thrive, acquire freshness and delicacy, become green and bear fruit. This hidden secret is well known to the gardener, but those souls who are unaware of this bounty suppose that the gardener, in his anger and wrath, hath uprooted the shrub. Yet to those who are aware, this concealed fact is manifest, and this predestined decree is considered a bounty.'*[84] Once more the Bahá'í texts

---

82. *Promulgation*, p.226.
83. ibid. p.47.
84. *Selections*, pp.199–200.

show a Benign Reality which in its often inscrutable Rationality and Providential Order is guarantee of rationality and order in its creation. And whoever understands and complies with the meaning of that rationality and the harmony of that order will say: 'there is nothing more wonderful than which already exists',[85] and in that awareness will find fulfilment and happiness.

Relations between human souls in the world of the Kingdom

As to the relations among human souls in the world of the Kingdom, Bahá'u'lláh writes that whoever has lived in conformity with the divine will will have blissful joy: *'the Maids of Heaven, inmates of the loftiness mansions, will circle around [him], and the Prophets of God and His chosen ones will seek his companionship. With them that soul will freely converse, and will recount unto them that which it hath been made to endure in the path of God, the Lord of all worlds.'*[86] When 'Abdu'l-Bahá was asked *'whether the souls will recognize each other in the spiritual world'*, He answered: *'This fact is certain: for the Kingdom is the world of vision where all the concealed realities will become disclosed. How much more the well-known souls will become manifest. The mysteries of which man is heedless in this earthly world, those he will discover in the heavenly world, and there will he be informed of the secret truth; how much more will he recognize or discover persons with whom he hath been associated . . . Even they will manifestly behold the Beauty of God in that world. Likewise will they find all the friends of God, both those of former and recent times, present in the heavenly assemblage.'*[87]

However, mutual awareness among the souls in that world depends on the grade of their development: *'They that are of the same grade and station are fully aware of one another's capacity, character, accomplishment and merits. They that are of a lower grade, however, are incapable of comprehending adequately the station, or of estimating the merit, of those that rank above them.'*[88]

Thus a hierarchy exists in the world of the Kingdom: there is a great difference between those who, having attained the life of the spirit during their earthly life, are closer to God; and those who, having not made spiritual progress, are as dead. 'He who is deprived of these divine favours, although he continues after death, is considered as dead by the people of truth,' says 'Abdu'l-Bahá: and moreover: 'For those who believe in God, who have love of God, and faith, life is excellent – that is, it is eternal; but to those

---

85. *Some Answered Questions*, p.177.
86. *Gleanings*, p.156.
87. *Tablets*, p.205.
88. Bahá'u'lláh, *Gleanings*, p.170.

souls who are veiled from God, although they have life, it is dark, and in comparison with the life of believers it is nonexistence.'[89]

Relationship between human souls in this world and in the other

The Bahá'í texts also describe the relationship between those souls who have traversed earthly life and ascended into that Kingdom, and mankind which is wearily making its way here on the earth. 'Abdu'l-Bahá says: 'those who ascended have different attributes from those who are still on earth, yet there is no real separation.'[90] In fact, pure and holy souls in the Kingdom are — in the words of Bahá'u'lláh — *'the pure leaven that leaveneth the world of being, and furnisheth the power through which the arts and wonders of the world are made manifest.'* 'The light which these souls radiate', He writes moreover, *'is responsible for the progress of the world and the advancement of its peoples. They are like unto leaven which leaveneth the world of being, and constitute the animating force through which the arts and wonders of the world are made manifest. Through them, the clouds rain their bounty upon men, and the earth bringeth forth its fruits . . . These souls and symbols of detachment have provided, and will continue to provide, the supreme moving impulse in the world of being.'*[91]

As the souls of the Kingdom have an influence upon this world, so the contrary is true as well. 'In prayer there is a mingling of station, a mingling of condition', says 'Abdu'l-Bahá. Then He adds: 'Pray for them as they pray for you.'[92] These concepts need to be carefully studied and pondered so that both 'the despairing slough of materialism' and 'the quagmire of superstition'[93] may be avoided.

These are certainly not all the signs of the world of the Kingdom that may be discovered in the world of creation, within man, within society, or in the Holy Scriptures. This brief discussion is just intended as a starting point, as an encouragement. Seekers will undoubtedly discover other traces, understand other metaphors, and in so doing will foster such attraction toward the world of the Kingdom within their own selves as will kindle the eagerness to tread the path of spirituality, both within their own hearts and in those of others.

89. *Some Answered Questions*, pp.225, 243.
90. *'Abdu'l-Bahá in London*, p.96.
91. *Gleanings*, p.157.
92. *'Abdu'l-Bahá in London*, p.157.
93. *Paris Talks*, p.143.
94. For a deeper discussion of this topic *see* J. S. Hatcher, *The Purpose of Physical Reality*.

11 God: The Beginning and the End of All Things

The knowledge of God – *'the beginning of all things'* – is, in the words of Bahá'u'lláh, *'the purpose of God in creating man'*.[1] Therein the Bahá'í scholar's or would-be philosopher's journey may come to a close. From the rational proof of God's existence to the feelings ensuing from the awareness of His existence the circle is completed.

The knowledge of God

The knowledge of God, as a theoretical and intellectual knowledge, is little more than a trifle. Whenever it remains in the realm of thought it is utterly useless, as is any other thought. In this sense 'Abdu'l-Bahá says: 'People speak of Divinity, but the ideas and beliefs they have of Divinity are, in reality, superstition . . . Divinity is not what is set forth in dogmas and sermons . . .'[2]

In fact, what else could our theoretical and intellectual knowledge of God be if not the fruit of our own imagination? 'For example,' says 'Abdu'l-Bahá, 'if we form a conception of Divinity as a living, almighty, self-subsisting, eternal Being, this is only a concept apprehended by a human intellectual reality. It would not be the outward, visible, Reality, which is beyond the power of human mind to conceive or encompass.' 'Divinity is the effulgence of the Sun of Reality, the Manifestation of spiritual virtues and ideal powers . . . it essentially means the wisdom and knowledge of God, the effulgence of the Sun of Truth, the revelation of reality

1. *Gleanings*, pp.5, 70.
2. *Promulgation*, p.326.

God: The Beginning and the End of All Things

and the divine philosophy.'[3] In the light of what has been previously said, these words can now be understood more easily. The knowledge of God is rather in the awareness and consciousness of His qualities; in other words, it is in the effulgence of His active attributes from human hearts, from the universe and, above all, from the Manifestation of God. These three aspects of our knowledge of God have been briefly discussed already. They will now be studied once more, in the hope of outlining a more comprehensive description of their nature and of making a deeper analysis of their meaning in human life, i.e. in the feelings they evoke and in the attitudes they imply and qualify.

God within human hearts

From the 'love of reality'[4] that God 'has deposited' within man proceed two kinds of human needs. On the one hand is the need to know and comprehend reality. When this need is met, man becomes aware of and feels his own powerlessness in front of that extraordinary reality which he is trying to know and in which he is discovering an infinite dimension and a perfect order. On the other hand, this feeling generates a second need in man; the need to be comprehended, to feel a part of a greater Reality which somehow may fulfil and satisfy him.[5] To such great Reality the name of God is given.

The knowledge of God is therefore founded first upon an awareness of human limitation and upon an obscure and confused feeling that there must be a 'source' whence such 'virtues' as will satisfy human needs may come forth.[6] This awareness, this feeling, are indeed a way of being, an inner attitude issuing from a complicated combination of cognitive data and beliefs, which in their turn find their origin in the personal knowledge and experience gained by each individual in different ways and under different circumstances. Therefore, that feeling is an act of faith, according to our previously-mentioned concept of faith. Bahá'u'lláh even says that when this faith leads man *'to submit to the Will of God'*, it is the *'essence of understanding'*.[7]

---

3. ibid. pp.192, 326.
4. ibid. p.49.
5. For a discussion of these concepts, *see* W. S. Hatcher, 'The Unity of Religion and Science', in *World Order*, IX, no.3, p.22.
6. *Promulgation*, p.83. 'Abdu'l-Bahá says: '. . . demand and supply is the law, and undoubtedly all virtues have a centre and a source. That source is God, from Whom all these bounties emanate.' ('Abdu'l-Bahá, *Promulgation*, p.83.) *See* above, pp.86–7.
7. *Tablets*, p.155. The entire aphorism says: *'The essence of understanding is to testify to one's poverty, and submit to the Will of the Lord, the Sovereign, the Gracious, the All-Powerful.'* (pp.155–6.)

Whoever is aware that God is the 'source' of all perfections and that anyone may freely draw therefrom if he wants to, has founded his life upon a bedrock and will live in certitude and joy, and will love life and action. In fact, he will trust that — if he does his utmost and avails himself of his own powers with purity of motive — all his deeds will have their prize, at least in their fruits. This feeling pervades many Bahá'í prayers, where God is implored as *'Haven in distress . . . Shield . . . Shelter . . . Asylum and Refuge in time of need and in . . . loneliness . . . Companion! In . . . anguish . . . Solace, and in . . . solitude a loving Friend.'*[8]

Such an attitude is viewed by most atheists as a sign of weakness, and such a faith in God is considered as a quality of an infant humanity, wholly unnecessary for an intellectually adult mankind, even prejudicial to its development. There might be some truth in these ideas: undoubtedly such a faith in God is founded upon an awareness of one's own weaknesses. However, it is suggested that there may be presumption in a man who thinks he may dispense with the Divinity and with faith in it. In fact, the feeling of human omnipotence implied in this concept is undoubtedly less mature than an adult and proved feeling of inadequacy and dependence. Perhaps a man who believes any problem can be solved through unaided human reason can be likened — such is the idea that clearly transpires from the Bahá'í teachings[9] — to an adolescent with his adolescent excesses, typical of someone who has recently gained the paramount use of reason and therefore ascribes to it greater powers than those it actually has — and those powers are certainly not few. But very soon life will show him its limits and will persuade him to a more moderate view.

Others, having observed the behaviour of self-styled or so-called ancient and modern mystics, are afraid that a faith in a God Who is Lord of all things may be conducive to a paralysis of will, bringing man to forsake this world for the sake of the transcendent one, and to surrender himself to a fancied will of God requiring him to renounce any action and initiative. But all that has no place in a truly religious view of life. Spiritual growth, as inculcated and recommended by the Manifestations, depends upon active efforts aimed at promoting unity and peace in the world. Any deed which

---

8. 'Abdu'l-Bahá, in *Bahá'í Prayers*, p. 108.

9. Shoghi Effendi writes: 'The long ages of infancy and childhood, through which the human race had to pass, have receded into the background. Humanity is now experiencing the commotions invariably associated with the most turbulent stage of its evolution, the stage of adolescence, when the impetuosity of youth and its vehemence reach their climax, and must gradually be superseded by the calmness, the wisdom, and the maturity that characterize the stage of manhood.' (*World Order of Bahá'u'lláh*, p. 202.)

is conducive to unity and peace is a tangible expression of faith in God as well as of knowledge of God. Such deeds cannot be described as the actions of a man who has forsaken this world.

While a man performs such spiritual deeds, he will have the inner experience of those spiritual qualities which belong to the divine world and to which he has the capacity of giving concrete expression in his daily life. This is a further aspect of the knowledge of God in human hearts: the knowledge of the divine attributes of the world of the Kingdom through a direct experience of their effulgence as feelings and deeds manifesting them. Bahá'u'lláh writes: *'Could ye apprehend with what wonders of My munificence and bounty I have willed to entrust your souls, ye would, of a truth, rid yourselves of attachment to all created things, and would gain a true knowledge of your own selves – a knowledge which is the same as the comprehension of Mine own Being.'*[10] Through these words two fundamental aspects of life can be understood: on the one hand, the inner struggle which is required for self-purification; on the other, the knowledge of one's own true self. The former is simply the effort exerted to release oneself from the attachment to the natal self with its natural emotions; however, the natal self is not an enemy, but an instrument which we must learn how to turn in the right direction so that it may be properly used. The latter is the result, the outcome of the struggle and it is the expression of the virtues realized through it. This is the key – we repeat – to the understanding of the famous Islamic tradition: 'He hath known God who hath known himself', and of the ancient Greek saying: 'Know thyself'. Knowing oneself means knowing one's divine nature; and this can be attained through the knowledge of that divine nature in its expressions through daily deeds. This is how we can know God. Such knowledge is no theory, no intellectual abstraction. It is a spiritual, mystical experience; it is a joy resulting from the harmonious growth of the powers of knowing, loving and willing which have been vouchsafed to all human beings. Therefore, once more the Bahá'í texts dispel that esoteric aura which has up to now enveloped certain aspects of religion, making them disagreeable to rationalists. Nevertheless, the texts do not suggest that man can penetrate all the mysteries of the infinite universe God has created. This is 'the mystic way' trodden 'with practical feet'[11] which has been previously mentioned, because this mystical knowledge of spiritual attributes of the world of the Kingdom is obtained through a daily practice of service.

10. *Gleanings*, pp. 326–7.
11. D. S. Jordan, quoted in *Bahá'í World*, VI, p. 480.

This recognition of the image of God within man is a mighty spur to action, because it confirms the hope that there is always a chance for man to grow better, to amend past mistakes. In *The Promise of World Peace*,[12] ignorance of true human nature and the consequent firm belief that man is inherently quarrelsome and warlike is viewed as the main reason for the 'paralysis of will'[13] which has for so long kept mankind from any practical measures for the realization of a lasting peace among the nations of the world. Whereas whoever recognizes the image of God in his fellow-beings will be a staunch advocate of human perfectibility, an attitude which will have far-reaching consequences upon human relations: no longer personality against personality, but an image of God beside another image of God. This recognition of a common identity – without denying the individuality of each human being – this consciousness of one God reflected in the different hearts, is the strongest tie which may bind together human beings. It could be metaphorically likened to those nuclear interactions (described in the Bahá'í texts as 'affinity' among the 'elemental atoms') which support the entire fabric of the universe. The same thing is true in the world of humanity; the tie of spiritual identity among human beings, the foundation of the consciousness of the unity of mankind, is the only guarantee of a peaceful and united society.[14]
This is the most important awareness mankind is going to acquire in its new stage of development – the stage of spiritual maturity – towards which it is moving as a whole, according to the ancient plan of God.

God within the universe

In our quest we have sought the traces of God throughout the universe: we will now proceed to describe the feelings evoked within human hearts whenever those traces are discovered.

Whoever has recognized the traces of God in the universe feels himself no longer as a knowing, feeling and willing creature

---

12. The Universal House of Justice writes: '. . . so much have aggression and conflict come to characterize our social, economic and religious systems, that many have succumbed to the view that such behaviour is intrinsic to human nature and therefore ineradicable.' (*Promise*, p.3.)

13. *Promise*, pp.4, 350.

14. 'Abdu'l-Bahá says: 'And when through the breaths of the Holy Spirit this perfect fraternity and agreement are established amongst men – this brotherhood and love being spiritual in character, this loving-kindness being heavenly, these constraining bonds being divine – a unity appears which is indissoluble, unchanging and never subject to transformation. It is ever the same and will forever remain the same.' (*Promulgation*, p.391.)

God: The Beginning and the End of All Things

forsaken, a tiny meaningless atom, upon a grain of dust wandering about through unbounded space. The world around is no longer threatening and awesome, unknown and hostile as it is to a man who has not yet understood his own place in its context. Whoever has found God in the universe feels the joy of being a part of a total harmony which may sometimes be incomprehensible in some of its aspects, but which it is always fundamentally a friendly reality because it is moving towards a known goal, which is the expression of virtues he knows, because they are enshrined, albeit potentially, in his innermost heart. In addition, he feels serene in his heart, as one who can rely upon the support of mighty powers which are at the disposal of anyone who wants to seize them, lavished by an all-loving Creator for the progress of His creatures. These powers emanate from the same Source which radiates those forces which bind together quarks and leptons, which make lichens grow in the most hostile environments, which enable animals to perceive sensible reality and to react to it, which bestow a knowledge upon man that ranges from the perception of an earthly reality to the inner perception of a reality which, though it cannot be known through the senses, nevertheless may be certainly perceived by anyone who makes an effort to discover it within his own self and in the universe.

This man does not feel that earthly life is vain; he feels the soundness and the joy of a creative commitment which is bound to yield its fruit of inner growth and which will therefore win its intended, longed-for prize. He understands how this never-ending postponement of the most cherished goals is difficult only in relation to a need for immediate satisfaction, which he will overcome as soon as he becomes able to see the end in the beginning; for each present condition is a seed which already contains in itself its fruit.[15]

Whoever discovers God in the universe discovers a perfect and marvellous order in sensible reality, a subtle, miraculous equilibrium whereby that apparently discordant world appears as an organic unit; thus he understands and feels the necessity both of creating such an ideal order in his own personal microcosm as well, and of attuning his own microcosm to all the microcosms which make up society. Willingly therefore will he shoulder the challenging responsibility of following the standards of inner personal and outer social order Revelation sets for him, showing to him as much of 'the essential connection which proceeds from the realities of

---

15. Bahá'u'lláh writes: '. . . *those who journey in the garden-land of knowledge, because they see the end in the beginning, see peace in war and friendliness in anger.*' (*Seven Valleys*, p.28.)

things'[16] as he can profit from — because he can understand it. In this way he will achieve the development of his own potentialities and — through the creation of a harmonious society — contribute to those of other human beings. This is the foundation and the mainspring of civilization.

Last but not least, a man who has discovered an order and a harmony in both macrocosm and microcosm will be able to harmonize the objective reality of creation with the subjective reality of his experience of his own self and of the cosmos, and thus he will 'live in conscious at-one-ment with the eternal world'.[17] This 'at-one-ment' is the essence of joy: the aesthetic enjoyment of a common origin, of belonging to one and the same order, whose conscious experience is conducive to a deep love, to an attraction founded upon the same divine fatherhood. This joy is identical, whether it comes from the contemplation of the wonders of existence or from the observation and study of the fruits of man's efforts to express through his own means the beauty that has been plentifully lavished upon creation by the bountiful hand of a divine Creator. Thus Bahá'u'lláh pours out the ecstasy of His heart, enraptured before the widespread traces of God in this world: *'Every time I lift up mine eyes unto Thy heaven, I call to mind Thy highness and Thy loftiness, and Thine incomparable glory and greatness: and every time I turn my gaze to Thine earth, I am made to recognize the evidences of Thy power and the tokens of Thy bounty. And when I behold the sea, I find that it speaketh to me of Thy majesty, and of the potency of Thy might, and of Thy sovereignty and Thy grandeur. And at whatever time I contemplate the mountains, I am led to discover the ensigns of Thy victory and the standards of Thine omnipotence . . . I swear by Thy might, O Thou in whose grasp are the reins of all mankind, and the destinies of the nations! I am so inflamed by my love for Thee, and so inebriated with the wine of Thy oneness, that I can hear from the whisper of the winds the sound of Thy glorification and praise, and can recognize in the murmur of the waters the voice that proclaimeth Thy virtues and Thine attributes, and can apprehend from the rustling of the leaves the mysteries that have been irrevocably ordained by Thee in Thy realm.'*[18]

God in His Manifestations

This is the apex of the knowledge of God within the reach of human creatures. The Manifestation of God reveals to human beings as much of their Creator as they are able to understand.

---

16. *Some Answered Questions*, p.158.
17. *Promulgation*, p.328.
18. *Prayers and Meditations*, pp.207–8.

The meeting with the Manifestation of God is a deep and touching mystical experience within the reach of any human being, if he only is willing to have it. This century has been particularly generous to us, for crowning the ancient religious models God sent Bahá'u'lláh, the latest of His Messengers, no more than a hundred years ago.

The traces of His physical presence in the world are still all accessible; the memory of His life is still alive. It is not difficult to trace the places where He lived and passed away, objects which belonged to Him.[19] Apart from all that, He left a hundred volumes of His Writings, written in His own handwriting or authenticated by His seal. It is through the reading of these writings that we can really meet Him; it is through this experience that anyone can find the way leading him unto His Lord and, through Him, unto his own inner being.[20]

The experience of the meeting with the Manifestation of God through the reading of His Words — which Bahá'u'lláh recommends as a daily practice[21] — may be, in the writer's view, better understood and conveyed in the light of the following passages of Bahá'u'lláh's writings, describing the impact of His Revelation upon the entire creation.

Bahá'u'lláh writes: '*Consider the hour at which the supreme Manifestation of God revealeth Himself unto men. Ere that hour cometh, the Ancient Being, Who is still unknown of men and hath not as yet given utterance to the Word of God, is Himself, the All-Knower, in a world devoid of any man that hath known Him. He is indeed the Creator without a creation. For at the very moment preceding His Revelation, each and every created thing shall be made to yield up its soul to God . . .*'[22] This is the condition of mankind immediately before the beginning of any Revelation of God. At that time the former religion is wholly

---

19. Bahá'u'lláh was born in Tehran on 12 November 1817, and passed away in Bahjí ('Akká) on 28 May 1892. Many of the houses He occupied, the house where he was born and the Mansion where He passed away are still in existence. Objects which belonged to Him are preserved in Haifa in the International Bahá'í Archives as historic pieces of exceptional interest. Most of His writings are preserved in the Archives of the Bahá'í World Centre.

20. As to the meeting with God, Bahá'u'lláh devotes a few passages of His *Kitáb-i-Íqán* to the explanation of the meaning of the locution '*Divine presence*' used to indicate the same concept. (pp.141–6.)

21. In his *Kitáb-i-Aqdas*, Bahá'u'lláh writes: '*Recite ye the verses of God every morning and evening. Whoso reciteth them not hath truly failed to fulfil his pledge to the Covenant of God and His Testament and whoso in this day turneth away therefrom, hath indeed turned away from God since time immemorial.*' And He adds: '*Recite ye the verses of God in such measure that ye be not overtaken with fatigue or boredom.*' (quoted in *The Importance of Prayer, Meditation and the Devotional Attitude* (comp.), p.3.)

22. *Gleanings*, p.151.

submerged in its desolate winter, and mankind is dead. Likewise, any man whose heart has not yet been directly touched by the quickening influence of the Word of the Manifestation of God is himself as though dead. Bahá'u'lláh refers to this particular human condition as the *'plane of heedlessness'*,[23] a stage in which a man has not yet hearkened to the Word of God.

But as soon as the Manifestation of God utters His word, a great upheaval is stirred up, an upheaval which He describes with several metaphors: *'Verily, We have caused every soul to expire by virtue of Our irresistible and all-subduing sovereignty. We have, then, called into being a new creation, as a token of Our grace unto men.'* And yet: *'In every age and cycle He hath, through the splendorous light shed by the Manifestations of His wondrous Essence, recreated all things, so that whatsoever reflecteth in the heavens and on the earth the signs of His glory may not be deprived of the outpourings of His mercy, nor despair of the showers of His favours.'*[24] And moreover: *'Immeasurably exalted is the breeze that wafteth from the garment of thy Lord, the Glorified. For lo, it hath breathed its fragrance and made all things new.'*[25] And in His *Kitáb-i-Aqdas*, He writes: *'. . . when We manifested Ourselves to all in the world with Our most Comely Names and Our Exalted Attributes, all things have been submerged in the Sea of Pureness.'*[26] These Words describe the effect of the revelation of the Word of God as a universal regeneration of all things, which are divested of their former characteristics and then appear again purified, renewed, re-created. This is one of the meanings of the metaphors of the succession of seasons, viewed as the succession of the Manifestations of God. This is why Bahá'u'lláh refers to His Own Advent as *'the Divine Springtime'*. This *'Divine Springtime'*, this re-creation, this purification, this renewal are for the individual, as soon as he meets His Lord through the reading of His Words. Such 'reading' is obviously not a mere verbal or mental reading. It is rather the inner perception of the deep quickening power of the Divine Word. Through this perception, a man undergoes an inner transformation whereby he will no longer be the same. And yet, human souls do not all respond to the Word of God in the same way. *'Some'*, writes Bahá'u'lláh, *'have made haste to attain the court of the God of Mercy, others have fallen down on their faces in the fire of Hell, while still others are lost in bewilderment.'*[27]

23. *Seven Valleys*, p.5.
24. *Gleanings*, pp.29–30, 62.
25. Quoted in Shoghi Effendi, *Promised Day*, p.47.
26. Quoted in Mírzá Abu'l-Fadl, *Bahá'í Proofs*, p.86.
27. *Gleanings*, pp.27, 41–2. As to the concepts of paradise and hell, *see* above, p.213, n. 43.

Bahá'u'lláh likens the outpourings of His Word to the breaths of *'fertilizing winds'*. In the same vein He writes: *'The whole earth is now in a state of pregnancy. The day is approaching when it will have yielded its noblest fruits, when from it will have sprung forth the loftiest trees, the most enchanting blossoms, the most heavenly blessings.'*[28] The Word of God fertilizes mankind, setting a process in motion which yields its fruit in the flourishing of a new civilization. Likewise, that Word fertilizes any individual who has understood its quickening power, inasmuch as it sets in motion an inner process within him which is the essence of his spiritual growth.[29] The time of the meeting with the Word of God is therefore of vital importance in the life of every man, who – since God has bestowed upon him the gift of freedom in his own choices – runs the risk of missing this wonderful opportunity.[30] In the light of these concepts the following exhortation uttered by Bahá'u'lláh will be more easily understood: *'O Brother! Not every sea hath pearls; not every branch will flower, nor will the nightingale of the mystic paradise repair to the garden of God, and the rays of the heavenly morning return to the Sun of Truth – make thou an effort, that haply in this dust-heap of the mortal world thou mayest catch a fragrance from the everlasting garden and live forever in the shadow of the peoples of this city. And when thou hast attained this highest station and come to this mightiest plane, then shalt thou gaze on the Beloved,*[31] *and forget all else . . . Now hast thou abandoned the drop of life and come to the sea of the Life-Bestower.*[32] *This is the goal thou*

---

28. Quoted in Shoghi Effendi, *Promised Day*, p.47.
29. *See* above p.115, etc. For a deeper discussion of the concept of spiritual growth, *see* A. Taherzadeh, *The Revelation of Bahá'u'lláh*, vol. I, pp.73–4.
30. That is why this time is described in the Holy Writings as the *'Day of Judgement'*. At that time, souls are judged by their capacity and willingness to respond to the Word of God.
As to the reasons why some understand these Words and others do not, Bahá'u'lláh said the following enlightening words to Nabíl, the great historian of the Bahá'í Faith: 'Be thankful to God for having enabled you to recognize His Cause. Whoever has received this blessing must, prior to his acceptance, have performed some deed which, though he himself was unaware of its character, was ordained by God as a means whereby he has been guided to find and embrace the Truth. As to those who have remained deprived of such a blessing, their acts alone have hindered them from recognizing the truth of His Revelation. We cherish the hope that you, who have attained to this light, will exert your utmost to banish the darkness of superstition and unbelief from the midst of people. May your deeds proclaim your faith and enable you to lead the erring into the paths of eternal salvation.' (Words uttered by Bahá'u'lláh, recorded in Nabíl, *The Dawn-Breakers*, p.586.)
31. The 'Beloved' is the Manifestation of God.
32. It is a reference to the famous Apologue of the Pearl, from Sa'di's *Golestan*, thus epitomized by A. Bausani: 'A drop of water fell down from a cloud and, as it saw the great ocean, it was dumbfounded. If the ocean exists, I am nothing,it said. But the ocean welcomed the drop in its wide bosom and the shell trained and nourished it by its vital power, as a prize for its humility, until the humble drop turned into a famous, kingly pearl.' (*Persia Religiosa*, p.316.)

didst ask for; if it be God's will, thou wilt gain it.'[33] He adds: '*How strange that while the Beloved is visible as the sun, yet the heedless still hunt after tinsel and base metal. Yea, the intensity of His revelation hath covered Him, and the fullness of His shining forth hath hidden Him.*

> *Even as the sun, bright hath He shined,*
> *But alas, He hath come to the town of the blind!*'

Experiences of such a meeting have been described in words. There is so much privacy in this event that its experience can hardly be conveyed to others. And yet, one of its manifold aspects seems to be shared by all those who describe it: the reading of that Word becomes a real meeting as soon as the ideas and feelings which those Words convey evoke such an echo from the heart, produce such vibrations in its inmost chords, that it seems as though they are coming forth from the heart's innermost essence. In those Words, the seeker meets his own self, he re-discovers truths that he had always vaguely felt in his innermost heart and that now he finds clearly explained.[34] This is one of the deepest experiences of mystical union a man may go through, if he only is willing to. It is as the ancient tradition says: '*A servant is drawn unto Me in prayer until I answer him: and when I have answered him, I become the ear wherewith he heareth . . .*'[35]

---

33. *Seven Valleys*, pp.38–9.

34. A famous testimony of this meeting has been handed down by Mullá Ḥusayn, the first person who believed in the Báb, the Herald of the Bahá'í Dispensation. In his detailed account of the experience of his first meeting with the Báb, in Shiraz on the evening of 22 May 1844, he said: 'This Revelation, so suddenly and impetuously thrust upon me, came as a thunderbolt which, for a time, seemed to have benumbed my faculties. I was blinded by its dazzling splendour and overwhelmed by its crushing force. Excitement, joy, awe, and wonder stirred the depths of my soul. Predominant among these emotions was a sense of gladness and strength which seemed to have transfigured me. How feeble and impotent, how dejected and timid, I had felt previously! Then I could neither write nor walk, so tremulous were my hands and feet. Now, however, the knowledge of His Revelation had galvanized my being. I felt possessed of such courage and power that were the world, all its people and its potentates, to rise against me, I would, alone and undaunted, withstand their onslaught. The universe seemed but a handful of dust in my grasp . . .' (Nabíl, *The Dawn-Breakers*, p.65.)

Another very interesting testimony has been handed down by Queen Marie of Romania. She was not privileged to attain the presence of the Manifestation of God, but she accepted the Bahá'í Faith after she read Bahá'í texts. Thus she describes the feelings which were stirred up in her heart through that reading: 'If ever the name of Bahá'u'lláh or 'Abdu'l-Bahá comes to your attention, do not put their writings from you. Search out their Books, and let their glorious, peace-bringing, love-creating words and lessons sink into your hearts as they have into mine . . . Seek them, and be the happier.' '. . . these books have strengthened me beyond belief and I am now ready to die any day full of hope . . .' 'The Bahá'í teaching brings peace and understanding. It is like a wide embrace gathering together all those who have long searched for words of hope . . . To those in search of assurance the words of the Father are as a fountain in the desert after long wandering.' (Quoted in *Bahá'í World*, v, pp.323–4.)

35. *Seven Valleys*, p.22.

It is the time of the 'second birth':[36] that time when the inner being of man is regenerated. All of a sudden he catches a glimpse, according to his capacities, of that personal and individual reality which the Manifestation of God lays bare in front of him. Through that vision a force is generated that, if he will only make an effort, will guide him during all his life, nourished by all the means and methods recommended for his spiritual progress, along the thorny path of self-purification, of sacrifice, of love, up to self-effacement, perfect service, and finally to the stage of unconditional love.[37]

Through that meeting the heart is transformed, the feelings are re-created, the urge to act is stirred up. And if man will conquer every fear, and overcome any other attraction, and will give up himself to that love, and persistently act according to that Word — then in each of his actions and of their fruits he will again and again meet the Manifestation of God, and in the Manifestation he will meet with God. He will live for ever in Paradise.[38]

---

36. *Promulgation*, p. 305.

37. Referring to the meeting between the soul and the Word of the Manifestation of God, 'Abdu'l-Bahá writes: '*The blessings of Bahá'u'lláh are a shoreless sea, and even life everlasting is only a dewdrop therefrom. The waves of that sea are continually lapping against the hearts of the friends, and from those waves there come intimations of the spirit and ardent pulsings of the soul, until the heart giveth away, and willing or not, turneth humbly in prayer unto the Kingdom of the Lord.*' (*Selections*, pp. 192–3.)

38. '*Know thou for a certainty that whoso disbelieveth in God is neither trustworthy nor truthful . . . Nothing whatever can deter such a man from evil, nothing can hinder him from betraying his neighbour, nothing can induce him to walk uprightly.*' (*Gleanings*, pp. 232–3.)
This is R. Rabbani's comment upon these stern words: 'How unbelievably stern are these words — so stern, indeed, that we are tempted to discount them. But when we pass on to His dire warnings regarding the state of human society and what its general delinquency may well lead to, we begin to grasp the subtle depths of this statement and we enter a field that merits profound contemplation, for it analyses and explains, warns and prophesies about the period we ourselves are living in. "*This is the Day whereon every man will fly from himself, how much more from his kindred, could ye but perceive it . . .*". Split personalities? Broken homes, divorce, shattered societies? "*This is the Day on which all eyes shall stare up with terror, the Day in which the hearts of them that dwell on earth shall tremble . . .*". A giant mushroom in the sky? The sound of gunfire and bombs?' (*The Desire of the World*, pp. 69–70.)
These stern words by Bahá'u'lláh on atheism, and the brief but touching comment by R. Rabbani, may appear more clear in the light of the concepts of religion, religiousness and knowledge of God which have been previously mentioned.

A Conclusion

Upon a thread of words we have tried to cover a long way in our efforts aimed at 'comprehending the reality of things as they exist, according to the capacity and the power of man'.[1] Whoever treads this path will undoubtedly run the risk of exceeding in knowledge, of lacking in love, of forgoing action. These are the pitfalls he will have to avoid as he treads that path, all the more so in a modern Western world where 'philosophy, it has been said, is talk about talk'.[2]

We are reminded of the following stern admonition uttered by Bahá'u'lláh: '. . . *he whose words exceed his deeds, know verily his death is better than his life.*'[3] Should the Bahá'í would-be philosopher or scholar refrain today from his search? Should he give up his efforts to understand the world and himself? When 'Abdu'l-Bahá was asked: 'Shall we devote much time to the study of philosophy?' He answered: 'Everything must be done moderately. Excess is not desirable. Do not go to extremes. Even in thinking do not go to excess, but be moderate. If there is too much thinking, you will be unable to control your thoughts.'[4] Therefore, once again the answer lies in moderation, balance, harmonious growth, wisdom. Knowledge, volition and action — active expressions of the three fundamental capacities of the soul, to know, to love and to will — are the three indispensable factors for any realization in human life.[5] They must be harmoniously developed so that none of them

---

1. *Some Answered Questions*, p.221.
2. A. J. Ayer, *The Concept of a Person*, p.3.
3. *Tablets*, p.156.
4. Quoted in A. Kunz, 'Some Questions about Science and Religion' in *Star of the West*, XIII, p.143.
5. See *Promulgation*, p.157.

A Conclusion

will overcome the others. This is one of the most important practical conclusions of our search.

Our words are therefore intended as an invitation to a study of reality; as a provision for the execution of those practical, preliminary exercises that life assigns to each of us so that our capacities of knowing, loving and willing may be trained; an encouragement and an incentive in the performance of such deeds as will enable us to test – before the tribunal of life – any achieved knowledge, and perceived attraction. But we will always be ready to renounce any of those thoughts and attachments which – though they have been already weighed and meditated upon – prove themselves in the light of facts to be remote from reality, inasmuch as they will not be able to contribute to that world of love and unity, peace and justice God is teaching us how to build.

Bibliography

ABBAGNANO, N. *Dizionario di Filosofia*. Torino: UTET, 1984.
— *Storia della Filosofia*. 2 vols. Torino: UTET, 1982.
ABU'L-FAḌL, MÍRZÁ. 'The Heart. Lesson given to Mrs. Corinne True, summer of 1904.' *Star of the West*, Vol. X, p. 115.
— *The Bahá'í Proofs and A Short Sketch of the History and Lives of the Leaders of This Religion*. Wilmette, Illinois: Bahá'í Publishing Trust, 1983.
'ABDU'L-BAHÁ. *'Abdu'l-Bahá in London*. London: Bahá'í Publishing Trust, 1982.
— *'Abdu'l-Bahá on Divine Philosophy*. Boston: The Tudor Press, 1918.
— *Paris Talks: Addresses Given by 'Abdu'l-Bahá in Paris in 1911–1912*. 11th edn. London: Bahá'í Publishing Trust, 1969.
— *The Promulgation of Universal Peace. Talks delivered by 'Abdu'l-Bahá during His visit to the United States and Canada in 1912*. Comp. Howard MacNutt. 2nd edn. Wilmette, Illinois: Bahá'í Publishing Trust, 1982.
— *Some Answered Question*. Trans. Laura Clifford-Barney. 3rd edn. Wilmette, Illinois: Bahá'í Publishing Trust, 1981.
— *The Secret of Divine Civilization*. Trans. Marzieh Gail. Wilmette, Illinois: Bahá'í Publishing Trust, 1957.
— *Selections from the Writings of 'Abdu'l-Bahá*. Trans. Marzieh Gail. Haifa: Bahá'í World Centre, 1978.
— 'Tablet to Dr. August Forel'. *The Bahá'í World*, Vol. XV, pp. 37–43.
— *Tablets of 'Abdu'l-Bahá Abbas*. Vols. I, II and III. New York: Bahá'í Publishing Society, 1909–1915.
— *Tablets of the Divine Plan*. Rev. edn. Wilmette, Illinois: Bahá'í Publishing Trust, 1977.
— *The Will and Testament of 'Abdu'l-Bahá*. Wilmette, Illinois: Bahá'í Publishing Trust, 1971.

* * *

From *Star of the West*:
— 'Become Lamp of the True One.' Vol. IX, p. 162.

Bibliography

- 'Divine Contentment. Tablet to Mr. and Mrs. Rabb of San Francisco.' Vol. XIV, p. 168.
- 'Extracts from Tablets of Abdul-Baha to Mrs. Isabella D. Brittingham.' Vol. XIV, p. 353.
- 'A Fortune that Bestows Eternal Happiness. Knowledge, Purity of Thought and Love. Talks given by Abdul-Baha on Mount Carmel to a group of college students during their summer vacation.' Vol. XIII, p. 102.
- 'The Greatest of the Gifts of God.' Vol. IX, p. 163.
- 'How is it possible to imagine life after death? Recent Tablet from Abdul-Baha to J. Isbrucker.' Vol. XI, p. 316.
- 'It is the time which His Holiness Christ calls the "Days of Marriage".' Tablet from Abdul-Baha. Vol. XII, p. 194.
- 'Progress in Religion. The Question of Evolution.' Vol. XIII, p. 99.
- 'Recent Tablets to Bahais in America.' Vol. XII, pp. 58, 194.
- 'Some Questions Answered by Abdul-Baha.' Vol. XIV, p. 37.
- 'Survival and Salvation. Words of Abdul-Baha from Diary of Mirza Ahmad Sohrab.' Vol. VI, p. 190. Vol. XIV, p. 11.
- 'Tablets of Abdul-Baha recently revealed.' Vol. X, p. 7.
- 'Talks by Abdul-Baha in the Holy Land.' Vol. IX, p. 135.
- 'The Three Realities. Address by Abdul-Baha at "The White Lodge", Wimbledon, England, Friday Evening, January 3, 1913.' Vol. VII, p. 117.
- 'The Worst Enemies of the Cause are in the Cause. Utterances of Abdul-Baha in answer to questions asked by Dr. Edward G. Getsinger during brief meetings at Haifa, Syria, January 26 to February 5, 1915, and recorded by Dr. Getsinger at the time.' Vol. VI, p. 43.

Airone: Vivere la natura, conoscere il mondo. A monthly magazine on nature and civilization. Milan: Giorgio Mondadori e Associati.

ANONYMOUS AUTHORS. 'Join the Army of Peace,' *Star of the West*, Vol. XIII, p. 112.
- 'The Need of a Universal Program,' *Star of the West*, Vol. XIII, p. 131.
- 'Studies in Immortality,' *Star of the West*, Vol. XIV, pp. 11, 37.
- 'References to the Bahá'í Faith.' *The Bahá'í World*, Vol. VI, p. 480; Vol. VIII, p. 270.

ATTAR, FARID UD-DIN. *The Conference of the Birds.* Translation and Introduction by Afkhan Darbandi and Dick Davis. London: 1984.

AYER, A. J. *The Concept of a Person and Other Essays.* London: 1966.

BÁB, THE. *Selections from the Writing of the Báb.* Trans. Habib Taherzadeh. Haifa: Bahá'í World Centre, 1976.

BAHÁ'Í INTERNATIONAL COMMUNITY. *The Bahá'í Statement on Nature.* New York: Bahá'í International Community, 1987.

Bahá'í News. A monthly news journal published by the National Spiritual Assembly of the Bahá'ís of the United States. Wilmette, Illinois, USA.

Bahá'í Studies. A publication of the Canadian Association for Studies of the Bahá'í Faith.

Bahá'í World, The. An International Record.
- Vol. VI, 1934–1936. Wilmette, Illinois: Bahá'í Publishing Trust, 1937.
- Vol. VIII, 1938–1940. Wilmette, Illinois: Bahá'í Publishing Trust, 1941.
- Vol. XV, 1968–1973. Haifa: Bahá'í World Centre, 1976.
- Vol. XVII, 1976–1979. Haifa: Bahá'í World Centre, 1981.

BAHÁ'U'LLÁH. *Epistle to the Son of the Wolf.* Trans. Shoghi Effendi. 2nd edn. Wilmette, Illinois: Bahá'í Publishing Trust, 1953.
- *Gleanings from the Writings of Bahá'u'lláh.* Trans. Shoghi Effendi. Rev. edn. Wilmette, Illinois: Bahá'í Publishing Trust, 1952.

- *The Hidden Words of Bahá'u'lláh.* Trans. Shoghi Effendi. Wilmette, Illinois: Bahá'í Publishing Trust, 1975.
- *Kitáb-i-Íqán. The Book of Certitude.* Trans. Shoghi Effendi. 2nd edn. Wilmette, Illinois: Bahá'í Publishing Trust, 1970.
- *Prayers and Meditations.* Comp. and trans. Shoghi Effendi. London: Bahá'í Publishing Trust, 1957.
- *The Proclamation of Bahá'u'lláh to the Kings and Leaders of the World.* Trans. Shoghi Effendi. Comp. The Universal House of Justice. Haifa: Bahá'í World Centre, 1967.
- *The Seven Valleys and the Four Valleys.* Trans. Marzieh Gail. Rev. edn. Wilmette, Illinois: Bahá'í Publishing Trust, 1952.
- *A Synopsis and Codification of the Kitáb-i-Aqdas.* Comp. The Universal House of Justice. Haifa: Bahá'í World Centre, 1973.
- *The Tablet of the Holy Mariner and the Tablet of Fire.* Hofheim-Langenhain: Bahá'í-Verlag, 1980.
- *Tablets of Bahá'u'lláh Revealed after the Kitáb-i-Aqdas.* Trans. Habib Taherzadeh. Haifa: Bahá'í World Centre, 1978.

From *Star of the West*:
- 'The Federation of the World. A Tablet of Bahá'u'lláh.' Vol. XIV, p.296.
- untitled. Vol. VII, p.100.

BAHÁ'U'LLÁH and 'ABDU'L-BAHÁ. *Bahá'í World Faith: Selected Writings of Bahá'u'lláh and 'Abdu'l-Bahá.* Rev. edn. Wilmette, Illinois: Bahá'í Publishing Trust, 1956.

BAHÁ'U'LLÁH, 'ABDU'L-BAHÁ and THE BÁB. *Bahá'í Prayers: A Selection of Prayers.* Wilmette, Illinois: Bahá'í Publishing Trust, 1981.

BALYUZI, H. M. *The Báb: The Herald of the Day of Days.* Oxford: George Ronald, 1973.
- *'Abdu'l-Bahá: The Centre of the Covenant of Bahá'u'lláh.* London. George Ronald, 1971.
- *Bahá'u'lláh: The King of Glory.* Oxford: George Ronald, 1980.

BATTAGLIA, S. *Il Grande Dizionario della Lingua Italiana.* Turin: UTET. Vol. III, 1964; Vol. IX, 1975.

BAUSANI, A. 'Cuore, cervello, mistica, religione.' *Opinioni Bahá'í*, Vol. II, no. 1, p.55.
- 'La nascita di Bahá'u'lláh.' *Opinioni Bahá'í*, Vol. VIII, no. 4, p.3.
- *Persia Religiosa.* Milan: Il Saggiatore, 1959.
- 'Some Aspects of the Bahá'í Expressive Style.' *World Order*, Vol. 13, no. 2, p.36.
- 'Unità delle Religione'. To be published.

CABANIS, P. *Rapports du physique et du moral.* 1802.

COLE, J. R. 'The Concept of Manifestation in the Bahá'í Writings.' *Bahá'í Studies.* Vol. 9, 1982.
- 'Problems of chronology in Bahá'u'lláh's Tablet of Wisdom.' *World Order*, Vol. 13, n. 3 p.24.

Compilations. prepared by the Universal House of Justice.
- *Bahá'í Education: A Compilation.* London: Bahá'í Publishing Trust, 1976.
- *Bahá'í Institutions.* New Delhi: Bahá'í Publishing Trust, 1973.
- *The Establishment of The Universal House of Justice.* London: Bahá'í Publishing Trust, 1984.
- *Health and Healing: Some Aspects.* Auckland: National Spiritual Assembly of the Bahá'ís of New Zealand, 1981.
- *Huqúqu'lláh: The Right of God.* London: Bahá'í Publishing Trust, 1986.
- *The Heaven of Divine Wisdom.* London: Bahá'í Publishing Trust, 1978.

Bibliography

— *The Importance of Prayer, Meditation and the Devotional Attitude.* London: Bahá'í Publishing Trust, 1981.
— *Living the Life. A Compilation.* London: Bahá'í Publishing Trust, 1974.
— *Peace.* London: Bahá'í Publishing Trust, 1985.
COY, G. *Counsels of Perfection. A Bahá'í Guide to Mature Living.* Oxford: George Ronald, 1978.
DAHL, A. L. *A Bahá'í Perspective on Nature and the Environment.* New York: Bahá'í International Community, 1986.
DANESH, H. B. 'Conflict-free Conflict Resolution. Integrating the Principles of Bahá'í Consultation, Group Dynamics and Human Development.' Unpublished.
— 'Health and Healing.' *World Order,* Vol. 13, no. 3. p.15.
— *The Violence-Free Society. A Gift for Our Children. Bahá'í Studies,* Vol. 6, 1979.
DELAUNAY, A. 'Vita.' *Enciclopedia della Scienza e della Tecnica,* Vol. XII, p.673.
Enciclopedia Italiana di Scienza, Lettere ed Arti. Milan: Istituto Giovanni Treccani. Vol. I, 1929; Vol. IV, 1929; Vol. V, 1930; Vol. XII, 1931.
ESSLEMONT, J. E. *Bahá'u'lláh and the New Era.* 4th rev. edn. Wilmette, Illinois: Bahá'í Publishing Trust, 1980.
EST: *Enciclopedia della Scienza e della Tecnica.* Vol. II, IV, XII. Milan: Arnoldo Mondadori Editore, 1970. English edition: *Encyclopaedia of Science and Technology.* McGraw-Hill, 1960–1971.
EYFORD, G. A., 'Aesthetics and Spiritual Education.' *World Order,* Vol. 14, no. 1, p.36.
FACCHINI, F. *Il cammino dell'evoluzione umana. Le scoperte e i dibattiti della paleoantropologia.* Milan: Jaca Book, 1985.
FERMI, E. 'Atomo.' *Enciclopedia Italiana,* Vol. V, p.245.
GHISELLI, A. and C. CASAGRANDE. *Lingua e Parola. Grammatica, sintassi e avviamento allo studio della letteratura.* Florence: Sansoni, 1974.
GIACHERY, U. R. *Shoghi Effendi: Recollections.* Oxford: George Ronald, 1973.
GRATTON, L. 'Cosmologia.' *Enciclopedia della Scienza e della Tecnica,* Vol. IV, p.338.
GRUNDY, J. M. *Ten Days in the Light of 'Akká.* Wilmette, Illinois: Bahá'í Publishing Trust, 1979.
HAECKEL, E. *Generelle Morfologie der Organismen.*
HATCHER, J. S. *The Metaphorical Nature of Material Reality. Bahá'í Studies,* Vol. 3, 1977.
— *The Purpose of Physical Reality. The Kingdom of Names.* Wilmette, Illinois: Bahá'í Publishing Trust, 1987.
HATCHER, W. S. *The Concept of Spirituality. Bahá'í Studies,* Vol. 11, 1982.
— 'A Logical Solution to the Problem of Evil. *Zygon,* Vol. 9, no. 3, 1974.
— *Science and the Bahá'í Faith. Bahá'í Studies,* Vol. 2, 1977.
— 'Science and Religion.' *World Order,* Vol. 3, no. 3, p.7.
— 'The Unity of Religion and Science.' *World Order,* Vol. 9, no. 3, p.22.
HELLABY, W. and M. *Prayer: A Bahá'í Approach.* Oxford: George Ronald, 1985.
HOBBES, T. *Leviathan.* London, 1651.
JAHODA, M. 'Uomini e Orsi. Ma è possible convivere?' *Airone,* No. 51, 1985, p.71.
JORDAN, D. *Becoming Your True Self.* Wilmette, Illinois: Bahá'í Publishing Trust, 1971.
— *The Meaning of Deepening.* Wilmette, Illinois: Bahá'í Publishing Trust, 1973.

JORDAN, D. S. in 'References to the Bahá'í Faith.' *The Bahá'í World*, Vol. VIII, p.270.
KAWAI, M. 'Newly acquired precultural behaviour in the natural troops of Japanese monkeys of Koshima Islet.' *Primates* 1965, Vol. VI, pp.1–30.
KOLSTOE, J. E. *Consultation. A Universal Lamp of Guidance*. Oxford: George Ronald, 1985.
KUNZ, A. 'Some Questions about Science and Religion. An Interview with 'Abdu'l-Bahá at Tiberias and Haifa.' *Star of the West*, Vol. XIII, p.139.
LASZLO, E. *Evolution, The Grand Synthesis*. Boston, 1987.
LORENZ, K. *The Waning of Humaneness*. London, 1988.
MAHMOUDI, J. 'The Institutionalization of Religion.' *World Order*, Vol. 2, no. 1, p.16.
MCLEAN, J. 'The Knowledge of God: An Essay on Bahá'í Epistemology.' *World Order*, Vol. 12, no. 3, p.38.
MARIE OF ROMANIA in 'References to the Bahá'í Faith.' *The Bahá'í World*, Vol. VI, pp.449–53.
MELCHIORRI, F. and B. OLIVO MELCHIORRI. 'La cosmologia del big bang.' *Scienza e Tecnica* 80/82, p.35.
MERTON, T. *New Seeds on Contemplation*. Abbey of Gethsemani, Inc., 1961.
MOFFETT, R. *Du'a: On Wings of Prayer*. Naturegraph Publishers, Inc., 1984.
MORENO, M. M. *Antologia della Mistica Arabo-Persiana*. Bari: Laterza, 1951.
MURCHIE, G. *The Seven Mysteries of Life. An Exploration in Science and Philosophy*. Boston: Houghton Mifflin Company, 1978.
NABÍL-I-A'ZAM (Muḥammad-i-Zarandí). *The Dawn-Breakers: Nabíl's Narrative of the Early Days of the Bahá'í Revelation*. Trans. Shoghi Effendi. New York, Bahá'í Publishing Committee, 1932.
NASH, G. *The Phoenix and the Ashes. The Bahá'í Faith and the Modern Apocalypse*. Oxford: George Ronald, 1984.
New Day. The national Bahá'í periodical of the Bahá'ís of Ireland. Dublin, Ireland.
NICHOLSON, R. A. *Selected Poems from the Divani Shamsi Tabriz*. Cambridge, 1952.
N. S. F. 'Capacity and Spiritual Revelation.' *Star of the West*, Vol. XIII, p.214.
Opinioni Bahá'í. A quarterly magazine published by the Italian Casa Editrice Bahá'í. Rome.
PIATTELLI PALMARINI, M. 'Sui limiti della razionalitá.' *Scienza e Tecnica* 75, p.180.
POPPER, K. *The Logic of Scientific Discovery*. London, 1968.
PRIGOGINE, Y. and A. DANZIN. 'Quale scienza per domani?' *Corriere Unesco*, no. 2, 1982.
RABB, M. M. 'The Divine Art of Living. A Compilation.' *Star of the West*, Vol. VIII, pp.149, 177; Vol. VIII, pp.5, 17, 41, 57, 84, 121, 123, 136, 228, 234, 238.
RABBANI, R. *The Desire of the World. Materials for the contemplation of God and the Manifestation of this Day*. Compiled from the Words of Bahá'u'lláh. Oxford: George Ronald, 1983.
— 'The Prayers of Bahá'u'lláh.' *The Bahá'í World*, Vol. IX, p.792.
— *The Priceless Pearl*. London: Bahá'í Publishing Trust, 1969.
RECAMI, E. 'Particelle elementari come microuniversi.' *Scienza e Tecnica* 79, p.60.
ROOT, M. 'Happiness from the Bahá'í Viewpoint.' *Star of the West*, Vol. XIII, p.101.
SAVI, J. 'Alcuni aspetti del rapporto fra religione e medicina.' *Opinioni Bahá'í*, Vol. V, no. 1, p.24.

— *The Child and Spiritual Life in the Family: A Bahá'í Perspective*. Geneva: Bahá'í International Community, 1986.
— 'La meta della giustizia sociale.' *Opinioni Bahá'í*, Vol. III, no. 2. p.6.
— 'La purezza: attributo della anime devote.' *Opinioni Bahá'í*, Vol. IV, no. 2. p.3.
— 'Salute e guarigione negli Scritti Bahá'í.' *Opinioni Bahá'í*. Vol. V, no. 2, p.13.
SCHAEFER, U. *The Imperishable Dominion. The Bahá'í Faith and the Future of Mankind*. Oxford: George Ronald, 1983.
Scienza e Tecnica. Annuario dell'Enciclopedia della Scienza e della Tecnica. Milan: Mondadori. 75, 1975; 79, 1979; 80–82, 1982.
SHOGHI EFFENDI. *The Advent of Divine Justice*. Rev. edn. Wilmette, Illinois: Bahá'í Publishing Trust, 1984.
— *Arohanui. Letters from Shoghi Effendi to New Zealand*. Suva: Bahá'í Publishing Trust, 1971.
— *Call to the Nations*. Comp. The Universal House of Justice. Haifa: Bahá'í World Centre, 1977.
— *Dawn of a New Day: Messages to India 1923–1957*. New Delhi: Bahá'í Publishing Trust, 1970.
— *The Faith of Bahá'u'lláh. A World Religion*. Wilmette, Illinois: Bahá'í Publishing Trust, 1980.
— *God Passes By*. Wilmette, Illinois: Bahá'í Publishing Trust, 1957.
— *High Endeavours: Messages to Alaska*. Anchorage: National Spiritual Assembly of the Bahá'ís of Alaska, 1976.
— *The Light of Divine Guidance*. Hofheim-Langenhain: Bahá'í-Verlag, 1982.
— *The Light of Divine Guidance*. Volume 2. Hofheim-Langenhain: Bahá'í Verlag, 1985.
— *Principles of Bahá'í Administration*. 3rd edn. London: Bahá'í Publishing Trust, 1976.
— *The Promised Day Is Come*. Wilmette, Illinois: Bahá'í Publishing Committee, 1941.
— *Unfolding Destiny. The Messages from the Guardian to the Bahá'ís of the British Isles*. London: Bahá'í Publishing Trust, 1981.
— *The World Order of Bahá'u'lláh. Selected Letters*. Wilmette, Illinois: Bahá'í Publishing Trust, 1955.
SHOOK, G. A. *Mysticism, Science and Revelation*. Oxford: George Ronald, 1974.
Star of the West. The first Bahá'í magazine in the Western world, published from 1910 to April 1924. Reprint. Oxford: George Ronald, 1978.
TAHERZADEH, A. 'Notes on Bahá'í Concept of Spirituality.' *New Day*, May–June 1984.
— *The Revelation of Bahá'u'lláh. Baghdád 1853–63*. Oxford: George Ronald, 1974.
TERTULLIAN, Q. S. F. *De Carne Christi*.
TOWNSHEND, G. *Christ and Bahá'u'lláh*. Oxford: George Ronald, 1972.
— *The Mission of Bahá'u'lláh*. London: George Ronald, 1965.
— 'Solving the Christian Enigma.' *Bahá'í News*, no. 534, September 1975.
UNIVERSAL HOUSE OF JUSTICE, THE. 'The Challenge and Promise of Bahá'í Scholarship.' *The Bahá'í World*, Vol. XVII, pp.195–6.
— *The Promise of World Peace*. Haifa: Bahá'í World Centre, 1985.
VAIL, A. 'Teach the Cause of God. The Most Important Work. A Compilation of the Words of Abdul-Baha from Talks and Tablets.' *Star of the West*, Vol. IX, p.161.

VAN LAWICK-GOODALL, J. 'The Behaviour of Free-Living Chimpanzees in the Gombe Stream Reserve.' *Animal Behaviour Monographs*, no. 1, part 3, 1968.
VEGNI, G. 'Atomo.' *Enciclopedia della Scienza e della Tecnica*, Vol. II, p.373.
WEIL, H. A. *Closer than your Life Vein. An Insight into the Wonders of Spiritual Fulfilment*. Anchorage: National Spiritual Assembly of the Bahá'ís of Alaska, 1978.
WINTERBURN, G. *Table Talks with Abdul-Baha*. Chicago: Bahá'í Publishing Society, 1908.
WORLD HEALTH ORGANIZATION. *Alma-Ata 1978. Primary Health Care*. Report of the International Conference on Primary Health Care, Alma-Ata, USSR, 6–12 September 1978. Geneva: World Health Organization Publications, 1978.
World Order. A quarterly Bahá'í magazine published by the National Spiritual Assembly of the Bahá'ís of the United States. Wilmette, Illinois, USA.
ZOHOORI, E. *The Throne of the Inner Temple*. Jamaica, 1985.
Zygon. Journal of Religion and Science. The University of Chicago.

Index

This index is designed to refer the reader to the Bahá'í texts wherever possible, and not only to the relevant pages in this book. For this reason, most subheadings are direct quotations from the Bahá'í Writings.

A

Abbagnano, N., 19n, 144n, 147n, 170, 212n
'Abdu'l-Bahá, xvi, xvii, 1, 2, 4, 5, 20, 37n
   definitions of religion by, 18n
   excellent horseman, 80
   His address at the Friends' Meeting House, 159
   and perfections of man in activity, 2
   a practical mystic, 2
   Secret of Divine Civilization, The, 17
   'Tablet on Purity', so-called, 185n
   Tablets of the Divine Plan, 216n
   travels in North America, xv
   visits Stanford University, 2
Abraham, 100, 196
Abu'l-Faḍl, Mírzá, 111, 232
Action (actions), 167–70
   spiritual, 174
   thought and, *see* Thought
Adam, 41, 109, 196
Addiction, *see* Habits
Adrons, 55n, 74
Affinity
   chemical, 75
   selective in animals, 81, 161
   of the atoms, *see* Atom
   of the elements, 51
   the cause of life, 51, 77
Agnosia to pain, 162n
Agnosticism, 70
Alcohol, 186n
Algae, blue-green, 78
'Alí, Commander of the Faithful, 171n
Alma Ata, Conference of, 185n
Animals, 63–4, 78
   difference between men and, 44n, 80–83, 93, 101–2, 137, 160
   feelings of, 63, 79, 156
   freedom of, 83
   king of the world of nature, 79, 82, 83
   learning in, 80–81
   limitations of, 81–3
   man
      does not come from the, 79, 190
      perfect animal, 137
   memory in, 64, 79–80
   origin of, 78–9
   qualities of, 79–81

sense perception of, *see* Perception, sensory
Apes, *see* Pongides
Aquinas, St. Thomas, 24n, 143n
Arandas, 194
Arc of existence, *see* Plotinus
Archetype, *see* Exemplar
  archetypal virtues, 106
Aristotle, 15, 16n, 24n
  Eastern philosopher, 16n, 93n
Atheism, 235n
Atom (atoms)
  affinity of, 51–2, 54, 77, 97, 205
    expression
      of love, 54, 77, 205
      of spirit, 54–5
    conception of
      of 'Abdu'l-Bahá, 51–6
      of scientists, 53–4
    elemental, 51, 53, 57, 77
    and intrinsic oneness of all phenomena, 55, *see also* World material
    is indestructible, 55
    is totipotent, 54, 57
    motion of, 54
      expression of the dynamism of the spirit, 54, 77
Atomic bomb, 54
Attachment, 167n, 170–71
  conscious, 160
  of the heart, 167n
Attainment of any object, 19, 155
Attraction, 51
  atomic, *see* Atom, affinity of
  power of, 40, 61, 63, 67, 77, 205
  toward the natal self, 131
  toward the world of creation, 126, 127, 161, 170–71
  toward the world of the Kingdom, 115, 126, 127, 134, 161, 169, 217
    conscious, 160
Attributes of God, 32–5, 56n
  active, 33–4
  essential, 33
    identical with the Essence of God, 33
    incomprehensible to man, 33
  infinite, 125
  within created things, 32–3
  within man, *see* Man
Augustine, 8n, 143n

Australopithecus, 193, 194, 203
Avicenna, 24n
Ayer, A.J., 21, 236

B

Báb, The, 20 and n, 100, 133, 172–3, 185n, 213n, 234n
Bayán, 14n
Bacon, R., 204
Backbiting, 129
Bahá'í Community as model for study, 194n
Bahá'í Faith, xv
  scientific in its method, 8
Bahá'u'lláh, 1n, 2, 20, 41, 100, 197, 230, 231–3
  quotations from
    Epistle to the Son of the Wolf, 105, 122, 128, 130, 147
    Gleanings from the Writings of Bahá'u'lláh, xvin, 22, 24, 27, 28, 32, 35, 37, 38, 39, 43, 44, 45, 46, 49, 50, 56, 65, 70, 86, 87, 88, 91, 95, 99, 102, 104, 105, 106, 107, 108, 109, 110, 111, 112, 113, 119, 120, 122, 126, 127, 130, 144, 145, 147, 148, 149, 150, 152, 153, 154, 155, 160, 165, 167, 168, 173, 175, 182, 183, 184, 196, 199, 202, 205, 208, 209, 215, 216, 219, 220, 222, 223, 224, 227, 231, 232, 234
    Hidden Words, 7, 36, 87, 118, 127, 129, 134, 161, 177, 209, 215
    Kitáb-i-Aqdas, 14, 120, 184, 185, 186, 208, 231
    Kitáb-i-Íqán, 7, 13, 28, 56, 60, 87, 98, 107, 112, 120, 122, 126, 129, 138, 147, 171, 175, 215
    Proclamation of Bahá'u'lláh, 107
    Seven Valleys and Four Valleys, 7, 26, 92, 105, 120, 126, 134, 164, 171, 177, 210, 211, 229, 232, 234
    Tablet of Wisdom, 71

Tablet of the Holy Mariner, 216, 217
Tablets of Bahá'u'lláh, 15, 31, 34, 36, 44, 61, 71, 107, 129, 163, 172, 175, 180, 186, 187, 213, 214, 225
texts of other authors:
Compilations
Bahá'í Education, 184
Ḥuqúqu'lláh, 124
Shoghi Effendi
Advent of Divine Justice, 126
Promised Day Is Come, 163, 232, 233
World Order of Bahá'u'lláh, 105
Star of the West, 37, 146, 150, 152, 153, 156, 165
Battaglia, S., 24n, 128n
Bausani, A., 38, 120n, 233n
Beauty, 121, 204, 208, 230
Big Bang, 72
Bird, *see* Metaphor
Birth, second, *see* Progress, spiritual
Body
  heavenly, of man, 135, 146–7
  human, 87, 137, 138, 141–2, 154–5, 168, 172
    animal nature of man, 87, 135
    instrument of the soul, 154
    magnet for the spirit, 153
    mirror of the spirit, 64, 153
    temple of the soul, 172, 185
    the most perfect existence, 64
    veil, 218
Bounty
  of God, *see* Grace
Boyle, Charles, Earl of Orrery, 69–70
Brain, *see* Mind
Buddha, 100

C

Cabanis, P., 135
Capacity (capacities)
  of created things, 43, 56, 136
  of the kingdoms, 63–4
  of man, *see* Man
Carnot, principle of, 76
Cave, myth of the, *see* Plato
Chain of Revelations, *see* Revelation
Chance, 76–7
Chastity, 125

Children, 183, 184, 188–9
Choice, 165–6
  and knowledge, 165–7
  between the world of creation and the world of the Kingdom, 125–6, 165–6
  dynamics of, 169–70
  freedom of, 165–6
Choppers and chopping tools, 193
Corinthians, *see* Paul
Christ, *see* Jesus
Chilon of Sparta, 213
Cicero, 144n
Circle of existence, *see* Plotinus
Circumstances of human life, 166
Civilization
  divine, 14, 111, 112n, 195–6, 197, 214
  divine and material
    develop together, 198
    harmony between, 19
    coming efflorescence of, 196, 200, 203–4, 209, 214, 228
  material, 12, 195–6, 214
  modern, 95
    disharmony of, 214
  origin of, 101
  spiritual, *see* Civilization, divine
  twofold aspect of, 12–17, 213
Cleanliness, 185
Cole, J.R., 26–7n, 33n, 37n, 43n, 100n
Collective Centre, *see* Soul, Man
Command of God, *see* God
Competition, 203
Confirmations, 95, 170
Consciousness, 147n, 159–60, 168
  of the Manifestation of God, 103
  purposes of, 159–60
Conscious knowledge, 9, 169
Consensus gentium, 144–5
Conservation
  of energy, 55
  of species, 66
  principles or theorems of, 46
Consultation, 10, 159, 175–6
Contemplation, 121, 159
Cooperation and unity, 10, 122, 128, 170, 174, 187n, 195, 202, 203, 214
Coordinator of the body, *see* Soul
Cosmological principle, 47
Cosmology, 24 and n

Courage, 131, 164, 212
Creation, 31pp
  and motion, 59
  as emanation, 34
  had no beginning, 44
  is continuous, 44–6
  knowledge, will and love, and creation, *see* Knowledge
  laws of, 45pp
  purpose of, 56–7
Creationism, 6
Creativity, 187n, 204
Cult of the dead, earliest traces of worship, 234
Culture
  and man's success on the earth, 194
  international, 188
Cycles, 58, 60, 109–10
  universal, 199n

D

Danesh, H.B., 155n, 175n, 187n, 201n, 210
Dante, 20n
Day
  of Judgment, 232n, 235n
  of God, 110, 197, 202
Death
  as a lower degree of existence, 59, 92
  as motionless and inert objects, 57, 59
  as decomposition, 51, 59, 142
  as transference from one degree to another, 59–60, 141
  of the body, 135, 218, 221
  of the spirit, 60, 92, 93n
Deeds, *see* Action
Deity, *see* God
Delaunay, A., 76
Delphi, Temple of, 213
Demand and supply, 86–7, 162n
Democritus, 51
Desire, 92, 150
Detachment, 7, 125, 131–2, 134, 182, 226–7
Devil, *see* Satan
Dinosaurs, 67
Dispensation, 139
Dreams, 139n
Drugs, habit-forming, *see* Health

Dual nature of man, *see* Man
Dualism
  religion-science, 18, 30, 188
  spirit-matter, 4, 18, 30, 33, 49, 188, 208
Dynamism
  of the universal energy, 59, 205
  of the world of creation, 10, 59, 205

E

Earth, origin of, 73–5
  see Metaphor
Ecological balance, 48
Education of man, 99n, 136, 151–2n, 182pp, 203
  intellectual, 187–8
  limitations of, 99
  material, 184–7
  prerequisite of progress, 184
  spiritual, 188–9
  universal compulsory education, 184, 187
  universal, of things, 50, 65, 136, 183
Effort,
  for the realization of self, 96–9, 135–7, 152n, 166, 167–8
  to acquire knowledge, 3, 6
Ego, *see* Self
Einstein, A., 5
Electrons, 53
Elephant and the blind men, 31
Elijah, 41
Emanation, 34–5, 104–5, 115, 146, 148, 149
  and soul, *see* Soul
  and creation, *see* Creation
  and manifestation, 34–5
  First Emanation, 36, 102, 105
Emotions, 135, 160, 186
  conscious, 160
  natural
    and brain, 92
    in animals, 63, 81
    of the natal self, 88, 92, 96n, 205, 227
Endeavour, 119, *see also* Effort
  direction of human, 119–20
  for the realization of self, 96–9, 135–7, 152n, 166, 167–8

Index 249

Enlightenment, 8–9
Environment, 187n, 214
  natural
    devastation of, 12, 214
    protection of, 214
Envy, 129
Essence, 146n
  see also Substance
Estrangement, 128
Evil, 46n, 89
Evolution, 43–6, 56pp
  as education, 50, 65, 183
  biological, of living systems, 75
  conscious and voluntary process in man, 98–9, 136
  expression of the spirit, 57, 205
  general, of the world of creation, 97
  general systems, theory of, 58n, 110, 219n
  gradual, cyclical, relative and infinite growth, 58
  guided by an Intelligent Being, 69, 72, 73
  in nuce, 43
  in the mineral kingdom, 73–4
  is discontinuous, 199
  made possible through spirit, 60–61
  mistakes of, 68
  of individuals, 179–89
  of mankind, 190–204
    intellectual, 193–6
    material, 190–93
    spiritual, 196–204
  spiritual
    of individuals, 96–9, 181–2
    of society, 200–204
  unconscious and involuntary process in nature, 98, 136
Exceeding in words, 11, 129–30
Exemplar, 135, 147, 212n, 213
Existence
  conditions of, 35
  is ever existence, 58–9
  nonexistence cannot become, 45, 59
  spiritual condition of, 84–5
Eyford, G.A., 209n

F

Facchini, F., 6n, 194, 200n, 201, 202n
Faculty (faculties)
  common, 155
  mental, *see* Soul
Faith, 9, 24, 69, 77, 125, 169, 170, 226
  and reason, 17–18, 188
Faithfulness, 125
Falsification, method of, *see* Popper, K.
Fanaticism, 10
Fate, 98n
Faust, 208
Feed-back, 169, 171
Feelings, spiritual, 172–4
Fermi, E., 47n, 53n
Fidelity, 125
Force, active, 72
Form, 141–2
  ethereal, 146–7
Free will, 48, 114
Freedom
  in animals, 82–3
  of choice, 165–6
  in men, 166

G

Galileo, 5, 29
Gamov, G. 72n
Genesis, 6, 122n, 227
God,
  attributes of, *see* Attributes
  Command of, 44, 61, 98
  Creator, 31–5
  Divine Presence, 453 and n. i
  Essence of, 104–5
  existence of, 15
    rational proofs of
      cosmological, 24–5
      limited value of, 27
      teleological, 25–6
  Grace of, *see* Grace of God
  Identity of, 35–6, 37, 65, 102n
  image of, 91n
  knowledge of, 28, 70, 119, 125–6, 134, 147n, 275–6
  love of, *see* Love
  meeting with, 231–5
  motive Power, 25
  Names of, *see* Attributes of God
  nature of, theme of divine philosophy, 14
  preexistence of, 34

Self of, 35, 39, 130, 166
Soul of, 35n, 39, 65, 102n
Supreme Centre, 35, 39, 64–5
traces of, 28, 50, 70, 206, 228
unknowable, 22–3, 36, 104–5n
will of, *see* Will
Word of, 35, 44, 65, 72–3, 97, 102n, 106n
Good and evil, Bahá'í concept of, 46, 89
Gospel, *see* Jesus
Grace of God, 36n, 40
as spirit, xvii, 40
Manifestations, vehicle for the transmission of, 104
Gratton, L., 73
Growth, 58
and progress, *see* Progress
as evolution, *see* Evolution
power of, 40, 63, 67, 76, 97–8, 206
spiritual, *see* Progress

H

Habits, 163, 186n
Haeckel, E.H., 180n
Happiness, *see* Joy
Hatcher, J.S., 35n, 38n, 120n, 206n, 223n
Hatcher, W.S., 8n, 9n, 46n, 76n, 77n, 126n, 147n, 150n
Health, 184–7
and emotions, 186n
and natural environment, 187
and social environment, 187
habit-forming drugs, 186n
hygiene, 184–7
alcohol, 186n
prevention of disease, 185n, 186
psychosomatic diseases, 155n
smoking, 186n
spiritual sicknesses, 163
Hellaby, W. and M., 121n
Hell, 171n, 213n, 232
History, tribunal of, 10, 11, 113
Hobbes, T., 204n
Holiness, 125, 129
Holy Alliance, 201
Holy Writings
criterion of knowledge, 5–6, 31
false interpretation of, 6
infallibility of, 6, 120–21

reading of, 121, 124, 231pp literally, 6
meditation upon, 120
metaphors of, *see* Metaphors
Homo
erectus, 194, 203
habilis, 194, 203
homini lupus, 204
sapiens, 194, 203
Humanity, *see* Mankind
Humility, 125
Hygiene, 225, 226

I

Identity of God, *see* God
Illuminati, 5
Image of God, *see* God
Imagination, 157
Incarnation, 104–5n
Individuality, 50, 116n, 181
of the soul, 116n, 148–50, 153
after physical death, 218
the greatest bestowal of God to man, 116n, 149
of things, 206
of the Manifestations, 103
Industries, primitive lithic, 193
Infallibility
of the Holy Scriptures
of the Manifestations, *see* Manifestations, infallibility of,
Insight, *see* Knowledge, intuitive
Inspiration, *see* Knowledge, intuitive
Instinct (instincts)
guided through reason, 203
in animals, 80, 81, 82
spiritual, 143, 161n
Intellect, *see also* Mind; Perception, rational
criterion of knowledge, 4
limitations of, 4, 93–6, 157
the most precious gift bestowed upon man, 89, 116n, 171
and spiritual reality, 4
Intellection, 157
Intelligence
in animals, 63, 80
in man, 64, 115

intermediary between body and spirit, 91
Intercession, 220
Intuition, *see* Knowledge, intuitive

J

Jahoda, M., 80n
Jesus, 41, 93n, 100, 103, 105n, 106n, 113, 125, 129, 132, 137, 143, 145, 171, 196, 202n, 203, 209, 210
  Gospels of, 60, 93n, 113, 125, 171, 181, 196, 210
  parable of the wedding feast, xv
  Sermon on the Mount, 209
John the Baptist, 41
John of the Cross, 210
Jordan, D.C., 150n
Joy, 37n, 161–2, 186, 189
  essence of, 230
  human birthright, 70
  material (happiness), 173
  of a creative commitment, 230
  of spiritual growth, 134
  spiritual, 173–4, 189
    the animal can never attain, 83n, 174
Justice, 7
Judas Iscariot, 129

K

Kawai, M., 80n
Keniahs, 194
Kingdom (kingdoms), 38–40 62–4, 66, 77, 190 *see also* World
  animal, 40, 63, 64, 67, 190, 206
  differences among, 63
  divine, entrance into, 137
  human, 40, 63, 64, 67, 161, 190
  mineral, 40, 63, 64, 67, 74–5, 161, 190
  vegetable, 40, 63, 64, 67, 161, 190, 206
  world of, *see* World of the Kingdom
Kitáb-i-Íqán, *see* Bahá'u'lláh, quotations from

Knowing, loving and willing, 37, 155, 169
Knowledge
  acquired, 7, 9
  and civilization, 19
  criteria of, 3–6, 8, 81–2
  divine and satanic, 13n, 170–71
  divine gift, 3, 8, 12, 19, 172
  efforts to acquire, 3, 6, 9
  human, 103
  love and will, *see* Knowledge, volition and action
  and enlightenment, 8–9
  intuitive, 97–8, 135–6, 139–40, 156, 157–8, 172, 206
    and spiritual progress, 27–8
    criterion of knowledge, 4–5
    practice of, 5, 158, 160
    value of, 5n
  of the essence, 8, 104, 145–6
  of God, *see* God
  of the heart, 158n
  of the Manifestation of God, 104
  of oneself, 127n, 131, 147n, 171, 213, 227
  of the qualities, 8, 23–4, 146
  power of the soul, 156–62
  spiritual, 172
  volition and action, 19, 98, 155, 169, 176, 236
    and creation, 37
Krishna, 100

L

Language
  international auxiliary, 188
Laszlo, E., 58n, 110, 179n
Lavoisier, 46n
Laws
  of nature, *see* nature, laws of
Leptons, 53, 75
Life
  all beings are endowed with, 59
  in stellar bodies, 45
  on earth,
    preparation for the life beyond, 219
  very ancient, 78
Logos, *see* God, Word of
Lorenz, K., 68n, 203

Love, 36–7, 37n, 50, 52, 54n, 134, 160–65, 205, 235
  cause of the creation of the phenomenal world, 37
  cause of the existence of all phenomena, 52, 161
  growth of, 164–5
  in animals, 81, 161
  in the world of creation, 50, 52, 54n, 161, 205
  laws of, 50, 161
  of exaltation, 90
  of God, 37, 117–18, 125, 165, 189
    towards the Self of God, 37, 161, 165, 166
  of reality, 6, 21, 189, 225
  a spiritual power of the soul, 160–66
  unconditional, 235
Lucifer, 209
Lunar cycle, see Metaphor

M

Macrocosm, 85–6
  man should be regarded as the greater world, 86n
Mahmudi, J., 100n
Maieutic, Socratic see Socrates
Malice, 128–9
Man
  after his physical death, 218pp
  and animals, 79–83, 87–9, 137, 139, 161, 191, 192
  and attributes of God, 107, 148–9
  artist of his own self, 209
  as letter, 106n
  brotherhood of, 202
  capacity of, 97–8, 108, 119, 121, 136, 149, 151, 161, 168, 173, 198
  character of a true, 123
  characters of, 151–2n
  collective centre
    of all human virtues, 135
    of spiritual as well as material forces, 84
  contradictions in, 92
  creator of his own self, see artist of his own self
  definitions of, 84–6
  dual endowment of, 93
  evolution of, 84–6, see also origin of
  fruit of evolution, 67, 84, 115, 179, 181
  has existed from all eternity, 74
  highest development in man, 137
  highest point in creation, 64, 84
  image of God, 91, 135, 149
  lofty aspirations of, 90
  lowest point of the arc of descent, 65
  maturity of, xv, 182, 188, 189, 190n, 194, 200–204
  nature of
    animal, 87–9, 135, 166
    divine, 91–3, 96–9, 135, 166
    human, 89–90
      greatness and limitations of, 93–6
    tension between animal and divine, 91–2, 162–3
  origin of, 190–93, 199
  part of physical and metaphysical world, 86
  Perfect, see Manifestation of God
  perfect animal, see Animal
  perfectibility of, 201–2, 228
  possesses certain virtues of which nature is deprived, 26
  powers of,
    knowledge, 156–60
    love, 160–65
    will, 165–7
  progress of, see Progress
  purpose of, 136–7
  quickening of, 234
  supreme gift conferred by God on man, 116n, see also 135–7, 149, 173
  temple of God, 85
  three realities of, 86pp, 181–9
  two natures of, 151, 161
  virtues of, see Virtues
Manifestation
  different from emanation, 34–5
Manifestation of God
  and philosophers, see Philosophers
  and Soul of God, 102, 194
  and spirit
    intermediary of, 99
    visible expression of, 105
  and world of the Kingdom, 41, 102, 136
  deeds of, as proof of their mission, 112–13

denial of, 114
differences among, 103, 108, 111–12
Divine Physician, 107
divinity of, 106–7
double station of, 108–13
educators of mankind, 110–13
  as proof of their mission, 113
emanation of God, 104–5
founders of civilization, 102, 196–8
  of divine civilization, 111–12
iconoclastic, 114
in the history of mankind, 100–101
individuality of, 103
infallibility of, 107–8, 119–20
love for, 130, 134
meeting with, 135
Messengers, 106
miracles of, 113
mirrors of God, 103, 105, 107
names of, 106–7
perfect image of God, 65
Perfect Man, 65, 106–7, 176, 183, 191, 193
pre-existence of, 103
preliminary, 198
progressivity of, 109–10, 198
proof of, 112–13
prophecies of, 112–13
  as proof of their mission, 113
Prophets, 106
purpose of, 110–11
rational soul of, 103
recognition of, 116, 119, 130, 134
Soul of, 102–3
spiritual power of, 102, 115–16
submitted unto God, 106
submission to the will of, 130pp
Sun of Reality, 106, 109
teachings of, 102
threefold reality of, 102–4
unity of, 107–8, 110, 198
universal, 41
Universal Mind, divine see Mind, Universal
vehicles of the Grace of God, see Grace
very ancient, 108–9, 199
Word of God, 106
words of, 101, 119–20
  as proof of their mission, 112–13
  spiritual meanings of, 119–20
Mankind
  capacity of cooperation of, 194, 200–202

evolution of, 199–200
  intellectual, 193–6
  not homogeneous in the world, 194
  material, 190–93
  spiritual, 196–8
infancy of, 191
maturity of,
  approaching, 200
oneness of, 203
selfish and aggressive, 202
Martyrs, 101, 113, 132
Marx, K. 110
Marie, Queen of Romania, 234n
Materialism, 28, 30
  causes of, 4n, 110
  criticism of, 15–16
Matter, see also World, material; World, of creation
  and sensible reality, 41–3, 56–8
  original, 41, 45, 56, 57, 67, 72, 73, 85
Maturing, see Progress, spiritual
Maturity
  of created things, 59, 62
  of humanity, 123, 196–7, 198, 200–204, 202n, 228
  of human beings, 67, 180, 182, 188, 189, 190n, 194, 200–204
McLean, J., 13n, 158n
Medicine, 184–7
Meditation, 5, 120, 121, 158–9
Melchiorri, F., 72n
Memory, 156–7
  nature is devoid of, 79n
  in animals, see Animals
Mendeleév Table, 74, 78
Merton, T., 210
Mesons, 74
Metaphor, 5, 120–21, 206
  definition of, 206n
  in the Bahá'í texts, 38n, 206–9
  bird, 208
  cage, 127n
  dawn, 117, 207
  dust, 117, 127n, 208
  earth, 117, 127n, 207
  fire, 127n
  light, 117
  lunar cycle, 117, 207
  mirror, 103, 105, 107, 207
  pilgrimage, 208
  rain, 42

rust, 127
sea, 117, 208
seasons, 109, 207
seed, 117, 207
spring, 109, 232
stone, 117
sun, 38n, 39, 72, 106, 109, 110, 117, 206
  and earth, 42
veil, 126n
water, 208
Method, scientific, 8n
Microcosm, 85–6
Mind
  and brain, 89, 135, 142, 152, 155–6, 157, 159, 180–81, 186n, 218n
  and intellect, 4–5, 89–90, 103, 135, 157–8, 180
  factor of progress, 194–5, 197
  First, 35–6, 65
  inner, 157
  recent use of, xv–xvi, 194
  the thinker, the comprehender, 40, 152
  Universal, 95, 103, 165
Mirror, see Metaphor
Moderation, 185, 236
Moffett, R., 121
Moral proof of the immortality of the soul, see Soul
Moses, 41, 100, 103, 105n, 112n, 196
Motion, 57n
  atomic, 51, 52, 53–6
  essential, 57–8, 140
  is life, 53, 57, 59
  logic of, 44
  proof of the immortality of the soul, 140–41
  voluntary, 63–4, 81, 166
Motive Power, see God
Muhammad, 41, 100, 196
Mullá Ḥusayn, 234n
Murchie, G., 69–70
Mysticism, 2, 5, 136, 210–12, 226–7

N

Nabíl-i-A'ẓam, 173, 233n, 234n
Nash, G., 110
Nationalism, 201–2
Nations, 201–2
Naturalist, see Philosophers
Nature
  definition of, 44
  laws of, 42, 46, 47, 54–5, 62, 76, 98
  world, see World, of nature
Nearness to God, 117, 127, 133, 135, 216, 217
Needs, 86–7, 118–19, 162n, 167, 225
  human
    of being comprehended, 225
    of comprehending, 225
    material, 86
    spiritual, 86–7
Neo-platonism, see Plotinus
Neutrins, 53
Neutron, 53, 74
  bomb, see Atomic bomb
Newton, I., 5, 69
Nuclear interactions, 54
Nucleosynthesis, 74

O

Objective, attainment of, 19
Oneness
  of being see Pantheism
  of mankind, 203
  of phenomena, theme of divine philosophy, 11, see also World, material
Orrery, see Boyle

P

Pain, 130–32, 134, 161–2, 166–7, 210–12
Paleontology, 194–5, 203
Pantheism, 49n, 52, 55
  true explanation of, 55
Parable, 121
  see also Jesus
Paradise, 171n, 213n, 235
Particles, subatomic, 53–4, 76
Passion, 92, 150
Paul, St., 6n, 196
Peace, xv, 174, 175
  Most Great Peace, 190n
  universal, 111

Index

Pearl, apologue of the, 233n
Pedagogy, Bahá'í, 182
Perception
  inner, see Knowledge, intuitive
  intellectual, see rational
  rational, 40, 63, 67, 81, 97, 136, 139, 156–7
    criterion of knowledge, see Intellect
  sense or sensory, 79, 138, 139, 206
    criterion of knowledge, see Sense perception
  power of, 40, 61, 63, 67, 79
  spiritual, 67 see also Knowledge, intuitive
Perfecting, see Progress, spiritual
Persecutions, see Martyrs
Personality, 149
Pessimism, 70
Peter, St., 129
Philosophy, 1–3
  and Bahá'í teachings, 2–3, 16–17, 21, 24–5, 28, 31, 51
  definitions of, 3
  divine, 13–15
    praise of, 16
  Eastern, 4, 16, 89, 93n
  Greek, 4n, 15
  natural, 11–13, 25n
  of reality, 11, 19–20
  value of, 11
  Western, 16n
Philosophers
  and the Prophets, 15, 98n
  Eastern, 4, 89, 93n
  founders of material civilization, 2–3
  Greek, 4n, 15
  ideal, 16–17
  materialists, see Materialism
  of Central Europe, 16n
  of the New World, 16n
  Persian, 93n
  Western, 16n
  philosophical tradition, 16, 20
Piattelli Palmarini, M., 88n
Pigmies, 194
Pillars of Hercules, 20
Plan of God,
  creative, 56–7
    general features of, 57–8
    individual responsibility in, 149
    power of execution of, 56, 96
Planets,
  beginning and end of, 74

Plato, 15–16, 27n, 93n, 141n, 143n, 170n
  dualism in, 49
  Eastern philosopher, 16n, 93n
  myth of the cave, 31
  philosopher-king, 27n
  world of Ideas, 49
Plautus, 204
Plotinus, 27n, 36
  arc of existence
    of ascent, 65, 86
    of descent, 65, 86
  bringing forth, 65, 86
  circle of existence, 58, 67, 85, 101, 199n
  and emanation, 27n
  evolution, 64–5
  exemplar, 212n
  Neoplatonism, founder of, 27n
  producing something new, 67, 86
  and Universal Intellect, 27n
  and unknowability of God, 27n
Pongides, 78, 87
Popper, K., 77
  method of falsification, 10
  principle of refutability, 10
Positivism, 4n
Prayer, 120–21, 124, 223
  and material means, 124
  daily, 120
Predestination, 98n
Pre-existence
  essential, 33, 34
  of God, 33, 34
  of the world of the Kingdom, 37–8
  of time, 33, 34
Prejudice, 7, 16
  and imitation, 7
  definition of, 7
  freedom from prejudice, 188
  cause of war, 10
Pride, 7, 13, 14, 216n
Prigogine, I., 4n
Progress, 68
  expression of spirit in the world of matter, 62
  fruit (outcome) of knowledge, 19
  fruit (outcome) of effort, 227
  future, 195, 198, 202, 228
  intellectual, 195
  material, 12, 195
  spiritual, 14, 93, 96, 98, 105, 116, 118, 125, 127, 127n, 130,

133–7, 158, 170, 176, 181, 189, 196–8, 233
  and physical health, 186
  conscious and willing, 98–9
  is infinite, 140–41, 181
  means for, 125
  moved by the Holy Spirit, 97n
  obstacles to, 126–30
Prophecies, *see* Manifestation of God
Prophet, *see* Manifestation of God
Protons, 53, 74
Protoplasm, 193
Proto-universe, 72, 73, 76
Purification, 133
Purity, 118–19, 125, 128–9, 162–3, 185, 219, 227, 235

Q

Quark, 53, 75
Qur'án, 125–6, 128, 172–3

R

Rabbani, R., 107n, 123, 235n
Reading the Writings, *see* Writings, Holy
Reality
  love of, *see* Love
  collective, *see* Soul
  definition of, 18–19
  essential unknown, 8
  is one, 1, 9, 18
  is pure spirit, 43
  is truth, 10
  material or sensible, 1, 3, 11–12, 41
    educational meaning of, 208
    metaphorical meaning of, 35, 206, 208
  metaphysical or spiritual, 1, 41
  philosophy of, 19
  science of, 104
  universal, 36
Reason
  and brain, *see* Mind and brain
  faith and, 17–18
  rational faculty, *see* Intellect; Perception, rational
  Supreme, 77

Recami, E., 55n
Refutability, principle of, *see* Popper, K.
Reincarnation, 50n
Religion (religions), 106
  and science, 17–18, 94, 188
    separation between religion and scientific truth, 29–31
  cause of civilization, 14
  cause of unity, 214n
  cycles of, 101, 109
  decline of, 110, 214n
  definitions of, 17–18
  science of reality, 104
  science of the love of God, 165
  the greatest bestowal of God in the world of humanity, 116n
  two aspects of, 111
Repose, absolute, does not exist in nature, 53
Research method, 6–8
Retro-action, *see* Feed-back
Revelation
  as guidance for man, 19, 30–31, 95–6, 99
  as elixir, 111
  chain of, 108, 196
  of the Soul of God, 102
  progressive, 101, 108–10, 196, 198
Rewards and punishments of the other world, 144
Righteousness, 212
Rumi, 177–8
Rutherford, E., 53

S

Sacrifice, 125
  meaning of, 132–3, 169, 173, 235
  of life, 125
  of self, 132–3, 136, 171
Sa'di, 233n
Sana'i, 31n
Satan, 88–9, 92, 150, 151
Satanic self, *see* Self
Schaefer, Hans, 94
Science, 2, 11–12, 17–18, 94
  abuse of, 12–13
  and insight, 99
  and religion, 17–18, 29–30, 188
  and virtue, 170
  and natural philosophy, 12

Index

divine, 13
  limitations of, 94
  man of, 12
  method of, 8n, 11–12
  of reality, 13, 30–31, 104
  spiritual, 13
  use of, 124
  useful, 2n
  useless, 2n
Scientific method, 8n, 11–12, 16–17
Scriptures, Holy *see* Holy Writings
Search
  free and unfettered, 1, 16, 188
  method of, 6–8, 145
Seasons, *see* Metaphor
Scholars, Bahá'í
  fundamental principles for, xix, 21, 30n
Second brith, *see* Progress, spiritual
Self
  attraction toward, *see* Attraction
  cause of sorrows, 131
  dying from the, 132, 134
  elimination of, 127
  love of, 126–7
  natal, 87–8, 92, 96, 127, 132, 134, 148, 170–71, 211, 227
  natural emotions of, *see* Emotions, natural, of natal self
  of God, *see* God
  realization of, 147n
  sacrifice of, 127, 132, 211–12
  satanic, 88n, 92, 134, 150–51, 211
  selfish disorders, 127–8n, 163
  struggle against, 128
  two meanings of, 127n, 140
Self-centredness, 127, 170
Self-sacrifice, 132–3
Sense perception, 79
  criterion of knowledge, 3–4, 15–16
  lowest degree of perception, 3
Sensibility in animals, 63, 79
Service, 122–3, 134, 235
Shame, sense of, 163
Shoghi Effendi, 3n, 20
  quotations
    from writings of,
      The Faith of Bahá'u'lláh, 202
      The World Order of Bahá'u'lláh, 8, 198, 226n
    from letters written on behalf of, 3, 5, 7, 14, 15, 16, 20, 40–41n, 46n, 79n, 89n, 99n, 103, 127, 128, 139, 183, 191n, 219n
Shook, G., 121n
Sickness, 154
  spiritual, 163
Silence, 159
Simplicity, 142–3
Singleness, mathematical, 73
Sleep, 139
Society
  development of, 200–204
  likened to the human organism, 189, 200
  modern, 195–6
Socrates, 15n, 170n, 184n
  identification of science and virtue, 170
  maieutic of, 184n
Sorrow, 130–32, 134
Soul (souls), 28, 35, 40, 67, 83, 86, 90, 102–3, 138pp, 153
  after physical death, 218–23
  capacity of feeling joy and pain, 161–2
  collective centre, 84, 106, 147–8, *see* Man, collective centre
  comes into being with conception of physical body, 140, 153
  coordinator and motor of the body, 154–5
  dual nature of, *see* Man, dual nature of
  emanation of God, 40, 140
  enlightened
    qualifications of, 125–6
  existence of the
    denial of the, 138
    proofs of the, 138–40
      limited value of, 145
  faculties of the, *see* powers of the
  immortality of the, 64, 86, 181
    proofs of the
      limited value of, 145
      metaphysical, 140–43, 181
      moral, 143–5
  imperfect, 201
  individuality of the, *see* Individuality
  journey of the, 20, 176–8
  mental faculties, *see* Soul, powers of the
  mirror of human choice, 171–2
  not subject to change, 149 *see also* Substance, innate
  passionate, 150

pleasing and tranquil, 150
powers of the, 154–76
   spiritual, or mental faculties,
      156–7
      appearance of, 199
   rational, 89, 103
   relation between body and, 103,
      153–5
   spiritual qualities of the, 155pp,
      212–13
   as substance, 141–3
   unknowable, 145–6
Soul of God, see God
Soul of the Manifestation of God, see
   Manifestation of God
Species
   conservation of, 66
   phenomenal, 67n
Spin, 54
Spirit, 40–43, 52, 55, 57, 59, 60–61,
   72, 97–9, 105, 146, 148,
   152, 153, 165, 172
   action of upon things, 60–61
   and matter, unity of, 43, 49
   animal, 40, 59, 60, 63, 67, 156
   definition of, 40–41 and n
   degrees of, 40, 61n
   divine, 147, 151, 157, 158, 159
   emanates from the world of the
      Kingdom, 43
   Holy, 42–3, 65, 96, 97n, 104,
      116n, 119, 130, 136, 159,
      169, 170, 172, 179n
      light and knowledge, 8
   human, 40, 63, 67, 89–91, 148,
      149, 153–4, 156–7, 158
      is eternal, 64
      powers of, 90
   indwelling, 27–8
   is the greater power, 52
   is progressive, 43, 57, 61
   mineral, 59, 60, 63, 67
   Most Great, 41, 65
   of faith, 41, 65, 93n, 116n
   quickening, 52
   reality is, 43, 50
   unity of, 43, 152
   vegetable, 40, 59, 60, 63, 67
Spiritual feelings, 172–4
Spiritual world, see World, spiritual
Spirituality, 116n, 134, 137, 181, 206
Spiritualization of mankind, 176, 196
Spring, divine, see Metaphor

Steadfastness, 125, 168n
Struggle
   for existence, 88, 170, 195, 203–4
   inner, 227
Subconscious, 96n
Submission to the Will of God, 118,
   119, 210
Substance
   innate, transformation of, is
      impossible, 60, 141, 146,
      183
   inorganic, 75
   organic, 75
   simple, 51, 141–3, 158
Sun
   metaphor, 38n, 39, 106n
   of Reality, 105, 106, 109
   of Truth, 105, 106
Superstition, 17, 30n, 95
Sympathetic nerve, see Faculty, common
Systems,
   living, 75–8
      biological evolution of, 78pp
   pre-biotic, 78

T

Taherzadeh, A., 120n, 233n
Teaching the Faith, 120, 121–2, 175
   prerequisites for, 122
Teleology, 25n
Teresa of Avila, St., 210
Terminology
   Bahá'í
      devil, see Satan
      dispensation, 108
      emotions, natural, 88
      faith, 9
      fate, 98n
      good and evil, 46n
      hell, 213n
      Identity of God, 35
      individuality, 116n
      knowledge, 8–9
      Logos, 35
      love, 37n
      man, 84
      Manifestations of God, 99
      mind, 40
         First, 35
      natal self, 87

natural law, 44
nature, 44n
  divine, of man, 135
  paradise, 213n
  personality, 150
  philosophy, 2
  predestination, 98n
  reality, 6–7, 9, 18
  religion, 17–18, 165
  Satan, 88–9, 92
  science, 2, 11–12
  scientific method, 8
  second birth, 93
  self, 127n
  Self of God, 35
  soul, 145–8
  Soul of God, 35n
  Spirit
    Holy, 41, 116n
    Most Great, 41
  spirit of faith, 116n
  spiritual progress, 96, 133
  spirituality, 134
  theology, 24–6
  Trinity, 36n
  will, 98
    of God, 32, 44
  Word of God, 35, 44
  world of the Kingdom, 35–7
Tertullian, 6
Texts, Bahá'í
  philosophical language of, 26, 36, 64, 145
Thales, 213
Theology, 107n
  'science of Divinity', xvin, 24
Theorems of conservation, 46n
Thought and action, 10–11, 121
Townshend, G., 70n, 198n
Traces of God, see God
Tradition
  criterion of knowledge, see Holy Writings
  philosophical and religious, see Philosophy
Transformation, 96–7, 98n
  of substance, depends upon divine bounty, 60, 77
  of man, 95–6, 115pp, 136–7
  spiritual, see Progress, spiritual
Tribunal of life and history, 10, 11, 113
Tripartition of being, 36n
Truth, see also Reality

absolute, 9
free and independent search after, see Search
Truthfulness, 125

U

Ulysses, 19, 20n
Unconscious, 96n
Understanding
  essence of, 89–90, 91, 95–6, 104, 172, 225
  power of, 89–90, 91, 95–6, 115, 135, 157
  and spiritual vision, 172
  limitations of, 23, 94–5
  the most praiseworthy power of man, 91
Uniqueness of phenomena, 50, 206
Unity
  and cooperation, 10, 170, 213–14
  as moral criterion, 10, 170, 174
  collective expressions of, 200
  of being, see Pantheism
  of the human race, 11, 122, 129, 174, 175, 188
  of phenomena, 47–50, 55
  of religion, 188
  of spirit and matter, 42
  of worlds of nature and spirit, 43
  theme of divine philosophy, 11
Universal House of Justice, 20n, 21, 30n, 184n
  The Promise of World Peace, 123, 187n, 194n, 196, 202, 214n, 228
Universality, 17n, 127n
Universe
  free from imperfection, 46, 191
  infinite, 45, 206
  is not fortuitous, 69–70
  laboratory, 25, 47, 52, 55
  oneness of the laws of, 47
  origin of, 71–5
  workshop, 25, 55, 144
Upright position, 197

V

Values, 70, 82, 94–5, 96n, 123

Van Lawick-Goodall, J., 80
Vegni, G., 53
Via eminentiae, 32
Via negationis, 32, 34
Virtues
  archetypal, 106
  divine, 84, 135, 136
    potential in man, 85, 169
  human, *see* of man
  of humanity, *see* of man
  of man, 95, 169–70, 181
Vision, inner (spiritual), 135–6, 157n, 180 *See also* Knowledge, intuitive

W

Wai-wais, 194
War
  religious, 6
  prejudice, cause of, 10
Water, *see* Metaphors
Weil, H., 159n
West, *see* World, modern Western
Will, 98
  free, *see* Free will
  First, 35, 36, 65
  of God, 39, 44, 118, 166–7
  power of the soul, 165–7
  Primal, *see* First
Winterburn, G., 64n
Wisdom
  Tablet of, *see* Bahá'u'lláh
Word (words)
  exceeding in, 11, 129–30, 175
  meaning of, 174
  of God, *see* God, word of
  power of, 174–5
Work, 186
World (worlds)
  material or of creation, 41–50, *see also* Universe
    balance of phenomena, 48
    change, essential attribute of, 50
    deathless in its duration, 44
    educational meaning of, 166, 208
    evidences that proclaim the perfection of God, 35
    evolution of, 58pp
    facsimile of the inner kingdom of the spirit, 49
    illusion, 44n, 60
    imperfect, 46, 50
    inequality in degree, 62
    infinite in its range, 45
    interdependence of phenomena, 77
    intrinsic oneness of phenomena, 47, 55, 58
    is always growing and evolving, 57
    metaphor of spiritual world, 35, 42, 206–9, 216–17
    mirror of the image of God, 56
    multiplicity of, 43
    order and perfection of, 35–7, 46, 49, 191, 206
    perpetual motion of, 53–4
    reality of, 43, 49–50, 60
    shadow stretching out of the world of the Kingdom,
    show, vain and empty, 43, 49
  metaphysical, 42
  modern Western, 4, 30, 94–5, 96n, 101
  of creation, *see* World, material
  of existence,
    degrees of, 35–6
  of God, 32–4
    countless, 45
  of nature
    and of reason, 44n, 79–83, 93n
    is imperfect, 46, 50
  of reason, *see* World of nature and world of reason
  of the Kingdom, 35–41, 205pp
    acquiring the qualities of, 133
    creative forces of, 99, 115–16
    entrance into, 125–6
    laws and truths of, 115
  qualities of, 171
  spiritual, 43, 49–50
Writings, *see* Holy Writings

Z

Zoroaster, 100
Zohoori, E., 187n
Zygote, 153, 193–4

About the Author

Julio Savi is the translator into Italian of most of the major Bahá'í texts published in the last twenty years in Italy. Beginning with *The Dawn-Breakers*, he went on to translate *Epistle to the Son of the Wolf, Tablets of Bahá'u'lláh Revealed after the Kitáb-i-Aqdas, Tablet of the Holy Mariner, The Long Healing Prayer, Selections from the Writings of the Báb, Selections from the Writings of 'Abdu-l-Bahá, Tablets of the Divine Plan, The Will and Testament of 'Abdu'l-Bahá, The Advent of Divine Justice*, and numerous compilations. This work provided the backbone of the comprehensive and detailed knowledge of Bahá'í Writings that went into the writing of *The Eternal Quest for God*.

Two early influences were important for Savi: his father's encouragement to study philosophy, and his own love of the unspoiled wilderness of Ethiopia where he was born and grew up. He received a classical education and then studied medicine at the Universities of Bologna and Florence. He earns his living as a specialist in the public hospital in Bologna, the city where he lives with his wife and two sons.

Much in demand as a lecturer on Bahá'í subjects, he has written about Baḥíyyih Khánum, the Greatest Holy Leaf; and about the spiritual education of children, the theme of a Bishops' Conference in Rome where he represented the Bahá'í International Community. He is a regular contributor of articles to *Opinioni Bahá'í*, the quarterly magazine, and has served as a member of the National Spiritual Assembly of the Bahá'ís of Italy for the last fourteen years.

www.ingramcontent.com/pod-product-compliance
Lightning Source LLC
Chambersburg PA
CBHW021847300426
44115CB00005B/51